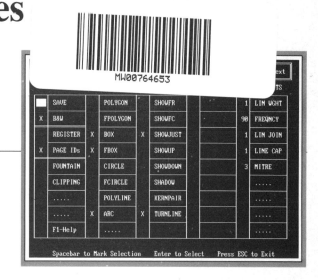
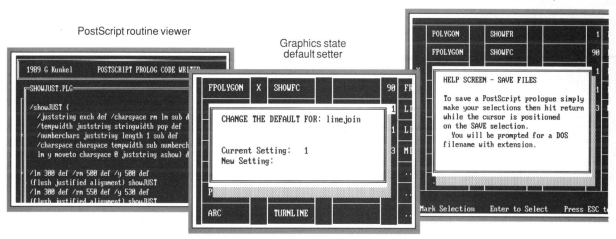

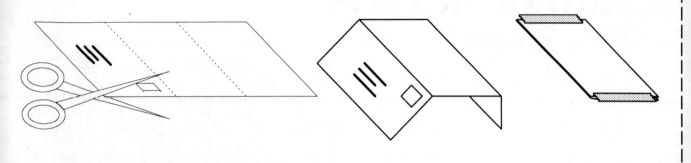

FOLD HERE

FOLD HERE

L&K Communications
PO Box 208
Morrisville, PA 19067-0208

graphic design with POSTSCRIPT

graphic design with PostScript

Gerard Kunkel

Scott, Foresman and Company
Glenview, Illinois   London

Library of Congress Cataloging-in-Publication Data

Kunkel, Gerard.
    Graphic design with PostScript / Gerard Kunkel.
       p.   cm.
    ISBN 0-673-38794-1
    1. Desktop publishing.   2. PostScript (Computer program language)
    3. Printing, Practical—Layout—Data processing.   I. Title.
    Z286.D47K87   1990
    686.2′2544536—dc20   89-24195
                                                     CIP

1 2 3 4 5 6 RRC 94 93 92 91 90 89

ISBN 0-673-38794-1

Notice of Liability

Scott, Foresman professional books are available for bulk sales at quantity discounts. For more information, please contact Marketing Manager, Professional Books Group, Scott, Foresman and Company, 1900 E. Lake Avenue, Glenview, IL 60025.

Dedication

This book is dedicated to Heather Luchak, my wife, for patiently waiting while the months of designing, programming, and writing monopolized my attention.

There are many other people who must be thanked for helping me complete this book. Without these professionals, this book would be incomplete: Bill Machrone, Publisher and Editor-in-Chief, *PC Magazine*, for giving me my first PostScript printer and a direction to follow; John Dickinson, Executive Editor, *PC Magazine* for always pointing me towards the right technology; Bill Howard, Executive Editor, *PC Magazine*, for always including me in the search for new technologies; Bill Lohse, President, Ziff-Davis Publishing Company, for allowing me the opportunity to explore my ideas; Dr. George Luchak, Princeton University, for being a constructive critic; Dr. John Warnock, Adobe Systems, for extending a welcome visit and sharing his thoughts; Paul and George Grayson, Micrografx, for providing their latest technological advances; Charles Humble, Hastings and Humble Public Relations, for introducing me to the world of color PostScript; Stanford Davis, Tektronix, for being my technical adviser on the Tektronix Phaser CP; Peter DeBlass and Michael Christie of Gerard Associates Phototypesetting, for providing an essential test-bed on the Linotronic 300; Mike Sherwood, Aldus Corporation, for providing detailed help on interacting with PageMaker; and of course, Tabatha and Samantha, my programming lap-cats, for keeping me company.

Also of note: Toshiba, for creating an affordable, readable, portable computer; and Amtrak, for providing a daily workspace between Pennsylvania and New York.

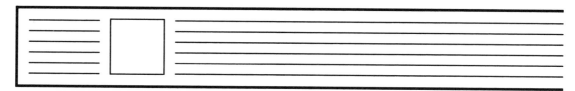

Contents

Chapter

2   **PostScript Principles**   **29**

Chapter

3   **Typographic Solutions**   **53**

Chapter

4 **Graphics** **120**

Chapter

5 **Data Driven Graphics** **132**

Chapter

6 **Color** **255**

Appendix

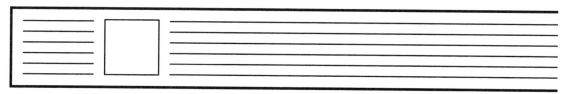

Introduction

Any book on the PostScript language should acknowledge, and indeed praise, Dr. John E. Warnock and Dr. Charles M. Geschke for the development of such a versatile and flexible page-description language. John and Charles created the PostScript language back in 1982, when they recognized a need for standards in the printing and graphic arts industry. From this vision and commitment, PostScript is quickly becoming the standard for describing the electronic page.

The initial implementation of PostScript on a wide scale was in the Apple Laser-Writer. Within its circuitry was placed the licensed PostScript interpreter, the heart of any PostScript imaging system. This interpreter is a chip. The chip contains the software necessary to read and process PostScript code.

PostScript is an interpreted, not compiled, language. It cannot be independently executed. It creates images only when interpreted by the PostScript Language Interpreter. Why do we need a software language that is dependent on a piece of hardware for printing? The answer to this question will become acutely obvious as you read this book.

I have tapped into my experience at *PC Magazine* and in other endeavors to create what I believe is the most useful book for understanding and using PostScript to create graphics and other quality designs. My challenges at *PC Magazine* have made me fully aware of the potential of many computerized graphics systems and programming languages. The challenge at *PC Magazine* is one of quantity and deadlines. Designing and producing approximately 5,000 editorial pages per year have led to interesting and extremely efficient solutions.

Working with computers to design and create graphics is extremely rewarding. For computer jocks like me, this is fun. For the publication I work for, this is business—big business. PostScript implementations often mean substantial savings in typesetting and art creation. They also mean greater control over quality. Our "three-dimensional" bar charts are terribly complex arrays of information. When numbers are translated into graphics, conventional drawings may take days. Computer drawings now take minutes, and the quality of plot and line are far superior to any hand-drawn work.

Some of you have probably been using PostScript for some time without realizing it. The introduction of PageMaker for the Macintosh, combined with the Apple Laser-Writer, put application-level PostScript control in the hands of tens of thousands. And, in turn, desktop publishing was born.

This book is written exclusively for you, the desktop publisher. AND Linotronic output houses, graphic designers, graphic artists, publication designers, cartographers, statisticians, stock analysts, and programmers. I have intentionally put programmers last because PostScript is a programming language that allows all creative individuals to become electronic publishing "power users" (as we fondly call them at *PC Magazine*). The reason this language is so accessible to so many people is its format, ASCII. It is pure text. You do not have to be a binary-format wizard to start programming in PostScript. This is, quite simply, a text-based language that does not require a programming language application to compile and run. Since it is straight ASCII, it can be created and edited in almost any word processor, electronic notepad, or even the ultra-simplistic, PC-based DOS EDLIN.

This book is organized in a theory-and-example structure that first discusses the reason "why" and then shows "how." Sample code is shown both in complete form and fragmented with comments for easier understanding.

In creating an outline for this book, I looked at the current market to determine what subjects should be covered. Halfway through the manuscript, however, I saw the market changing and PostScript's role expanding. An ever-increasing interest in desktop publishing and PostScript device support has created a PostScript clone industry in itself. As the clones were being developed, color thermal-transfer printers were becoming a reality. QMS had already launched its pricey ColorScript 100, and Tektronix was readying the Phaser system of color and black-and-white printers.

New devices and new interest from users mean new chapters. So, away we plunge into the world of color PostScript. And, of course, everyone handles it differently. I will not suggest that our way is the latest and greatest, but it is clean and efficient. I have added a number of sections that address color from some traditional standpoints. I have also taken a careful look at file and image control when working in multiple colors. Terminologies used in this section are those of the printing and publishing industry. The translation into PostScript coding should go smoothly for anyone who has traditional publishing experience.

With all this evolution and revolution in printing technologies, it's no wonder that this book wouldn't stop growing. Smaller and more efficient PostScript code solutions will continue to be developed. I hope that this book will offer a stable foundation for your own growth. I have tried to adhere to the Adobe PostScript Document Structuring Conventions in all cases. Any variation from these conventions has been done to save valuable printing space, by avoiding the repetitive comment lines. Please read the chapter on structuring carefully, and your code will stay error-free across many computer platforms.

Where Are We Going?

The conventional paste-up artist is on the way out. Desktop publishing, or as I prefer to call it, electronic publishing, puts the combined control of design and execution in the hands of one person. At *PC Magazine*, I have seen the demand for paste-up or mechanical artists go from an average of 40–80 hours per week to zero.

There are some negative implications when the role of the paste-up artist is eliminated. This position typically operated as an apprentice opportunity for a young artist directly out of a college, university, or vocational school. Now, much more of the creative responsibility is placed directly in the hands of the artist.

In addition, these computerized systems allow the designer to be the paste-up artist. In reality, both positions are coming much closer together. In a structured creative environment, there could well be a design director, art director, associate art directors, assistant art directors, graphic artists, layout artists, and paste-up artists. With exactly the same hardware and software in front of each person on each level, what makes them different?

Creativity in various forms is the only distinguishing factor among these different job responsibilities. Working directly in PostScript allows you to break out of some of the limitations imposed by the DTP (desktop publishing) software.

Limitations programmed into applications software are not a reflection of the PostScript programming language. Indeed, as I mentioned earlier, your imagination is your only limitation.

If you are a seasoned desktop publisher with little or no previous experience in conventional publishing, seek out a broader understanding of the conventional methods of design and production. If you are a seasoned conventional publishing professional in design or production, with little computer experience, seek out that desktop publisher. The synergy of the two professionals can and will be rewarding for both, and the end product will also benefit.

This melding of talents will inevitably happen. If you are wondering how soon, that's hard to tell. I see the signs of it today and can see that *all* major publishers will use these tools as we proceed through the '90s.

Testing Equipment

The code written for this book was tested in a number of environments. Even though PostScript is a generic page-description language with device independence, some devices have specific code requirements. In Chapter 6 I go into detail on the differences between the devices that output color and those that interpret color into black and white. The equipment used for creation and testing was:

Computers:

- IBM PC
- Toshiba T1100 Plus
- Compaq 386/20
- Dell System 200
- Apple Macintosh SE

Printers:

- Apple LaserWriter IINT
- Apple LaserWriter IINTX
- Tektronix Phaser CP (color PostScript printer)
- Linotronic 300

Once again, let me thank Dr. John E. Warnock and Dr. Charles M. Geschke for developing a tool for the 1990s, one that I am sure you will relish and that will make you wonder, "How did we ever do without it?"

CHAPTER 1

A Quick Start

1-1 Getting Started with PostScript

To make this an enjoyable exercise in learning, I will use this chapter to teach you the basics of PostScript by example.

In order for you to begin programming in PostScript with some understanding of what you will be typing, the next few sections outline the basics you will need to get started with PostScript.

1-2 Where Do You Work?

The best and easiest way to get started in PostScript programming is to open up a new file in your favorite word processor. If you have a Macintosh, start up MacWrite. If you have an IBM, start up WordPerfect or even the Windows Notepad or any ASCII-based text editor. When you start typing in the PostScript code that I am providing, you will be programming in PostScript.

You will realize the fruits of your labors when you send that text file down to your PostScript printer. If you are unfamiliar with sending files to a PostScript printer or wish to program interactively with the printer, refer to chapter 2, "PostScript Principles."

1-3   Units of Measure

It is important to note at this time that the PostScript system of measurement is in relative units. However, these units are equivalent to the points/picas system used in traditional American publishing. A pica is equivalent to 1/6 of an inch, and a point is 1/72 of an inch. Therefore, a pica is 12 points, and an inch is 72 points. Working in points will give you a one-to-one relationship with the page you are printing on.

1-4   Coordinate System

For the examples in this book, I will work with an 8.5 × 11-inch page, or 612 × 792 points. The PostScript coordinate system directly reflects these points. Figure 1–1 shows the dimensions of an 8.5 × 11-inch page and where PostScript locates its point of origin.

1-5   Locating a Point

Text and graphics both require a starting point. To locate the point of origin for a line of text, a single PostScript operator is required. The *moveto* operator requires two numbers in order to be effective, the x and y coordinates. In order to move to the point one inch to the right and two inches up from the lower left corner, the following command must be used.

```
72 144 moveto
```

You should note at this point that the first value, "72," represents the x coordinate, and the second value, "144," represents the y coordinate. Both of these numbers have a specific location in the program line. PostScript can be thought of as a "backwards" language. Since PostScript is a stack-based language (a stack of memory), the location points appear *before* the procedural call to use them. This type of programming is called Post-Fix Notation.

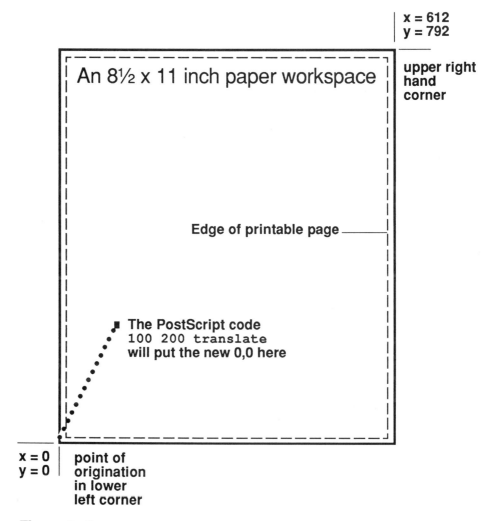

An 8½ x 11 inch paper workspace

x = 612
y = 792

upper right
hand
corner

Edge of printable page

The PostScript code
`100 200 translate`
will put the new 0,0 here

x = 0
y = 0

point of
origination
in lower
left corner

Figure 1—1

1-6 Working in Inches

If you prefer working in inches, you can take the same PostScript code, add an *inch* routine, and get the same results:

```
/inch 72 mul def
1 inch 2 inch moveto
```

The first line of code multiplies whatever is on the stack by 72. Since the units that we are putting on the stack are typically thought of as points, if we multiply them by 72 they become inches. The second line of code shows the inch procedure in action.

1-7   Path Construction

In drawing a graphic, I first need to instruct PostScript to construct a path for my graphic to be drawn on. This process of path construction can be thought of as a pencil sketch before going to ink. PostScript contains numerous path-construction operators to help in the creation of graphical outlines. Unlike other high-level languages, however, PostScript has no operators for a box, circle, or other geometric shapes.

A path begins by using one of the PostScript path-constructing operators. It implicitly ends with the *closepath* operator or by drawing a line along the path defined by using the *stroke* operator. Creating a path does not draw the path onto the page. It merely creates the invisible path and waits for further instructions.

1-8   Drawing a Line

Now that I have located a point on the page, I can begin creating a path to be drawn. Starting simply, I will path a line. The PostScript operator for defining a line is *lineto*. The *lineto* operator also requires two values, the x and y coordinates of the new point on the page. This operator will draw an invisible line to that point from wherever the current point is. To create a path 30 picas long directly across the page, we would need to add the following line of code.

```
72 144 moveto
432 144 lineto
```

The *lineto* operator performs a second task for me. The original point was located at 72,144. In Figure 1–2, I drew a line to 432,144. In order to continue the path up from that location, all I need to do is add another *lineto* operation. This is possible because the current point has been updated by the first *lineto* operation. In Figure 1–3, a second line is drawn straight up

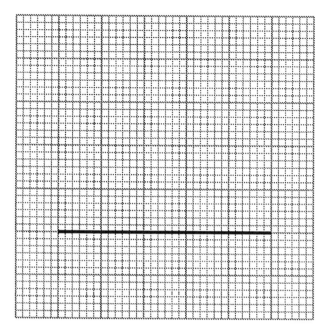

Figure 1—2

from this new point when the following line of code is added to the program.

```
72 144 moveto
432 144 lineto
432 216 lineto
```

1-9 Drawing an Arc

In Figure 1–4, I have added an arc to this drawing with the use of the PostScript *arcn* operator.

```
72 144 moveto
432 144 lineto
432 216 lineto
252 216 180 90 180 arcn
```

This operation will continue the path in the form of an arc to the left connected to the last point in the path. This operation is not determined by the current point, however. The five numbers that are placed on the stack

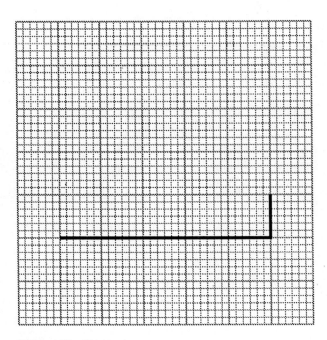

Figure 1—3

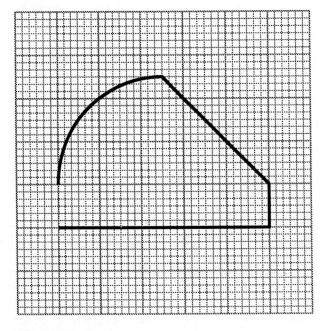

Figure 1—4

prior to the operator call are: x location and y location for center of arc, starting rotation (zero is at 3 o'clock), ending rotation, and radius of arc.

PostScript also has an *arc* operator that accepts the same amount of data as the *arcn* operator. The difference is in the direction of drawing the arc. The *arcn* operator, as you have seen, draws an arc in a counterclockwise direction. The *arc* operator draws in a clockwise direction.

1-10 Creating a Polygon

So far, I have defined a path with two lines and an arc. To connect the last point with the first point (72, 144), all I need to do is call on the PostScript operator *closepath*. This operator takes all of the path construction instructions and connects them into a polygon. The last connecting line between the end of the arc and the point of origin need not be defined.

```
72 144 moveto
432 144 lineto
432 216 lineto
252 216 180 90 180 arc
closepath
```

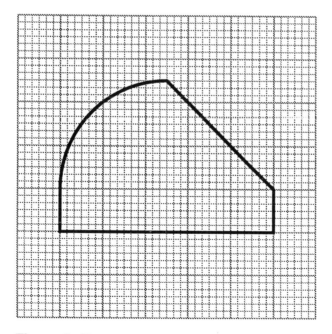

Figure 1—5

1-11   Stroking the Line

Once a path has been defined, the line can be drawn by using the *stroke* operator. As mentioned before, the path operators simply define the location of lines but do not actually draw them. Whether or not the path is closed, the line still needs to be stroked.

1-12   Printing and Ejecting the Page

All of the exercises so far have not actually printed a page. The initial operations defined a path for eventual stroking. The actual printing on paper does not take place unless specifically requested. The *showpage* operator handles this. This operator requires no preceding values and cannot produce an error. The *showpage* operator copies the image to the paper, ejects the page, and resets the system to its default values.

```
72 144 moveto
432 144 lineto
432 216 lineto
252 216 180 90 180 arc
closepath
stroke
showpage
```

1-13   Adjusting the Line Weight

The line that is stroked has certain characteristics that can be defined by operators in PostScript. The most often used of these operators is *setlinewidth*. This operator takes one value as its argument, the width of the line in points. In Figure 1–6 I have adjusted the line weight up to 10 points from the default of .5 points.

```
72 144 moveto
432 144 lineto
432 216 lineto
252 216 180 90 180 arc
closepath
10 setlinewidth
stroke
showpage
```

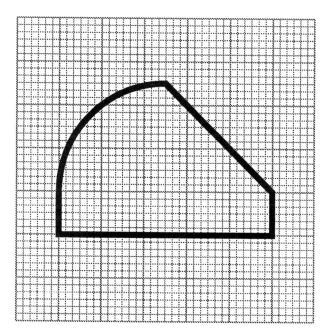

Figure 1—6

1-14   Filling a Polygon

So far, I have created a path and stroked it. Since this path has been closed to create a polygon, it can be filled. In Figure 1–7, I have taken the same path and closed it. This time, however, I will fill the area inside the polygon rather than stroking the line. The *fill* operator is used to paint the area within the defined fully connected path. An error will occur if you attempt to fill without a closed path.

```
72 144 moveto
432 144 lineto
432 216 lineto
252 216 180 90 180 arc
closepath
fill
showpage
```

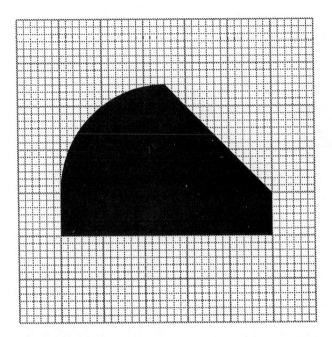

Figure 1—7

1-15   Shades of Gray

If I wished to take the same polygon and paint it gray rather than black, I would have to employ another PostScript operator, *setgray*. The *setgray* operator accepts one value as its argument. The value preceding the operator can range from 0 to 1, with 0 being equal to black and 1 being equal to white. The gray values in between can be thought of as the percentage of white dot added to a black field. For instance, .9 *setgray* will produce a 10% black paint, and .1 *setgray* will produce a 90% black paint. This seems awkward to me, and it may seem backwards to you as well. However, I overcame my initial confusion during practical use of the language and forgot about it until reviewing the subject in this book. Figure 1—8 shows the effect of using the *setgray* operator.

```
72 144 moveto
432 144 lineto
432 216 lineto
252 216 180 90 180 arc
closepath
```

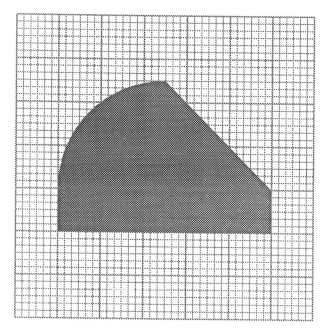

Figure 1—8

```
.5 setgray
fill
showpage
```

1-16 Printing Text

Up to this point, we have worked with the graphics operations available in PostScript. The text operations, however, are probably the most familiar to you. Since PostScript defines its text characters as outlines (point-to-point instructions constructing the letter form), they can be scaled and manipulated in any direction or form.

Printing text on a page requires a few simple steps. The first requirement is the same as for the graphics example, a starting point. In the graphics example, a *moveto* operation was performed. Once again, the *moveto* operator is used to locate the left-hand edge, baseline of the text to be drawn.

The second requirement is the text itself. Text in PostScript is in string form. Strings are identified by parentheses. Any text character within the parentheses is assumed to be part of that text string. Finally, the PostScript *show* operator is called on to print the text string to the page.

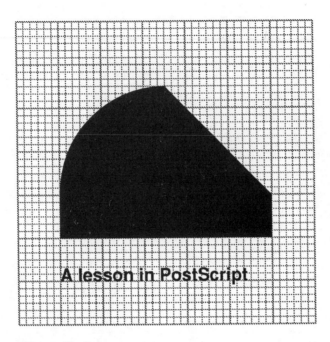

Figure 1—9

Figure 1–9 shows the results of the following code listing.

```
72 144 moveto
432 144 lineto
432 216 lineto
252 216 180 90 180 arc
closepath
fill

72 72 moveto
/Helvetica-Bold findfont 30 scalefont setfont
(A lesson in PostScript) show
showpage
```

1-17   Using Algebra (Did You Wonder When This Would Be Useful?)

If you study the numbers in the example code being used in this chapter, you will see some obvious relationships. There are some repetitive numbers, and there are relationships between different numbers, notably that they are all divisible by 72 (by the inch). In the following section, the same figure is rendered with multiples of 72 defined as letters. For long code segments this can save many keystrokes.

1.17.1 Defining a Variable

Using simple algebra we can reduce the number of characters in the program. Since many lines lengths and other sizes become related to one another, modifications to the original variable definitions will result in more global changes to the final image. If we were to change the original 72 to 36 the resulting image would be one-half as large. If we changed 72 to 288 the resulting image would be 4 times as large. In this case we would not have to change all of the values, only one. Figure 1–10 shows the results of the following code listing.

```
/a 72 def
/b a 2 mul def
/c a 6 mul def
/d a 3 mul def
/e a 3.5 mul def

a b moveto
c b lineto
c d lineto
e d 180 90 180 arc
closepath
fill

a a moveto
/Helvetica-Bold findfont 30 scalefont setfont
(A lesson in PostScript) show
showpage
```

1.17.2 From Idea to Print

In a typical exercise in design, I would start with an idea, usually sketched on paper. Yes, paper. Even though these computerized systems can create fabulous graphics at incredible speeds, they are not that good at replacing a design tool such as a pencil.

The design I am seeking will be simple, a logotype for some company. To keep it simple, I will use my initials as the basis of a logo for the company name, "Gerry's Global Graphics."

Figure 1–11 shows the original pencil sketch for the logo design. Note that the design is sketched on grid paper. This is a typical approach for a mechanical-looking design.

Computerized systems often reflect traditional methods. It makes sense in this case to reflect the traditional design process. A computerized grid would therefore be helpful in plotting out this rendering.

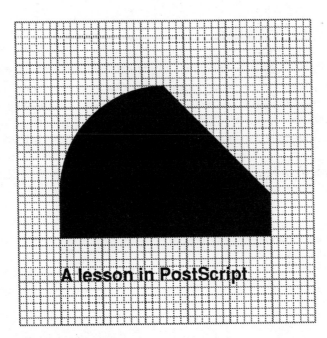

Figure 1—10

1.17.3   Set Up a Grid

Print a points/picas grid 42 × 42 picas (504 × 504 points). The grid should
be equally spaced in both directions, with each line in the grid representing
1 pica (12 points).

```
50 50 translate        % move lower left corner up
/grid {/GS exch def     % exchange value from stack
  .6 setgray            % set gray to 40%
  .8 setlinewidth       % .8 points line thickness
%  HORIZONTAL LINES 12 POINTS APART
  /x 0 def              % x=0
  0 12 GS{              % begin for loop
    /y exch def         % y=current value
    x y moveto          % locate point
    GS y lineto         % draw line
    stroke}for          % stroke line repeat till GS
%  VERTICAL LINES 12 POINTS APART
  /y 0 def
  0 12 GS{/x exch def x y moveto x
    GS lineto stroke}for
  2 setlinewidth
%  HORIZONTAL LINES 72 POINTS APART
```

```
  /x 0 def
  0 72 GS{/y exch def x y moveto
    GS y lineto stroke}for
%  VERTICAL LINES 72 POINTS APART
  /y 0 def
  0 72 GS{/x exch def x y moveto x
    GS lineto stroke}for
  0 setgray 1 setlinewidth
}def

504 grid
```

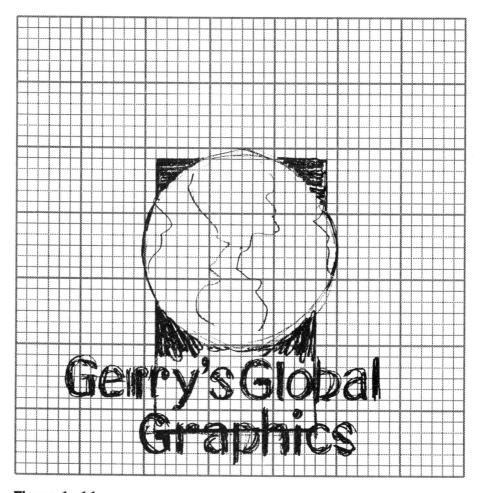

Figure 1—11

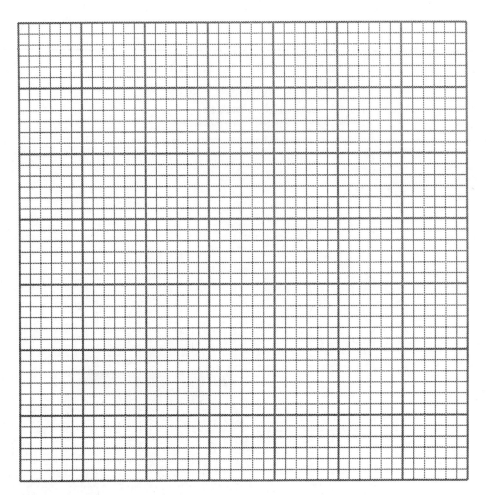

Figure 1—12
Grid

The operators and techniques used to create the grid are explained later in this book. For the sake of teaching the design process with PostScript, I will skip over a detailed explanation of the *grid* procedure.

With the grid in place I can easily measure and locate the plot points that my design requires. The first and simplest object to be drawn is the background box. Figure 1–13 shows the gray box in place. The listing below creates that box.

```
%  ----- draw back panel in gray -----
.2 setgray       % set gray to 80%
156 48 moveto    % locate first point
```

```
156 348 lineto    % path to second point
348 348 lineto    % path to third point
348 48 lineto     % path to fourth point
closepath         % connect to first point
fill              % fill with gray
```

The next step will be to draw a circle representing the space for a globe. Since PostScript does not have a circle routine, I will use the *arc* routine, draw a complete 360-degree arc, and fill it. Figure 1–14 shows the effect of the following code added to the *grid* and *graybox* procedures.

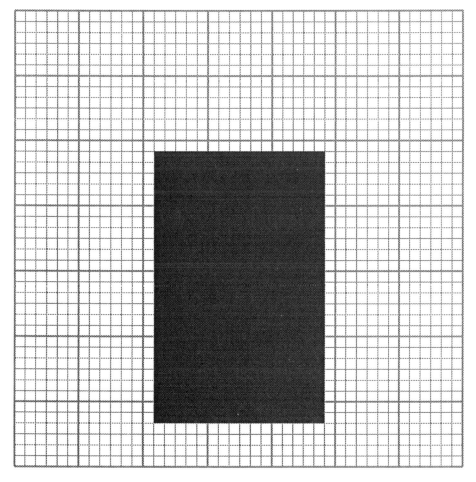

Figure 1–13
Back Panel

```
%  ----- draw inner circle for globe -----
1 setgray          % set gray to white
252 252 108 0 360 arc  % draw a complete circle
fill               % fill the circle with white
```

The only step remaining is to place the text on the art. Normally, a graphic artist would specify this type "on center." However, there is no such command in PostScript. Such alignment operations must be coded. To simplify the presentation of this graphic, I will simply measure and place the text according to the grid. Figure 1–15 shows the first line of text placed. The following code executes this procedure.

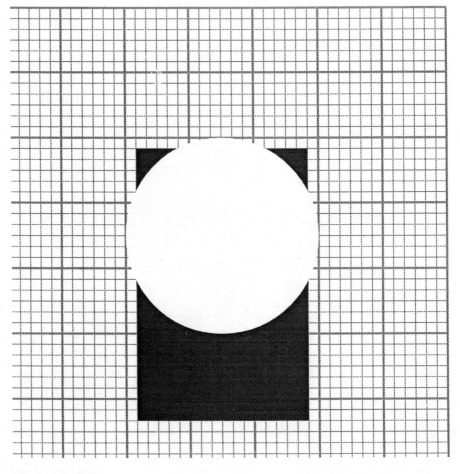

Figure 1—14
Global Space

```
%   ----- place text on page ------------
/Helvetica-Bold findfont 58 scalefont setfont
60 84 moveto      % move to starting location
0 setgray         % set color to black
(Gerry'sGlobal)   % text to print
show              % place text on page
```

The last line of text is placed according to the grid. In printing this page I found that an adjustment of a few points was necessary. After two or three printings, I found the correct position. This repetitive printing is common in perfecting PostScript code, since the first printing may not give you the result you want. PostScript screen *display* interpreters are quickly coming

Figure 1—15
Global Type

to market. This computer screen preview should help save untold reams of paper. Figure 1–16 shows the near completed artwork.

```
126 36 moveto      % move to starting location
(Graphics)         % text to print
show               % place text on page
showpage
```

Below is the complete listing for Figure 1–17. In this figure, I have changed the background tint and altered the circle routine to add an outline.

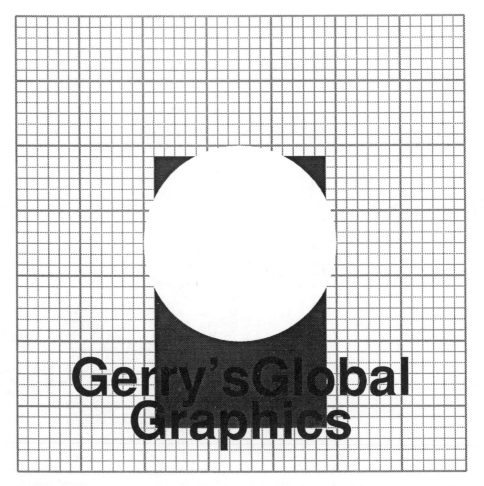

Figure 1–16
Graphics

```
/grid {/GS exch def
50 50 translate
.6 setgray
.8 setlinewidth /x 0 def 0 12 GS{
  /y exch def x y moveto GS y lineto stroke}for
/y 0 def 0 12 GS{
  /x exch def x y moveto x GS lineto stroke}for
2 setlinewidth /x 0 def 0 72 GS{
  /y exch def x y moveto GS y lineto stroke}for
/y 0 def 0 72 GS{
  /x exch def x y moveto x GS lineto stroke}for
0 setgray 1 setlinewidth
}def

504 grid
%  ----- draw back panel in gray -----
.8 setgray        % set gray to 20%
156 48 moveto     % locate first point
156 348 lineto    % path to second point
348 348 lineto    % path to third point
348 48 lineto     % path to fourth point
closepath         % connect to first point
fill              % fill with gray

%  ----- draw inner circle for globe -----
1 setgray         % set gray to white
252 252 108 0 360 arc  % draw a complete circle
gsave             % save graphics state
fill              % fill the circle with white
grestore          % restore graphic
.8 setgray        % set gray to 20%
4 setlinewidth    % line thickness 4 points
stroke            % stroke line of arc

%  ----- place text on page -----------
/Helvetica-Bold findfont 58 scalefont setfont
60 84 moveto       % move to starting location
0 setgray          % set color to black
(Gerry'sGlobal)    % text to print
show               % place text on page
126 36 moveto      % move to starting location
(Graphics) % text to print
show               % place text on page
showpage
```

1-18   The imagemask Operator

A scanned image of a globe would be helpful. However, inserting a scanned image into your art brings the PostScript interpreter to its knees. The time to process a bit-mapped image can be prohibitive. For this reason I have not

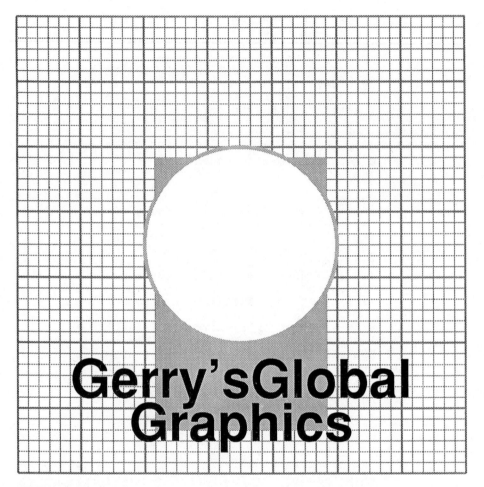

Figure 1—17
Change Gray

gone to any lengths to explain or use scanned images in this book. Figures 1–18 and 1–19 show the same graphic with a scanned image in place.

With the addition of this image, the print time was increased from 10 seconds to 5 minutes, using an Apple LaserWriter IINTX for output. The same image on a Linotronic 300 would take approximately 20 minutes to process at 1270 dpi resolution.

The following code utilizes the *imagemask* operator which differs from the *image* operator in the way it is painted onto the page. The *imagemask* operator creates an opaque mask of the black dots which make up the image, the white areas of the image are left transparent. The *image* operator paints a black and white opaque image in its rectangular area.

```
%  ----- draw back panel in gray -----
.8 setgray        % set gray to 20%
156 48 moveto     % locate first point
156 348 lineto    % path to second point
348 348 lineto    % path to third point
348 48 lineto     % path to fourth point
closepath         % connect to first point
fill              % fill with gray

%  ----- draw inner circle for globe -----
1 setgray         % set gray to white
252 252 108 0 360 arc  % draw a complete circle
gsave             % save graphics state
fill              % fill the circle with white
grestore          % restore the graphic
2 setlinewidth    % width of line
.8 setgray        % 20% gray
stroke            % stroke line

/imagestring 1225 7 add 8 idiv string def
0 setgray
13 10 translate
.6 .6 scale
1225 797 true [1 0 0 1 0 0]
{currentfile imagestring readhexstring pop}
imagemask
8880880008880008880088880808800088800000000000000000000
00000000000000000137FFF007FFFFF01FFFF737FFFE1F80000000000
00001FFFFFFFFFFFFFFFFFFF1133FFFFFFFFFFFFFFFFFFFFFFFFFFFFFF
FFFFF7000000000000000000000000000000000000000000000000000
00000000000000000000000000000000000000000000000000000000000
00000000000000000000000000000000000000000000000000000000000
000000000000000000000111B90001900000000000000000000111111F9
001B9B901BB9911199819000000000000001199999999999999991
91111119999999999999999999919199991B9110000000000000000
00000000000000000000000000000000000000000000000000000000000
00000000000000000000000000000000000000000000000000000000000
00000000000000000000000000000000000000000000000000000000011
1FD001D10000000000000001111111F9001FDF901FF911111FF81D
100000000000011F991119DFFDFF9DD19111115DDDDDFD1199DFF9
11111111119F91FD11100000000000000000000000000000000000000
00000000000010191001100100000000000010178000000000000
...stream of hexidecimal information, 122,783 in length
...00000000000

initgraphics     % reset graphics state

%  ----- place text on page ------------
/Helvetica-Bold findfont 58 scalefont setfont
0 setgray         % set color to black
60 84 moveto      % move to starting location
(Gerry'sGlobal)   % text to print
show              % place text on page
126 36 moveto     % move to starting location
(Graphics)        % text to print
```

```
show              % place text on page
.9 setgray         % set color to black
56 80 moveto      % move to starting location
(Gerry'sGlobal)   % text to print
show              % place text on page
122 32 moveto     % move to starting location
(Graphics)        % text to print
show              % place text on page
showpage
```

In Figure 1–19, the scanned image has been flipped to create a better composition. This type of manipulation is simple in PostScript. Only one line of code was affected and one added. The original translation of the image was increased by approximately 500 in each direction to move the point of origin to the upper right. Then the entire graphic was rotated 180 degrees. The changes are reflected in the code fragment that follows:

Figure 1—18

Figure 1—19

```
/imagestring 1225 7 add 8 idiv string def
0 setgray
513 510 translate % change point of origination
.6 .6 scale
180 rotate         % rotate image 180 degrees
1225 797 true [1 0 0 1 0 0]
{currentfile imagestring readhexstring pop}
imagemask
```

1-19   The image Operator

The *image* operator in PostScript is typically used to print scanned halftones. However, the same operator can be used to create synthetic images. The following code is not of a scanned image. Instead, I chose to hand-code the hexidecimal information for an image of a letter G. Figure 1–20 shows the image scaled at 50%, 100%, 200%, and 1,000%. The code shown on the following page reflects the image printing at 1,000%.

Figure 1–20
Image Operator

```
gsave
100 50 translate
400 420 scale
/DataString 40 string def
40 42 8 [40 0 0 -42 0 42]
{currentfile DataString readhexstring pop}
image
000000000000000000000000000113264afcfcfcfaf64321100000
0000000000000000000000000000000000000000000003264af
cfffffffffffffffffcfaf643200000000000000000000000000
000000000000113264affffffffffffffffffffffffffffaf6432
1100000000000000000000000000000113264affffffffffffe66
432113264ffffffffffffffaf64321100000000000000000000000
003264affffffffffffe664321100000112232fffffffffffffffaf6
43200000000000000000000003264affffffffffffe6641100000000
0000001132ffffffffffffffffaf643200000000000000000003264aff
ffffffffffe66400000000000000000000000032ffffffffffffffffaf64
320000000000003264afffffffffffff64000000000000000000000
000000032fffffffffffffffaf64320000000000113264afffffffffff
ffe66400000000000000000000000032ffffffffffffffffaf64321
100000003264afffffffffffff640000000000000000000000000
000032fffffffffffffffaf643200000113264affffffffffffe6640
00000000000000000000000000032fffffffffffffffaf64321100
003264affffffffffffff6400000000000000000000000000000000
032fffffffffffffffaf643200003264affffffffffffff6400000000
0000000000000000000000000032fffffffffffffffaf64321111326
4afffffffffffffe66400000000000000000000000000000000032ff
fffffffffffffaf6432223264afffffffffffff6400000000000000000
000000000000000000003232fffffffffffffffaf64323264affff
ffffffff6400000000000000000000000000000000000000000000
00000000000000003264affffffffffffff64000000000000000000000
0000000000000000000000000000000000000003264affffffffff
fff6400000000000000000000000000000000000000000000000000
000000003264affffffffffffff640000000000000000000000000
0000000000000000000000000000000003264affffffffffff64
001a2a3a4a5a6a7a8a9aaabacadaeafafffffffffffffffffffffffa
f64323264afffffffffffff64001a2a3a4a5a6a7a8a9aaabacadaea
fafffffffffffffffffffffffaf64323264affffffffffffff64001a2
a3a4a5a6a7a8a9aaabacadaeafafffffffffffffffffffffffffaf6432
3264affffffffffffff64001a2a3a4a5a6a7a8a9aaabacadaeafafff
fffffffffffffffffffaf64323264afffffffffffff64001a2a3a4a
5a6a7a8a9aaabacadaeafafffffffffffffffffffffffffaf64323264a
fffffffffff64001a2a3a4a5a6a7a8a9aaabacadaeafaffffffff
fffffffffffffaf64323264affffffffffffff64001a2a3a4a5a6a7
a8a9aaabacadaeafafffffffffffffffffffffffaf64323264afffff
fffffff6400000000000000000000000000000011325364fffff
fffffffffaf6432113264afffffffffffe664000000000000000000
000000000000000064e6ffffffffffffaf643211003264afffffffff
fffff64000000000000000000000000000000000064ffffffffffff
ffaf643200003264afffffffffffff64000000000000000000000
0000000000064fffffffffffffffaf64320000113264afffffffffff
e664000000000000000000000000000064e6ffffffffffffffaf643
2110000003264afffffffffffff64000000000000000000000000000
000064fffffffffffffffaf643200000000113264afffffffffffe66
400000000000000000000000000064e6ffffffffffffffaf6432110000
```

```
0000003264affffffffffff640000000000000000000000000064f
ffffffffffffaf6432000000000000003264afffffffffffe66400
000000000000000000064e6fffffffffffffaf64320000000000000
000003264affffffffffffe66432000000000000003264e6ffffffff
ffffaf6432000000000000000000000000113264affffffffffffe6643
21111113264e6ffffffffffffaf6432110000000000000000000000
000000113264affffffffffffff6e6e6e6f6ffffffffffffffaf6432110
0000000000000000000000000000000113264afffffffffffffff
ffffffffffffaf6432110000000000000000000000000000000000000
000000000113264afffffffffffffffffffffaf6432110000000000000
00000000000000000000000000000000000000011111132326464643
23211110000000000000000000000000000000000000000000000000
00000000000000000000000000000000000000000000000000000000
00000
grestore
showpage
```

You can see by the amount of data supplied to the *image* operator that a photograph can be a tremendously large file and that processing can take forever.

A couple of things have to happen in order for the *image* operator to function properly. Before the operator and its values are executed, the space for that image must be defined. The *scale* operator is used to define the *x* and *y* coordinates of the image's rectangular space. A null string equal to the length of the data strings must also be defined.

The *image* operator itself requires five objects to be on the stack at the time of calling. The first two objects are the *x* and *y* dimensions of the image. The next object, "8", represents the bit depth of the image. An image of one-bit depth can address two colors: black or white. An eight-bit image will allow 256 levels of gray. The next object is an array of information in matrix form. This matrix represents the transformation from user space to the image coordinate system. Notice the use of the *x* and *y* dimensions of the data as values within the matrix.

Finally, the fifth item on the stack prior to calling the *image* operator is the procedure to be followed for each string of hexidecimal data.

The current hex file is read via the PostScript *currentfile* operator. The *DataString* null string is used to hold the 40 elements of hexidecimal information placed there by *readhexstring*. The string remains on the stack, so it must be popped off (removed) after its use.

```
400 420 scale
/DataString 40 string def
40 42 8 [40 0 0 -42 0 42]
{currentfile DataString readhexstring pop}
image
```

2

PostScript Principles

2-1   What is PostScript?

PostScript is the best tool that a graphic designer could possibly have. Once you have realized that the computer is nothing more than a sophisticated tool, you will be more accepting of the fact that a programming language can also be a designer's tool. If you look at the conventional tools used by the graphic artist and how the graphic artist uses them, you will see that there are direct comparisons between the conventional graphic-arts tools and the capabilities of PostScript.

For instance, the triangle and T square allow the graphic artist to draw a straight line, almost. A computer can draw the same line, only better. PostScript as a tool for the designer offers a text-based description of that line or any other graphic. I don't believe that the computer should or even could replace the artist. In fact, I believe that the computer, when used correctly, is a tool that allows the artist to explore many more ideas than was ever possible with conventional tools. The simple fact is that the computer can perform the same tasks, but with a higher degree of precision. And assuming that the hardware and software are readily available, PostScript will perform the same task better *and* in a fraction of the time.

PostScript is a tool. To the programmer, it is a language that talks to a PostScript-compatible printer, which allows for high quality output. To the artist, it is a flexible design tool that allows for complex renderings to be realized with exact precision. For the businessperson, PostScript is the answer for high-quality business graphics in the office.

PostScript is defined as a page-description language. By "page description," I mean that the operations of the code describe what a printed page will look like. The nice thing about this language is the fact that whatever you can imagine on a printed page can be described in PostScript code. That sounds a little like pie in the sky, but it's true. As you look over the examples in this book and study the set of operators in the language, you will see that the only things holding back an extraordinary graphic are your ability to program efficiently and your imagination.

This language is interpreted rather than compiled. Programs written in BASIC, C, or FORTRAN become self-executable after being compiled. PostScript, on the other hand, is not self-executable. It relies completely on an interpreter to execute the code. This interpreter is usually software that is permanently placed in a computer chip. That chip is then placed in a printing device or in a separate host that sends information to the printer engine. The page description is sent to that printing device, interpreted there, and imaged onto paper or film.

PostScript is available in many places. In fact, you may already have been using PostScript without even knowing it. Popular DTP software uses PostScript to communicate to PostScript laser printers, such as the Apple LaserWriter. Many word processors now support PostScript. These word processors are taking advantage of the rich set of scalable fonts available in the PostScript printer's ROM (read-only memory).

Just as these programs have printer drivers to address the PostScript interpreter, you can have your own application that creates the code necessary to do the same. Why would you want to do this? As you go through the examples in this book, you will find that I have presented many design solutions that are not readily available in off-the-shelf software. Your ability to create PostScript code means that you can circumvent the limitations of today's DTP and drawing packages.

Figure 2–1 shows the basic relationship between an operator and the final output of a PostScript-generated page. As you can see, there are some very basic relationships between what happens at the PostScript code-writing stage and the final output stage. No matter where it comes from, PostScript is text-based. You can easily open a PostScript output file from some other program and study the code. Once the interpreter gets the text-based (ASCII) code, it scans the code and draws the image in memory. As it does this, it layers each new operation onto the imaginary page. This is now being performed in a raster, or pixel format. You may have heard some of your peers referring to a Linotronic RIP at the type supplier. RIP

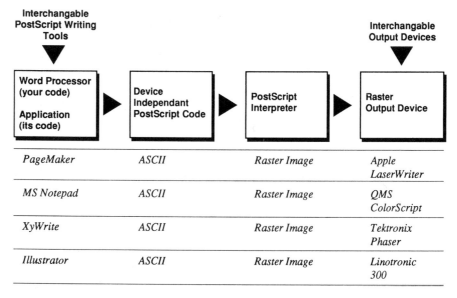

Word Processor (your code) Application (its code)	Device Independant PostScript Code	PostScript Interpreter	Raster Output Device
PageMaker	ASCII	Raster Image	Apple LaserWriter
MS Notepad	ASCII	Raster Image	QMS ColorScript
XyWrite	ASCII	Raster Image	Tektronix Phaser
Illustrator	ASCII	Raster Image	Linotronic 300

Figure 2–1

stands for Raster Image Processor. This is where the code is interpreted into a raster format. The final section of Figure 2–1 points out the device independence of PostScript. Theoretically, PostScript code from any source will run on any PostScript output device. While this is mostly true, there are some exceptions. Just as a distributor for a late-model Chevrolet will not fit into the engine of a 1952 Chevrolet, newer PostScript code will not necessarily run on an older PostScript printer. Chapter 6, "Color Post-Script," addresses these issues.

2-2   Working With Word Processors

You will more than likely use a word processor as the primary source of PostScript code input. I prefer to use XyWrite III + from XyQuest. Figure 2–2 shows a XyWrite screen with PostScript code opened as a text file.

I have also used Microsoft Windows Notepad and MS-DOS's primitive EDLIN and have even copied directly from the keyboard console to a file by utilizing the MS-DOS COPY CON command. The only requirement is that the code be pure ASCII (American Standard Code for Information Interchange) text. Most word processors either store their text in this format or have an option to do so, either in the *save* function or the *export* function.

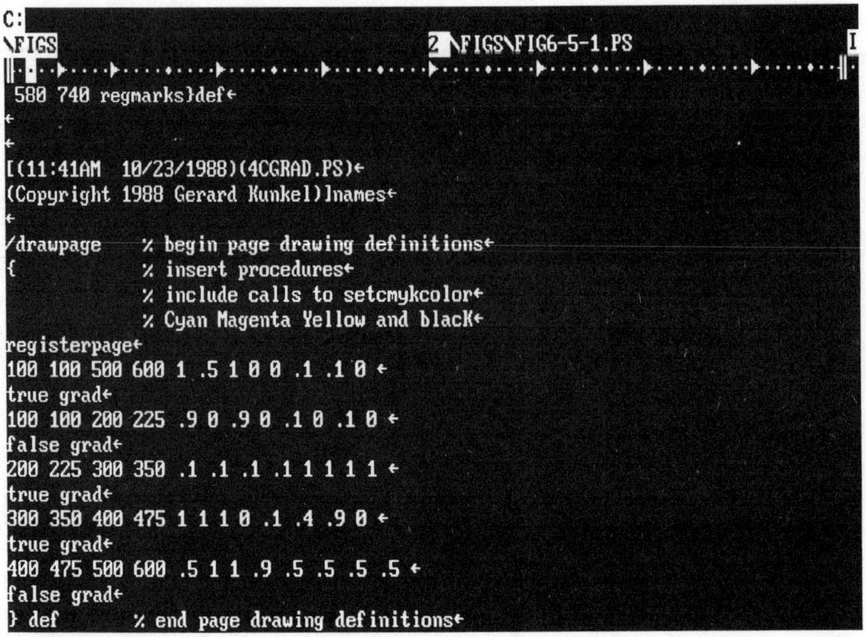

```
C:
\FIGS                              2 \FIGS\FIG6-5-1.PS              I
||·|·|·▶····▶····▶····▶····▶····▶····▶····▶····▶····▶···|·|·||
 580 740 regmarks}def←
←
←
[(11:41AM  10/23/1988)(4CGRAD.PS)←
(Copyright 1988 Gerard Kunkel)]names←
←
/drawpage      % begin page drawing definitions←
{              % insert procedures←
               % include calls to setcmykcolor←
               % Cyan Magenta Yellow and black←
registerpage←
100 100 500 600 1 .5 1 0 0 .1 .1 0 ←
true grad←
100 100 200 225 .9 0 .9 0 .1 0 .1 0 ←
false grad←
200 225 300 350 .1 .1 .1 .1 1 1 1 1 ←
true grad←
300 350 400 475 1 1 1 0 .1 .4 .9 0 ←
true grad←
400 475 500 600 .5 1 1 .9 .5 .5 .5 .5 ←
false grad←
} def          % end page drawing definitions←
```

Figure 2—2

On the Macintosh, I have used Teach Text and MacWrite. I have even used Z-BASIC and Microsoft BASIC as a form of text input. Once again, whatever text-processing tool you have will work as long as it can export unformatted ASCII. On the Macintosh, the file type should always be set to EPSF. That will enable you to import the graphic into Adobe's Illustrator, Aldus' PageMaker, or Quark Express.

Once you have the code, you can send it to the PostScript interpreter in a number of different ways. Here is where I greatly prefer the IBM environment. I typically create my code on an IBM-compatible, either a Compaq 386 or a Dell 286, and connect to the PostScript interpreter via Microsoft Windows' Terminal. The objective here is to go interactive with the interpreter so that any errors are seen as they occur.

Figure 2–3 shows a Microsoft Windows screen with both the Notepad and Terminal applications running. The terminal is communicating with an Apple LaserWriter IINTX via an RS-232 communications port. Using the RS-232 port is preferable to the 32K packet transmissions of AppleTalk, although I often share my Apple printer between a PC and a Macintosh. In

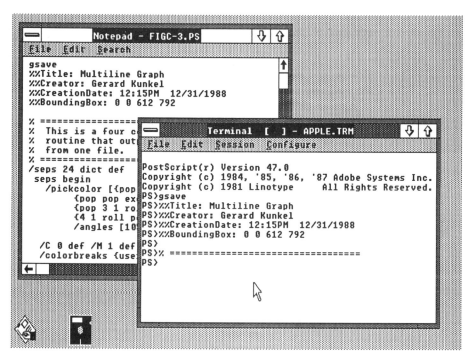

Figure 2–3

that case, I will always use AppleTalk on both the PC and the Macintosh, to avoid having to reset the Apple LaserWriter for each system.

Another form of sending a PostScript code file to the interpreter is to use the DOS COPY command. The following DOS prompt command line will send our imaginary TEST.PRN file to the printer.

```
COPY TEST.PRN COM1:
```

This works with the assumption that your printer is hooked up with a serial connection to COM1. The same would be true if you were working with LPT1 and adjusted the DOS command line to reflect this.

Another option for downloading is to use Adobe's Downloader program. It comes packaged with their downloadable fonts. This utility will control the communications to the printer and alert you if it encounters an error. The only drawback to this approach is that you cannot see exactly where the error has occurred. When you go interactive in Microsoft Windows, you can watch each line of your PostScript code get interpreted and see exactly where code modification needs to take place.

2-3   Resolution Independence

PostScript is a resolution-independent language. All descriptions of size and location are relative to the printing space. Being relative rather than absolute means that the description of a line is a point-to-point connection. The points on the line that are between the end-points need not be described. This is a vector-based instruction set that thinks in terms of connecting points rather than painting picture elements on a screen (as a paint program would define pixels). Since the two end-points of a line are the only two pieces of information for this line, the information can be used on any PostScript device at any resolution to produce the same line.

There is a one-to-one relationship of code to paper that is equal to points and picas, the standard form of measurement in the printing and graphic arts industry. Converted into inches, there are 72 points per inch. A pica is equal to 12 points, and 6 picas equal one inch. You will see the following definition in many PostScript programs.

```
/inch 72 def
```

This definition sets up the use of inches as a form of measurement. You would then see this type of program instruction to apply inches:

```
1 inch 1 inch moveto
1 inch 3 inch lineto
```

This set of instructions draws a two-inch vertical line from the starting coordinate of $x = 1$ inch, $y = 1$ inch. The PostScript interpreter recalculates these coordinates to:

```
72 72 moveto
72 216 lineto
```

This code will draw the same two-inch vertical line on an Apple LaserWriter, a QMS PS-810, or a Linotronic 300 typesetting system.

2.3.1   Scan Conversion

At some point between the creation of vector information and the final printed paper, there must be a conversion from vectors to raster information. Raster information is nothing more than a specific instruction to paint a pixel black or white, a shade of gray, or some color. The total space that an output device can image is defined as an array of pixels. An 8.5 × 11-inch printable space is equal to 612 × 792 points or 2550 × 3300 pixels.

The PostScript interpreter performs this vector-to-raster conversion. At this point, the resolution of the device becomes a deciding factor in the process. The number of pixels painted in our two-inch line example on a LaserWriter is significantly lower than the number on a 2540 dpi Linotronic 300. The Linotronic's resolution is 8.46 times as great as the 300 dpi LaserWriter. So, there would be 8.46 times as many pixels to paint. The result, however, is a line of the same length but different degrees of quality.

2-4   Opaque Painting

As the interpreter calculates the exact pixels to be painted, it places the results into an array in memory that is equal to the number of pixels on an output page. As each subsequent instruction is performed, new pixels are painted. This is an opaque operation that actually layers an image together. Since layering takes place, a white box can overlap a black box, and so on. There is no transparent feature to PostScript, so any surprint treatments must be programmed explicitly.

Understanding that the process is layered and opaque, your PostScript code must be positioned to accommodate the structure of events. For instance, a black box with white type in it, over a gray background, must be structured as follows:

- code to draw gray background
- code to draw black box
- code to draw white type

Figure 2–4 demonstrates the effect of layering. On the left is the correct way to get to the image desired. If the sequence of code is out of order, the result could be the image on the right. Seeing your PostScript code output as shown on the right could lead you to believe that the procedure in the prologue has problems. However, the only problem is the way it was ordered. The following code demonstrates both right and wrong.

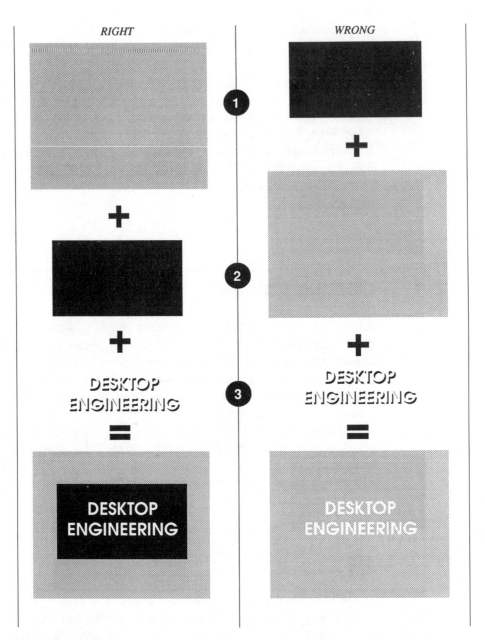

Figure 2—4

The Prologue:

```
%%BeginPrologue
/graybox
```

```
{.8 setgray
newpath
0 0 moveto
200 0 lineto
200 150 lineto
0 150 lineto
closepath
fill
}def

/blackbox
{0 setgray
newpath
24 32 moveto
176 32 lineto
176 118 lineto
24 118 lineto
closepath
fill
}def

/whitetype
{1 setgray
/Helvetica-Bold findfont 18 scalefont setfont
100 80 moveto
(DESKTOP) centershow
100 60 moveto
(ENGINEERING) centershow
}def
%%EndProlog
```

The right script:

```
%%BeginScript
graybox
blackbox
whitetype

showpage
```

The wrong script:

```
%%BeginScript
blackbox
graybox
whitetype

showpage
```

2-5 Structure

The fact that PostScript paints its pages opaquely forces you to structure your code in the order that you want your text and graphics layered. There is an even more important structuring convention that should be adhered to. Figure 2–5 illustrates the PostScript structuring convention in broad strokes.

You will notice that there are major sections to this code. Following these conventions will aid in debugging and offer some portability to the procedures that you define. In addition, if you intend to encapsulate your code for import into a desktop publishing package, the importing package will look for these structuring conventions.

The first section is the header. As in other file formats, the header indicates what the file type is and where it came from. There is also some

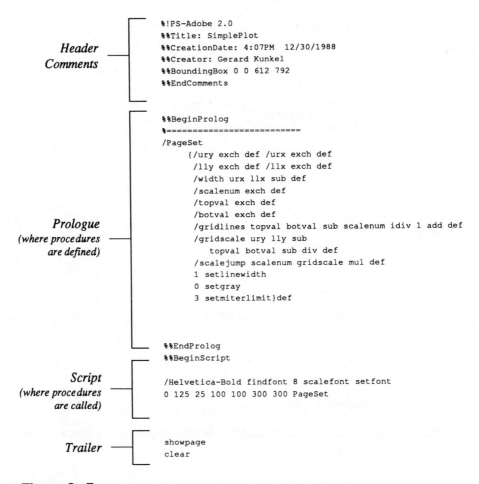

Header Comments

```
%!PS-Adobe 2.0
%%Title: SimplePlot
%%CreationDate: 4:07PM  12/30/1988
%%Creator: Gerard Kunkel
%%BoundingBox 0 0 612 792
%%EndComments
```

Prologue
(where procedures are defined)

```
%%BeginProlog
%============================
/PageSet
    {/ury exch def /urx exch def
     /lly exch def /llx exch def
     /width urx llx sub def
     /scalenum exch def
     /topval exch def
     /botval exch def
     /gridlines topval botval sub scalenum idiv 1 add def
     /gridscale ury lly sub
        topval botval sub div def
     /scalejump scalenum gridscale mul def
     1 setlinewidth
     0 setgray
     3 setmiterlimit}def
```

```
%%EndProlog
%%BeginScript
```

Script
(where procedures are called)

```
/Helvetica-Bold findfont 8 scalefont setfont
0 125 25 100 100 300 300 PageSet
```

Trailer

```
showpage
clear
```

Figure 2–5

basic file "furniture," such as date and time of creation. In addition there is *BoundingBox* information to tell an importing package what the exterior dimensions of the graphic are.

The second section is the Prologue. This is where all of your procedures are written. Procedures carry out the specific drawing tasks by being fed information prior to calling them from the script.

The third section, the Script, is where all of the actual program execution takes place.

Following these conventions will help you and anyone else who needs to work with your code. Ultimately, the debugging process will be a lot easier when each process is broken down into procedures, procedure calls, and data.

2-6 Operators

Within the prologue and script are PostScript operators. An operator is a command that is built into the language. For instance, *moveto* is an operator. This operator commands the interpreter to move the current point to the location specified by the two top numbers on the operand stack. Many PostScript operators require that there be a specific number of stack elements available in memory. The *moveto* operator requires that an *x* and *y* coordinate be available. The *makefont* operator requires that a six-element array be present at the top of the operand stack.

Since operators have specific requirements of the stack prior to execution, the preceding elements must somehow get onto the stack. Usually, your input will feed the operator.

The following code segment demonstrates what is termed *postfix* notation.

```
100 100 moveto
```

The two 100s that precede the *moveto* operator are called *operands*. If you are familiar with BASIC, the opposite is true—the operator precedes the operand, as in:

```
pset (100,100)
```

There is a rich set of PostScript operators that perform all types of graphical manipulations. There are currently no operators for specifically addressing a computer display. There is however, Display PostScript, a separate derivation of PostScript that specifically addresses computer displays.

PostScript operators rely completely on the output device's ability to interpret the raw code. Within this set of operators are three families of application. The applications include graphics, text, and sampled images. Sampled images are scanned photos or user-created raster graphics, such as a patterned background.

2-7   The Stack

PostScript is a stack-based language. All operations, mathematical or otherwise, take place on a stack. PostScript actually handles four stacks. They are the operand, dictionary, execution, and graphics-state stacks. Items are pushed onto a stack or popped off a stack. Pushing an item onto the stack is performed explicitly by putting it there. Removing an item from the stack is performed by popping it off using the PostScript operator *pop*, or through any other PostScript operator that requires the existence of elements on the stack in order to be executed properly.

The stack that you will use most of the time is the operand stack. The line of code

```
10 14 moveto
```

pushes the integers 10 and 14 onto the operand stack. The *moveto* operator requires two numbers to be executed. It pops these two integers off the stack and uses them for execution. The result is an empty operand stack, as it was before pushing the two integers onto it.

These stacks have limits. It is possible to reach the limits of these stacks, at which time a *stackoverflow* error will occur. A *stackunderflow* error is also possible. This occurs when the stack does not hold the required number of elements for an operator. The following brief descriptions of stacks include the memory limits of each stack.

- The operand stack: This is where you will place all of your active elements or data. Maximum number of elements: 500.

- The dictionary stack: This is where all of your dictionary definitions (procedures that are specifically sent to the dictionary stack) are stored. There are two dictionaries present in the dictionary stack, the *systemdict* and *userdict*. Your definitions are placed in the *userdict*. The *systemdict* contains all of the standard PostScript operators, such as *moveto* and *lineto*. Maximum depth: 20. Maximum depth of *userdict*: 200. The maximum capacity of a dictionary (where all of the specific key-value pairs (definitions that you create) are stored): 65,535. Userdict is where definitions and procedures are stored, such as:

```
/tintvalue .5 def
```

- The execution stack: This is governed by the interpreter. It is where it stores all of its pending operations and your user-defined procedures. Maximum depth: 250.

- The graphics-state stack: This stack is used to maintain a record of the current graphics state. This is useful when there is a need to temporarily alter the current graphics state and then return to it. An example would be setting a line color to black and then temporarily setting the color to 50% black to fill a box. Saving the original state and later returning there are accomplished by use of the *gsave* and *grestore* operators. This stack is managed completely by the interpreter.

In Figure 2–6, the PostScript operator *pstack* is used to show the operand stack contents. Here I have shown the results of the *dup* operator and the *add* operator. It is strongly recommended that you try going interactive with the PostScript interpreter when learning about the operand stack. Getting the immediate feedback of the *pstack* operator will speed your understanding of the stack.

In Figure 2–7, a procedure has been defined and then called. Here I am showing the proper use of the stack. Always try to keep the operand stack free of unwanted elements. This will help ensure that a *stackoverflow* error will not occur. This example shows that a procedure was defined that required an integer or real number to be present on the stack prior to execution. Just in front of the procedure call is the integer 12. This satisfies the procedure's stack requirements, and the subsequent *pstack* shows that the stack is empty.

If you are unsure if there are elements on the stack after executing a procedure, and none are required afterwards, the *clear* operator can be used to empty all elements from the operand stack. Keeping the stack clean will help avoid a stack overflow.

Figures 2–8 through 2–16 demonstrate the effect different operators have on the operand stack by showing before-and-after looks at the stack.

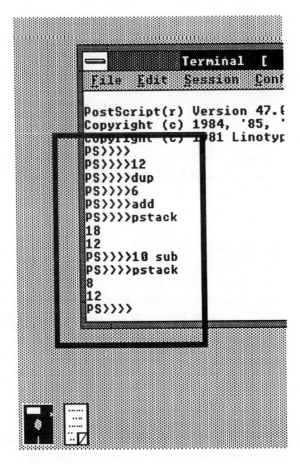

Figure 2—6

2-8   PostScript Dictionaries

2.8.1   Operand Dictionary—Key Name References

As noted earlier, PostScript is a stack-based language. All computation takes place via the operand stack. This, however, is only part of the picture. The greatest resource within this language is actually its set of dictionaries. The term *dictionary* does not refer to a location with operator definitions, although this analogy is fine to work from. The PostScript dictionary is a modifiable location in memory that can be called upon to execute tasks.

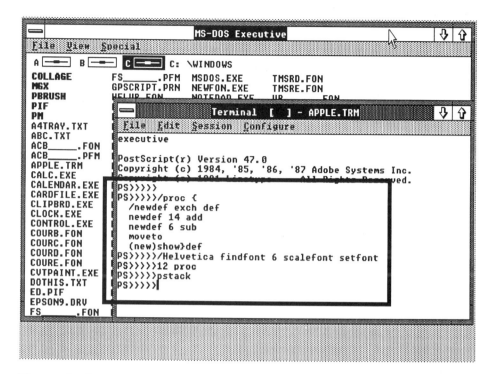

Figure 2–7

When initiating a PostScript program, the PostScript environment sets up an unnamed dictionary that accepts any definitions put there with the *def* operator.

While a definition can be as simple as:

```
/x 130 def
```

the typical dictionary definition contains a series of operations grouped together by a key name. The key name may be complex, containing groups of operations and definitions, such as:

```
/complex {
  /x 130 def
  /y 245 def
  /Helvetica findfont 10 scalefont setfont
  x y moveto
  (new location) show}def

%%EndProlog

complex
```

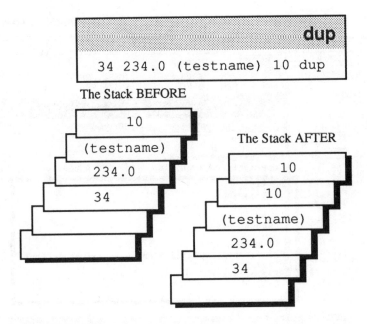

Figure 2—8

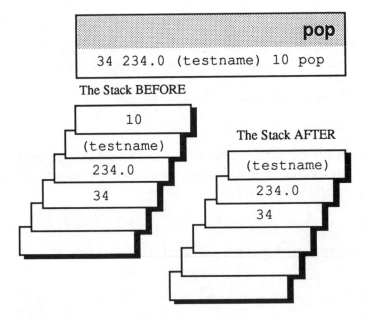

Figure 2—9

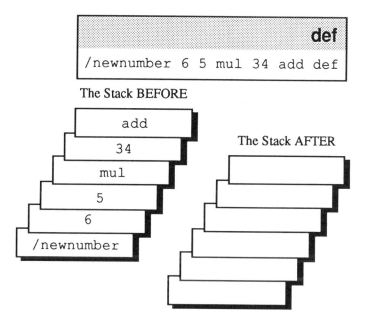

Figure 2–10

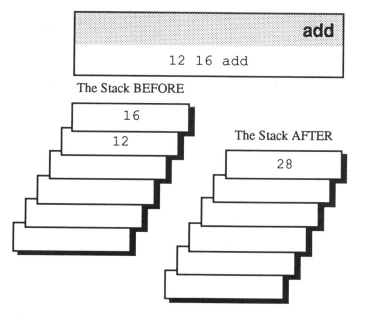

Figure 2–11

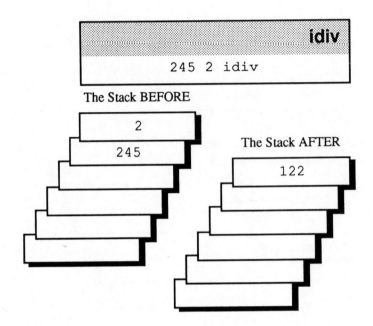

Figure 2—12

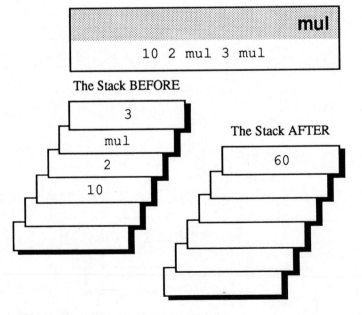

Figure 2—13

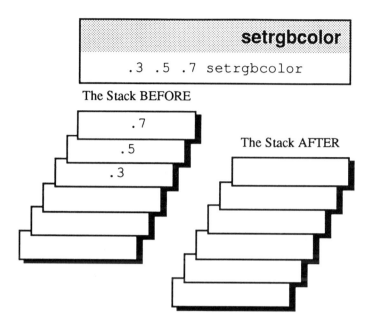

Figure 2—14

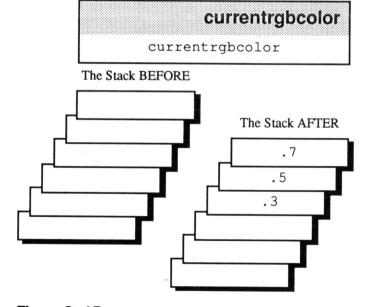

Figure 2—15

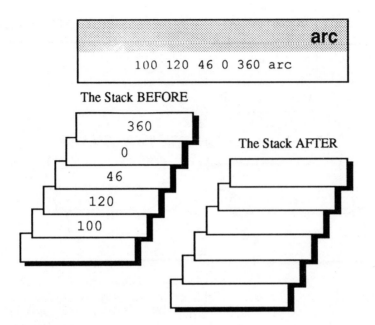

Figure 2—16

This key name definition, *complex*, itself contains two key name definitions, a font setup procedure, a *moveto* operation, and the printing of a text string. By simply calling this key name from the script, all of these operations will take place.

Taking this process one step further, we can put variables within the *complex* key name definition. The most likely objects to make variables would be the *x* and *y* coordinates and the text string. The following modification shows the *complex* routine with variables.

```
complex {
  /x exch def
  /y exch def
  /Helvetica findfont 10 scalefont setfont
  x y moveto
  show}def

%%EndProlog
(new location) 245 130 complex
```

Note that in this new procedure the *x* and *y* coordinates are exchanged on the stack and given their key name references. The text string is not. This is because the string is already sitting on the operand stack waiting for something to happen. Since the two preceding operations, the font call and the *moveto*, do not affect the contents of the stack, we can simply call the *show* operator, which will pull the top item off the stack. The advantage of creating a key name definition out of a procedure is the ability to modify the output effects by building in variables.

Here is the same PostScript program with some added text strings.

```
/complex {
  /x exch def
  /y exch def
  /ps exch def
  /Helvetica findfont ps scalefont setfont
  x y moveto
  show}def

%%EndProlog

(first location) 10 245 130 complex
(second location) 8 315 230 complex
(third location) 12 445 330 complex
(fourth location) 15.5 535 430 complex
```

When adding the three additional text strings, a new variable was added to accommodate a change in type size for each line. The key name definition *ps* was added to be inserted in front of the *scalefont* operator. Now this routine has the ability to locate, scale, and print a text string.

2.8.2   User-Defined Dictionaries

It is possible to take this key name definition and some others and put them into a user-defined dictionary. The advantage of doing so is to organize your definitions into logical groups and make them easier to work with. By creating your own dictionary, you can place definitions there and then push the dictionary onto the top of the dictionary stack when it is needed (otherwise leaving it where it is and executing all other tasks). If you then create multiple user-defined dictionaries, you can push the currently needed dictionary onto the top of the dictionary stack by pushing the name of the dictionary onto the stack, followed by the *begin* operator. Let's look at the same key name routine when put into a user-defined dictionary called *gkkdict*.

```
/gkkdict 4 dict def

gkkdict begin
/complex {
  /x exch def
  /y exch def
  /ps exch def
  /Helvetica findfont ps scalefont setfont
```

```
    x y moveto
    show)def
end

%%EndProlog

gkkdict begin
(first location) 10 245 130 complex
(second location) 8 315 230 complex
(third location) 12 445 330 complex
(fourth location) 15.5 535 430 complex
end
```

The first line of the program defines a dictionary called *gkkdict*, which will contain four definitions, one for each unique key name definition within the procedure.

```
/gkkdict 4 dict def
```

The PostScript operator *dict* is placed after the integer and before the *def* call to tell the interpreter that this is a key name definition for a dictionary. It is important to allow the proper number of key name objects within the dictionary when defining it. If you are short, you will get the PostScript error *dictstackoverflow*. Providing a larger number when defining the dictionary will waste some memory space but will not cause an error.

The line following the dictionary definition marks the beginning of the dictionary. The lines that follow are simply the lines that we used previously. The difference here is that the definitions that follow are being placed within the *gkkdict* dictionary. The *end* operator tells the PostScript interpreter that we have finished writing information into this dictionary.

In order to use the definitions within this dictionary, we must push the dictionary to the top of the dictionary stack. This is done by the line

```
gkkdict begin
```

Immediately following the *begin* operator are the script calls to the key name definitions within the dictionary.

2.8.3 User Dictionary

The user dictionary, *userdict*, is very useful for modifying PostScript operators, and you can see examples of this later in the book. The user dictionary has a maximum limit of 200, although according to Adobe, some objects are already present in this dictionary. The user dictionary resides directly above the system dictionary on the dictionary stack.

If you were picking up some existing PostScript code and wanted the line widths to be modified overall, such a procedure could be accomplished by redefining the *setlinewidth* operator in the *userdict*.

```
userdict begin
/setlinewidth
   {systemdict begin .7 add setlinewidth end}def
```

This piece of code takes all references to the *setlinewidth* operator and adds .7 point to the requested line width. The effect is a heavier line weight for all lines.

2.8.4 System Dictionary

The *systemdict* is on the bottom of the dictionary stack. Objects cannot be redefined at this level. There is no need to, since objects can be redefined at a higher level dictionary such as the *userdict*. The *systemdict* is used by the interpreter to find system-wide definitions, such as *setgray*. If *setgray* had been redefined elsewhere in your program, you could access the default operation of *setgray* by pushing the system dictionary to the top of the dictionary stack. Once the dictionary is there, the default operation for *setgray* could be called and then the current dictionary returned. The following line of code demonstrates this procedure.

```
systemdict begin .5 setgray end
```

Without this line of code, the *setgray* operator would be sought out in the current dictionary, then in *userdict*, and finally in the system dictionary.

2.8.5 Font Dictionary

Another dictionary available to you is the font dictionary. This is a noneditable dictionary that contains the PostScript font matrix and outline information for a given font. Each font has a dictionary. By executing a *findfont* operator, the dictionary font name desired is pushed onto the stack, like any other dictionary, so that the interpreter can read the information concerning each character. A font dictionary may also be created via the *definefont* operator.

The *makefont* operator takes the current font and allows a transformation on its font matrix. It does not create a new font dictionary; rather, it makes a copy of the font selected and performs the transformation. So the font dictionary that was pushed onto the stack is modified and then kept track of by the interpreter. The *setfont* operator sets the modifications that have been performed to the current font dictionary.

2.8.6 Checking the Current Status

All system parameters are stored in a dictionary called *statusdict*. Access to this dictionary is performed as with any dictionary, by invoking a *begin* and an *end*. Here is where you can set up communication parameters, enable or disable the start page, and set page type and other output-device-specific parameters. Care should be taken if you want to access this dictionary, since this may make your code device-dependent. To avoid any dependencies, always use the *known* operator when entering modifications to the *statusdict*. The following lines of code demonstrate this technique.

```
statusdict begin
/setpageparams known {612 792 0 0 setpageparams}if
end
```

This *if* operation first looks into the status dictionary to see if the *setpageparams* operator exists. If a Boolean *true* is returned, the operator call within the braces is executed; otherwise, the procedure is ignored. This code will work on both the Apple LaserWriter line of printers and the Linotronic line, even though the *setpageparams* operator does not exist in the LaserWriter line.

CHAPTER 3

Typographic Solutions

3-1   Introduction

PostScript is by far the most popular solution for integrated pages in the DTP market. As you review this page-description language, you will see an extensive number of graphically oriented operators. This should not obscure the fact that PostScript is also the best typographic solution for DTP.

If someone were to strip away all graphical possibilities in my designs, I would still choose PostScript for the standard output file. The library of fonts is certainly not the largest, but graphically it may be the best. The fonts (35 resi dent in the LaserWriter IINT's interpreter, hundreds downloadable) are created from outlines. The characters themselves are created out of lines and curves connected to form an outline that is then filled. This outline may be mani pulated by mathematical computations. The size, rotation, skew, and fill color are some of the many modifications that can be applied to the character.

From a designer's viewpoint, too much control over a well-designed typeface can be bad. All too often someone distorts an elegantly designed typeface into something that is disproportionate and unbalanced. The power that is handed to you in PostScript should be handled with care. A little knowledge in this area can be dangerous. I am referring to aesthetic disasters, not programming disasters (although it is possible to produce some temporary programming problems in the current state of the interpreter).

The process of instructing the PostScript interpreter to image characters onto a page is a simple one. It can be expressed in the following sequence of events.

1. Define the font that you wish to use.
2. Define the point size of that font.
3. Provide the x and y coordinates for the left-hand baseline of text.
4. Provide a text string.
5. Image that text string.

In the simplest form of typesetting in PostScript, consider the following code:

```
/Helvetica-Bold findfont 12 scalefont setfont
200 200 moveto
(line of text)show
showpage
```

These four lines of code will locate an origin, draw a line of text flush left to that point, image the page, and eject it. Nothing could be simpler. The first line,

```
/Helvetica-Bold findfont 12 scalefont setfont
```

simply tells the interpreter which font to use and at what size. The name */Helvetica-Bold* is a legal PostScript font name. The name reference is permanantly stored in the PostScript interpreter. By pushing the correct name onto the operator stack and then following it with the *findfont* operator, PostScript will look into its font dictionary for that font's outline information. The *scalefont* operator does exactly what it says it will. *Scalefont* requires that a font be previously found and that it be immediately preceded by a number representing the unit size.

If you have multiple lines of text, or if you separate your text strings with other PostScript manipulations and do not wish to change the current typeface, you need only define the typeface once. For instance:

1. Define the font that you wish to use.
2. Define the point size of that font.
3. Provide the x and y coordinates for the left-hand baseline of text.
4. Provide a text string.
5. Image that text string.
6. Provide the x and y coordinates for the left-hand baseline of text.

7. Provide a text string.

8. Image that text string.

Essentially, items 6, 7, and 8 have located a new point at which to image text and have done so. The same process in PostScript would look like this:

```
/Helvetica-Bold         % legal PostScript font name
findfont                % establish font
12 scalefont            % set unit size
setfont                 % set font
200 200 moveto          % goto starting location
(line of text)show      % print text
200 400 moveto          % goto new location
(another line of text)show   %print text
showpage                % image and print page
```

The definition of a font sets a reference in the current graphics state of the interpreter. Any call to image text after that setup will use that font. In the following sections I will show how to create some rudimentary typographic solutions and some more elaborate ones. If you are just starting out and need some instant gratification, try this next program listing.

```
% ----- DEFINE X LOCATION ----------------------
/x 50 def

% ----- SETUP A FOR LOOP TO CREATE -------------
% ----- INCREMENTAL POINT SIZES ----------------

10 20 130 {
  /ps exch def
% ----- DEFINE FONT WITH VARIABLE FOR ----------
% ----- POINT SIZE -----------------------------

  /Helvetica-Bold findfont ps scalefont setfont
  x y moveto
  (Gerard Kunkel)show     % replace with your name

% ----- USE POINT SIZE TO LOWER THE ------------
% ----- CURRENT LOCATION ON THE PAGE -----------

  /y y ps sub def
  }for

showpage
```

The typeface, */Helvetica-Bold,* should be on your PostScript printing device. Not all PostScript printers have the same fonts resident in ROM (read-only memory, permanently stored on a computer chip inside your printing device). Figure 3–1 shows the available fonts in three popular

Typeface	Font	PostScript Programming Name	Laser-Writer	Laser-Writer IINT/X	Lino-tronic 300
Avant Garde	Regular	AvantGarde-Book	☐	■	☐
	Regular Italic	AvantGarde-BookOblique	☐	■	☐
	Medium	AvantGarde-Demi	☐	■	☐
	Medium Italic	AvantGarde-DemiOblique	☐	■	☐
Bookman	Light	Bookman-Light	☐	■	☐
	Light Italic	Bookman-LightItalic	☐	■	☐
	Medium	Bookman-Demi	☐	■	☐
	Medium Italic	Bookman-DemiItalic	☐	■	☐
Courier	Regular	Courier	■	■	■
	Regular Italic	Courier-Oblique	■	■	■
	Bold	Courier-Bold	■	■	■
	Bold Italic	Courier-BoldOblique	■	■	■
Helvetica	Regular	Helvetica	■	■	■
	Regular Italic	Helvetica-Oblique	■	■	■
	Bold	Helvetica-Bold	■	■	■
	Bold Italic	Helvetica-BoldOblique	■	■	■
	Narrow Regular	HelveticaNarrow	☐	■	☐
	Narrow Regular Italic	HelveticaNarrow-Oblique	☐	■	☐
	Narrow Bold	HelveticaNarrow-Bold	☐	■	☐
	Narrow Bold Italic	HelveticaNarrow-BoldOblique	☐	■	☐
New Century	Regular	NewCenturySchlbk-Roman	☐	■	☐
Schoolbook	Italic	NewCenturySchlbk-Italic	☐	■	☐
	Bold	NewCenturySchlbk-Bold	☐	■	☐
	Bold Italic	NewCenturySchlbk-BoldItalic	☐	■	☐
Palatino	Regular	Palatino-Roman	☐	■	☐
	Italic	Palatino-Italic	☐	■	☐
	Bold	Palatino-Bold	☐	■	☐
	Bold Italic	Palatino-BoldItalic	☐	■	☐
Symbol	--	Symbol	■	■	■
Times	Regular	Times-Roman	■	■	■
	Italic	Times-Italic	■	■	■
	Bold	Times-Bold	■	■	■
	Bold Italic	Times-BoldItalic	■	■	■
Zapf Chancery	Medium Italic	ZapfChancery-MediumItalic	■	■	☐
Zapf Dingbats	--	ZapfDingbats	■	■	☐

Figure 3—1
Table of available fonts

PostScript laser-printing devices. If your printer is not on this list, it is probably compatible with one of the three. The PostScript font name must be input with the exact spelling. If it is misspelled, the interpreter will give you an error and default to Courier.

3-2   Putting Text Exactly Where You Want It

In Figure 3–2 there are multiple references to typeface and location. This program would be excellent practice for understanding how to position your type and print it. If you are not familiar with measurements in points and picas, this code will also help you understand the process by working in inches.

This program relies on two activities to place type on a page. One is the *moveto* operator. The *moveto* operator repositions the current point to the *x* and *y* coordinates provided prior to executing itself. The other activity is the use of the *show* operator.

```
%!PS-Adobe 2.0
%%Title: SampleText
%%Creator: Gerard Kunkel
%%CreationDate: 3-2-89
%%BoundingBox: 0 0 612 792
%%EndComments

/inch {72 mul} def    % convert units to inches
0 setgray             % black type

% page size 8.5 x 11 inches

% ---- HEADLINE --------------------------------
/Times-Bold findfont 36 scalefont setfont
3 inch 9 inch moveto
(Company Name) show

% ---- NAME AND ADDRESS ----------------------
/Times-Roman findfont 12 scalefont setfont
1 inch 8 inch moveto
(Gerard Kunkel) show
1 inch 7.75 inch moveto
(PC Magazine) show
1 inch 7.5 inch moveto
(1 Park Avenue) show
1 inch 7.25 inch moveto
(New York, NY  10016) show

% ---- LIST HEADLINE -------------------------
```

```
/Helvetica findfont 16 scalefont setfont
2 inch 6.5 inch moveto
(COMPUTER HARDWARE REQUIREMENTS) show

% ---- LIST TEXT ------------------------------
/Helvetica findfont 10 scalefont setfont
2 inch 6.3 inch moveto
(25 MHz 386 computer with 5 MB of RAM) show
2 inch 6.1 inch moveto
(Super VGA controller and display) show
2 inch 5.9 inch moveto
(Microsoft Mouse, or compatible) show
2 inch 5.7 inch moveto
(Hayes 2400 baud modem, or compatible) show
2 inch 5.5 inch moveto
(Apple LaserWriter IINTX, or compatible) show

% ---- PRINT PAGE ------------------------------
showpage
```

Figure 3–2 implicitly positions text according to the measurements provided to the interpreter. This is a rather long-winded but efficient method for placing text on a page. In the first two lines of this code, some basic parameters are set up.

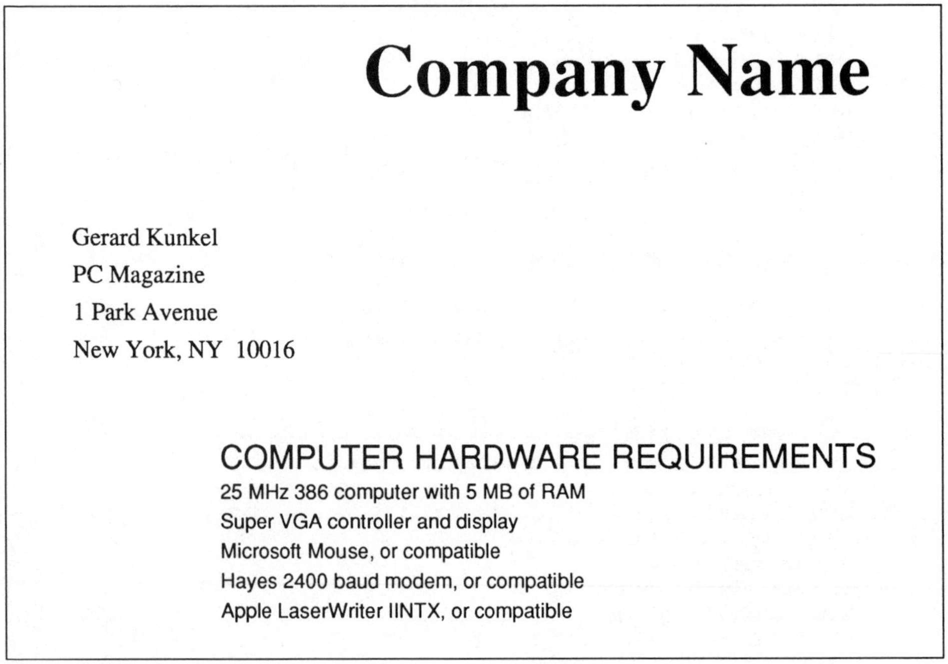

Company Name

Gerard Kunkel

PC Magazine

1 Park Avenue

New York, NY 10016

COMPUTER HARDWARE REQUIREMENTS

25 MHz 386 computer with 5 MB of RAM

Super VGA controller and display

Microsoft Mouse, or compatible

Hayes 2400 baud modem, or compatible

Apple LaserWriter IINTX, or compatible

Figure 3—2
Moveto and show

```
/inch {72 mul} def      % convert units to inches
0 setgray               % black type
```

The first line takes the standard unit measure and creates a definition with the name *inch*, whose dictionary definition is *72 mul*. When this name is pushed onto the stack following any integer or real number, that value is multiplied by 72. Hence, all points are converted to inches when this dictionary name is called. The second line sets the current color to black. Text, just as with any graphic, can be painted on the page in varying degrees of black, or as white. Reverse or knockout type would be expressed as

```
1 setgray
```

Of course, this would be pointless unless there were some value of black already imaged in that area to paint white characters onto.

The headline example is the same as all other examples in this code, so we will focus in on this area. The first line of this section is a comment

```
% ---- HEADLINE ------------------------------
/Times-Bold findfont 36 scalefont setfont
3 inch 9 inch moveto
(Company Name) show
```

The next line is the string of commands necessary to set up a particular font. In this case I have chosen Times-Bold, at 36 point. The line of code immediately following the typeface is the location setup. The *moveto* operator is used in conjunction with the *inch* definition that I set up in the beginning of the program. By utilizing the *inch* definition, both integers 3 and 9 are multiplied by 72 on the stack. If you were to look at the stack at this time it would look like this:

```
216 648 moveto
```

Converting all movements from points to inches may help you position items on the page. I am so used to working in points and picas that I prefer to deal directly in points. If you prefer to work in picas, the following definition would apply.

```
/pica {12 mul} def
```

You can easily see the similarities between the *inch* definition and our *pica* definition. The same movement in picas would now be:

```
18 pica 54 pica moveto
```

The remainder of the routines are structured exactly like the first. This is far from a structured program, though. This is merely a linear program that affects the page with each instruction. The more logical way to approach a page that has repetitive operations is to define those operations as definitions that accept some variable input. Input in this case is the information that is on the stack when an operation is called. In PostScript, these operations are called *procedures*. I often refer to them as routines. They are one and the same. A *procedure* is a collection of operations or a single operation that can be called repeatedly. Procedures are stored in the userdict dictionary in the interpreter's memory. Each time the *def* operator is used, a key name and a value are pushed onto the dictionary stack. An example would be

```
/x 23 def
```

A procedure, however, is an expanded version of the simple definition. We have used one already:

```
/inch {72 mul} def
```

The initial slash alerts the interpreter that a definition will follow. This is immediately followed by a name. There is no space following the slash, and the name itself is case-sensitive, so two different key names can have the same spelling but use different capitalization without any errors. Sandwiched between the name and the final *def* operator is the procedure. The series of operations is contained in braces. Many operations may take place within the braces. For instance:

```
% ---- LIST TEXT ------------------------------
/listshow {
  /strg exch def
  x y moveto
  show
  y y .2 inch sub def
  }def

/Helvetica findfont 10 scalefont setfont
/x 2 inch def
/y 6.3 inch def
(25 MHz 386 computer with 5 MB of RAM) listshow
(Super VGA controller and display) listshow
(Microsoft Mouse, or compatible) listshow
(Hayes 2400 baud modem, or compatible) listshow
(Apple LaserWriter IINTX, or compatible) listshow
```

This rewrite of the list portion of our earlier example will produce the same output. However, I have created a procedure called *listshow* that repeatedly lowers the *y* coordinate by .2 inch to get set for the next line of copy. This is extremely helpful if my line of copy grows longer. Rather than continually provide a new coordinate, I simply add to my list and follow the text string with a call to *listshow*.

3.2.1   Using Routines to Correctly Position your Text

In subsequent program listings, you will see that I look for repetitive operations and turn them into procedures.

Sometimes putting type directly on the page as it was given to you is not good enough. For instance, newspapers and magazines use justified columns to help structure articles on a page. You may also need to structure titles and subtitles to fit your design typographically. A technique often used in recent years is the exaggerated letterspacing of headlines and other display type. Figure 3–3 addresses this need by using the *ashow* operator. This operator places a space between each character according to the values that you place on the operand stack prior to calling it.

The *ashow* operator requires three variables to be on the operand stack when called. The topmost item is the string of characters making up your headline or display type. The second is a number representing the amount of vertical displacement to be applied between each character. The third and most important in this example is the amount of horizontal displacement to be applied between each character. The two numbers representing *x* and *y* can be either positive or negative.

As you may have guessed by now, this is a process that can get us to justified type if we know a few other variables. By establishing the width of our display area, or column, and the width of our text string, we can then divide the difference by the number of characters in that string to come up with either the positive or negative number that is required to space each character to fit the column evenly. We can read the width of our unaltered text string by utilizing the *stringwidth* operator. *Stringwidth* reads the width of the string that is on the stack when it is called. The result of this operation leaves two numbers on the stack. They are the *x* and *y* values of the outermost dimensions of the string. Since we will be needing the width only, the height information can be popped off the stack with the *pop* operator.

The following is the complete listing for Figure 3–3.

```
%!PS-Adobe 2.0
%%Title: JUSTified Type
%%Creator: Gerard Kunkel
%%CreationDate: 2-20-89
%%BoundingBox: 0 0 612 792
%%EndComments

%%BeginProlog

% ----- Exchange basic parameters ---------------------------
```

```
/JUSTify {
  /leading exch def
  /JUSTright exch def
  /startingy exch def
  /JUSTleft exch def
  /JUSTwidth JUSTright JUSTleft sub def % width of text column
  }def

% ----- Justified type routine --------------------------------
/JUSTshow {
  JUSTleft startingy moveto
  /JUSTstring exch def
  JUSTstring stringwidth pop
  /JUSTstringwidth exch def
  /fillspace JUSTwidth JUSTstringwidth sub def
  /JUSTchars JUSTstring length 1 sub def
  /microspace fillspace JUSTchars div def
  microspace 0 JUSTstring ashow
  /startingy startingy leading sub def
  JUSTleft startingy moveto
  }def

%%EndProlog
%%BeginScript

/Times-Roman findfont 10 scalefont setfont

% ----- Put parameters on stack, call JUSTify ----------------
100 400 200 15 JUSTify

% ----- Print characters on page  ----------------------------
(This is JUSTified type) JUSTshow
(The second line is too) JUSTshow
(The third line is not.) show

% ----- Create new column of type ----------------------------
/Times-Roman findfont 11 scalefont setfont
220 400 320 12 JUSTify
(This is JUSTified type) JUSTshow
(The second line is too) JUSTshow
(The third line is not.) show

% ----- Create another column of type
----------------------------
/Times-Roman findfont 14 scalefont setfont
340 400 500 15 JUSTify
(This is JUSTified type) JUSTshow
(The second line is too) JUSTshow
(The third line is not.) show

% ----- Create display type ----------------------------
/Helvetica findfont 11 scalefont setfont
100 300 500 14 JUSTify
(LETTER SPACING) JUSTshow
/Helvetica-Bold findfont 42 scalefont setfont
```

```
100 260 500 42 JUSTify
(MADE EASY) JUSTshow
/Bookman-Demi findfont 25 scalefont setfont
100 200 500 30 JUSTify
(EXCELLENT FOR DISPLAY TYPE) JUSTshow

%%Trailer
showpage

% ===============================================
```

The first procedure that I have defined is called *JUSTify*. This routine exchanges data from the operand stack and gives a dictionary key name to it. The total width is then calculated by utilizing the new definitions.

```
/JUSTify {
/leading exch def
/JUSTright exch def
/startingy exch def
/JUSTleft exch def
/JUSTwidth JUSTright JUSTleft sub def
}def
```

The total width, saved as *JUSTwidth*, is calculated using simple math. The left margin, defined as *JUSTleft*, is subtracted from the right margin, *JUSTright*. The remainder of this calculation is then stored with the

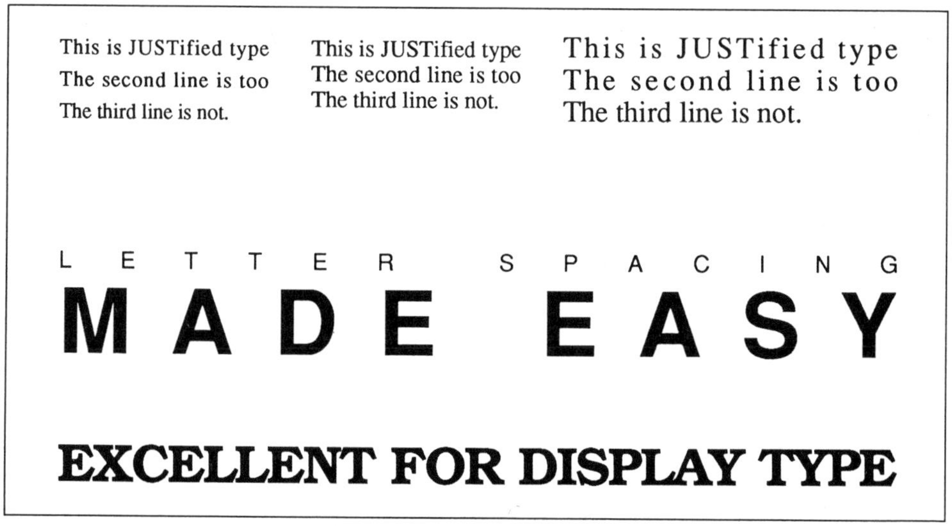

Figure 3–3
Ashow, Kshow

dictionary key name *JUSTwidth*. This new dictionary definition will be used in subsequent operations.

```
/JUSTwidth JUSTright JUSTleft sub def
```

The next routine performs the actual placement and imaging of text. *JUSTshow* goes through a series of operations that determine the starting coordinate, the amount of intercharacter spacing, and the final painting of characters on the page.

```
% ----- Justified type routine ------------------------------
/JUSTshow {
  JUSTleft startingy moveto
  /JUSTstring exch def
  JUSTstring stringwidth pop
  /JUSTstringwidth exch def
  /fillspace JUSTwidth JUSTstringwidth sub def
  /JUSTchars JUSTstring length 1 sub def
  /microspace fillspace JUSTchars div def
  microspace 0 JUSTstring ashow
  /startingy startingy leading sub def
  JUSTleft startingy moveto
  }def
```

The first operation is the *moveto*. The two numbers needed by this operator are picked up from our key names defined in the previous routine, *JUSTify*. *JUSTleft* and *startingy* each push their associated values onto the stack prior to the *moveto* operator.

```
JUSTleft startingy moveto
```

The second line of this routine exchanges the string from the script and places it on the dictionary stack with the key name *JUSTstring*. This object is immediately used in the next operation. The *stringwidth* operator pushes both the *x* and *y* dimensions of the string. The *pop* operator removes the unwanted *y* value and leaves the *x* value sitting on the top of the stack. The next line immediately picks up the *x* value and stores it in the dictionary with the key name *JUSTstringwidth*.

```
/JUSTstring exch def
JUSTstring stringwidth pop
/JUSTstringwidth exch def
```

Now that we have the proper ingredients, we can perform the intercharacter spacing. The *fillspace* definition is calculated for use in the *ashow* operator. This number will be the amount of space difference between column width and the actual text-string width. *Fillspace* is the remainder of *JUSTwidth* less *JUSTstringwidth*. If *JUSTstringwidth* is less than *JUSTwidth*, then *fillspace* will be a positive number; if not, then *fillspace* will be a negative number. The next line of code determines the number of characters in the string. The *length* operator reads a text string off the stack and leaves an integer on the stack equal to the number of characters in the text string. Since we are dealing with the spaces between characters and not the characters themselves, we need to subtract one character from the product of the *length* operation.

```
/fillspace JUSTwidth JUSTstringwidth sub def
/JUSTchars JUSTstring length 1 sub def
```

With all of the calculations now in hand, there is still one more. We now have the total amount of space to be adjusted and the number of characters that need to be affected. The final bit of information is the remainder when *fillspace* is divided by *JUSTchars*. This result is defined as *microspace*. The actual painting of characters on the page is done using the *ashow* operator. The three requirements are pushed onto the stack prior to calling the routine. They are: *microspace*, followed by a zero (since there will be no vertical adjustment) and *JUSTstring*, the original text string.

```
/microspace fillspace JUSTchars div def
microspace 0 JUSTstring ashow
```

The last operation in this procedure sets up the next line of text by reducing the value of *startingy* by *leading*. This product of subtraction is then stored as *startingy*, replacing the original value. The new *startingy* value is used in positioning the next line of text with the *moveto* operator.

```
/startingy startingy leading sub def
JUSTleft startingy moveto
}def
```

In the script portion of the program the typeface definition is followed by four integers representing the variables required by the *JUSTify* procedure.

```
/Times-Roman findfont 10 scalefont setfont

% ----- Put parameters on stack, call JUSTify ----------------
100 400 200 15 JUSTify
```

The text strings to be printed are followed by the *JUSTshow* procedure call. Note that the last line is followed by the standard *show* operator, so that this line will print flush left.

```
% ----- Print characters on page  ----------------------------
(This is JUSTified type) JUSTshow
(The second line is too) JUSTshow
(The third line is not.) show
```

3-3   Some Primitive Text Operations

When I first used the PostScript language for placing text on a page, I searched for the "flush right" operator. Unfortunately, there is no such operator. However, there are some simple routines that you can use to create the alignments that you need. In Figure 3–4, I have set up a standard example of flush-left type.

```
.5 setlinewidth
0 setgray
300 100 moveto
300 500 lineto
stroke

/Palatino-Bold findfont 21 scalefont setfont
300 200 moveto
(normal flush left alignment) show

showpage
```

There are no mysteries here. PostScript naturally aligns its typography to the point of origin as provided in the *moveto* operator. Figure 3–4 also has a line drawn at the vertical point of origin to help you see the actual alignment.

```
.5 setlinewidth
0 setgray
300 100 moveto
300 500 lineto
stroke
```

The first five lines of code simply set up and draw a half-point black line along the vertical axis to help you see the text alignment.

```
/Palatino-Bold findfont 21 scalefont setfont
300 200 moveto
(normal flush left alignment) show
```

The *show* operator takes the string value that precedes it and places it at the coordinates $x = 300$, $y = 200$, using the typeface Palatino-Bold.

3.3.1   Aligning Type to the Right

As I mentioned earlier, I longed for a flush-right operator in PostScript. Since PostScript allows you to define dictionary procedures, we can make up for what we view as shortcomings by writing a procedure. Thus, we can write a procedure that performs the way an operator would.

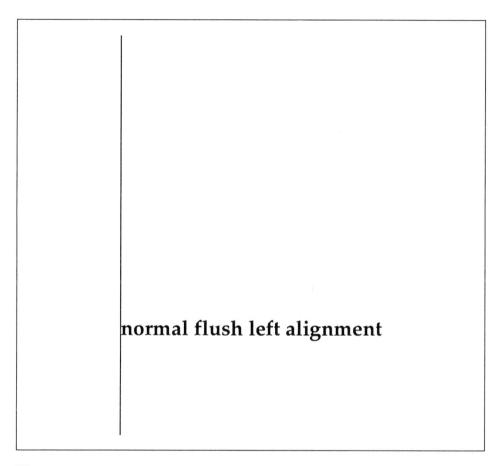

Figure 3—4
Flush Left

Figure 3–5 shows the addition of text flush right to the vertical alignment rule, using a new procedure called *showFR*.

```
/showFR
  {dup
   stringwidth
   pop
   neg
   0 rmoveto
   show}def

.5 setlinewidth
0 setgray
300 100 moveto
300 500 lineto
```

```
stroke

/Palatino-Bold findfont 21 scalefont setfont
300 200 moveto
(normal flush left alignment) show
300 300 moveto
(flush right alignment) showFR

showpage
```

As you can see in the program listing for Figure 3–5, there is the new procedure defined as *showFR* and a call to that procedure in the script portion of our program.

```
/showFR
(dup
 stringwidth
 pop
 neg
 0 rmoveto
 show)def
```

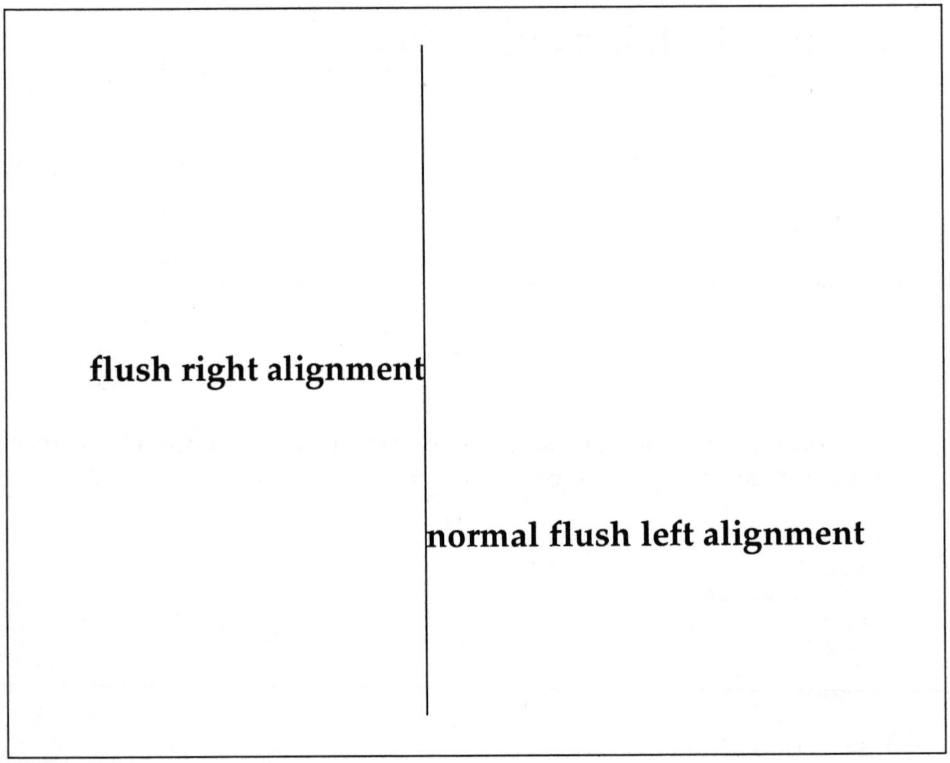

Figure 3—5
Flush Right

The procedure *showFR* is a straightforward stack manipulation. As we go through it line by line, you will see that line 1 simply duplicates the text string using the *dup* operator.

The second line of the procedure uses the duplicate string to satisfy the *stringwidth* operator. At this point, the stack contains the *y* and *x* dimensions of the string and the original string, in that order from the top down. We do not need the *y* value, so that is *pop*ped off the stack in the third line of the routine. The fourth line takes the *x* value and makes it a negative number. The fifth line adds a zero to the stack. This zero represents the amount of vertical space to be utilized by the *rmoveto* operator. *Rmoveto* takes the now-negative horizontal value, moves that much to the left, and makes no change vertically relative to the current point.

Now that the current point has been moved to the left an amount equal to the string's width, we can use the *show* operator to paint the text.

3.3.2   Centering Type

Flush-left and flush-right are useful design tools but are certainly not the complete set of tools. Centering type on a given point is equally important. And no, there is not a PostScript operator for centering type. But as you can well guess, there is a simple routine that we can write to handle this (see Figure 3–6).

```
/showFR
  {dup
   stringwidth
   pop
   neg
   0 rmoveto
   show}def

/showFC
  {dup
   stringwidth
   pop
   2 div
   neg
   0 rmoveto
   show}def

.5 setlinewidth
0 setgray
300 100 moveto
300 500 lineto
stroke

/Palatino-Bold findfont 21 scalefont setfont
```

```
300 200 moveto
(normal flush left alignment) show
300 300 moveto
(flush right alignment) showFR
300 400 moveto
(flush center alignment) showFC

showpage
```

For comparison's sake, I have added to the existing alignment program. The additional material is the *showFC* procedure and the call to that procedure in the script.

```
/showFR
{dup
 stringwidth
 pop
 neg
 0 rmoveto
 show}def

/showFC
   {dup
    stringwidth
    pop
    2 div
    neg
    0 rmoveto
    show}def
```

The *showFC* procedure is exactly the same as the *showFR* routine, with one important exception. After the width of the string has been determined with the *stringwidth* operator and the *y* value is discarded, the remaining *x* value is divided by two. The fourth line in this routine handles this with the *2 div* instruction. That number is then turned into a negative number in the next line. The result is a relative move to the left equal to half the width of the string, thus centering it on the point of origin.

If multiple lines are to be centered on the same axis, the *moveto* operation that precedes the *showFC* call in the script should have the same *x* coordinate.

3.3.3   Flush Justified

We now have flush left, right, and center under our belt. Let's tackle justified type in the same exercise. In the previous section, a routine for justification was used to show a letter-spacing effect. That same routine can be modified for this example.

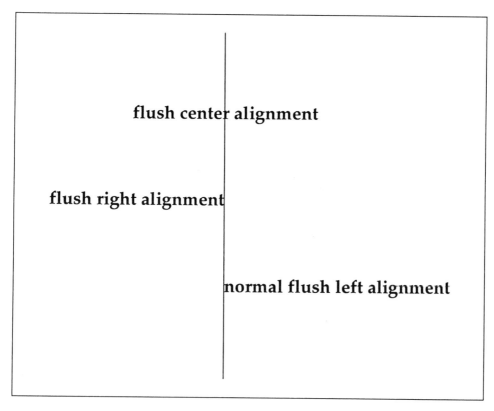

Figure 3—6
Flush Center

```
/showJUST {
  /juststring exch def
  /charspace rm lm sub def
  /tempwidth juststring stringwidth pop def
  /numberchars juststring length 1 sub def
  /charspace charspace tempwidth sub
      numberchars div def
  lm y moveto charspace 0 juststring ashow} def

/showFR
  {dup
   stringwidth
   pop
   neg
   0 rmoveto
   show}def
/showFC
  {dup
```

```
        stringwidth
        pop
        2 div
        neg
        0 rmoveto
        show}def

.5 setlinewidth
0 setgray
300 100 moveto
300 500 lineto
stroke

/Palatino-Bold findfont 21 scalefont setfont
300 200 moveto
(normal flush left alignment) show
300 300 moveto
(flush right alignment) showFR
300 400 moveto
(flush center alignment) showFC

/lm 300 def
/rm 500 def
/y 500 def
(flush justified alignment) showJUST
/lm 300 def
/rm 550 def
/y 530 def
(flush justified alignment) showJUST

showpage
```

Figure 3–7 takes the alignment sample page and adds the flush-justified routine.

The *showJUST* procedure is very different from the other routines that we have gone through. In an overview, it would be fair to say that they all exchange text strings and modify the current location. But in the case of the justification procedure, the eventual *show* operator is replaced by the *ashow* operator. *Ashow* affects the amount of space placed between each character in a string. The amount provided to the operator via the operand stack is applied equally between all characters in that string. Using this operator will allow us to space characters evenly. The value supplied to the *ashow* operator may be different for each line, to accommodate different line lengths while maintaining the same column width. The left and right margins, *lm* and *rm*, respectively, are defined prior to executing this procedure. The remaining calculations read the string length, determine the space difference between the column width and the unaltered string width, and provide a value to the *ashow* operator for letter spacing.

For a more in-depth look at this procedure refer to Figure 3–3.

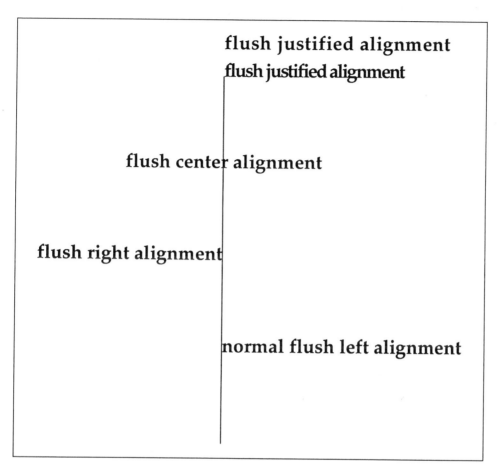

Figure 3—7
Flush Justify

3.3.4 Line Breaking

The previous examples of justification deal with line breaks that have already been determined. But what happens when you need to calculate where to break a longer line to fit the column? There are a couple of PostScript operators that help out. Some PostScript text string modifiers are:

- *anchorsearch*
- *copy*

- *get*
- *getinterval*
- *length*
- *put*
- *putinterval*
- *search*
- *string*

We will concern ourselves mostly with *getinterval* and *search*. These two operators are used in Figure 3–8. The complete listing follows.

```
%!PS-Adobe 2.0
%%Title: TurnLineFL
%%CreationDate: 2-25-88
%%Creator: Gerard Kunkel
%%BoundingBox: 0 0 612 792
%%EndComments

%%BeginProlog

% ----- DEFINE SPACE AS EMPTY SPACE ----------------
/space ( )def

% ----- BEGIN LINE BREAKING PROCEDURE --------------
/TurnLineFL
 {/T exch def
  /spacewidth space stringwidth pop def
  /currentw 0 def
  /wordspace_count 0 def
  /restart 0 def
  /remainder T def

% ----- SEARCH THE STRING FOR THE FIRST SPACE ------
 {remainder space search

% ----- IF SPACE IS FOUND --------------------------
    {/nextword exch def pop
     /remainder exch def
     /nextwordwidth nextword stringwidth pop def

% ---------- CHECK THE WIDTH STATUS ----------------
    currentw nextwordwidth add lw gt

% ---------- IF THE CURRENTWIDTH PLUS THE ----------
% ---------- WIDTH OF THE NEXT WORD IS GREATER -----
% ---------- THAN THE COLUMN WIDTH DO THIS ---------
       {T restart wordspace_count restart sub
        getinterval showline
        /restart wordspace_count def
```

```
          /currentw nextwordwidth spacewidth add def}

% ---------- IF TOTAL WIDTH IS STILL LESS THAN -----
% ---------- THE COLUMN WIDTH THEN DO THIS ---------
      {/currentw currentw nextwordwidth add
       spacewidth add def}
    ifelse

% ----- ADD TO WORD SPACE COUNTER -----------------
     /wordspace_count wordspace_count
        nextword length add 1 add def}

% ----- IF SPACE IS NOT FOUND --------------------
    {pop exit}
  ifelse

% ----- SET UP PARAMETERS ------------------------
 }loop

% ----- SET UP PARAMETERS ------------------------
/lastchar T length def
T restart lastchar restart sub getinterval lm y moveto show
}def

% ----- SET UP PARAMETERS ------------------------
/parms {
  /y exch def
  /lm exch def
  /rm exch def
  /leading exch def
  /pointsize exch def
  /lw rm lm sub def
  findfont pointsize scalefont setfont
  /showline {lm y moveto show
            /y y leading sub def} def
  lm y moveto
  }def

% ----- IDENTIFY THE OUTPUT PAGE ----------------
/names {/namearray exch def}def
/F {findfont exch scalefont setfont}def
/idpage
 {/colr exch def 0 setgray
 8 /Helvetica-Bold F
 90 665 moveto
 namearray {show 50 0 rmoveto}forall
 colr show .5 setlinewidth
 80 675 moveto 0 -15 rlineto 430 0 rlineto
 0 15 rlineto closepath stroke
}def

[(FIG3-8.PS)(Gerard Kunkel)(12:01PM  3/05/1989)]names
(black) idpage

%%EndProlog
```

```
% ----- DEFINE A LONG TEXT STRING ---------------
/testlines (IBM PS/2 Model 80-111 with cache software \
is one of the more expensive IBM personal \
computers. It uses the Intel 80386 processor \
operating at 20 MHz.) def

% ----- SET EACH BLOCK OF COPY ------------------
/NewCenturySchlbk-Roman
8 9 180 100 600 parms
testlines TurnLineFL

/Helvetica-Bold
8 10 180 100 500 parms
testlines TurnLineFL

/Times-Roman
9 12 180 100 400 parms
testlines TurnLineFL

/AvantGarde-Demi
24 27 500 200 600 parms
testlines TurnLineFL

/Helvetica-Oblique
14 18 430 200 400 parms
testlines TurnLineFL

/ZapfChancery-MediumItalic
18 18 500 100 280 parms
testlines TurnLineFL

/Times-Bold
18 20 500 100 200 parms
testlines TurnLineFL

showpage
```

This program works with a long text string that needs to be broken according to a maximum column width. Below is the sample text string used in the next few figures, as it appears in the script portion of the program. This is a continuous text string that is separated by back-slashes to clean up the presentation. PostScript interprets these four lines of text as one continuous string, discarding the back-slashes as it reads the string.

```
% ----- DEFINE A LONG TEXT STRING ---------------
/testlines (IBM PS/2 Model 80-111 with cache software \
is one of the more expensive IBM personal \
computers. It uses the Intel 80386 processor \
operating at 20 MHz.) def
```

IBM PS/2 Model 80-111 with cache software is one of the more expensive IBM personal computers. It uses the Intel 80386 processor operating at 20 MHz.

IBM PS/2 Model 80-111 with cache software is one of the more expensive IBM personal computers. It uses the Intel 80386 processor operating at 20 MHz.

IBM PS/2 Model 80-111 with cache software is one of the more expensive IBM personal computers. It uses the Intel 80386 processor operating at 20 MHz.

IBM PS/2 Model 80-111 with cache software is one of the more expensive IBM personal computers. It uses the Intel 80386 processor operating at 20 MHz.

IBM PS/2 Model 80-111 with cache software is one of the more expensive IBM personal computers. It uses the Intel 80386 processor operating at 20 MHz.

IBM PS/2 Model 80-111 with cache software is one of the more expensive IBM personal computers. It uses the Intel 80386 processor operating at 20 MHz.

IBM PS/2 Model 80-111 with cache software is one of the more expensive IBM personal computers. It uses the Intel 80386 processor operating at 20 MHz.

Figure 3—8
Line Breaking

Column width is provided by the user as a left and right margin. Other information, such as typeface and point size, is passed through the *parms* procedure.

```
% ----- SET UP PARAMETERS -------------------------
/parms {
    /y exch def           % starting y position
    /lm exch def          % exchange left margin from script
    /rm exch def          % exchange right margin
    /leading exch def     % text baseline-to-baseline measure
    /pointsize exch def   % text pointsize
    /lw rm lm sub def     % linewidth
    findfont pointsize scalefont setfont

    /showline {lm y moveto show
                /y y leading sub def} def % show routine
    lm y moveto
    }def
```

Since we will be searching for spaces between words, we can define a key name object for a space. When performing the search, the key name *space* is used to represent the ASCII value of the space character.

```
% ----- DEFINE SPACE AS EMPTY SPACE ----------------
/space ( )def
```

The entire line-breaking operation is performed in a procedure called *TurnLineFL*.

```
% ----- BEGIN LINE BREAKING PROCEDURE --------------
/TurnLineFL
  {/T exch def
   /spacewidth space stringwidth pop def
   /currentw 0 def
   /wordspace_count 0 def
   /restart 0 def
   /remainder T def
```

The complete text string is exchanged and scanned by this procedure, searching for spaces.

```
% ----- SEARCH THE STRING FOR THE FIRST SPACE ------
  {remainder space search
```

```
% ----- IF SPACE IS FOUND --------------------------
    {/nextword exch def pop
     /remainder exch def
     /nextwordwidth nextword stringwidth pop def
```

When a space is found, the word prior to the space is stored with a key name, *nextword*. The remainder of the string is resaved as the key name *remainder*. This is the original string less the latest word, *nextword*.

The software must test the current string width against the maximum string width for each word that is scanned and printed. If the current string width is less than the column width, then the current string width is increased by the width of the next word, and the current word space count is increased by one.

```
% ---------- CHECK THE WIDTH STATUS ----------------
   currentw nextwordwidth add lw gt

% ---------- IF THE CURRENTWIDTH PLUS THE ----------
% ---------- WIDTH OF THE NEXT WORD IS GREATER -----
% ---------- THAN THE COLUMN WIDTH DO THIS --------
   {T restart wordspace_count restart sub
   getinterval showline
   /restart wordspace_count def
   /currentw nextwordwidth spacewidth add def}

% ---------- IF TOTAL WIDTH IS STILL LESS THAN -----
% ---------- THE COLUMN WIDTH THEN DO THIS ---------
   {/currentw currentw nextwordwidth add
   spacewidth add def}
   ifelse
```

After either process, the *wordspace_count* is increased by the number of characters in the *nextword* +1 for the space. This number is used in *show*ing the text line. If the original Boolean equation, searching for a space, is false, then the program loop is exited.

```
% ----- ADD TO WORD SPACE COUNTER ------------------
   /wordspace_count wordspace_count
      nextword length add 1 add def}

% ----- IF SPACE IS NOT FOUND --------------------
  {pop exit}
 ifelse

% ----- SET UP PARAMETERS ------------------------
}loop
```

The *getinterval* operator requires the exact location in a string where a break is to occur. The *wordspace_count* value is used in calculating the third number pushed onto the operand stack prior to calling the *getinterval* operator. The object left on the stack at the end of this operation is the text string to be painted for one line of text.

```
{T restart wordspace_count restart sub
getinterval showline
```

The script portion of this code is straightforward. Six objects are pushed onto the operand stack prior to calling the *parms* procedure. They are:

1. Typeface
2. Pointsize
3. Leading
4. Right margin

5.   Left margin

6.   Starting y coordinate

```
% ----- SET EACH BLOCK OF COPY -----------------
/NewCenturySchlbk-Roman
8 9 180 100 600 parms
testlines TurnLineFL
```

The last line in this block of operations pushes the long text string onto the operand stack and calls the *TurnLineFL* procedure.

3.3.5   Flush-Right Line Breaking

Figure 3–9 illustrates the same procedures as Figure 3–8, except that this time the output is flush right rather than flush left. This is accomplished through a simple modification to the original program for Figure 3–8.

There are only two changes to this code. One alteration, changing the procedure name, is done only for housekeeping purposes and has no effect on the output of the code. The other merely changes the final *showline* routine, which was set up in the *parms* procedure. (See the complete listing for Figure 3–9).

```
%!PS-Adobe 2.0
%%Title: TurnLineFL
%%CreationDate: 2-25-88
%%Creator: Gerard Kunkel
%%BoundingBox: 0 0 612 792
%%EndComments

%%BeginProlog
/space ( )def
/TurnLineFR
  {/T exch def
   /spacewidth space stringwidth pop def
   /currentw 0 def
   /wordspace_count 0 def
   /restart 0 def
   /remainder T def

  {remainder space search

     {/nextword exch def pop
      /remainder exch def
      /nextwordwidth nextword stringwidth pop def

      currentw nextwordwidth add lw gt
        {T restart wordspace_count restart sub
         getinterval showline
         /restart wordspace_count def
```

```
            /currentw nextwordwidth spacewidth add def}
            {/currentw currentw nextwordwidth add
            spacewidth add def}
        ifelse

        /wordspace_count wordspace_count
           nextword length add 1 add def}
        {pop exit}
    ifelse
    }loop
/lastchar T length def
% ----- MUST CHANGE SHOW TO SHOWLINE FOR FR ------
T restart lastchar restart sub getinterval
    lm y moveto showline
}def

/parms {
    /y exch def
    /lm exch def
    /rm exch def
    /leading exch def
    /pointsize exch def
    /lw rm lm sub def
    findfont pointsize scalefont setfont
    /showline {rm y moveto dup stringwidth
        pop neg 0 rmoveto show /y y leading sub def} def
    lm y moveto
    }def


% ==================================
/names {/namearray exch def}def
/F {findfont exch scalefont setfont}def
% ==================================
/idpage

 {/colr exch def 0 setgray
 8 /Helvetica-Bold F
 90 665 moveto
 namearray {show 50 0 rmoveto}forall
 colr show .5 setlinewidth
 80 675 moveto 0 -15 rlineto 430 0 rlineto
 0 15 rlineto closepath stroke
}def

[((FIG3-9.PS)(Gerard Kunkel)(12:04PM   3/05/1989)]names
(black) idpage
%%EndProlog

/testlines (IBM PS/2 Model 80-111 with cache software \
is one of the more expensive IBM personal \
computers. It uses the Intel 80386 processor \
operating at 20 MHz.) def

/NewCenturySchlbk-Roman 8 9 180 100 600 parms testlines
TurnLineFR
/Helvetica-Bold 8 10 180 100 500 parms testlines TurnLineFR
```

```
/Times-Roman 9 12 180 100 400 parms testlines TurnLineFR
/AvantGarde-Demi 24 27 500 200 600 parms testlines
TurnLineFR
/Helvetica-Oblique 14 18 430 200 400 parms testlines
TurnLineFR
/ZapfChancery-MediumItalic 18 18 500 100 280 parms testlines
TurnLineFR
/Times-Bold 18 20 500 100 200 parms testlines TurnLineFR
showpage
```

IBM PS/2 Model 80-111 with cache software is one of the more expensive IBM personal computers. It uses the Intel 80386 processor operating at 20 MHz.

IBM PS/2 Model 80-111 with cache software is one of the more expensive IBM personal computers. It uses the Intel 80386 processor operating at 20 MHz.

IBM PS/2 Model 80-111 with cache software is one of the more expensive IBM personal computers. It uses the Intel 80386 processor operating at 20 MHz.

IBM PS/2 Model 80-111 with cache software is one of the more expensive IBM personal computers. It uses the Intel 80386 processor operating at 20 MHz.

IBM PS/2 Model 80-111 with cache software is one of the more expensive IBM personal computers. It uses the Intel 80386 processor operating at 20 MHz.

IBM PS/2 Model 80-111 with cache software is one of the more expensive IBM personal computers. It uses the Intel 80386 processor operating at 20 MHz.

IBM PS/2 Model 80-111 with cache software is one of the more expensive IBM personal computers. It uses the Intel 80386 processor operating at 20 MHz.

Figure 3—9
Line Breaking FR

If you review the program listings for Figures 3–8 and 3–9, you will see that they are identical except for the *TurnLineFR* procedure name and the *showline* procedure code.

```
/showline {rm y moveto dup stringwidth
pop neg 0 rmoveto show /y y leading sub def} def
```

The code for the *showline* routine is the flush-right routine explained in the beginning of this chapter. As you can see, creating a structured program allows you to customize certain aspects of the graphic without rewriting the entire program.

3.3.6   A Justified Column of Type

The final example of this program modifies the *showline* procedure once again to come up with another look. In this case, I desired flush-justified columns (see Figure 3–10).

This was actually a much simpler process than it may seem. The string that has been determined by the line-breaking process is exchanged into this procedure and used to calculate widths. The difference in space between the string and the column width is divided by the number of characters in that string less one. That value is then used with the *ashow* operator to position each character with the new intercharacter spacing.

```
/showline {
    /juststring exch def
    /charspace rm lm sub def
    /tempwidth juststring stringwidth pop def
    /numberchars juststring length 1 sub def
    /charspace charspace tempwidth sub numberchars div def
    lm y moveto charspace 0 juststring ashow /y y leading
sub def} def
```

For reference, the complete listing for Figure 3–10 appears below.

```
%!PS-Adobe 2.0
%%Title: TurnLine
%%CreationDate: 12:10PM  3/05/1989
%%Creator: Gerard Kunkel
%%BoundingBox: 0 0 612 792
%%EndComments

%%BeginProlog
/space ( )def
/TurnLine
  {/T exch def
   /spacewidth space stringwidth pop def
   /currentw 0 def
   /wordspace_count 0 def
```

```
 /restart 0 def
 /remainder T def

{remainder space search

   {/nextword exch def pop
   /remainder exch def
   /nextwordwidth nextword stringwidth pop def

   currentw nextwordwidth add lw gt
      {T restart wordspace_count restart sub
      getinterval showline
      /restart wordspace_count def
      /currentw nextwordwidth spacewidth add def}
      {/currentw currentw nextwordwidth add
      spacewidth add def}
   ifelse

   /wordspace_count wordspace_count
      nextword length add 1 add def}
   {pop exit}
ifelse
}loop
/lastchar T length def
T restart lastchar restart sub getinterval lm y moveto show
}def

/parms {
  /y exch def
  /lm exch def
  /rm exch def
  /leading exch def
  /pointsize exch def
  /lw rm lm sub def
  findfont pointsize scalefont setfont
  /showline {
    /juststring exch def
    /charspace rm lm sub def
    /tempwidth juststring stringwidth pop def
    /numberchars juststring length 1 sub def
    /charspace charspace tempwidth sub numberchars div def
    lm y moveto charspace 0 juststring ashow /y y leading
sub def} def
  lm y moveto
  }def

% ==================================
/names {/namearray exch def}def
/F {findfont exch scalefont setfont}def
% ==================================
/idpage
 {/colr exch def 0 setgray
 8 /Helvetica-Bold F
 90 665 moveto
```

```
namearray {show 50 0 rmoveto}forall
colr show .5 setlinewidth
80 675 moveto 0 -15 rlineto 430 0 rlineto
0 15 rlineto closepath stroke
}def

[ (FIG3-10.PS)(Gerard Kunkel)(12:11PM  3/05/1989)]names
(black) idpage
%%EndProlog

/testlines (IBM PS/2 Model 80-111 with cache software \
is one of the more expensive IBM personal \
computers. It uses the Intel 80386 processor \
operating at 20 MHz.) def

/NewCenturySchlbk-Roman 8 9 180 100 600 parms testlines
TurnLine
/Helvetica-Bold 8 10 180 100 500 parms testlines TurnLine
/Times-Roman 9 12 180 100 400 parms testlines TurnLine
/AvantGarde-Demi 24 27 500 200 600 parms testlines TurnLine
/Helvetica-Oblique 14 18 430 200 400 parms testlines
TurnLine
/ZapfChancery-MediumItalic 18 18 500 100 280 parms testlines
TurnLine
/Times-Bold 18 20 500 100 200 parms testlines TurnLine
showpage
```

3-4   Modifying Your Typefaces

In working with many designers as they embark on the frustrating road to desktop publishing proficiency, I have seen a consistent desire for condensed and expanded typefaces. To satisfy this desire with the best quality typography, you would need to purchase the downloadable font to match your needs. However, even then the amount of condensing or expanding may not fit your design needs. PostScript offers a solution through its *makefont* operator. Since each font is defined within the guidelines of a six-element array, or matrix, the scaling and distortion of any PostScript font can be modified according to that matrix.

Before we jump into the use of the matrix, let's look at the matrix itself. In scaling a typeface to be 36 point, you would normally use this definition:

/Helvetica findfont 36 scalefont setfont

It is possible, however, to define the same point size utilizing the *makefont* operator.

```
/Helvetica findfont [36 0 0 36 0 0] makefont setfont
```

Note that the integer 36 appears twice within the font matrix. The first appearance of the 36 is the character width; the second is the character height. These are actually scaling values in the matrix.

The following table explains the function of the other values in the matrix.

IBM PS/2 Model 80-111 with cache software is one of the more expensive IBM personal computers. It uses the Intel 80386 processor operating at 20 MHz.

IBM PS/2 Model 80-111 with cache software is one of the more expensive IBM personal computers. It uses the Intel 80386 processor operating at 20 MHz.

IBM PS/2 Model 80-111 with cache software is one of the more expensive IBM personal computers. It uses the Intel 80386 processor operating at 20 MHz.

IBM PS/2 Model 80-111 with cache software is one of the more expensive IBM personal computers. It uses the Intel 80386 processor operating at 20 MHz.

IBM PS/2 Model 80-111 with cache software is one of the more expensive IBM personal computers. It uses the Intel 80386 processor operating at 20 MHz.

IBM PS/2 Model 80-111 with cache software is one of the more expensive IBM personal computers. It uses the Intel 80386 processor operating at 20 MHz.

IBM PS/2 Model 80-111 with cache software is one of the more expensive IBM personal computers. It uses the Intel 80386 processor operating at 20 MHz.

Figure 3—10

1	2	3	4	5	6
Scale Width	Sine	Negative Sine	Scale Height	Transform Horizontal	Transform Vertical

Position	Effect
1	Scales the width of a typeface. If your desired point size is 36 and you are looking for a condensed face, reduce this number by the percentage that you need. For instance, a 10% condensing will require this first number to be 32.4, and the fourth to be 36.
2	This position allows some interesting character distortions. It controls the sine value of the matrix, in which a positive number will result in stretching the right side of the character up while leaving the left side intact. A negative number will yield a character with the right side transformed down.
3	This position can help you create a custom oblique transformation. In this case the top of the character is transformed while the bottom remains intact. Hence, a positive number will yield an italic appearance, and a negative number will oblique the face to the left.
4	Scales the height of a typeface. If you desire a compressed typeface, this position gives you control over the relative height. In our 36-point example, you may want a 20% compression of the face. The value in the fourth position would then be 28.8, and the value in the first position would be 36.
5	Transforms the character's x position. By placing a 4 in this position, the character will be moved to the right by four points from its point of origin. A negative number will move its current point to the left.
6	Transforms the character's y position. By placing a 9 in this position, the character will be moved up by 9 points from its point of origin. A negative number will lower its current point.

By using the *makefont* operator, you can customize the existing typeface to fit your design needs. The next few figures will demonstrate some of the modifications that can be achieved while using standard ROM fonts from the Apple LaserWriter IINT.

In Figure 3–11, an unaltered font is achieved by applying the matrix:

```
%!PS-Adobe 2.0
%%Title: figure 3-11
%%CreationDate: 12:20PM  3/05/1989
%%Creator: Gerard Kunkel
%%BoundingBox: 100 100 436 712
%%EndComments

% ---- FONT DEFINITION ROUTINE -----------------
/F {findfont exch scalefont setfont}def
/names {/namearray exch def}def

% ---- PAGE IDENTIFICATION ROUTINE -------------
/idpage
 {8 /Helvetica-Bold F
 .5 setlinewidth
 0 setgray
 60 745 moveto
 namearray {show 50 0 rmoveto}forall
 50 755 moveto 0 -15 rlineto 500 0 rlineto
 0 15 rlineto closepath stroke
} def

% ---- REGISTER MARKS ROUTINE ------------------
/regmarks
  {.7 setlinewidth
  /Helvetica findfont 5 scalefont setfont
  /ym exch def
  /xm exch def
  xm 12 sub ym 17 sub moveto
  90 rotate
  (PC MAGAZINE) show
  -90 rotate
  newpath xm ym 10 add moveto
    xm ym 10 sub lineto closepath stroke
  newpath xm 10 sub ym moveto
    xm 10 add ym lineto stroke
    xm ym 5 0 360 arc stroke
 } def

% ---- LOCATE REGISTER MARKS ROUTINE -----------
/registerpage
 {40 740 regmarks
 40 50 regmarks
 580 50 regmarks
 580 740 regmarks
} def

% ---- FONT ALTERING ROUTINE -------------------
```

```
/distort {/type exch def
        /Times-Bold findfont
        .7 setlinewidth
        [120 0 0 120 0 0] makefont setfont
        100 120 moveto
        type show
        stroke
}def

% ---- CALL FONT ALTERING ROUTINE --------------
(Normal) distort

registerpage
[(FIG3-11.PS)(12:19PM  3/05/1989)(Copyright 1988 Gerard
Kunkel)]names
idpage
showpage
```

In Figure 3–12, two effects are created through the use of the *makefont* operator. Both obliquing and condensing are performed on the typeface. The first value in this matrix, 50, represents approximately 41% condensing of a 120 point type size (the fourth value). The third value, 50, is the negative sine of the fourth value and is user selected at random. The result of this matrix is the oblique characters that you see in Figure 3–12.

To save space on the next few listings I have omitted the program segments that draw the registration marks and identify the page. If you desire this portion, simply copy them from Figure 3–11. Regardless, these listings will work fine without them.

```
%!PS-Adobe 2.0
%%Title: Condensed Oblique FIGURE 3-12
%%CreationDate: 12:24PM  3/05/1989
%%Creator: Gerard Kunkel
%%BoundingBox: 100 100 436 712
%%EndComments

/distort {/type exch def
        /Times-Bold findfont
        .7 setlinewidth
        [50 0 50 120 0 0] makefont setfont
        120 120 moveto
        type show
        stroke
}def

(Condensed Oblique) distort

showpage
```

Figure 3–13 shows the effect of the *makefont* operator used for condensing the characters.

Normal

Figure 3—11
Normal makefont

```
%!PS-Adobe 2.0
%%Title: figure 3-13
%%CreationDate: 12:58PM  3/05/1989
%%Creator: Gerard Kunkel
%%BoundingBox: 100 100 436 712
%%EndComments

/distort {/type exch def
        /Times-Bold findfont
        .7 setlinewidth
        [50 0 0 120 0 0] makefont setfont
        120 120 moveto
        type show
        stroke
}def

(Condensed) distort
showpage
```

In Figure 3–14 the characters appear expanded. This can also be thought of as though the height of these characters has been condensed. By making the fourth value in the matrix smaller than the first, you effectively compress the characters down. In this case, the width of the character matrix is 100 points, and the height is 45% of its normal height. The *makefont* matrix reflects this directly:

```
[100 0 0 45 0 0] makefont
```

Condensed Oblique

Figure 3—12
Oblique makefont

Condensed

Figure 3–13
Condensed makefont

```
%!PS-Adobe 2.0
%%Title: figure 3-14
%%CreationDate: 1:10PM  3/05/1989
%%Creator: Gerard Kunkel
%%BoundingBox: 100 100 436 712
%%EndComments

/distort {/type exch def
          /Times-Bold findfont
          .7 setlinewidth
          [100 0 0 45 0 0] makefont setfont
          80 120 moveto
          type show
          stroke
}def

(Expanded) distort

showpage
```

If you are a Macintosh user, you have enjoyed the ability to create outline fonts on screen and in your printouts. On the MS-DOS platform there are few programs that have this capability. Figure 3–15 shows you how to create an outline of any PostScript typeface, even after it has been modified using the *makefont* operator.

To create an outline we must rely on another PostScript font operator, *charpath*. PostScript fonts are outline fonts. That is, they are created out of line segments that shape the edges of the character, and then the character

Expanded

Figure 3–14
Expanded makefont

is filled. The *charpath* operator pushes that outline of the character onto the stack. The outline is a path just like a path you might create for a box or any other shape. Because it is a path, it can be treated just like any other graphic. In the case of creating an outline, the fill operation is foregone, and the character outline is merely stroked.

```
(Outline) false charpath
```

The *charpath* operator requires two objects from the stack. The topmost object on the stack is a Boolean operand instructing the *charpath* operator what to do with the character path. If the operand is *false*, the path is set up for stroking the line only. If the operand is *true*, the path is set up for filling or clipping special effects, but not for stroking the outline. Since I was looking for an outline only, I chose *false*. The other item that must be on the stack is the character or string to be outlined. As you can see, an entire string can be outlined in one process.

```
%!PS-Adobe 2.0
%%Title: figure 3-15
%%CreationDate: 1:12PM  3/05/1989
%%Creator: Gerard Kunkel
%%BoundingBox: 100 100 436 712
%%EndComments

/outline {/Times-Bold findfont
        .7 setlinewidth
        [72 0 50 140 0 0] makefont setfont
        120 120 moveto
        (Outline) false charpath
        stroke
}def

outline

showpage
```

Figure 3—15
Outline

3.4.1   Type as a Clipping Region

In Figure 3–16 the typographic and programming techniques become a bit more complex. PostScript has a powerful set of operators that allow special effects to be created when you use some imagination. One of those operators is *clip*. *Clip* enables the programmer to specify a regular or irregular shape to act as a mask.

A clipping path can be thought of as the edge of a cookie cutter. The dough that is cut out to form the cookie would be analogous to that part of the page where something can be imaged. The areas that fall outside the clipping path are protected from anything being painted on them. If you have ever used an airbrush and created a mask to define an area to be painted, you will understand the effect of the *clip* operator. When creating an airbrush mask, you lay down the masking film and cut out those areas that are to be painted. The path, or edge, of this area is cut using a straight-edged razor or an Exacto knife. In PostScript, the area is cut out using path operators. To clip out a box area, you would create the following code.

```
/boxarea {100 0 rlineto
0 100 rlineto
-100 0 rlineto
closepath}def

/drawline{100 300 moveto
 400 y lineto stroke}def

2 setlinewidth
200 200 moveto
boxarea clip
newpath

0 20 600 {/y exch def drawline} for

showpage
```

The procedure *boxarea* is defined to precede the call to the *clip* operator. The only requirement of the *clip* operator is that there be a path defined that can be used for clipping. This procedure draws a closed path equal to a square and fills it.

The *drawline* procedure repeats a line-drawing operation that creates a fan of lines. The call to the *boxarea* routine is preceded by a *moveto* operation to establish the current point. Without the *moveto* operation performed, a *nocurrentpoint* error will occur.

Try running this code without the line *boxarea clip*. This will show you what is happening below the clipping area. Or, using our airbrushing analogy, this would show you what is below the masking film. By adding that line of code back in, you will clip the image and see only a fan of lines within the box dimensions.

Figure 3–16 shows the effect of text used as a clipping area. To paint a shadow of text I have introduced a clipping path equal to the characters' outline. As I have shown with the previous type examples, it is possible to create a path that is constructed from the character outline. That path can be used for stroking a line, filling the outline to form a solid character, or setting up a clipping path. When combining this with a special graphic trick, such as a graduated tint (elaborated in Chapter 6), this semirealistic image is produced.

```
%!PS-Adobe 2.0
%%Title: Figure 3-16
%%CreationDate: 21:45PM  2/19/1989
%%Creator: Gerard Kunkel
%%BoundingBox: 100 100 436 712
%%EndComments

/grad
  {/ud exch def
   /k1 exch def
   /k2 exch def
   /ury exch def /urx exch def /lly exch def /llx exch def
   ud{/range ury lly sub def}
     {/range urx llx sub def}ifelse
   /kgrad k2 k1 sub range div def
   1.1 setlinewidth
   k1 abs setgray
   ud{range{llx lly moveto urx lly lineto
     stroke /lly lly 1 add def grada}repeat}
     {range{llx lly moveto llx ury lineto
     stroke /llx llx 1 add def grada}repeat}ifelse
  }def

/grada {k1 abs setgray
        /k1 k1 kgrad add def
  }def

/F {findfont exch scalefont setfont}def
/names {/namearray exch def}def

/idpage
  {8 /Helvetica-Bold F
  .5 setlinewidth
  0 setgray
  60 745 moveto
```

```
    namearray {show 50 0 rmoveto}forall
    50 755 moveto 0 -15 rlineto 500 0 rlineto
    0 15 rlineto closepath stroke
  } def

/regmarks
   {.7 setlinewidth
   /Helvetica findfont 5 scalefont setfont
   /ym exch def
   /xm exch def
   xm 12 sub ym 17 sub moveto
   90 rotate
   (PC MAGAZINE) show
   -90 rotate
   newpath xm ym 10 add moveto
     xm ym 10 sub lineto closepath stroke
   newpath xm 10 sub ym moveto
     xm 10 add ym lineto stroke
     xm ym 5 0 360 arc stroke
  } def

/registerpage
  {40 740 regmarks
  40 50 regmarks
  580 50 regmarks
  580 740 regmarks
  } def

/shadow {/Times-Bold findfont
        [72 0 50 140 0 0] makefont setfont
        120 120 moveto
        (Shadow) false charpath
  }def

gsave
shadow clip
100 115 600 220 1 0 true grad
grestore

registerpage
[(2:50PM  2/19/1989)(FIG3-16.PS)(Copyright 1988 Gerard
Kunkel)]names
idpage
showpage
```

When a clipping path is defined and the *clip* operator is used, the current graphics state is updated to reflect this. If you wish to place anything outside the clipping path after it is defined, you must save the graphics state prior to using the *clip* operator. After the clipping area is defined and used, the graphics state can then be restored, and the entire page becomes available again. These four lines from Figure 3–16 demonstrate this technique:

Shadow

Figure 3—16
Shadow

```
gsave
shadow clip
100 115 600 220 1 0 true grad
grestore
```

This portion of code also demonstrates one of the advantages of defining procedures and creating a structured program. The entire process of imaging this effect takes place in the two lines between the *gsave* and *grestore*. Reviewing this code or making alterations can be done quickly and easily.

Figure 3–17 shows a much more elaborate treatment for a shadow font. Be forewarned that this program takes a considerable time to process. Once again, this is due primarily to the clipping for the shadow. The techniques used to create the foreground characters take a relatively short amount of time to process and can be lifted and used elsewhere.

In this figure, I have added all of the standard page identification and registration marks that are outlined in Chapter 6.

```
%!PS-Adobe 2.0
%%Title: Figure 3-17
%%CreationDate: 2:53PM  2/19/1989
%%Creator: Gerard Kunkel
%%BoundingBox: 100 100 436 712
%%EndComments

/grad
  {/ud exch def
   /k1 exch def
   /k2 exch def
   /ury exch def /urx exch def /lly exch def /llx exch def
   ud{/range ury lly sub def}
     {/range urx llx sub def}ifelse
   /kgrad k2 k1 sub range div def
   1.1 setlinewidth
```

```
    k1 abs setgray
    ud{range{llx lly moveto urx lly lineto
      stroke /lly lly 1 add def grada}repeat}
      {range{llx lly moveto llx ury lineto
      stroke /llx llx 1 add def grada}repeat}ifelse
 }def

 /grada {k1 abs setgray
       /k1 k1 kgrad add def
 }def

 /F {findfont exch scalefont setfont}def
 /names {/namearray exch def}def

 /idpage
  {8 /Helvetica-Bold F
  .5 setlinewidth
  0 setgray
  60 745 moveto
  namearray {show 50 0 rmoveto}forall
  50 755 moveto 0 -15 rlineto 500 0 rlineto
  0 15 rlineto closepath stroke
 } def

 /regmarks
   {.7 setlinewidth
   /Helvetica findfont 5 scalefont setfont
   /ym exch def
   /xm exch def
   xm 12 sub ym 17 sub moveto
   90 rotate
   (PC MAGAZINE) show
   -90 rotate
   newpath xm ym 10 add moveto
     xm ym 10 sub lineto closepath stroke
   newpath xm 10 sub ym moveto
     xm 10 add ym lineto stroke
     xm ym 5 0 360 arc stroke
 } def

 /registerpage
  {40 740 regmarks
  40 50 regmarks
  580 50 regmarks
  580 740 regmarks
 } def

 /shadow {/Times-Bold findfont
        [72 0 50 140 0 0] makefont setfont
        120 120 moveto
        (Shadow) false charpath
 }def

 /typeit {0 setgray
```

```
        /Times-Bold findfont
        72 scalefont setfont
        6 {120 120 moveto
          (Shadow) show
          -.5 -1 translate}repeat
        120 120 moveto
        2 setlinewidth 0 setgray
        (Shadow) true charpath stroke
        120 120 moveto
        .4 setlinewidth 1 setgray
        (Shadow) true charpath stroke
}def

gsave
shadow clip
100 115 600 220 1 0 true grad
grestore

typeit

registerpage
[(2:50PM  2/19/1989)(FIG3-17.PS)(Copyright 1988 Gerard
Kunkel)]names

idpage
showpage
```

3.4.2   Special Effects

Once you have a good grasp of the workings of text in PostScript, you can start to explore some of the special effects that are possible. Figure 3–18 illustrates a simple technique in repeating an outlined text string at different sizes. The zoomed type is the same string repeated many times. Each time the string is repeated, it is increased in size and is made a little darker using the *setgray* operator.

Figure 3–17
Fancy Shadow

This program includes all of the code necessary to identify the page and place crop marks and registration marks. This portion of the code is not necessary for its successful imaging. If you omit it, be sure to omit the reference to it in the script portion of the code.

Let's look at the entire listing.

```
%!PS-Adobe 2.0
%%Title: ZoomType Figure 3-18
%%Creator: Gerard Kunkel
%%CreationDate: 1:21PM  3/05/1989
%%BoundingBox: 0 0 612 792

/names {/namearray exch def}def
/F {findfont exch scalefont setfont}def

/idpage
 {/colr exch def 0 setgray
 8 /Helvetica-Bold F
 90 665 moveto
 namearray {show 50 0 rmoveto}forall
 colr show .5 setlinewidth
 80 675 moveto 0 -15 rlineto 430 0 rlineto
 0 15 rlineto closepath stroke
 registerpage
 30 63 translate
 cropmarks
 -30 -63 translate
 }def

/regmarks
  {.7 setlinewidth
  /ymark exch def
  /xmark exch def
  /Helvetica findfont 5 scalefont setfont
  xmark 10 sub ymark 32 sub moveto 90 rotate
  (LUCHAK COMMUNICATIONS) show -90 rotate
  newpath
    xmark ymark 10 add moveto
    xmark ymark 10 sub lineto closepath stroke
  newpath
    xmark 10 sub ymark moveto
    xmark 10 add ymark lineto stroke
    xmark ymark 5 0 360 arc stroke
 }def

/registerpage
 {80 660 regmarks
 80 120 regmarks
 532 120 regmarks
 532 660 regmarks}def

/cropmarks {1 setlinewidth
   /width 549 def
   /height 666 def
```

```
   0  6 sub 0 moveto
   0 30 sub 0 lineto stroke
   0  0  6 sub moveto
   0  0 30 sub lineto stroke

   0  6 sub height moveto
   0 30 sub height lineto stroke
   0 height 6 add moveto
   0 height 30 add lineto stroke

   width 6 add 0 moveto
   width 30 add 0 lineto stroke
   width 0 6 sub moveto
   width 0 30 sub lineto stroke

   width 6 add height moveto
   width 30 add height lineto stroke
   width height 6 add moveto
   width height 30 add lineto stroke

}def
[(FIG3-18.PS)(Gerard Kunkel)(1:20PM  3/05/1989)]names
(black) idpage

/ZOOM
 {/Helvetica-Bold findfont z scalefont setfont
 /name (ZOOM) def name dup stringwidth pop
 2 div neg 0 rmoveto
 name true charpath stroke}def

/drawZOOM
 {0 0 moveto 18 {x setgray ZOOM /x x .05 sub def
 /z z 2 add def 0 0 moveto}repeat}def

300 400 translate
/z 60 def /x .9 def
3 setmiterlimit
2 setlinejoin
3 setlinewidth
drawZOOM
showpage
```

Figure 3—18
Zoom Type

Taking a look at the details of this code, we should first look at the *ZOOM* procedure. The objective of this procedure is to set the typeface, position the center of the text string, and stroke the outline of the text string.

```
/ZOOM
{/Helvetica-Bold findfont z scalefont setfont
/name (ZOOM) def name dup stringwidth pop
2 div neg 0 rmoveto
name true charpath stroke}def
```

The second line of the procedure defines the text string. Then the *stringwidth* operator pushes the width of that string object, called *name*, onto the operand stack. The third line of the procedure takes the width value of the string, divides it in half, and converts it to a negative number. The new value on the stack is then used as the *x* value in the *rmoveto* operation.

The last line in this procedure places the string object on the operand stack again and performs a *charpath* operation on it. The Boolean value *true* is used to tell the *charpath* operator that this path will be used for an outline. The final *stroke* is required to paint the line on the page.

The *ZOOM* procedure call is made within the next procedure, *drawZOOM*. This procedure has two main purposes. The first is to call the *ZOOM* routine; the second is to redefine the gray value and the point size of the type.

```
/drawZOOM
{0 0 moveto 18 {x setgray ZOOM /x x .05 sub def
/z z 2 add def 0 0 moveto}repeat}def
```

DrawZOOM is a routine that relies on the PostScript *repeat* operator. This operator is used after an integer and a procedure are placed on the operand stack. The integer represents the number of times the interpreter should repeat the following procedure. The procedure is any legal Post-Script operation. This procedure performs the following tasks.

- Sets the gray value
- Calls the *ZOOM* procedure
- Adds .05 to the value of x
- Adds 2 to the value of z
- Moves to the location 0,0

The final few lines of code set the page up before calling the *drawZOOM* routine. I have annotated these lines with trailing comments to tell the story.

```
300 400 translate % translate the point of origin
/z 60 def /x .9 def % set the point size and gray value
3 setmiterlimit % define the miterlimit for outline type
2 setlinejoin  % define the line join for outline type
3 setlinewidth  % define the line width for the outline
drawZOOM    % call the drawZOOM procedure
showpage    % eject page, reset parameters
```

It should be obvious from this code that it would not take much modification to come up with some different visual effects. Figure 3–19 shows another possibility, working with the same code as used in Figure 3–18.

To create this new effect, the *drawZOOM* procedure was modified slightly to create the rotated effect. In detail, the process was increased to 36 repeats, the amount of gray value increase was changed to .025, and a new operator, *rotate*, was introduced. The *rotate* operator requires one number on the operand stack, between −360 and 360. Since this operator deals in degrees, numbers greater than 360 or less than −360 would simply involve one complete revolution, which would be pointless but would not cause an error. The operator rotates the entire page so that, in the case of typography, the characters will continue to read across in a line. To return to the original angle of rotation, you must perform a *gsave* or *save* with *restore* of the current state, or explicitly perform a negative *rotate* equal to your positive rotation.

In this case I have rotated the type by 1.3 degrees for each pass through the repeated procedure.

```
%!PS-Adobe 2.0
%%Title: RotateZoomType Figure 3-19
%%Creator: Gerard Kunkel
%%CreationDate: 1:35PM  3/05/1989
%%BoundingBox: 0 0 612 792

/ZOOM
  {/AvantGarde-Demi findfont z scalefont setfont
  /name (PostScript) def name dup stringwidth pop
  2 div neg 0 rmoveto
  name true charpath stroke}def

/drawZOOM
  {0 0 moveto 36 {x setgray ZOOM /x x .025 sub def
  /z z 2 add def 0 0 moveto 1.3 rotate}repeat
}def

300 400 translate
/z 50 def /x .9 def
3 setmiterlimit
0 setlinejoin
5 setlinewidth
```

```
drawZOOM
1 setgray ZOOM
0 0 moveto
1 setlinewidth
0 setgray ZOOM
showpage
```

Figure 3—19
Rotate Type

3-5   Helpful Tools for Working with Text

In some cases you may need to have character-width information available in advance of programming. For instance, if you were trying to program a complete desktop publishing application, you may need to show text on screen relative to the character size of the actual output font. This is no simple task, and I will not try to address these requirements in this book. On a smaller scale, you may wish to create a simple *BoundingBox* for a single line of type. This can be accomplished by borrowing the character-width information directly from the interpreter in your printer.

The next few programs print out useful font information. The output may be customized to fit your needs by changing the font call and point size. Since these next few programs are useful productivity tools and not necessarily art or design tools, I have chosen to give brief descriptions.

Figure 3–20 prints out a complete set of character widths for the Helvetica-Bold typeface at 50 points. The complete listing is shown for Figure 3–20.

```
/x 30 def
/y 670 def
/numb1 20 string def

/showchars {30 1 240 {
  /charnum exch def
  fontname findfont ps scalefont setfont
  /tempstring (x)def
  tempstring 0 charnum put
    newpath x y moveto
    tempstring true charpath flattenpath pathbbox
    y sub numb1 cvs /charury exch def
    x sub numb1 cvs /charurx exch def
    y sub numb1 cvs /charlly exch def
    x sub numb1 cvs /charllx exch def
    charury length 5 gt{/charury charury 0 5 getinterval def}if
    charurx length 5 gt{/charurx charurx 0 5 getinterval def}if
    charlly length 5 gt{/charlly charlly 0 5 getinterval def}if
    charllx length 5 gt{/charllx charllx 0 5 getinterval def}if
    clear
    x y moveto
    fontname findfont 12 scalefont setfont
    tempstring showchar
    /Helvetica findfont 6 scalefont setfont
    charllx showchar
    charlly showchar
    charurx showchar
    charury showchar
  nextchar
  }for
```

```
}def
/showchar {
  show /x x 20 add def x y moveto}def
/nextchar {/x x 100 sub def
  y 55 ge
  {/y y 15 sub def}
  {/y y 630 add def /x x 107 add def}ifelse
}def

/showfont {/fn 40 string def
  x 720 moveto
  fontname findfont ps scalefont setfont
  fontname fn cvs show
  ( )show
  ps fn cvs show
  (pt)show
  /Helvetica-Bold findfont 10 scalefont setfont
  x 700 moveto
  (Character widths: llx, lly, urx, ury in points)show}def

/ps 50 def
/fontname {/Helvetica-Bold} def
showfont
showchars
showpage
```

Taking a closer look at the listing for Figure 3–20, we can see that it is broken down into four major procedures. The first procedure, *showchars*, is where the character widths are pulled from the interpreter, the characters are shown, and the character widths are printed to the right of the actual character. The *showchar* routine prints a single text string representing one of the character's width values.

The *nextchar* routine resets the current position so that the next character line may be printed. The appropriate *x* and *y* positions are determined, and the current point is moved there.

The final routine, *showfont*, is merely window dressing. This routine puts an identifying line at the top of the page.

Let's take a closer look at the *showchars* routine, since this is where some new operators are introduced.

```
/x 30 def
/y 670 def
/numbl 20 string def

/showchars {30 1 240 {
  /charnum exch def
  fontname findfont ps scalefont setfont
  /tempstring (x)def
  tempstring 0 charnum put
    newpath x y moveto
    tempstring true charpath flattenpath pathbbox
```

```
      y sub numb1 cvs /charury exch def
      x sub numb1 cvs /charurx exch def
      y sub numb1 cvs /charlly exch def
      x sub numb1 cvs /charllx exch def
      charury length 5 gt{/charury charury 0 5 getinterval def}if
      charurx length 5 gt{/charurx charurx 0 5 getinterval def}if
      charlly length 5 gt{/charlly charlly 0 5 getinterval def}if
      charllx length 5 gt{/charllx charllx 0 5 getinterval def}if
      clear
      x y moveto
      fontname findfont 12 scalefont setfont
      tempstring showchar
      /Helvetica findfont 6 scalefont setfont
      charllx showchar
      charlly showchar
      charurx showchar
      charury showchar
    nextchar
   }for
}def
```

Up in front of the routine is the definition of an empty string called *numb1*. This empty string is called on later to temporarily hold a value used in other definitions. The string value, called by a number between 30 and 240, is picked up during the *for* loop. That number is *put* into a string, and a character path is obtained using the *charpath* operator.

The result of a *charpath* operation includes any bezier curve points that may have been used in the construction of the character. Leaving these points in will cause odd results when trying to find a character's bounding box. Another PostScript operator will help in finding the actual bounding box of a character. The *flattenpath* operator will eliminate the inclusion of control points in bezier curves. The subsequent *pathbbox* operator will then return a bounding box that more closely resembles the outer edges of the character.

The numbers that are pushed onto the stack as a result of that operation will then be stored in key name definitions for later use in printing. This is where the *numb1* empty string becomes useful. The width information that is now sitting on the stack is subtracted from its corresponding *x* or *y* coordinate. The numerical result is then converted to a string using the *cvs* operator. This operator requires that an empty string of equal or greater length be placed on the stack prior to the *cvs* call.

The new text-string definitions are then clipped to a maximum length of five characters using the *getinterval* operator. This operator requires three elements on the operand stack before calling. The first is the text string; the second is a number representing the starting point for the new substring;

Helvetica-Bold 50pt

Character widths: llx, lly, urx, ury in points

Char	llx	lly	urx	ury
	13.9	13.90	13.9	13.90
	13.9	13.90	13.9	13.90
	13.9	13.	13.9	13.
!	5.49	5.497	5.497	5.497
"	2.43	2.430	2.430	2.430
#	0.184	0.184	0.184	0.184
$	1.18	1.184	1.184	1.184
%	1.195	1.195	1.195	1.195
&	2.670	2.670	2.670	2.670
'	3.345	3.345	3.345	3.345
(	2.08	2.080	2.080	2.080
)	1.04	1.041	1.041	1.041
*	1.25	1.253	1.25	1.253
+	2.42	2.420	2.420	2.42
,	3.09	3.097	3.097	3.097
-	1.3	1.318	1.34	1.340
.	3.09	3.099	3.099	3.099
/	0.175	0.175	0.175	0.175
0	1.42	1.423	1.423	1.423
1	3.48	3.488	3.488	3.488
2	1.38	1.384	1.384	1.384
3	1.4	1.494	1.494	1.494
4	1.140	1.140	1.140	1.140
5	1.445	1.445	1.445	1.445
6	1.546	1.546	1.546	1.546
7	1.445	1.445	1.445	1.445
8	1.297	1.297	1.297	1.297
9	1.440	1.440	1.440	1.440
:	5.73	5.734	5.734	5.734
;	5.73	5.738	5.738	5.738
<	1.925	1.925	1.925	1.925
=	2.5	2.599	2.59	2.59
>	2.005	2.005	2.005	2.005
?	3.306	3.306	3.306	3.306
@	1.414	1.414	1.414	1.414
A	1.19	1.198	1.198	1.198
B	4.05	4.055	4.055	4.055
C	2.11	2.118	2.118	2.118
D	3.81	3.815	3.815	3.815
E	4.05	4.054	4.05	4.054
F	3.81	3.815	3.815	3.815
G	2.181	2.181	2.181	2.181
H	3.46	3.469	3.469	3.46

Char	llx	lly	urx	ury
I	3.13	3.139	3.139	3.13
J	1.209	1.209	1.209	1.209
K	3.850	3.850	3.85	3.85
L	4.09	4.094	4.094	4.094
M	3.37	3.379	3.379	3.37
N	3.37	3.378	3.378	3.378
O	1.934	1.934	1.934	1.934
P	3.850	3.850	3.850	3.850
Q	2.174	2.174	2.174	2.174
R	4.09	4.097	4.097	4.097
S	1.72	1.720	1.720	1.720
T	0.720	0.720	0.720	0.720
U	3.850	3.850	3.850	3.85
V	1.145	1.145	1.145	1.145
W	0.689	0.689	0.689	0.68
X	1.139	1.139	1.139	1.139
Y	1.39	1.390	1.390	1.39
Z	1.539	1.539	1.539	1.539
[	3.365	3.365	3.365	3.365
\	-0.62	-0.62	-0.62	-0.62
]	0.934	0.934	0.934	0.934
^	3.205	3.205	3.205	3.205
_	-1.06	-1.06	-1.06	-1.06
`	3.384	3.384	3.384	3.384
a	1.435	1.435	1.435	1.435
b	2.899	2.899	2.899	2.899
c	1.743	1.743	1.743	1.743
d	1.435	1.435	1.435	1.435
e	1.150	1.150	1.150	1.150
f	0.779	0.779	0.779	0.77
g	1.671	1.671	1.671	1.671
h	3.38	3.388	3.388	3.388
i	3.38	3.380	3.380	3.380
j	0.320	0.320	0.320	0.320
k	2.899	2.899	2.899	2.89
l	3.38	3.382	3.382	3.382
m	3.14	3.149	3.149	3.149
n	3.14	3.148	3.148	3.148
o	1.769	1.769	1.769	1.769
p	2.899	2.899	2.899	2.899
q	1.533	1.533	1.533	1.533
r	3.14	3.148	3.148	3.148
s	1.400	1.400	1.400	1.400

Char	llx	lly	urx	ury
t	0.690	0.690	0.690	0.690
u	2.94	2.947	2.947	2.947
v	0.854	0.854	0.854	0.854
w	0.330	0.330	0.330	0.330
x	0.879	0.879	0.879	0.879
y	0.529	0.529	0.529	0.529
z	1.129	1.129	1.129	1.129
{	1.985	1.985	1.985	1.985
|	5.160	5.160	5.160	5.160
}	3.615	3.615	3.615	3.615
~	3.105	3.105	3.105	3.105
	13.9	13.95	13.9	13.95
	13.9	13.	13.9	13.
	13.9	13.	13.9	13.
	13.9	13.95	13.9	13.95
	13.9	13.	13.9	13.
	13.9	13.	13.9	13.
	13.9	13.95	13.9	13.95
	13.9	13.95	13.9	13.95
	13.9	13.	13.9	13.
	13.9	13.95	13.9	13.95
	13.9	13.95	13.9	13.95
	13.9	13.	13.9	13.
	13.9	13.95	13.9	13.95
	13.9	13.95	13.9	13.95
	13.9	13.	13.9	13.
	13.9	13.95	13.9	13.95
	13.9	13.95	13.9	13.95
	13.9	13.95	13.9	13.95
	13.9	13.90	13.9	13.90
	13.9	13.97	13.9	13.97
	13.9	13.95	13.9	13.95
	13.9	13.97	13.9	13.97
	13.9	13.97	13.9	13.97
	13.9	13.97	13.9	13.97
	13.9	13.97	13.9	13.97
	13.9	13.95	13.9	13.95
	13.9	13.97	13.9	13.97
	13.9	13.97	13.9	13.97
	13.9	13.98	13.9	13.98
	13.9	13.95	13.9	13.95
	13.9	13.95	13.9	13.95
	13.9	13.95	13.9	13.95
	13.9	13.97	13.9	13.97
	13.9	13.97	13.9	13.97

Char	llx	lly	urx	ury
	13.9	13.90	13.9	13.90
	13.9	13.90	13.9	13.90
¡	3.449	3.449	3.449	3.449
¢	2.043	2.043	2.043	2.043
£	1.595	1.595	1.595	1.595
/	-8.61	-8.61	-8.61	-8.61
¥	0.404	0.404	0.404	0.404
f	1.170	1.170	1.170	1.170
§	1.699	1.699	1.699	1.699
¤	1.490	1.490	1.490	1.490
'	2.549	2.549	2.549	2.549
"	3.684	3.684	3.684	3.684
«	4.445	4.445	4.445	4.44
‹	4.185	4.185	4.185	4.185
›	4.024	4.02	4.024	4.024
fi	0.619	0.619	0.61	0.61
fl	0.619	0.619	0.61	0.619
	13.9	13.	13.9	13.
—	-0.33	-0.33	-0.33	-0.33
†	1.59	1.593	1.593	1.593
‡	1.59	1.596	1.596	1.596
·	3.260	3.260	3.260	3.260
	13.9	13.95	13.9	13.95
¶	1.149	1.149	1.149	1.149
•	2.724	2.724	2.724	2.724
‚	3.465	3.465	3.465	3.465
„	3.704	3.704	3.704	3.704
"	3.704	3.704	3.704	3.704
»	4.584	4.584	4.584	4.584
…	4.649	4.649	4.649	4.649
‰	0.614	0.614	0.614	0.614
	13.9	13.97	13.9	13.97
¿	2.709	2.709	2.709	2.709
	13.9	13.97	13.9	13.97
`	0.905	0.905	0.905	0.905
´	6.069	6.069	6.069	6.069
^	0.540	0.540	0.540	0.540
˜	-0.42	-0.42	-0.42	-0.42
¯	0.920	0.920	0.920	0.920
	1.794	1.794	1.794	1.794
	5.649	5.649	5.649	5.649
¨	1.09	1.099	1.099	1.099
	13.9	13.97	13.9	13.97

Char	llx	lly	urx	ury
°	3.814	3.814	3.814	3.814
¸	1.224	1.224	1.224	1.224
	13.89	13.	13.89	13.
"	-2.29	-2.29	-2.29	-2.29
˛	2.179	2.179	2.179	2.17
˳	0.364	0.364	0.364	0.364
—	-0.42	-0.42	-0.42	-0.42
	13.89	13.89	13.89	13.89
	13.89	13.	13.89	13.
	13.89	13.89	13.89	13.89
	13.89	13.89	13.89	13.89
	13.89	13.89	13.89	13.89
	13.89	13.	13.89	13.
	13.89	13.	13.89	13.
	13.89	13.	13.89	13.
	13.89	13.89	13.89	13.89
	13.89	13.	13.89	13.
	13.89	13.89	13.89	13.89
	13.89	13.89	13.89	13.89
	13.89	13.89	13.89	13.89
Æ	0.0	0.004	0.004	0.004
	13.89	13.89	13.89	13.89
ª	1.515	1.515	1.515	1.515
	13.89	13.89	13.89	13.89
	13.89	13.89	13.89	13.89
Ł	-0.05	-0.05	-0.0	-0.05
Ø	1.515	1.515	1.515	1.515
Œ	1.360	1.360	1.360	1.360
º	1.035	1.035	1.035	1.035
	13.89	13.89	13.89	13.89
	13.89	13.89	13.89	13.89
	13.89	13.89	13.89	13.89
	13.89	13.89	13.89	13.89
	13.89	13.89	13.89	13.89

Figure 3—20
Font widths

and the third represents the number of characters to be stored in that substring.

The remainder of operations in the *showchars* procedure simply locate and print the information.

There are numerous similarities between the code for Figure 3–21 and that for Figure 3–20. Here I have illustrated some of the character bounding boxes by calling upon the font character-width information extracted with the techniques used in the previous program. Again, I will be terse in my descriptions, since this is not necessarily a design tool.

Primarily, this program calls on fewer characters to be rendered in its *for* loop. The major difference between the two programs is that this program draws a character the same size as specified in the script portion of the code. In addition, the bounding box information that is acquired for this character is used to draw a box outlining the bounding box. Those values are then used as text strings to print the actual numbers next to the lower left corner and the upper right corner.

```
/x 100 def
/y 600 def
/numbl 20 string def

/showcharacter {
  76 1 105{/counter counter 1 add def
  /charnum exch def
  fontname findfont ps scalefont setfont
  /tempstring (x)def
  tempstring 0 charnum put
    newpath 0 0 moveto
    tempstring true charpath flattenpath pathbbox
    /ury exch def
    /urx exch def
    /lly exch def
    /llx exch def
    /charury ury numbl cvs def
    /charurx urx numbl cvs def
    /charlly lly numbl cvs def
    /charllx llx numbl cvs def
    charury length 5 gt{/charury charury 0 5 getinterval def}if
    charurx length 5 gt{/charurx charurx 0 5 getinterval def}if
    charlly length 5 gt{/charlly charlly 0 5 getinterval def}if
    charllx length 5 gt{/charllx charllx 0 5 getinterval def}if
    fontname findfont ps scalefont setfont
    /Helvetica findfont 6 scalefont setfont
    llx lly moveto llx ury lineto urx ury lineto urx lly lineto
    closepath stroke
    llx lly 10 sub moveto
    charllx show (, )show charlly show
    urx 2 div ury 4 add moveto
    charurx show (, )show charury show
    ps 0 translate
```

```
     counter 4 gt {ps 5 mul neg ps 10 add neg translate
                   /counter 0 def}if
}for}def

/showfont {/fn 40 string def
  x 720 moveto
  fontname findfont 24 scalefont setfont
  fontname fn cvs show
  ( )show
  ps fn cvs show
  (pt)show
  /Helvetica-Bold findfont 10 scalefont setfont
  x 700 moveto
  (Character widths: llx, lly, urx, ury in points)show}def

.5 setlinewidth
/counter 0 def
/ps 100 def
/fontname {/ZapfChancery-MediumItalic} def
showfont
75 600 translate
showcharacter
showpage
```

3-6   Typefaces Back-to-Back

One area that should be discussed is the proper placement of characters relative to one another. Figure 3–22 illustrates another approach to positioning a string of text. It is possible to line up a string of characters without having them expressed as one string. In fact, in Figure 3–22, each character is an independent string. If there is no explicit change to the current point, the current point will be the right offset of the preceding character. For instance, the following two program fragments will produce the same results.

```
100 100 moveto
(type) show

100 100 moveto
(t) show
(y) show
(p) show
(e) show
```

The benefit of breaking up a text string as shown in this example is that other operations may be inserted between characters that could not be inserted otherwise. Figure 3–22 does just that. A change in typeface was the most obvious change that I could come up with that would illustrate the point.

ZapfChancery-MediumItalic 100pt

Character widths: llx, lly, urx, ury in points

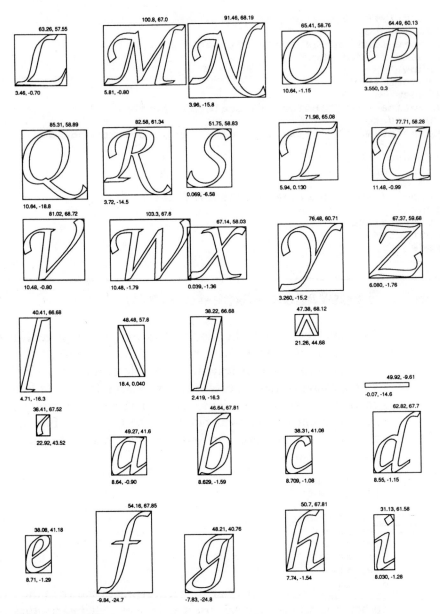

Figure 3—21
Character BBox

```
%!PS-Adobe 2.0
%%Title: Figure 3-23
%%CreationDate: 2:22PM  3/05/1989
%%Creator: Gerard Kunkel
%%BoundingBox: 100 100 436 712
%%EndComments


/F {findfont exch scalefont setfont}def
/names {/namearray exch def}def

/idpage
 {8 /Helvetica-Bold F
 .5 setlinewidth
 0 setgray
 60 745 moveto
 namearray {show 50 0 rmoveto}forall
 50 755 moveto 0 -15 rlineto 500 0 rlineto
 0 15 rlineto closepath stroke
} def

/regmarks
  {.7 setlinewidth
  /Helvetica findfont 5 scalefont setfont
  /ym exch def
  /xm exch def
  xm 12 sub ym 17 sub moveto
  90 rotate
  (PC MAGAZINE) show
  -90 rotate
  newpath xm ym 10 add moveto
    xm ym 10 sub lineto closepath stroke
  newpath xm 10 sub ym moveto
    xm 10 add ym lineto stroke
    xm ym 5 0 360 arc stroke
} def

/registerpage
 {40 740 regmarks
 40 50 regmarks
 580 50 regmarks
 580 740 regmarks
} def

100 100 moveto
70 /Times-Bold F
(V) show
70 /Helvetica-Bold F
(A) show
70 /Times-Roman F
(R) show
70 /Palatino-Roman F
(I) show
70 /Times-Italic F
```

```
(A) show
70 /Helvetica-Narrow F
(T) show
70 /Palatino-Bold F
(I) show
70 /Helvetica F
(O) show
70 /Times-Roman F
(N) show
70 /Courier F
(S) show

registerpage
[(2:22PM  3/05/1989)(fig3-23.ps)(Copyright 1988 Gerard
Kunkel)]names
idpage
showpage
```

Looking at the script portion of this code, you should note that there is only one *moveto* operation. The remainder of the characters shown rely upon a resetting of the current point, based upon the character last shown. A typeface change has been inserted between each character.

```
100 100 moveto
70 /Times-Bold F
(V) show
70 /Helvetica-Bold F
(A) show
70 /Times-Roman F
(R) show
70 /Palatino-Roman F
(I) show
70 /Times-Italic F
(A) show
70 /Helvetica-Narrow F
(T) show
70 /Palatino-Bold F
(I) show
70 /Helvetica F
(O) show
70 /Times-Roman F
(N) show
70 /Courier F
(S) show
```

VARIATIONs

Figure 3—22
Variations

Figure 3–23 uses the same technique to kern character pairs. There are two examples in this code: before kerning and after kerning. The top example has no change. This is the same letter spacing you would expect to receive if you supplied a single text string to the *show* operator. The second example performs a *moveto* operation between each character. The amount of space that is being moved is determined by the character's width.

In the complete listing for Figure 3–23, the code for page identification, registration marks, and crop marks has been removed to make this program easier to read.

```
%!PS-Adobe 2.0
%%Title: fig3-24
%%CreationDate:03-05-1989 Time: 14:33:16
%%Creator: Gerard Kunkel 1988
%%BoundingBox: 0 -59  151.2 30

/F {findfont exch scalefont setfont}def

0 setgray
0 setlinewidth
3 setmiterlimit /y 0 def
/T {dup stringwidth pop /tw exch def
    false charpath gsave fill grestore stroke
    /kfactor exch def
    /tw tw kfactor mul def /track track tw add def
    track y moveto }def
/newline {/y y 30 sub def /track 0 def track y moveto}def

/Helvetica findfont [30.00 0 0.00 30.00 0 0]
makefont setfont
100 400 translate
/track 0 def
0 y moveto
 1 (A)T
 1 (n)T
 1 ( )T
 1 (e)T
 1 (x)T
 1 (a)T
 1 (m)T
 1 (p)T
 1 (l)T
 1 (e)T
 1 ( )T
 1 (o)T
 1 (f)T
 1 ( )T
 1 (k)T
 1 (e)T
 1 (r)T
 1 (n)T
 1 (i)T
```

```
1 (n)T
1 (g)T

0 -50 translate
/track 0 def
0 y moveto
.9 (A)T
.9 (n)T
.9 ( )T
.9 (e)T
.9 (x)T
.9 (a)T
.95 (m)T
.9 (p)T
.85 (l)T
.9 (e)T
.9 ( )T
.9 (o)T
.9 (f)T
.9 ( )T
.9 (k)T
.9 (e)T
.9 (r)T
.9 (n)T
.85 (i)T
.9 (n)T
.9 (g)T

showpage
```

If we look a little closer at this code, we can see that each text string is preceded by a numerical value and followed by the procedural call *T*. The number represents the value used in multiplying the current character width. When a value less than 1 is used, the current character width is reduced; hence, the intercharacter space is tightened, or kerned. If this number is greater than 1, the width is increased, making the intercharacter space wider.

A few graphics-state parameters are set in the beginning of the program. Specifically, the gray value, line width, and miter limit are all set

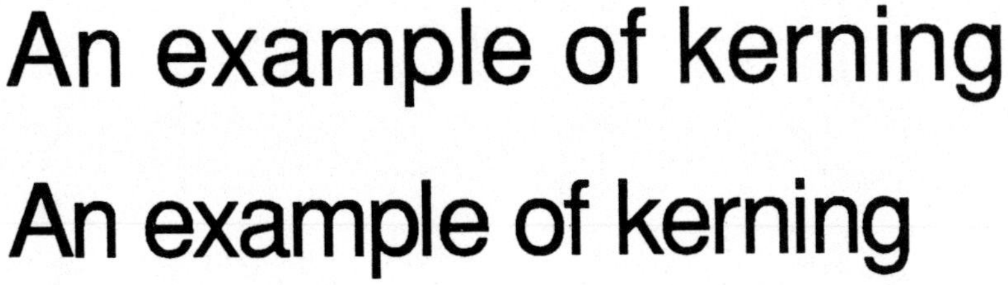

An example of kerning

An example of kerning

Figure 3—23
Kerning from KERN.EXE

to accommodate an outlined character. The *T* procedure performs the spacing calculation, with the width multiplier and string value supplied, and then shows the character.

```
0 setgray
0 setlinewidth
3 setmiterlimit /y 0 def
/T {dup stringwidth pop /tw exch def
    false charpath gsave fill grestore stroke
    /kfactor exch def
    /tw tw kfactor mul def /track track tw add def
    track y moveto }def
/newline {/y y 30 sub def /track 0 def track y moveto}def
```

The first operation in this procedure is the duplication of the topmost object on the operand stack, the text string. Next, the width of that string is obtained with the *stringwidth* operator. The *y* value of that width information is discarded with the *pop* operator. The remaining width information is stored with the key name *tw*.

The next line shows the current character via the *charpath* operator. (I have chosen to use this method rather than *show* in preparation for the next figure, on character bolding.) The defined character path is then filled and stroked.

The number that preceded the text string is finally picked off the stack in the next line and stored with the key name *kfactor*. The character width that was obtained previously, *tw*, is now multiplied by *kfactor*. This value is added to a running total of string width defined as *track*. This object keeps track of the current *x* position by starting at zero and increasing according to the widths that are calculated for each character. The last line of this procedure performs a *moveto* operation that then sets the starting point for the character to follow.

Figure 3–24 illustrates a technique for bolding existing typefaces. Use of this technique should be extremely limited. This does not always create an attractive-looking font. In broad strokes, this program acquires the character outline information to draw the character; the character is then filled and stroked. In stroking the character, I have introduced a wider line width. The result is a fat character. This technique works fine with small adjustments to the line width. Some typefaces react better than others. Courier will not work with this technique, since it is not an outline font but a stroke font.

Since outline fonts are created from connected lines and curves, miter limits and line-join parameters play a role in making this technique effective. Experiment with these operators in using this code. The best results may be obtained with different values for different fonts. This experimentation may also yield some serendipitous results that can be used in your design.

Below is the complete listing for Figure 3–24.

```
%!PS-Adobe 2.0
%%Title: fig3-25
%%CreationDate:2:47PM  3/05/1989
%%Creator: Gerard Kunkel 1989
%%BoundingBox: 0 -59   151.2 30

/F {findfont exch scalefont setfont}def

0 setgray
0 setlinewidth
3 setmiterlimit /y 0 def
/Tbold {false charpath gsave fill grestore stroke
    }def

/Helvetica-Bold findfont [30.00 0 0.00 30.00 0 0]
makefont setfont
100 600 translate

/drawtext {
0 -50 translate
0 y moveto
  (An example of bolding)Tbold
}def

0 setlinewidth drawtext
.5 setlinewidth drawtext
1 setlinewidth drawtext
1.5 setlinewidth drawtext
2 setlinewidth drawtext
2.5 setlinewidth drawtext
3 setlinewidth drawtext

showpage
```

The final figure in this chapter (Figure 3–25) is introduced to help you understand the workings of the font matrix as used with the *makefont* operator. Since I do not see this as a design tool, I will not go into detailed explanation of the code used to generate the graphic. I have included the code as a reference should you desire to use it.

```
%!PS-Adobe 2.0
%%Title: Makefont figure
%%Creator: Gerard Kunkel
%%CreationDate: 2-27-89
%%BoundingBox: 0 0 612 792
%%EndComments

%%BeginProlog
```

```
/x 100 def
/y 650 def
0 setgray
.5 setlinewidth


/drawmake
  {x y moveto
  font findfont [ps1 ps2 ps3 ps4 ps5 ps6] makefont setfont
  char show
  x y ps .3 mul sub moveto
  /Helvetica-Narrow findfont 7 scalefont setfont
  ([) show ps1 pst cvs show
  ( ) show ps2 pst cvs show
  ( ) show ps3 pst cvs show
  ( ) show ps4 pst cvs show
  ( ) show ps5 pst cvs show
  ( ) show ps6 pst cvs show
  (]) show
  /x x ps add def
  x 500 gt{
    /x 100 def
    /y y ps ps .6 mul add sub def}if
}def

%%EndProlog

/reset {
  /pst 6 string def
  /ps 60 def
  /jump ps 10 div def
  /char (A) def
  /ps1 ps def /ps2 0 def /ps3 0 def
  /ps4 ps def /ps5 0 def /ps6 0 def
}def

/drawbbox {
    llx x add lly y add moveto llx x add ury y add lineto
    urx x add ury y add lineto urx x add lly y add lineto
    closepath stroke}def

/definebbox {0 0 moveto
    font findfont [ps1 ps2 ps3 ps4 ps5 ps6] makefont setfont
    char true charpath flattenpath pathbbox
    /ury exch def
    /urx exch def
    /lly exch def
    /llx exch def
    newpath}def

/font {/Helvetica-Bold}def

/loopmake
  {reset definebbox 0 jump ps
  {/ps3 exch def drawmake drawbbox}
```

```
     for}def
loopmake
/loopmake
  {reset definebbox 0 jump ps
  {/ps5 exch def drawmake drawbbox}
  for}def
loopmake
/loopmake
  {reset definebbox 0 jump ps
  {/ps2 exch def drawmake drawbbox}
  for}def
loopmake
/loopmake
  {reset definebbox 0 jump ps
  {neg /ps2 exch def drawmake drawbbox}
  for}def
loopmake
showpage
```

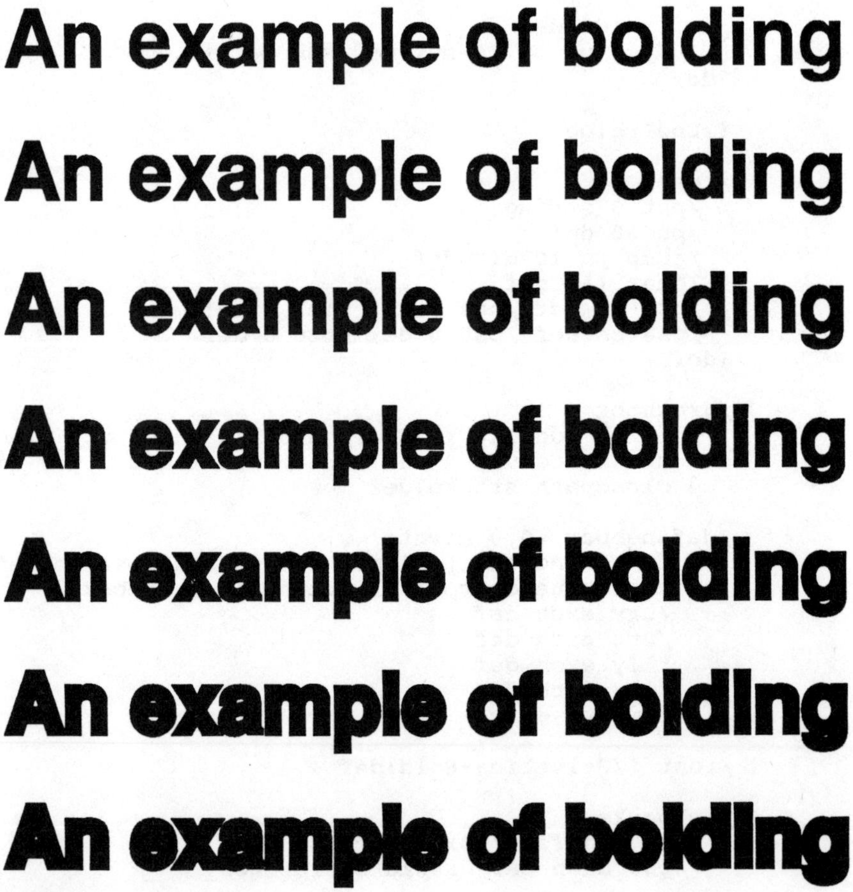

An example of bolding

An example of bolding

An example of bolding

An example of bolding

An example of bolding

An example of bolding

An example of bolding

Figure 3—24
Bolding

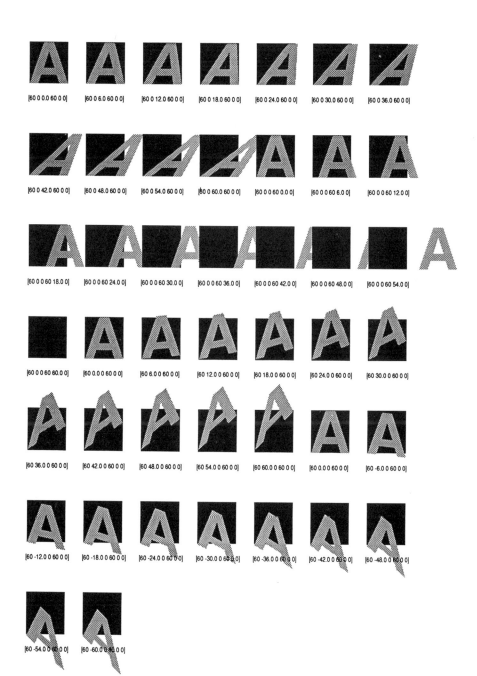

Figure 3—25
Letter "A" Font Matrix Chart

Graphics

4-1   Creating Art from Code

The reason that many of you have picked up this book, I'm sure, is to investigate the graphical capabilities of PostScript. PostScript certainly has an expansive control of typography. The benefits of using PostScript for type is immediately obvious when you print your first document with Times-Roman, Palatino, or any other ROM font. The characters are sharp, well designed, and instantly accessible.

Graphics, on the other hand, need to be programmed or drawn in order to realize the full potential. Many of the examples that you have seen probably consisted of simple images, generally in black and white. What I will present in the next chapters is a set of images that take advantage of the rich set of graphics commands in the PostScript language. In addition, PostScript is as much a programming language as it is a page-description language. Standard math operators allow for complex calculations to determine image placement, size, rotation, color content, and more.

Color is playing a big role in the creation of graphics. The black-and-white graphic is quickly becoming a thing of the past. Color reproduction in all forms is coming down in price as the time needed to reproduce is also falling. With these facts in mind, I believe it is important to consider the impact of color reproduction on all of your PostScript code. In Chapter 6 I go into greater detail concerning color models and color specification in PostScript. In this chapter, there will be sporadic reference to color usage in graphics. I apologize for any confusion that this brings. However, it is critical that we plan ahead properly.

The world would be truly wonderful if there were one standard programming language. It would be equally wonderful if there were one standard PostScript. Unfortunately, there are PostScript clones that for the most part do most everything that they are supposed to. But worse than that is the fact that each PostScript output device is in some way unique. The Apple LaserWriter, the Linotronic 300, the QMS Color-Script, and the Tektronix Phaser System all have their specific code requirements.

The code in this book attempts to address all of these needs. The chapter on color clearly points out the basic differences between what will be interpreted and what will not. The actual drawing routines in this chapter are very basic. Size, relative to resolution, is not an issue. These images will all print at the same size on each device. The major areas to be cognizant of are device resolution, page orientation, ability to interpret color operators, font availability, and memory requirements.

If you follow the images in this book through their construction, you will see that there are numerous routines that have been created to help draw the image. Once you have an understanding of these routines, you will be able to modify them or create new ones that will fit your needs.

As in most PostScript programs that I write, and especially in data-driven graphics programs, flexibility is built in. Quite often you will see the need to change certain design specifications within your code. If you can predict where some of that flexibility is needed, build in some variables that can be passed from your script to those prologue routines that require flexibility.

A number of **graphics** routines that you create will rely on some programming language primitives to draw the image. For instance, a logo that appears inside a box naturally requires a box routine to draw it. Unlike in high-level languages such as BASIC, graphics primitives are unavailable in PostScript. In order to draw a box in PostScript you would need to write the following code:

```
0 0 moveto
100 0 lineto
100 100 lineto
0 100 lineto
closepath stroke
```

The same set of commands could be combined in a routine that reads only the variables from your script.

```
%%BeginProlog
/box {
        /ury exch def
        /urx exch def
        /lly exch def
        /llx exch def
        llx lly moveto
        llx ury lineto
        urx ury lineto
        urx lly lineto
        closepath stroke }def
%%EndProlog
%%BeginScript
0 0 100 100 box
showpage
```

This is a rather long-winded routine that can be expressed in numerous other ways, some more efficiently than others. The following routine is much shorter in the prologue, yet it requires more information in the script.

```
%%BeginProlog
/box {
        moveto
        lineto
        lineto
        lineto
        closepath stroke }def
%%EndProlog
%%BeginScript
0 45 0 100 123 100 123 45 box
showpage
```

The same routine may need to be a filled box, with one of the variables being the line color and another being the fill color. The quantity of numbers required to draw the box increases again. However, we are not creating any further definitions with this routine, so we are not consuming much additional dictionary space.

```
%%BeginProlog
/box {moveto lineto
        lineto lineto
        closepath
        gsave setgray fill
        grestore setgray stroke }def
%%EndProlog
%%BeginScript
 0 .5 0 45 0 100 123 100 123 45 box
100 100 translate
.7 .2 0 45 0 100 123 100 123 45 box
100 100 translate
 0 .8 0 45 0 100 123 100 123 45 box
showpage
```

4.1.1   Graphics Operators

As was discussed earlier, PostScript's operators can be broken down into groups according to use. Graphics has a unique set of operators. That set includes:

- *setlinewidth*
- *setmiterlimit*
- *setgray*
- *setcmykcolor* (extended color operator)
- *setrgbcolor*
- *sethsbcolor*
- *lineto*
- *arcto*
- *arc*
- *fill*

For a complete review of these operators look in the appendix on PostScript operators under the heading "Graphics Operators."

4-2   Graphics Primitives

For the next few pages I will present a number of graphics routines that can be used as primitives to create a more elaborate graphics image. Examples of these routines in use exist throughout the book. At the end of this chapter, I will put these routines to use. Most of these routines are written with line weights and colors as variables.

4.2.1   Box

A box routine can be expressed many different ways, as illustrated earlier in this chapter. The following routine consumes no additional dictionary space when executed and performs the least number of stack manipulations.

```
/Box {moveto lineto
        lineto lineto
        closepath
        gsave setgray fill
        grestore setgray stroke }def
```

```
0 .5 0 45 0 100 123 100 123 45 Box
```

4.2.2   Circle

To create a circle in PostScript, you cannot fall back on a circle operator. Unlike BASIC, PostScript has no such graphics primitive. However, if your artwork requires the use of a circle in one form or another, it is simple to program a circle routine that will handle this.

The following routine uses the *arc* operator drawn from 0 to 360 degrees. In calling this routine, the user specifies the stroke color, fill color, radius, and finally the *x, y* center of the circle.

```
/Circle {
        newpath 0 360 arc
        gsave setgray fill
        grestore setgray stroke}def
```

```
0 .5 100 100 25 Circle
```

4.2.3   Polyline

Polylines, straight line segments that are joined end-to-end, are extremely useful in plotting graphs. Creating this user definition is also quite simple. You may also choose to add some other line type operators to the formula to control line endings, dash size, or miter limits. In this routine, we simply specify line weight and color and then add an array that contains the *x* and *y* coordinates for each plot point on the polyline. The array contents are counted, divided in half, and decremented by one to come up with the number of iterations that must be performed to complete the line.

The line is drawn, its color is set, and finally it is stroked. The path is not closed, since we are not attempting to create a polygon.

```
% ------- routine to draw polylines -------------------
/Polyline {
  setlinewidth
  /polyarray exch def
```

```
/pcount polyarray length
       2 idiv 1 sub def      % get # of plot points
polyarray aload pop          % get array remove copy
moveto                       % move to first point
pcount {lineto} repeat       % connect remaining points
setgray stroke}def           % stroke without
                             %   closing path
% -------- the script --------------------------------
0 [20 100 30 126 40 129 50 224 60 105 70 45] 3
Polyline
```

4.2.4   Polygon

The polygon is exactly the same as the polyline, except that the path is closed and both line and fill colors are specified.

```
% ------- routine to draw polygons --------------------
/Polygon {
  setlinewidth
  /polyarray exch def
  /pcount polyarray length
         2 idiv 1 sub def      % get # of plot points
  polyarray aload pop          % get array remove copy
  moveto                       % move to first point
  pcount {lineto} repeat       % connect remaining points
  /fc exch def                 % define fill color
  closepath gsave              % save graphics state
  fc setgray                   % set fill color
  fill grestore                % fill, restore gr. state
  setgray stroke}def           % set line color, stroke

% -------- the script ---------------------------------
0 .5 [20 100 30 126 40 129 50 224 60 105 70 45] 3
Polygon
```

4.2.5   Grid

Grids are often well-used graphic devices. However, they can also be useful tools in developing your code, finding locations, or determining a bounding box for your soon-to-be-encapsulated code. This grid routine accepts x and y coordinates for the lower-left corner and the upper-right corner, the same as for a bounding box. It then requires the number of lines up-and-down and the number of grid lines left-to-right. Finally, it looks for the line width and color.

```
% ----- routine to draw a generic grid ---------------
/Grid {
  /ylines exch def     % # of vertical lines
```

```
/xlines exch def      % # of horizontal lines
/ury exch def         % upper right corner x
/urx exch def         % upper right corner y
/lly exch def         % lower left corner y
/llx exch def         % lower left corner x

% ----- determine distance between lines by  finding
% ----- total span and dividing by the # of lines
/yspace ury lly sub ylines div def
/xspace urx llx sub xlines div def

  llx lly moveto        % moveto starting location

% ----- draw the vertical lines
  ylines 1 add          % # steps to draw vertical lines
    {llx lly moveto
    urx lly lineto
    /lly lly yspace add def % add yspace to current y
    }repeat             % repeat until ylines + 1
  stroke                % image line on page

% ----- reset the lly value by removing
% ----- what has been added in the last procedure
  /lly lly yspace ylines 1 add mul sub def

% ----- do the same for the horizontal lines
  xlines 1 add
    {llx lly moveto
    llx ury lineto
    /llx llx xspace add def}repeat
  stroke
}def

% ----- the script ----------------------------------
0 setgray             % set up color
.5 setlinewidth       % set line weight

% ----- call Grid routine : needs 6 values on the stack
100 200 350 500 16 18 Grid
```

4.2.6   Graduated Tints

The following graduated tint routine is my own "down-and-dirty" code, which works just fine. The recommended way to create a graduated tint is via the *image* operator. However, the results in my routine are nearly as good in some cases—and just as good in most cases. See chapter 6, on color gradients, for a full discussion of this method and some tricks for getting the smoothest transition from one color to the next.

This routine takes seven arguments from the stack to complete the graphic. Working in reverse, as PostScript does, it first grabs a Boolean operator to determine the direction of the gradient. A *true* results in a tint from top to bottom. A *false* results in a tint from left to right.

The next two values are for the starting and ending gray values. The remaining four numbers provide the outer dimensions of the tint area.

```
% ----- abbreviate common operator names
---------------
/ld {load def} def
/l /lineto ld
/m /moveto ld
/a /add ld
/s /sub ld
/np /newpath ld
/rm /rmoveto ld
/rl /rlineto ld

% ----- the grad routine ----------------------------
/grad {
  /updown exch def        % exch boolean true/false
  /k1 exch def            % ending gray color
  /k2 exch def            % starting gray color
  /ury exch def           % upper right corner y
  /urx exch def           % upper right corner x
  /lly exch def           % lower left corner y
  /llx exch def           % lower left corner x

% ----- if updown is true then ... --------------------
  updown
    {/range ury lly s def} % true
% ----- else ------------------------------------------
    {/range urx llx s def} % false
  ifelse

% ----- calculate amount of change
% ----- required for each step
  /kgrad k2 k1 s range div def

  1.1 setlinewidth

% ----- setgray with positive number only
  k1 abs setgray
% ----- plot lines for grad -------------------------
  updown
    {range                % if up/down is true
      {llx lly m          % move to lower left
       urx lly l          % line to lower right
       stroke             % stroke line
       /lly lly 1 a def   % add 1 to lower left y
       grada}             % gosub grada
      repeat}             % repeat till range

    {range                % if not true
      {llx lly m          % move to lower left
       llx ury l          % line to upper left
```

```
        stroke              % stroke line
        /llx llx 1 a def % add 1 to lower left x
        grada}              % gosub grada
        repeat}             % repeat till range
    ifelse
}def

% ----- set new gray value for gradient ---------------
/grada {
  k1 abs setgray          % set positive gray value
   /k1 k1 kgrad a def    % increase gray for next line
}def
% ----- the script portion  --------------------------
100 100 350 200 1 0 false grad
```

This tint routine is used when the CMYK (cyan, magenta, yellow, and black) color model is required. Note that this routine contains its own color separator. Do not use with an output device that directly supports the *setcmykcolor* operator.

```
/ld {load def} def
/l /lineto ld
/m /moveto ld
/a /add ld
/s /sub ld
/np /newpath ld
/rm /rmoveto ld
/rl /rlineto ld

% ----- A four color separator ------------------------
/seps 24 dict def
  seps begin
        /pickcolor [{pop pop pop 1 exch s setgray}
        {pop pop exch pop 1 exch s setgray}
        {pop 3 1 roll pop pop 1 exch s setgray}
        {4 1 roll pop pop pop 1 exch s setgray}]d
        /angles [105 75 90 45]d end
   /C 0 def /M 1 def /Y 2 def /K 3 def

   /colorbreaks {
        userdict begin
        dup seps /pickcolor get exch get
        /setcmykcolor exch def
        seps /angles get exch get
        currentscreen
        exch pop exch pop freq 3 1 roll
        setscreen
        end
}bind def

% ----- the gradient routine in color ----------------
/grad {
  /updown exch def
  /k1 exch def
  /y1 exch def
```

```
/m1 exch def
/c1 exch def
/k2 exch def
/y2 exch def
/m2 exch def
/c2 exch def
/ury exch def
/urx exch def
/lly exch def
/llx exch def
updown
  {/range ury lly s def}
  {/range urx llx s def}ifelse
/cgrad c2 c1 s range div def
/mgrad m2 m1 s range div def
/ygrad y2 y1 s range div def
/kgrad k2 k1 s range div def

1.1 setlinewidth
c1 abs m1 abs y1 abs k1 abs setcmykcolor

updown
  {range
    {llx lly m
    urx lly l
    stroke
    /lly lly l a def
    grada}
  repeat}
  {range
    {llx lly m llx ury l
    stroke /llx llx l a def grada}repeat}ifelse}d

/grada {c1 abs m1 abs y1 abs k1 abs setcmykcolor
  /c1 c1 cgrad a def /m1 m1 mgrad a def
  /y1 y1 ygrad a def /k1 k1 kgrad a def}d

/drawpage {
100 100 150 500 1 .5 .2 .1 .4 0 0 .3 true grad
} def

/freq 60 def
C colorbreaks drawpage showpage
M colorbreaks drawpage showpage
Y colorbreaks drawpage showpage
K colorbreaks drawpage showpage
```

4.2.7 Triangle

Sometimes a simple little shape is one of the most difficult objects to create in a DTP package. For instance, there are no polygon tools in PageMaker and most other DTP software packages. In order to draw one, you must go to a separate drawing package and import the image. This can be costly in terms of storage space and, ultimately, the time it takes to print the image. Such instances cry out for encapsulated PostScript files that do nothing but address the current need. A small filled arrowhead is such a polygon. The next two routines create the pointer in its specific direction (since few packages allow for rotations, 90 degrees or otherwise).

```
/uppointer {
    setlinewidth                  % pick up linewidth
    setgray                       % pick up gray value
    dup 0 rlineto                 % stack manipulations to
    2 div neg exch rlineto        % find points
    closepath gsave               % close polygon
    setgray fill grestore         % fill polygon
    stroke)def                    % stroke line

100 200 moveto                    % must establish currentpoint
.5 12 24 0 1 uppointer            % procedure call

/rightpointer {
    setlinewidth
    setgray
    0 0 rmoveto
    neg 2 copy pop 2 div neg rlineto
    0 exch rlineto
    closepath gsave
    setgray fill grestore
    stroke)def

200 300 moveto
.5 22 12 0 1 rightpointer
```

4.2.8   Registration Marks

A common need in producing graphics in two or more colors is the need to register. Below is a simple procedure to print a single register mark. The code listing is shown as an encapsulated PostScript file. The reference to color is only as *setgray*, although all four colors could be set as well. To make this a full four-color registered mark, change the *setgray* operator to *setcmykcolor*, with all four preceding values as one. If you do this, be sure that you are using the latest version of the PostScript interpreter with color extensions. If not, be sure you download the *setcmykcolor* routine outlined in Chapter 6.

```
%!PS-Adobe 2.0
%%Title: Registration Mark
%%Creator: Gerard Kunkel
%%CreationDate: 2-15-89
%%BoundingBox: 0 0 40 40
%%EndComments
/regmark {
  .7 setlinewidth
  /ymark exch def
  /xmark exch def
% ----- print company name in registration mark -------
  /Helvetica findfont 5 scalefont setfont
  xmark ymark 17 sub moveto
  (COMPANY NAME) centershow
% ----- draw vertical line ---------------------------
  newpath
  xmark ymark 10 add moveto
  xmark ymark 10 sub lineto
  stroke
% ----- draw horizontal line -------------------------
  newpath
  xmark 10 sub ymark moveto
  xmark 10 add ymark lineto
  stroke
% ----- draw circle ----------------------------------
  xmark ymark 5 0 360 arc
  stroke
}def

% ----- generic text centering procedure -------------
/centershow {
  dup stringwidth pop
  2 div neg
  0 rmoveto
  show
}def
% ----- procedure call -------------------------------
0 setgray
20 30 regmark
```

CHAPTER 5

Data Driven Graphics

Introduction   One of the best applications of computer technology is in the generation of data-driven graphics. By "data-driven," I mean those graphical treatments, such as charts, graphs, and other plots, that are derived from data.

There are numerous off-the-shelf software packages available that will give you 10, 20, or even 100 chart types. Of these chart types, one or more may be exceptable to you. More often than not, however, you will find certain aspects of the chart unacceptable. For instance, we find it particularly annoying when a charting package will not allow us to change the scale on the x- or y-axis. Some prevent you from forcing a scale to start at zero, while others let you do nothing but that. And the most annoying feature we find is the lack of ability to change the look of the chart.

In any graphic, the look is determined by the relative size of objects, weights of lines, color, typography, and general composition. In most cases, off-the-shelf graphics charting software determines this for you.

By creating your own routines, or using the ones that we provide here, you can create any chart, at any size, with any line weights, any typography, and any color. In chapter 7 I will show you how to write an application to edit the PostScript data that draws the chart.

5-1   Conventional Approaches

The reason for creating an application at all would have to be the automation of the chart-production process. If a data set is large, or if numerous data sets are of like graphical treatment, then an automated production process would be most effective. We found that the time needed to design and render a "three-dimensional" chart was excessive. Depending upon the amount of data, this process could take anywhere from a day to a week when rendered by hand. This time did not include the time required to redraw the graphic when the result was not acceptable.

The same data set, when applied in a computerized system, took 15 to 60 minutes, depending on how many variations were desired. Variations are important. As with any design, the look of a chart or graph should be explored to find the best representation of data. This is especially true in three-dimensional data. Quite often, background data will be obscured by foreground data in a 3-D rendering. By rotating the chart and changing the relative spacing, the hidden data may be brought into view.

Having to find these answers by hand-drawing them can take days if there are a large number of data points. A computerized system will find the answer in seconds.

As you can see from Figure 5–1, there are some data points obscured. The artist would now have to start all over again to come up with a rendering in which all data points are seen.

In the computer rendering shown in Figure 5–2, a similar problem is seen. However, a single variable is changed to fix the problem, as shown in Figure 5–3.

As in any good design, many variations are explored. The computer allows us to look at many possibilities without very much labor. The transition from idea to paper is greatly reduced.

In Figure 5–4, we have rotated the chart by changing the relative dimensions of the routine that draws each bar. This also respaces them according to their dimensions.

In this final rendering Figure 5–5, a background has been added and a four-color separation routine has broken down into its component cyan, yellow, magenta, and black colors. Look to COLOR INSERT C-7 for a look at a similar full color image.

5-2 Programming a 3-D Chart

The code for producing these 3-D charts is rather complex. An extensive number of key name definitions are set up to hold values either permanently or temporarily. The values that set the parameters of the graphic

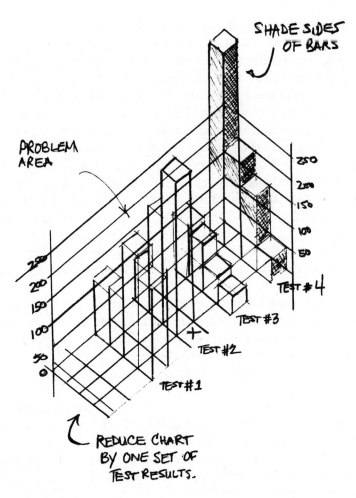

Figure 5—1
Hand Drawn Sketch Of 3-D Chart

can be thought of as the foundation, and the values captured from a spreadsheet are the building blocks that define the rest of the structure. When trying to understand how this graphic is being constructed, keep in mind that this is NOT true 3-D. This is a graphic technique that mimics 3-D by taking advantage of the PostScript opaque painting operation. Each bar in the chart—in fact, each section of a bar—is layered down on top of whatever has been painted in that space before. When performed in correct order, back-to-front, the illusion of three-dimensionality is obtained.

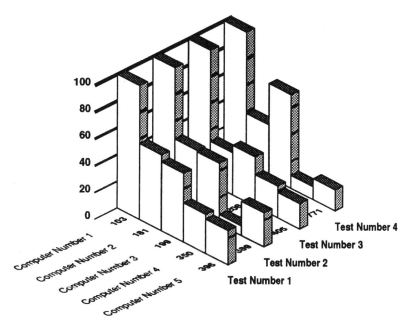

Figure 5—2

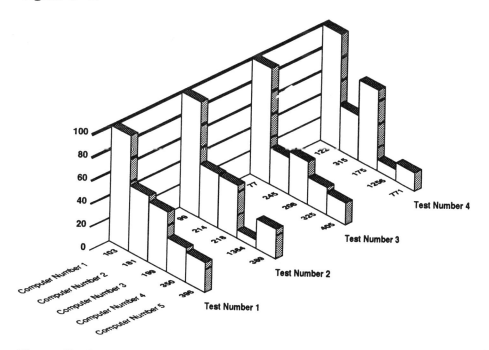

Figure 5—3

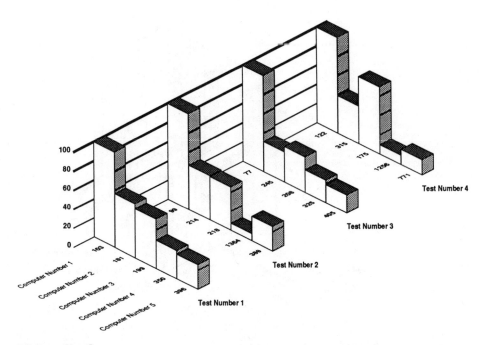

Figure 5—4

The code which follows is used to render these 3-D bar charts. The commenting within the code should explain some of the workings of the code. A complete application program is available for creating this type of chart and others from Lotus 1–2–3 spreadsheets. An order form is printed at the back of this book.

If you wish to create your own variations on this graphic, a detailed description of the code follows immediately after the complete listing. These descriptions should help you to understand the construction of this program better and allow enough comprehension to make your own modifications.

```
%%Title: PC Magazine New bar charts
%%Creator: Gerard Kunkel
%%CreationDate: 11:15PM  11/29/1988
%%BoundingBox: 0 0 612 792
%%EndComments

%%BeginProlog
/d {def} def /ld {load d} d /bd {bind d} d /l {lineto} d
/m {moveto} d /cl {closepath} d /rm {rmoveto} d
/rl {rlineto} d /color {setcmykcolor} d
```

```
/st {stroke} d /gr {grestore} d /s {sub} d /a {add} d
/sl {setlinewidth} d /lw .5 d
/separations 24 dict d
  separations begin
  /cmykprocs [{pop pop pop 1 exch s setgray}
             {pop pop exch pop 1 exch s setgray}
             {pop 3 1 roll pop pop 1 exch s setgray}
             {4 1 roll pop pop pop 1 exch s setgray}]d
  /screenangles [105 75 90 45]d end
  /C 0 d  /M 1 d  /Y 2 d /K 3 d %/setscreen {}d
  /setupcolor {userdict begin dup separations
  /cmykprocs get exch get /color exch d separations
  /screenangles get exch get currentscreen exch
  pop 3 -1 roll exch setscreen end
}bd

/idpage
  {1 1 1 1 color
  /Helvetica-Bold findfont 8 scalefont setfont
  60 740 m show 3{70 0 rm show}repeat
  }d

/regmarks
  {/ymark exch d /xmark exch d
  newpath xmark ymark m
  xmark ymark 20 s l cl st
  newpath xmark 10 s ymark 10 s m
  xmark 10 a ymark 10 s l cl st
  xmark ymark 10 s 5 0 360 arc st
  }d

/registerpage
  {1 setlinejoin 1 1 1 1 color
  40 740 regmarks 40 50 regmarks
  580 50 regmarks 580 740 regmarks}d

/h1 {/Helvetica-Bold findfont [7 0 -3.5 5 0 0]makefont setfont}d
/h2 {/Helvetica findfont [7 0 -3.6 6 0 0]makefont setfont}d

/newtest
  {/y y chtangle yangle div space mul s d
   /y y chtangle yangle div rows mul a d
   /x x chtangle xangle div rows mul s d
   /x x chtangle space mul s d
   x y startpoint /testnum testnum 1 a d}d

/newrow
  {/x x chtangle xangle div a d /y y chtangle yangle div s d
   x y startpoint /rowcount rowcount 1 a d}d

/bardims{
  /x2 x1 chtangle xangle div a d
  /x3 x1 chtdepth a d
  /x4 x2 chtdepth a d
```

```
 /y2 y1 chtangle yangle div s d
 /y3 y1 chtdepth yangle div a d
 /y4 y2 chtdepth yangle div a d
}d

/db
{/numb 6 string d
 /var exch d  /value exch d /product exch d
 /y1 exch d /mg exch d /cy exch d /tick 0 d
 % side of bar
 x2 y2 m x2 y2 var a l x4 y4 var a l x4 y4 l
 cl gsave cy mg yl .3 color fill gr 0 0 0 1 color st
 6{tick var lt{lw sl
 x2 y2 tick a m x4 y4 tick a l st /tick tick 20 a d
 /lw lw .4 a d}if }repeat /lw .5 d lw sl
 % top of bar
 x1 var yl a m x2 var y2 a l x4 y4 var a l x3 y3 var a l
 cl gsave cy mg yl .6 color fill gr  0 0 0 1 color st
 % front of bar
 x1 yl m x1 var yl a l x2 var y2 a l x2 y2 l
 cl gsave cy mg yl 0 color fill gr  0 0 0 1 color st
 % type
 h1 x1 chtangle xangle div 2 div a yl chtangle yangle div s m
 value 25 rotate rightshow -25 rotate
 h2 x1 chtangle s y2 chtangle yangle div s m
 product 25 rotate rightshow -25 rotate newrow
 }d

/centershow
 {/strg exch d strg dup numb cvs stringwidth pop
  2 div neg 0 rm numb show}d

/rightshow
  {dup stringwidth pop 0 exch s 0 rm show }d

/fbox
  {newpath m l l l cl fill}d

/headline
 {/head exch d
 0 0 0 1 color 550 696 550 712 40 712 40 696 fbox
 0 0 0 0 color /Helvetica-Bold findfont 10 scalefont setfont
 headx heady m head show}d

/startpoint
  {/y1 exch d /x1 exch d}d

/testname
   {/title exch d 0 0 0 1 color
    /Helvetica-Bold findfont [7 0 0 8 0 0] makefont setfont
    x1 y1 chtangle 2 div s 6 s m title show /rowcount 0 d}d


/gridlines
   {/scalenum 0 d 0 0 0 1 color /numb 6 string d
```

```
    /Helvetica-Bold findfont 8 scalefont setfont
    /yg y d 6{lw setlinewidth x chtdepth a
    yg chtdepth yangle div a m x gridx s yg gridy s l st
    x gridx s 3 s yg gridy s m scalenum dup numb cvs rightshow
    /scalenum scalenum step a d
    /yg yg step a d /lw lw .4 a d}repeat
    /lw .5 d lw sl}d

/grad
  {/lr exch def /ud exch def
   /k1 exch def /y1 exch def /m1 exch def /c1 exch def
   /k2 exch def /y2 exch def /m2 exch def /c2 exch def
   /ury exch def /urx exch def /lly exch def /llx exch def
   lr{/lns urx llx s d}if
   ud{/lns ury lly s d}if
   /cgrad c1 c2 sub lns div d
   /mgrad m1 m2 sub lns div d
   /ygrad y1 y2 sub lns div d
   /kgrad k1 k2 sub lns div d
   c2 c1 gt{/cgrad cgrad abs d}if
   m2 m1 gt{/mgrad mgrad abs d}if
   y2 y1 gt{/ygrad ygrad abs d}if
   k2 k1 gt{/kgrad kgrad abs d}if

   lr {lns {llx lly m llx ury l llx 1 a ury l
            llx 1 a lly l closepath c1 m1 y1 k1 color fill
            /llx llx 1 a d gradadd }repeat }if
   ud {lns {llx lly m urx lly l urx lly 1 a l
            llx lly 1 a l closepath c1 m1 y1 k1 color fill
            /lly lly 1 a d gradadd }repeat }if
  }def

/gradadd {
          c1 c2 lt{/c1 c1 cgrad add def}
          {/c1 c1 cgrad sub def}ifelse
          m1 m2 lt{/m1 m1 mgrad add def}
          {/m1 m1 mgrad sub def}ifelse
          y1 y2 lt{/y1 y1 ygrad add def}
          {/y1 y1 ygrad sub def}ifelse
          k1 k2 lt{/k1 k1 kgrad add def}
          {/k1 k1 kgrad sub def}ifelse
          }def
%%EndProlog
%%BeginScript
/chtangle 30 d    /chtdepth 6 d    /space 2.3 d
/rows 5 d         /tests 4 d       /step 20 d
/xangle 1.5 d       /yangle 2 d
/gridx chtangle space mul tests 1 s mul chtangle a d
/gridy chtangle yangle div space mul tests 1 s mul
  chtangle yangle div a d
/scalefactor 1 d /headx 50 d      /heady 701 d     /rowcount 0 d
/ids {(Gerard Kunkel: Benchmark Charts) (11:15PM  11/29/1988)
(Version:10)}d
/restart {/xstart 400 d  /ystart 500 d  /x xstart d  /y ystart d}d
bardims
```

```
/drawpage1
(40 200 550 712 0 0 0 .4 0 0 0 0 true false grad
(Benchmark Tests: 386 Computers)headline
registerpage restart gridlines x y startpoint /testnum 1 d
.5 .3 0   ()  (122)  100   db
.3 .1 0   ()  (315)  38.8 db
.1 0 .1   ()  (175)  69.7 db
.1 0 .3   ()  (1256) 9.7   db
.1 0 .5   ()  (771)  15.8 db
(Test Number 4)testname newtest }d
/drawpage2 {
.5 .3 0   ()  (77)   100   db
.3 .3 0   ()  (245)  31.4 db
.1 0 .1   ()  (208)  37 db
.1 0 .3   ()  (325)  23.7  db
.1 0 .5   ()  (405)  19 db
(Test Number 3)testname newtest}d
/drawpage3 {
.5 .3 0   ()  (99)   100   db
.3 .3 0   ()  (214)  46.6 db
.1 0 .1   ()  (218)  45.7 db
.1 0 .3   ()  (1364) 7.31  db
.1 0 .5   ()  (389)  25.6 db
(Test Number 2)testname newtest}d
/drawpage4 {
.5 .3 0   (Computer Number 1)  (103)  100 db
.3 .3 0   (Computer Number 2)  (181)  56.8 db
.1 0 .1   (Computer Number 3)  (199)  51.6 db
.1 0 .3   (Computer Number 4)  (350)  29.4   db
.1 0 .5   (Computer Number 5)  (396)  25.9 db
(Test Number 1)testname restart}d
/drawpage {drawpage1 drawpage2 drawpage3 drawpage4}d
K setupcolor ids (BLACK) idpage drawpage save showpage restore
C setupcolor ids (CYAN) idpage drawpage save showpage restore
Y setupcolor ids (YELLOW) idpage drawpage save showpage restore
M setupcolor ids (MAGENTA) idpage drawpage save showpage restore
grestoreall
%%EndScript
%%Trailer
```

Let's take this code a small piece at a time. The first area of the code should be familiar by now. The first five lines are the comments used to identify the program and make it ready for DTP packages, such as PageMaker, by including the *BoundingBox* information.

```
%%Title: PC Magazine New bar charts
%%Creator: Gerard Kunkel
%%CreationDate: 11:15PM  11/29/1988
%%BoundingBox: 0 0 612 792
%%EndComments
```

The first section of the prologue is a set of key name definitions that are set up to aid in condensing the overall space of the code. You will notice that

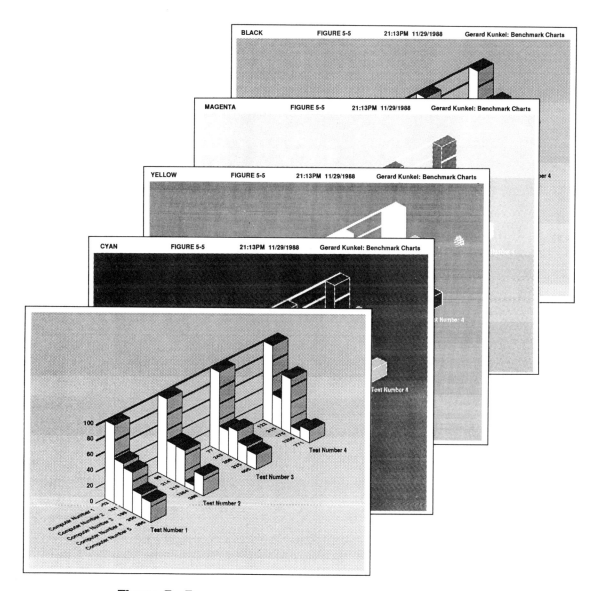

Figure 5–5

I have strived to reduce the standard operator names down to one or two characters. In many cases, this technique would cut the overall file size in half. If the size of the file is an issue, this should be the only name condensing required. At *PC Magazine,* file size is an issue because of the size and complexity of the graphics that we create, as well as the number of graphics that we create from month to month.

```
%%BeginProlog
/d {def} def /ld {load d} d /bd {bind d} d /l {lineto} d
/m {moveto} d /cl {closepath} d /rm {rmoveto} d
/rl {rlineto} d /color {setcmykcolor} d
/st {stroke} d /gr {grestore} d /s {sub} d /a {add} d
/sl {setlinewidth} d /lw .5 d
```

The next area of the code gets very complex. It is the color separator that breaks down the cyan, magenta, yellow, and black components of color specification into four separate outputs. Each output represents one of those colors and applies the necessary screen rotation for proper dot alignment in the printing process. Chapter 6 goes into extensive detail on color processing. Refer to that chapter for a closer look.

```
/separations 24 dict d
  separations begin
  /cmykprocs [{pop pop pop 1 exch s setgray}
              {pop pop exch pop 1 exch s setgray}
              {pop 3 1 roll pop pop 1 exch s setgray}
              {4 1 roll pop pop pop 1 exch s setgray}]d
  /screenangles [105 75 90 45]d end
  /C 0 d  /M 1 d  /Y 2 d /K 3 d
  /setupcolor {userdict begin dup separations
  /cmykprocs get exch get /color exch d separations
  /screenangles get exch get currentscreen exch
  pop 3 -1 roll exch setscreen end
}bd
```

The *idpage* routine performs a simple line of page identifiers, the first of which is the identification of the color being printed. Note that the color specification is comprised of four numbers representing cyan, magenta, yellow, and black. Specifying all 1s for these colors means that these words will print out as solid black for all four plates.

```
/idpage
  {1 1 1 1 color
   /Helvetica-Bold findfont 8 scalefont setfont
   60 740 m show 3{70 0 rm show}repeat
  }d
```

The register marks for the page rely on two routines. The first, *regmarks*, defines a single registration mark that still needs to be positioned. This routine requires that two numbers, which represent the x and y coordinates for the registration mark, be present on the operand stack. Once these two numbers have been exchanged and placed into key name definitions, they are used in the routine to draw a circle and two lines to make the registration mark.

```
/regmarks
  {/ymark exch d /xmark exch d
   newpath xmark ymark m
```

```
    xmark ymark 20 s l cl st
    newpath xmark 10 s ymark 10 s m
    xmark 10 a ymark 10 s l cl st
    xmark ymark 10 s 5 0 360 arc st
    }d
```

```
/registerpage
{1 setlinejoin 1 1 1 1 color
 40 740 regmarks 40 50 regmarks
 580 50 regmarks 580 740 regmarks}d
```

The second routine, *registerpage*, sets up some basic parameters and then pushes two numbers onto the stack prior to calling the *regmarks* procedure.

The next section sets the two type styles that are used in this graphic. Chapter 3 addresses the *makefont* operator, which is used here to distort the typography to look as though it is sitting on the same plane as the 3-D chart. These definitions are set up as procedures so that they may be easily called from the script portion of the code or from another procedure.

```
/h1 {/Helvetica-Bold findfont [7 0 -3.5 5 0 0]makefont
setfont}d
/h2 {/Helvetica findfont [7 0 -3.6 6 0 0]makefont setfont}d
```

The *newtest* procedure resets the current *x* and *y* coordinates to take into account a new column of data to be plotted.

```
/newtest
    {/y y chtangle yangle div space mul s d
     /y y chtangle yangle div rows mul a d
     /x x chtangle xangle div rows mul s d
     /x x chtangle space mul s d
     x y startpoint /testnum testnum 1 a d}d
```

Similarly, the *newrow* operator resets the *x* and *y* coordinates to accommodate a new data point within the same column of data points.

```
/newrow
    {/x x chtangle xangle div a d /y y chtangle yangle div s d
     x y startpoint /rowcount rowcount 1 a d}d
```

The *bardims* procedure defines the *x* and *y* dimensions of this two-dimensional representation of a three-dimensional object. If these values were to be plotted without the intervention of any data from our spreadsheet, the result would be a shape that looks like the top of one of the bars in the chart. This procedure relies upon some user input in the script portion to determine what *chtangle*, *chtdepth*, *xangle*, and *yangle* should be. These values are then used to calculate the specific plot points for each bar in the chart.

```
/bardims{
  /x2 x1 chtangle xangle div a d
  /x3 x1 chtdepth a d
```

```
  /x4 x2 chtdepth a d
  /y2 y1 chtangle yangle div s d
  /y3 y1 chtdepth yangle div a d
  /y4 y2 chtdepth yangle div a d
}d
```

The actual drawing of the bars takes place in the procedure defined as *db*. This procedure can be thought of as a compilation of several routines that render a single bar in the chart and place its label on it. The first few lines pull objects from the stack and give them key name definitions for use within the rest of the procedure. The first line defines an empty string six characters in length. This string will be used to temporarily store the value to be printed on the bar.

```
/db
{/numb 6 string d
 /var exch d  /value exch d /product exch d
 /y1 exch d /mg exch d /cy exch d /tick 0 d
```

The next portion of the *db* procedure draws the side of the bar. This portion and the next two portions may look very cryptic, but they are simple *moveto*, *lineto*, and other drawing operators at work under the condensed names that I defined in the beginning of the program. The values used in these lines of code are picked up from the *bardims* procedure and the script portion of the code.

Both the top-of-bar section and the front-of-bar section utilize the condensed operators and the values previously mentioned.

```
% side of bar
x2 y2 m x2 y2 var a l x4 y4 var a l x4 y4 l
cl gsave cy mg yl .3 color fill gr 0 0 0 1 color st
6{tick var lt{lw sl
x2 y2 tick a m x4 y4 tick a l st /tick tick 20 a d
/lw lw .4 a d}if }repeat /lw .5 d lw sl

% top of bar
x1 var y1 a m x2 var y2 a l x4 y4 var a l x3 y3 var a l
cl gsave cy mg yl .6 color fill gr  0 0 0 1 color st

% front of bar
x1 y1 m x1 var y1 a l x2 var y2 a l x2 y2 l
cl gsave cy mg yl 0 color fill gr  0 0 0 1 color st
```

The type section of this procedure calls upon *h1* and *h2* procedures, locates a starting point, and calls a routine called *rightshow*, which prints the text string *value* and *product* flush right.

```
% type
h1 x1 chtangle xangle div 2 div a y1 chtangle yangle div s m
value 25 rotate rightshow -25 rotate
h2 x1 chtangle s y2 chtangle yangle div s m
```

```
product 25 rotate rightshow -25 rotate newrow
}d
```

The *centershow* routine exchanges a string and calculates the width so that the center can be found. It then prints the text string on center from the current point.

```
/centershow
  {/strg exch d strg dup numb cvs stringwidth pop
  2 div neg 0 rm numb show}d
```

The *rightshow* routine, used in the *db* procedure, duplicates the current text string, calculates its width, and adjusts the current point that much to the left, so that the resulting string is flush right to the current point when shown.

```
/rightshow
  {dup stringwidth pop 0 exch s 0 rm show }d
```

The *fbox* routine is a very simple routine that paths out a box and fills it. This particular routine requires eight values to be on the stack when called. These eight numbers represent the box dimensions as *x* and *y* coordinates. See the beginning of this chapter for alternative approaches to this technique.

```
/fbox
  {newpath m l l l cl fill}d
```

The *headline* procedure exchanges a text string for the headline, then calls the *fbox* routine, and finally prints the headline in white type in the black box. With PostScript opaque layering, the characters are not actually reversed out of the box, but rather opaquely painted on top of the black box.

```
/headline
  {/head exch d
  0 0 0 1 color 550 696 550 712 40 712 40 696 fbox
  0 0 0 0 color /Helvetica-Bold findfont 10 scalefont setfont
  headx heady m head show}d
```

The *startpoint* routine is a "down-and-dirty" way of resetting the starting point of the graphic. After so many adjustments to the current point, defined most often as *x1* and *y1*, it becomes difficult to keep track of how to get back to the point of origin. By calling the *startpoint* routine, I can easily return to that point and begin a new operation.

```
/startpoint
{/y1 exch d /x1 exch d}d
```

The *testname* routine simply exchanges that title of the column of data, sets the typeface, locates the starting point, and shows the title. After showing this label, it resets the *rowcount* key name to zero.

```
/testname
  {/title exch d 0 0 0 1 color
   /Helvetica-Bold findfont [7 0 0 8 0 0] makefont setfont
   x1 y1 chtangle 2 div s 6 s m title show /rowcount 0 d}d
```

Gridlines is a routine that is called prior to imaging the bars. Since the grid sits behind the bars, it is important to place the lines on the page prior to the rest of the graphic. Note the placement of the procedure calls within the script.

```
/gridlines
  {/scalenum 0 d 0 0 0 1 color /numb 6 string d
   /Helvetica-Bold findfont 8 scalefont setfont
   /yg y d 6{lw setlinewidth x chtdepth a
   yg chtdepth yangle div a m x gridx s yg gridy s l st
   x gridx s 3 s yg gridy s m scalenum dup numb cvs rightshow
   /scalenum scalenum step a d
   /yg yg step a d /lw lw .4 a d}repeat
   /lw .5 d lw sl}d
```

The background for this graphic is printed with the *grad* routine, the first procedure to be called. This routine accepts a starting value and an ending value to create the sweep of color or gray from top to bottom. This routine is defined in detail in chapter 6.

```
/grad
  {/lr exch def /ud exch def
   /k1 exch def /y1 exch def /m1 exch def /c1 exch def
   /k2 exch def /y2 exch def /m2 exch def /c2 exch def
   /ury exch def /urx exch def /lly exch def /llx exch def
   lr{/lns urx llx s d}if
   ud{/lns ury lly s d}if
   /cgrad c1 c2 sub lns div d
   /mgrad m1 m2 sub lns div d
   /ygrad y1 y2 sub lns div d
   /kgrad k1 k2 sub lns div d
   c2 c1 gt{/cgrad cgrad abs d}if
   m2 m1 gt{/mgrad mgrad abs d}if
   y2 y1 gt{/ygrad ygrad abs d}if
   k2 k1 gt{/kgrad kgrad abs d}if

   lr {lns {llx lly m llx ury l llx 1 a ury l
           llx 1 lly l closepath c1 m1 y1 k1 color fill
           /llx llx 1 a d gradadd }repeat }if
   ud {lns {llx lly m urx lly l urx lly 1 a l
           llx lly 1 a l closepath c1 m1 y1 k1 color fill
           /lly lly 1 a d gradadd }repeat }if
  }def

/gradadd {
        c1 c2 lt{/c1 c1 cgrad add def}
        {/c1 c1 cgrad sub def}ifelse
        m1 m2 lt{/m1 m1 mgrad add def}
        {/m1 m1 mgrad sub def}ifelse
        y1 y2 lt{/y1 y1 ygrad add def}
```

```
{/yl yl ygrad sub def}ifelse
kl k2 lt{/kl kl kgrad add def}
{/kl kl kgrad sub def}ifelse
}def
```

```
%%EndProlog
%%BeginScript
```

The script for the 3-D graphic is nearly as long as the prologue. This is an extraordinarily long script, due to the amount of data that is being thrown at the prologue. With any data-driven graphic, you will have a long script portion. All of the procedures defined above are called in this script and finally imaged with the eight lines.

```
/chtangle 30 d
/chtdepth 6 d
/space 2.3 d
/rows 5 d
/tests 4 d
/step 20 d
/xangle 1.5 d
/yangle 2 d
/gridx chtangle space mul tests 1 s mul chtangle a d
/gridy chtangle yangle div space mul tests 1 s mul
  chtangle yangle div a d
/scalefactor 1 d
/headx 50 d
/heady 701 d
/rowcount 0 d
/ids {(Gerard Kunkel: Benchmark Charts) (11:15PM  11/29/1988)
(Version:10)}d
/restart
  {/xstart 400 d
   /ystart 500 d
   /x xstart d
   /y ystart d}d
bardims

/drawpage1
{40 200 550 712 0 0 0 .4 0 0 0 0 true false grad
(Benchmark Tests: 386 Computers)headline
registerpage restart gridlines x y startpoint /testnum 1 d
.5 .3 0  ()  (122) 100  db
.3 .1 0  ()  (315) 38.8 db
.1 0 .1  ()  (175) 69.7 db
.1 0 .3  ()  (1256) 9.7  db
.1 0 .5  ()  (771) 15.8 db
(Test Number 4)testname newtest }d
/drawpage2 {
.5 .3 0  ()  (77) 100  db
.3 .3 0  ()  (245) 31.4 db
.1 0 .1  ()  (208) 37 db
.1 0 .3  ()  (325) 23.7  db
.1 0 .5  ()  (405) 19 db
```

```
(Test Number 3)testname newtest}d
/drawpage3 {
.5 .3 0   ()  (99)  100   db
.3 .3 0   ()  (214) 46.6 db
.1 0 .1   ()  (218) 45.7 db
.1 0 .3   ()  (1364) 7.31  db
.1 0 .5   ()  (389) 25.6 db
(Test Number 2)testname newtest}d
/drawpage4 {
.5 .3 0   (Computer Number 1) (103) 100  db
.3 .3 0   (Computer Number 2) (181) 56.8 db
.1 0 .1   (Computer Number 3) (199) 51.6 db
.1 0 .3   (Computer Number 4) (350) 29.4  db
.1 0 .5   (Computer Number 5) (396) 25.9 db
(Test Number 1)testname restart}d
/drawpage {drawpage1 drawpage2 drawpage3 drawpage4}d
K setupcolor ids (BLACK) idpage drawpage save showpage restore
C setupcolor ids (CYAN) idpage drawpage save showpage restore
Y setupcolor ids (YELLOW) idpage drawpage save showpage restore
M setupcolor ids (MAGENTA) idpage drawpage save showpage restore
grestoreall
%%EndScript
%%Trailer
```

Note that this script has been broken down into four procedures that are then grouped into one procedure. This final procedure, called *drawpage*, contains all of the data and procedure calls to draw the chart. This chart is imaged four times, once for each color of the four-color separation process. The color to be imaged is defined by the call to the *setupcolor* procedure. The preceding character tells the procedure which color to look for in each reference to *setcmykcolor*, the extended color operator, which is used in only a few printing devices. Since this new operator is not found in all devices, (most importantly the Apple Laser-Writer family of printers), the *setupcolor* routine comes up with a definition for it. See chapter 6 for an in-depth look at this technique and others dealing with color separations.

5-3   High-Low Charts

Another reason for creating this type of program is if the chart-type is to be replicated many times. An example may be a weekly plot of stock information in the form of a "high-low-close" chart. The chart remains the same for each set of new data. The data may not be large, but the constant repetition supports the creation of such a program. Savings of small amounts of time multiplied by the number of times generated will justify its use.

Should the market jump up or down in value, a simple modification to the scale would accommodate the rise or fall. If the range of stock values exceeds the range on the chart, the scale and the plot-scaling factor may be adjusted to show a greater data range (See Figures 5–6, 5–7 and 5–8).

You will notice that in these various stock market charts, the overall dimensions have been changed. This can easily be done by changing the overall dimensions of the outer and inner boxes. All of the other routines are dependent on those dimensions for placement. Thus, while the reason for automation may be nothing more than gaining control over the quality of output, there is an added dimension of control over the graphical design.

As in previous examples of PostScript coding, flexibility should be an integral part of the programming process. Whether there exists a need to change the size, style, or content of a graphic, the means to do so should be readily accessible (see Figures 5–9, 5–10 and 5–11).

The best approach to determining where flexibility in code should be placed is to determine in conventional terms where constant changes will be required. Obviously, the data will change most frequently. Data ranges must change accordingly.

Routine by routine:

```
INSERT COMPLETE STOCK MARKET CODE
%%Title: Stock Market High-low graph
%%Creator: Gerard Kunkel
%%CreationDate: 10:00:00am 10-15-88
%%BoundingBox: 0 0 612 792


% ===================================
%  This is a four color separation
%  routine that outputs four plates
%  from one file.
% ===================================
/seps 24 dict def
 seps begin
   /pickcolor [{pop pop pop 1 exch sub setgray}
        {pop pop exch pop 1 exch sub setgray}
        {pop 3 1 roll pop pop 1 exch sub setgray}
        {4 1 roll pop pop pop 1 exch sub setgray}]def
        /angles [105 75 90 45]def end

  /C 0 def /M 1 def /Y 2 def /K 3 def
  /colorbreaks {userdict begin
        dup seps /pickcolor get exch get
        /CMYK exch def
        seps /angles get exch get
        currentscreen
        exch pop 3 -1 roll exch
        setscreen
        /setscreen {}def
        end
}bind def
```

```
% ==================================
%  regmarks is a routine for drawing
%  a registration mark
% ==================================
/regmarks
  {.7 setlinewidth
   /ymark exch def /xmark exch def
   /Helvetica findfont 5 scalefont setfont
    xmark 20 sub ymark 17 sub moveto 90 rotate
  (LUCHAK COMMUNICATIONS) show -90 rotate
    newpath xmark ymark 10 add moveto
    xmark ymark 10 sub lineto closepath stroke
    newpath xmark 10 sub ymark moveto
    xmark 10 add ymark lineto stroke
    xmark ymark 5 0 360 arc stroke}def


% ==================================
%  registerpage uses the regmark
%  routine to draw four registermarks
% ==================================
/registerpage
  {40 740 regmarks 40 50 regmarks
   580 50 regmarks 580 740 regmarks}def


% ==================================
%  an expanded box routine with
%  variables defined by exchanging
%  coordinate numbers allows for
%  those numbers to be used in later
%  calculations
% ==================================
/box
  {setlinewidth
   /ytbox exch def
   /xrbox exch def
   /ybbox exch def
   /xlbox exch def
   xlbox ybbox moveto
   xlbox ytbox lineto
   xrbox ytbox lineto
   xrbox ybbox lineto
  closepath gsave CMYK fill grestore stroke
  }def


% ==================================
%  this routine exchanges all the
%  parameters of the chart box and
%  grid. The grid is then further
%  broken down to horizontal ticks
%  or grid lines. The if questions
%  are looking for a Boolean true
%  or false. You may have horizontal
%  tick marks, lines, or niether if
%  both are false.
% ==================================
```

```
/chartgridbox
{setlinewidth
 /insidelines exch def
 /horizlines exch def
 /horiztick exch def
 /break exch def
 /yaxiscount exch def
 /xaxiscount exch def
 /yt exch def
 /xr exch def
 /yb exch def
 /xl exch def
 newpath
 xl yt moveto
 xr yt lineto
 xr yb lineto
 xl yb lineto
 closepath gsave
 CMYK fill
 grestore
 stroke
  /totalwidth xr xl sub def
  /vertjump totalwidth xaxiscount div def
  /totalheight yt yb sub def
  /horizjump totalheight yaxiscount div def
  insidelines setlinewidth
  /tick yb 6 add def
 drawvert
horizlines {/tick xr def drawhoriz}if
horiztick {/tick xl 6 add def drawhoriz}if
/ylegendline yb 20 sub def
}def

% ===================================
%  the horizontal grid line
%  or tick mark drawing routine
% ===================================
/drawhoriz
  {yaxiscount {newpath
  xl yb moveto tick yb lineto closepath stroke
  /yb yb horizjump add def}repeat
  /yb yb totalheight sub def
  }def

% ===================================
%  the vertical tick mark drawing
%  routine
% ===================================
/drawvert
  {/vertcount 1 def
  xaxiscount {newpath
  xl yb moveto xl
  vertcount 1 eq {tick 6 add}{tick} ifelse
  lineto closepath stroke
  /xl xl vertjump add def
```

```
   /vertcount vertcount 1 add def
   vertcount 6 eq {/vertcount 1 def}if
   }repeat
   /xl xl totalwidth sub def
   }def

% ==================================
%  a generic routine to centertype
% ==================================
/centertype
 {/strg exch def
  strg dup stringwidth pop
  2 div neg 0 rmoveto
  strg show}def

% ==================================
%  a routine to center the day-of-
%  week labels at the bottom of the
%  chart.
% ==================================
/centershow
  {/ax ax vertjump 2 div add def
  {ax y moveto centertype
  /ax ax vertjump add def} forall
  }def

% ==================================
%  a routine to print x label
% ==================================
/leftscale
 {/num 6 string def
  /xlabel exch def
  /scalestep topscale botscale sub xaxiscount div def
  7 /Helvetica-Bold F
  /x xl 18 sub def
  x yb moveto 90 rotate
  xlabel show -90 rotate
  /yscale yb def 0 yb moveto
  } def

% ==================================
%  a routine to print scale numbers
% ==================================
/scleft
  {num cvs dup stringwidth pop
  14 exch sub 0 rmoveto show
  /yscale yscale horizjump add def x yscale moveto
  } def

% ==================================
%  a routine to print y labels
% ==================================
/ylabels
{/labelarray exch def
  /y yb 10 sub def
```

```
    labelarray
    {xl y moveto
    /label exch def
    label aload pop
    dup stringwidth pop
    2 div sub neg 0 rmoveto show
    /xl xl vertjump add def
    }forall
    /xl xl vertjump yaxiscount mul sub def
}def

% ==================================
%   a routine to set up general
%   dimensions
% ==================================
/dimens
 {/topscale exch def
  /botscale exch def
  /scalefactor topscale botscale sub def
  /scalefactor scalefactor
    totalheight div def
  }def

% ==================================
%   a routine to draw a box
%   at the point of stock close
% ==================================
/drawclose
 {-2 -1 rmoveto 0 2 rlineto 4 0 rlineto
  0 -2 rlineto closepath fill /plotcount 0 def
  /xl xl vertjump add def
  /reversexl reversexl vertjump add def
 }def

% ==================================
%   a routine to locate and plot
%   the high, low, and close points
%   for the stock
% ==================================
/highlowplot
 {/plotarray exch def
  1.2 setlinewidth
  newpath
  /xl xl vertjump 2 div add def
  xl yb moveto
  /reversexl 0 def
  /plotcount 0 def

    plotarray    % use array of numbers

      {/plotcount plotcount 1 add def
       /plot exch def      % read numbers one at
                           % a time
       /y plot scalefactor div yb add def
       plotcount 1 eq
```

```
        {xl y moveto}if
      plotcount 2 eq
        {xl y lineto}if
      plotcount 3 eq
        {xl y moveto drawclose}if
      }forall

   /xl xl reversexl sub vertjump 2 div sub def
}def

% ==================================
%    a routine to headlines
% ==================================
/label
  {/Times-Bold findfont
     [17 0 0 14 0 0] makefont setfont
     xlbox ytbox moveto
     /headx xrbox xlbox sub 2 div def
     headx -18 rmoveto
     exch centertype pop
     xlbox ytbox moveto headx
     -32 rmoveto
     centertype pop
     /Times-Bold findfont
   [8 0 1 10 0 0] makefont setfont
   xlbox ytbox moveto headx -44 rmoveto
    centertype
  }def

% ==================================
%    a routine to define fonts
% ==================================
/F {findfont exch scalefont setfont}def

% ==================================
%    a routine to exch the name array
% ==================================
/names {/namearray exch def}def

% ==================================
%    a routine to print page ids
%    on each page of the separations
% ==================================
/idpage
  {/colr exch def 1 1 1 1 CMYK
  8 /Helvetica-Bold F
  60 745 moveto
  namearray {show 50 0 rmoveto}forall
  colr show .5 setlinewidth
  50 755 moveto 0 -15 rlineto 500 0 rlineto
  0 15 rlineto closepath stroke
  registerpage
  }def
```

```
% ====================================
%%EndProlog
% ====================================

[(11:10AM   12/3/1988)(HIGHLOW7.PS)(Copyright 1988 Gerard
Kunkel)]names
```

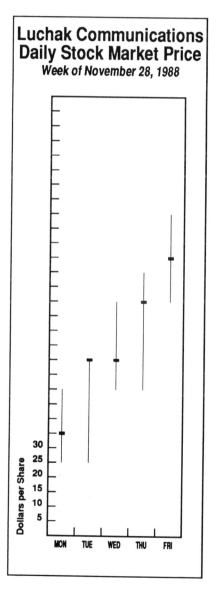

Figure 5—6
Week #1

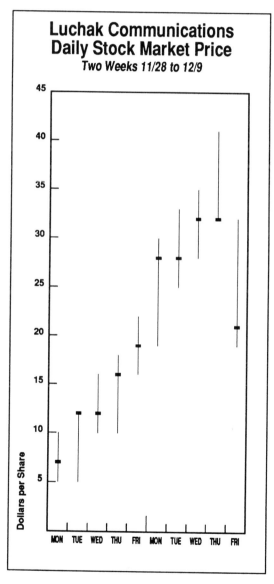

Figure 5—7
Week #2

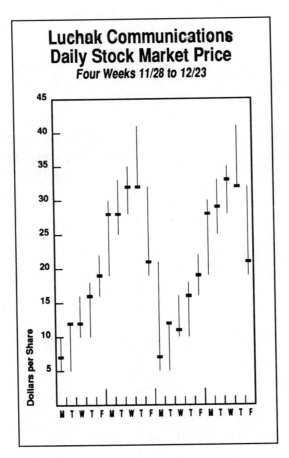

Figure 5—8
Week #3

5-4   A Simple Chart

5.4.1   Building a Chart from the Ground Up

When you begin to design any chart or graphic, you should first reduce the task to its most easily definable elements. For instance, in a simple plotting diagram the only necessary elements are the grid, the plot points, and the labels. Everything else in the design is "window dressing." Even the "window dressing" is often simple elements that merely direct the eye but avoid obscuring the data.

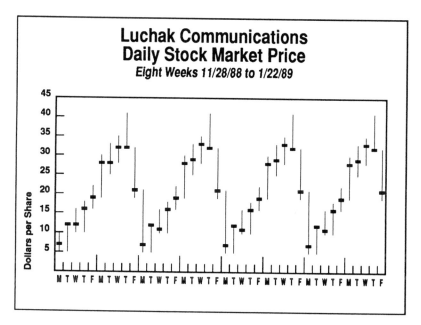

Figure 5—9
Stock Price Chart

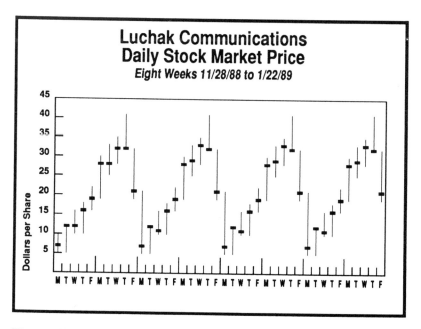

Figure 5—10
Change Line Weights

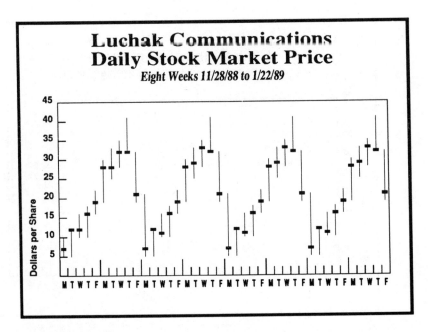

Figure 5—11
Change Type Styles

Our first concern, as always, should be the data and the way in which it is displayed. Above all, it should be displayed accurately. It is all too easy for even the best graphic artists to mislead a reader into believing an untruth about some data. With so much intentional fudging, let's make sure that the PostScript routines that we develop will not further cloud the truth.

The most important aspect of plotting data to a grid is that they relate one-to-one. In this programming environment it is very easy to plot numbers according to an x, y grid. Unfortunately, it is just as easy to plot inaccurately as it is to plot accurately. For example, a data value of 128 could plot as $x = 0$ and $y = 128$. This works fine as long as your underlying data grid is of the same point measure. That likelihood is very slim, however. So the obvious solution is to scale your number to match the underlying grid before plotting it.

Let's look at a simple plotting program, illustrated in Figure 5-12, to understand how to set up a correctly scaled data plot. First, be sure to enter the standard commenting to help you and others identify your code.

```
%!PS-Adobe 2.0
%%Title: SimplePlot
```

```
%%CreationDate: 4:07PM  12/30/1988
%%Creator: Gerard Kunkel
```

Enter a full 8.5 × 11-inch *BoundingBox* unless you need to encapsulate. The Bounding Box reference is only necessary when encapsulating your PostScript file. However, I always enter it into my standard PostScript files so that encapsulation is much easier later.

```
%%BoundingBox 0 0 612 792
%%EndComments

%%BeginProlog
%===========================
```

The *PageSet* procedure sets up the basic dimensions and default parameters of the graphic. The lower-left and upper-right coordinates are given, expressed as the standard *llx, lly, urx,* and *ury. Topval* and *botval* expect the top value and bottom value of the data grid. The *scalenum* definition looks for the increment between scale lines on the data grid.

```
/PageSet
{/ury exch def /urx exch def
 /lly exch def /llx exch def
 /width urx llx sub def
 /scalenum exch def
 /topval exch def
 /botval exch def
```

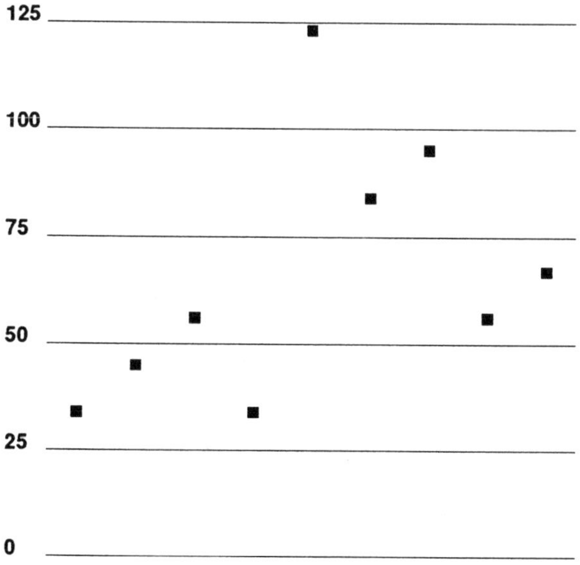

Figure 5—12

While still in the *PageSet* routine, I have defined a few more values that rely on the information just gathered from the first seven definitions. *Gridlines* determines the number of gridlines to be printed, by dividing the sum of the top of the scale, less the bottom of the scale, plus 1 by the scalenum definition. This enables the user to apply numbers that do not have to plot on a scale starting at zero.

```
/gridlines topval botval sub
    scalenum idiv 1 add def
/gridscale ury lly sub
    topval botval sub div def
```

Gridscale calculates the overall space, top to bottom, of the plotting area and then divides that by the sum of the top of the scale, less the bottom of the scale. This is a very important definition. *Gridscale* determines the accuracy of all your data plots to follow. In this example, your data scale runs from 0 to 125, and your plotting space, or *lly* and *ury,* runs from 100 to 300. Then,

$$300 - 100 = 200 \qquad ury - lly = t1$$
$$125 - 0 = 125 \qquad topval - botval = t2$$
$$200/125 = 1.6 \qquad t1/t2 = gridscale$$

Gridscale = 1.6.

```
\scalejump scalenum gridscale mul def
```

Scalejump is very straightforward. It is the sum of multiplying the supplied *scalenum,* in this case 25, by the product of the *gridscale* calculation. The following three lines are standard housekeeping. *Setmiterlimit* is a PostScript operator that will avoid any wild spikes when plotting data that jumps up and down.

```
1 setlinewidth
0 setgray
3 setmiterlimit)def
```

The *SimpleGrid* routine sets up and strokes the gridlines for the data. The definitions that we have calculated in the *PageSet* routine will come into use here.

```
%============================
/SimpleGrid
        {/ygrid lly def
        /num 6 string def
        /scnum botval def
    gridlines {
```

```
llx ygrid moveto llx width add ygrid lineto
llx 16 sub ygrid moveto
scnum dup num cvs show
/ygrid ygrid scalejump add def
/scnum scnum scalenum add def}repeat
}def
```

You may notice the routine to show some text within the *SimpleGrid* procedure. This line of code is inserted to print the scale numbers on the left-hand side of the grid lines. The PostScript line

```
scnum dup num cvs show
```

first pushes the value of *scnum* onto the stack. That number is *dup*ped (duplicated) and then converted to a text string by using the *cvs* operator. The preceding *num* definition is an empty string six characters in length. *Num* is defined earlier in the procedure with the PostScript line:

```
/num 6 string def
```

This definition does not store 6 as the definition of *num* but rather opens the space on the stack for six characters to be stored. Each time the procedure is *repeat*ed, the value of *scnum* is increased by adding *scalenum* to it. As the number grows, it is printed next to its corresponding gridline by these lines:

```
llx ygrid moveto llx width add ygrid lineto
llx 16 sub ygrid moveto
scnum dup num cvs show
/ygrid ygrid scalejump add def
```

The *PlotData* routine is quite simple. The array of numbers defined in the script is exchanged as a complete array and defined as *Dataarray*. The length of *Dataarray* is calculated by using the *length* operator. Once that number is determined, it is divided by the total width of the plotting area and stored as the definition *widthjump*.

```
%============================
/PlotData
        {/Dataarray exch def
        /widthjump width Dataarray length div def
        /x llx def
        /x x widthjump 2 div add def
        Dataarray
        {/Plot exch def
         /Plot Plot gridscale mul lly add def
         x Plot moveto Drawmark
         /x x widthjump add def
        }forall}def
```

Further into the *PlotData* routine, the *forall* operator is used to apply a routine to each plot point in the array called *Dataarray*. Within this routine is probably the most important line of code for assuring data accuracy. The PostScript code line

```
/Plot Plot gridscale mul lly add def
```

redefines the *Plot* definition as itself multiplied by the *gridscale* definition; then it adds the lower-left *y* coordinate, defined as *lly*. This is critical in guaranteeing an accurate plot, because you have previously defined *gridscale* as the scaling factor.

At the tail-end of the *PlotData* routine is a call to another procedure defined as *Drawmark*. This is a very straightforward procedure that draws a small four-point box centered on the plot point.

```
%==========================
/Drawmark
        {-2 2 rmoveto 0 -4 rlineto
      4 0 rlineto 0 4 rlineto closepath fill}def
```

It would be easy to change this routine and come up with a very different-looking graphic. For instance, you may want to try replacing the box with bullets by drawing and filling a complete 360-degree arc.

The remainder of the code is boilerplate. *Idshow* simply marks the page with file identifying information.

```
%===========================
/idshow {
   50 340 moveto show
   50 330 moveto show
   50 320 moveto show}def

%===========================
%%EndProlog
%%BeginScript
```

The script for this code calls the four procedures we just reviewed. *PageSet* exchanges and defines the dimensions of the graph and defines the parameters of the scale for the grid. *SimpleGrid* draws the grid. It does not exchange any values from the script. *PlotData* exchanges one array, which contains the data to be plotted. And, finally, *idshow* marks the page with its identifiers.

```
/Helvetica-Bold findfont 8 scalefont setfont
0 125 25 100 100 300 300 PageSet
```

```
SimpleGrid
[34 45 56 34 123 84 95 56 67] PlotData
(Date: 4:07PM  12/30/1988)
(FIG5-12.PS)
(gerard kunkel)idshow
showpage
clear
```

5.4.2   The Complete Program

And here is the complete listing, which will run fine as a stand-alone
PostScript program.

```
%!PS-Adobe 2.0
%%Title: SimplePlot
%%CreationDate: 4:07PM  12/30/1988
%%Creator: Gerard Kunkel
%%BoundingBox 0 0 612 792
%%EndComments

%%BeginProlog
%=========================
/PageSet
     {/ury exch def /urx exch def
     /lly exch def /llx exch def
     /width urx llx sub def
     /scalenum exch def
     /topval exch def
     /botval exch def
     /gridlines topval botval sub scalenum idiv 1
add def
     /gridscale ury lly sub
        topval botval sub div def
     /scalejump scalenum gridscale mul def
     1 setlinewidth
     0 setgray
     3 setmiterlimit}def

%=========================
/SimpleGrid
     {/ygrid lly def
     /num 6 string def
     /scnum botval def
     gridlines {
     llx ygrid moveto llx width add ygrid lineto
     llx 16 sub ygrid moveto
     scnum dup num cvs show
     /ygrid ygrid scalejump add def
```

```
        /scnum scnum scalenum add def}repeat
        }def

%==========================
/PlotData
        {/Dataarray exch def
        /widthjump width Dataarray length div def
    /x llx def
    /x x widthjump 2 div add def
        Dataarray
        {/Plot exch def
        /Plot Plot gridscale mul lly add def
        x Plot moveto Drawmark
        /x x widthjump add def
        }forall}def

%==========================
/Drawmark
        {-2 2 rmoveto 0 -4 rlineto
        4 0 rlineto 0 4 rlineto closepath fill}def

%==========================
/idshow {
    50 340 moveto show
    50 330 moveto show
    50 320 moveto show}def

%==========================
%%EndProlog
%%BeginScript

/Helvetica-Bold findfont 8 scalefont setfont
0 125 25 100 100 300 300 PageSet
SimpleGrid
[34 45 56 34 123 84 95 56 67] PlotData
(Date: 4:07PM  12/30/1988)
(FIG5-12.PS)
(gerard kunkel)idshow
showpage
clear
```

5.4.3   Making Your Plot Program PageMaker Compatible

In order to make this same program PageMaker-compatible, make the following changes to the code.

At the beginning of the file, the *BoundingBox* information must be filled in accurately. The current size, 612 x 792, is a standard letter-size page. If you wish to crop in on that image, use the outer dimensions of the chart, measured in points. These will be the same as the first four numbers exchanged by the *PageSet* routine—*llx, lly, urx,* and *ury.* At any time, a point gauge can be used to take a measurement off of the first-pass printout to accurately determine the *BoundingBox* coordinates.

At the end of the file is the most important line of code to be deleted, *showpage.* When this line is left in the code and encapsulated, an error will occur, and PageMaker will not print its page. You should add two lines of code to help ensure that you enter and leave the PageMaker file without damaging any part of that file. The *save* and *restore* operators will let you nest the entire encapsulated PostScript code. If you do this routinely, you will not have to worry about applications that do not automatically put *save* and *restore* around encapsulated files.

Beginning of file:

```
save
%!PS-Adobe 2.0
%%Title: SimplePlot
%%CreationDate: 4:07PM  12/30/1988
%%Creator: Gerard Kunkel
%%BoundingBox 0 0 612 792
%%EndComments

%%BeginProlog
.
.
.
```

End of file:

```
/Helvetica-Bold findfont 8 scalefont setfont
0 125 25 100 100 300 300 PageSet
SimpleGrid
[34 45 56 34 123 84 95 56 67] PlotData
(Date: 4:07PM  12/30/1988)
(FIG5-12.PS)
(gerard kunkel)idshow
clear
restore
```

5-5   Bar Charts

5.5.1   Drawing Bars instead of Dots

It should be relatively easy to switch from drawing dots on a grid to drawing bars. The basic change is in the routine that draws the mark on the page at the plot point. If you remember from the last example, *PageSet* set up a number of chart parameters that were useful in drawing the gridlines and plotting the points. These dimensions will also be very useful in drawing the bars.

In Figure 5–13, we have changed some of the definitions. At the same time, we have introduced some more definitions to help calculate other elements of the graphic. Let's walk through them one at a time.

First, set up the standard comment lines:

```
save
%%Title: Vertical Bars
%%CreationDate: 4:14PM  12/30/1988
%%Creator: gerard kunkel
%%BoundingBox: 0 0 612 792
%%EndComments
```

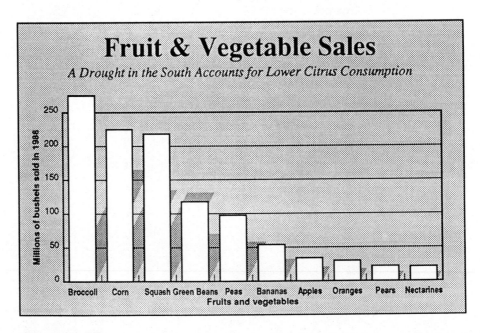

Figure 5—13

In the following six lines of code, commonly used operators are redefined to one- and two-character definitions and loaded into memory. This process will shorten the number of characters sent to the printer when processing. It also speeds the programming process and reduces file sizes at storage time.

```
%%BeginProlog
/ld {load def} def
/d /def ld /ex /exch ld
/l /lineto ld /m /moveto ld
/cl /closepath ld /st /stroke ld
/gs /gsave ld /gr /grestore ld
/rm /rmoveto ld
```

Dimens, like *PageSet* in our previous program, takes in the outer dimensions of the graphic. In this case, the outside box is also filled and stroked within the procedure.

```
/Dimens
{/ury ex d /urx ex d /lly ex d /llx ex d
 llx lly m llx ury l urx ury l urx lly l
 cl gs .9 setgray fill gr st}d
```

The *Gridbox* procedure sets up the interior gridlines but adds a lot more functionality than the previous *SimpleGrid* routine. The first line of this routine exchanges the value of the line weights for the interior lines. The next four lines exchange Boolean data types and assign definitions to be used within the *Gridbox* procedure. The two definitions *yaxiscount* and *xaxiscount* exchange the number of gridlines vertically and horizontally. Finally, the interior dimensions are exchanged to be used in drawing all gridlines and the interior box.

```
/Gridbox
{/insidelines ex d
 /vertlines ex d
 /horizlines ex d
 /verttick ex d
 /horiztick ex d
 /yaxiscount ex 1 sub d
 /xaxiscount ex 1 sub d
 /yt ex d /xr ex d /yb ex d /xl ex d
```

Further into *Gridbox* is an area where the space between gridlines is calculated. To do so, a few dimensions must be calculated first. The width of the plot area can be found by subtracting *xl* (140) from *xr* (480). This number (340) is then divided by the number of data points across the width (11), to define *vertjump* (30.9). The same operations take place for the horizontal gridlines, and the space between each line is defined as *horizjump*.

```
% calculations
 /totalwidth xr xl sub d
 /vertjump totalwidth xaxiscount div d
 /totalheight yt yb sub d
 /horizjump totalheight yaxiscount div d
```

At this point in the *Gridbox* procedure, the first call to the *Drawbars* routine is placed. The integer 1 is pushed onto the stack in advance of the routine to tell it that a shadow is to be drawn instead of the actual bar. The *Drawbars* routine is explained later in this code. This routine is accessed before drawing the gridlines so that the image is properly layered. The shadows, in this case, should appear behind the gridlines so as not to confuse the data plot points.

```
1 Drawbars
```

The first set of lines are drawn as the box defining the grid area, followed immediately by a group of *if* operators that determine the type of gridwork to be printed. Depending on the Boolean operators entered in the script, these subroutines enable the one larger routine, *Gridbox*, to have various line types. For instance, if *vertlines* is false and *vertticks* is true, then vertical tickmarks will be printed across the bottom of the chart. If the opposite were true, then vertical lines would print from bottom to top. Should you choose, both items could be false, and no vertical lines would print within the grid.

Boolean operators are also used to define the horizontal grid. If *horizlines* is true, the routine is performed, and horizontal lines are drawn.

```
% drawbox
  0 setgray
  newpath xl yt m  xr yt l xr yb l xl yb l
  cl st
% draw grid lines
insidelines setlinewidth
vertlines { xaxiscount {newpath
   xl yb m xl yt l closepath stroke
   /xl xl vertjump add d}repeat
   /xl xl totalwidth sub d
   }if
horizlines {insidelines setlinewidth
   yaxiscount {newpath
   xl yb m xr yb l closepath stroke
   /yb yb horizjump add d}repeat
```

```
   /yb yb totalheight sub d
   }if
verttick {/tick yb 6 add d
  insidelines setlinewidth
  xaxiscount {newpath
  xl yb m xl tick l closepath stroke
  /xl xl vertjump add d}repeat
  /xl xl totalwidth sub d
  }if
horiztick {/tick xl 6 add d
  insidelines setlinewidth
  yaxiscount {newpath
  xl yb m tick yb l closepath stroke
  /yb yb horizjump add d}repeat
  /yb yb totalheight sub d
  }if
```

After the gridlines are printed on top of the shadows, the *Drawbars* routine is called again. This time, a zero is pushed onto the stack in advance of the call. The zero is interpreted as a "no" to draw shadows and a "yes" to draw the data bars. This routine then prints the finished bars on top of the grid.

```
0 Drawbars
}d    % end Gridbox procedure
```

The *Bars* routine is where the actual bars are rendered.

```
/Bars
{/topscale ex d
 /botscale ex d
 /plotarray ex d
 /reverseyt 0 d
 /scalefactor topscale botscale sub d
 /scalefactor scalefactor totalheight div d
 /barwidth vertjump .7 mul d
 /barspace vertjump .15 mul d
 newpath
 xl yb m
 /x xl d
```

Within the *Bars* routine, *plotarray* is read and applied. Earlier in the prologue, *shadowtest* was defined. Here, it is used to define the existence of a shadow. The *ifelse* operator asks if *shadowtest* is equal to 1. If so, the first operation within the braces is executed. If not, the second operation within braces is executed.

```
plotarray
  {1 setlinewidth
  /plot ex d
```

```
 /x x barspace add d
 /y plot scalefactor div yb add d
shadowtest 1 eq
 { % shadow
 /sy plot scalefactor div .6 mul d
 /sx x sy 2 div add d
 /sy sy yb add d
 x yb m sx sy l
 /x x barwidth add d
 sx barwidth add sy l
 x yb l closepath .6 setgray fill
 /x x barspace add d
 }
 { %bar
 x yb m x y l
 /x x barwidth add d
 x y l x yb l closepath
 gs 1 setgray fill gr 0 setgray stroke
 /x x barspace add d
 }ifelse
 }forall
}def
```

An empty string is set up to accommodate the scale numbers when converted from integers to strings.

```
/num 6 string d
```

The *Scalenums* routine moves the *currentpoint* four points to the left of the left edge of the plot area and locates the *y* according to the value of *ypos*. This number is increased by *horizjump* each time *Scalenums* is executed. Once located, the scale value is converted from an integer into a string with the *cvs* operator. The *rightshow* routine is called to align all of the numbers to the right.

```
/Scalenums
 {xl 4 sub ypos m num cvs rightshow
 /ypos ypos horizjump add d }d
```

The next five routines place labels on the graphic. Each of these routines operates the same way. They exchange the label, calculate the position, go there, and *show* the type. The *Horizlabels* routine is a little different, in that it exchanges an array and executes an operation on each label in the array. The objective in this routine is to center the label under each bar of the bar chart.

```
/Horizlabels
 {/xpos xl barwidth 2 div add barspace add d
 /namesarray ex d
 namesarray{xpos yb 12 sub m
 /name ex d name centershow
 /xpos xpos barwidth add barspace 2 mul add d
}forall }d
```

```
/Head
 {/Times-Bold findfont 24 scalefont setfont
 llx ury m
 urx llx sub 2 div -30 rm
 centershow}d
/Subhead
 {/Times-Italic findfont 12 scalefont setfont
 llx ury m
 urx llx sub 2 div -48 rm
 centershow}d
/xlabel
 {/Helvetica-Bold findfont 8 scalefont setfont
 xl yb m
 xr xl sub 2 div -21 rm
 centershow}d
/ylabel
 {/Helvetica-Bold findfont 8 scalefont setfont
 llx yb m
 18 yt yb sub 2 div rm
 90 rotate
 centershow
 -90 rotate}d
```

The next two routines are generic routines to affect the placement of type. Each routine reads the total width of the text string and calculates a new position at which to start the text, based on the *currentpoint*. Note the *pop* after the *stringwidth* operator. Since *stringwidth* returns the x and y widths (width and height), the *pop* removes the unwanted y value. However, if you were centering a text string both left-to-right *and* top-to-bottom, you would then use the y value.

```
/centershow
 {dup stringwidth pop 2 div neg 0 rm show}d

/rightshow
 {dup stringwidth pop neg 0 rm show}d

/idpage
 {/Helvetica-Bold findfont 8 scalefont setfont
 60 740 moveto show
 70 0 rmoveto show
 70 0 rmoveto show
 70 0 rmoveto show
}def

%%EndProlog
%%BeginScript
(4:20PM  12/30/1988)
(Copyright 1988, Gerard Kunkel)
(black plate)(FIG5-13.PS) idpage

100 400 500 660 Dimens
(Fruit & Vegetable Sales)Head
```

```
(A Drought in the South Accounts for\
 Lower Citrus Consumption)Subhead
/Drawbars            % a routine within the script
 {/shadowtest ex d  % exchange the shadow boolean
 [275.33 224.83 218 117.5
 97.41 54.07 34 30 22 21 ] % data array
 0                    % bottom of scale
 250                  % top of scale
 Bars                 % call the Bars routine
 }d                   % end Drawbars routine
```

When inputting your numbers and other values, try changing the true/false operators listed below. They operate the subroutines within the *Gridbox* routine. You can create a variety of chart effects by changing these values and others.

```
140       % lower left x
430       % lower left y
480       % upper right x
580       % upper right y
11        % number of bars
6         % number of gridlines
false     % no to vertical lines
true      % yes to horizontal lines
true      % yes to vertical tick marks
false     % no to horizontal tick marks
.4        % linewidth of gridlines
Gridbox % call the Gridbox routine

(Fruits and vegetables)xlabel
(Millions of bushels sold in 1988)ylabel
/ypos yb d
/Helvetica findfont 8 scalefont setfont
0 50 250 {Scalenums} for
/Helvetica-Narrow-Bold findfont 8 scalefont
setfont
[ (Broccoli)(Corn)(Squash)
(Green Beans)(Peas)(Bananas)(Apples)(Oranges)
(Pears)(Nectarines)] Horizlabels
showpage
%%EndScript
%%Trailer
restore
```

Here is the complete listing for Figure 5–13:

```
save
%%Title: Vertical Bars
%%CreationDate: 4:14PM  12/30/1988
%%Creator: gerard kunkel
%%BoundingBox: 0 0 612 792
%%EndComments
%%BeginProlog
```

```
/ld {load def} def
/d /def ld /ex /exch ld
/l /lineto ld /m /moveto ld
/cl /closepath ld /st /stroke ld
/gs /gsave ld /gr /grestore ld
/rm /rmoveto ld
/Dimens
{/ury ex d /urx ex d /lly ex d /llx ex d
 llx lly m llx ury l urx ury l urx lly l
 cl gs .9 setgray fill gr st}d
/Gridbox
{/insidelines ex d
 /vertlines ex d
 /horizlines ex d
 /verttick ex d
 /horiztick ex d
 /yaxiscount ex 1 sub d
 /xaxiscount ex 1 sub d
 /yt ex d /xr ex d /yb ex d /xl ex d
% calculations
 /totalwidth xr xl sub d
 /vertjump totalwidth xaxiscount div d
 /totalheight yt yb sub d
 /horizjump totalheight yaxiscount div d

 1 Drawbars
% drawbox
 0 setgray
 newpath xl yt m  xr yt l xr yb l xl yb l
 cl st
% draw grid lines
 insidelines setlinewidth
 vertlines { xaxiscount {newpath
   xl yb m xl yt l closepath stroke
   /xl xl vertjump add d}repeat
   /xl xl totalwidth sub d
   }if
 horizlines {insidelines setlinewidth
   yaxiscount {newpath
   xl yb m xr yb l closepath stroke
   /yb yb horizjump add d}repeat
   /yb yb totalheight sub d
   }if
 verttick {/tick yb 6 add d
   insidelines setlinewidth
   xaxiscount {newpath
   xl yb m xl tick l closepath stroke
   /xl xl vertjump add d}repeat
   /xl xl totalwidth sub d
   }if
 horiztick {/tick xl 6 add d
   insidelines setlinewidth
   yaxiscount {newpath
   xl yb m tick yb l closepath stroke
```

```
   /yb yb horizjump add d}repeat
   /yb yb totalheight sub d
   }if
0 Drawbars
}d


/Bars
{/topscale ex d
 /botscale ex d
 /plotarray ex d
 /reverseyt 0 d
 /scalefactor topscale botscale sub d
 /scalefactor scalefactor totalheight div d
 /barwidth vertjump .7 mul d
 /barspace vertjump .15 mul d
 newpath
 xl yb m
 /x xl d
 plotarray
    {1 setlinewidth
    /plot ex d
    /x x barspace add d
    /y plot scalefactor div yb add d
   shadowtest 1 eq{% shadow
    /sy plot scalefactor div .6 mul d
    /sx x sy 2 div add d
    /sy sy yb add d
    x yb m sx sy l
    /x x barwidth add d
    sx barwidth add sy l
    x yb l closepath .6 setgray fill
    /x x barspace add d}
   {% bar
    x yb m x y l
    /x x barwidth add d
    x y l x yb l closepath
    gs 1 setgray fill gr 0 setgray stroke
    /x x barspace add d}ifelse
    }forall
 }def


/num 6 string d

/Scalenums
 {xl 4 sub ypos m num cvs rightshow
 /ypos ypos horizjump add d }d

/Horizlabels
 {/xpos xl barwidth 2 div add barspace add d
  /namesarray ex d
  namesarray{xpos yb 12 sub m /name ex d name
centershow
  /xpos xpos barwidth add barspace 2 mul add d
 }forall }d
```

```
/Head
 {/Times-Bold findfont 24 scalefont setfont
 llx ury m urx llx sub 2 div -30 rm centershow}d
/Subhead
 {/Times-Italic findfont 12 scalefont setfont
 llx ury m urx llx sub 2 div -48 rm centershow}d
/xlabel
 {/Helvetica-Bold findfont 8 scalefont setfont
 xl yb m xr xl sub 2 div -21 rm centershow}d
/ylabel
 {/Helvetica-Bold findfont 8 scalefont setfont
 llx yb m 18 yt yb sub 2 div rm 90 rotate
centershow -90 rotate}d

/centershow
 {dup stringwidth pop 2 div neg 0 rm show}d
/rightshow
 {dup stringwidth pop neg 0 rmoveto show}d
/idpage
 {/Helvetica-Bold findfont 8 scalefont setfont
 60 740 moveto show
 70 0 rmoveto show
 70 0 rmoveto show
 70 0 rmoveto show
}def

%%EndProlog
%%BeginScript
(4:20PM  12/30/1988)
(Copyright 1988, Gerard Kunkel)
(black plate)(FIG5-13.PS) idpage

100 400 500 660 Dimens
(Fruit & Vegetable Sales)Head
(A Drought in the South Accounts for\
 Lower Citrus Consumption)Subhead
/Drawbars {/shadowtest ex d
[275.33 224.83 218 117.5 97.41 54.07 34 30 22 21 ]
0 250 Bars}d
140 430 480 580 11 6 false true true false .4
Gridbox
(Fruits and vegetables)xlabel
(Millions of bushels sold in 1988)ylabel
/ypos yb d
/Helvetica findfont 8 scalefont setfont
0 50 250 {Scalenums} for
/Helvetica-Narrow-Bold findfont 8 scalefont
setfont
[ (Broccoli)(Corn)(Squash)
(Green Beans)(Peas)(Bananas)(Apples)(Oranges)
(Pears)(Nectarines)] Horizlabels

showpage
%%EndScript
%%Trailer
restore
```

In Figure 5–14, the overall size of the chart is changed. This is a very simple process in this program. Since almost all of the plot points in the graphic are relative rather than absolute, only those numbers that are absolute need be changed. In this case, I want to have a larger chart, so the four numbers that are fed to the *Dimens* routine are changed. The only other numbers that need be changed are the four numbers that define the lower left and upper right corners of the interior grid box.

```
50 100 500 660 Dimens
90 130 480 580
11 6
false true true false
.4 Gridbox
```

In Figure 5–15, the dimensions are changed once again. This time I have made some changes to make the graphic more dramatic. In all of these examples, the data has remained true to its scale. In this example, the location of the headline and subhead have been lowered into the chart.

In order to make some critical design changes, you may have to go back into the prologue of the program. I did just that in this example. The *Head* routine called for the type to be centered on the width of the chart. A simple addition of the code

```
24 add
```

moved the head sufficiently to the right to avoid the first bar, while adding to the aesthetics of the chart. The same was done to the subhead. Since the subhead was long, it was necessary to break it into two lines and create a second routine for the second line. This is the lazy man's way of getting a second line. In most cases, you would simply use the same routine for both and change only the value of the *y* location. Using my word processor, it was easier for me to copy the *Subhead* routine and create another routine.

```
/Head
  {/Times-Bold findfont 24 scalefont setfont
  llx ury m urx llx sub 2 div 24 add -40 rm
centershow}d
/Subhead
  {/Times-Italic findfont 12 scalefont setfont
  llx ury m urx llx sub 2 div 24 add -58 rm
centershow}d
/Subhead2
  {llx ury m urx llx sub 2 div 24 add -70 rm
centershow}d
```

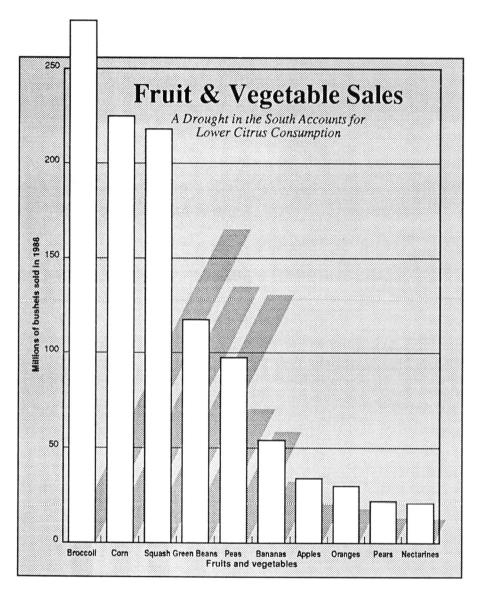

Figure 5—14

5.5.2   Turning the Chart on Its Side

Not every bar chart should be rendered from the base up. For instance, the measurement of time is more appropriately shown from left to right. A bar

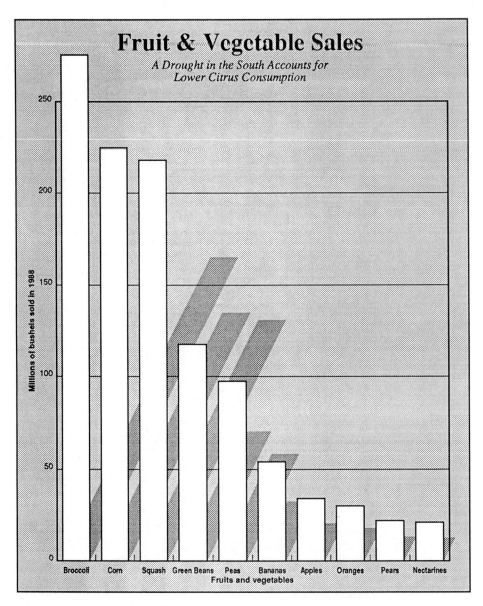

Figure 5–15

chart showing the time it takes to stop a speeding car is more easily conveyed horizontally than vertically. The shorter the time to stop the shorter the bar. Most people will look at a vertical bar chart and assume that shorter bars are less desirable values than the tall ones. The horizontal chart has less of impact on perceptions, and the reader will easily grasp the shorter-is-better concept. In Figure 5–16 the orientation of the bars has been rendered horizontally.

```
gsave
%%Title: Horizontal Bars
%%CreationDate: 5:57PM  12/30/1988
%%Creator: gerard kunkel
%%BoundingBox: 0 0 612 792
%%EndComments

%%BeginProlog
/ld {load def} def
/d /def ld /ex /exch ld /l /lineto ld /m /moveto
ld
/cl /closepath ld /st /stroke ld /gs /gsave ld /gr
/grestore ld
/rm /rmoveto ld

/Dimens
{/ury ex d /urx ex d /lly ex d /llx ex d
 llx lly m llx ury l urx ury l urx lly l
 cl gs .95 setgray fill gr st}d

/Gridbox
{/insidelines ex d
 /vertlines ex d
 /horizlines ex d
 /verttick ex d
 /horiztick ex d
 /yaxiscount ex 1 sub d
 /xaxiscount ex 1 sub d
 /yt ex d /xr ex d /yb ex d /xl ex d
% drawbox
 newpath xl yt m  xr yt l xr yb l xl yb l
 cl gs 1 setgray fill gr st
% calculations
 /totalwidth xr xl sub d
 /vertjump totalwidth xaxiscount div d
 /totalheight yt yb sub d
 /horizjump totalheight yaxiscount div d
% draw grid lines
insidelines setlinewidth
vertlines { xaxiscount {newpath
  xl yb m xl yt l closepath stroke
  /xl xl vertjump add d}repeat
  /xl xl totalwidth sub d
  }if
horizlines {insidelines setlinewidth
  yaxiscount {newpath
  xl yb m xr yb l closepath stroke
  /yb yb horizjump add d}repeat
  /yb yb totalheight sub d
  }if
```

```
verttick {/tick yb 6 add d
  insidelines setlinewidth
  xaxiscount {newpath
  xl yb m xl tick l closepath stroke
  /xl xl vertjump add d}repeat
  /xl xl totalwidth sub d
  }if
horiztick {/tick xl 6 add d
  insidelines setlinewidth
  yaxiscount {newpath
  xl yb m tick yb l closepath stroke
  /yb yb horizjump add d}repeat
  /yb yb totalheight sub d
  }if
}d


/Bars
{/topscale ex d
 /botscale ex d
 /plotarray ex d
 /reverseyt 0 d
 /scalefactor topscale botscale sub d
 /scalefactor scalefactor totalheight div d
 /barwidth horizjump .7 mul d
 /barspace horizjump .15 mul d
 newpath
 xl yb m
 /y yt d
 plotarray
    {/plot ex d
    /y y barspace sub d
    /x plot scalefactor div xl add d
    xl y m x y l
    /y y barwidth sub d
    x y l xl y l closepath
    gs 1 setgray fill gr 0 setgray stroke
    /y y barspace sub d
    }forall
}def

/num 6 string d

/Scalenums
 {xpos yb 12 sub m num cvs dup stringwidth pop
 2 div neg 0 rmoveto show /xpos xpos vertjump add
d }def

/Vertlabels
 {/ypos yt barwidth 2 div sub barspace sub d
  /namesarray ex d
    namesarray{xl ypos m /name ex d
    name dup stringwidth pop neg 4 sub 0 rmoveto
```

```
show
   /ypos ypos horizjump sub d }forall }d

/Head
 {/Times-Bold findfont 24 scalefont setfont
 llx ury m urx llx sub 2 div -30 rm centershow}d
/Subhead
 {/Times-Italic findfont 12 scalefont setfont
 llx ury m urx llx sub 2 div -48 rm centershow}d
/xlabel
 {/Helvetica-Bold findfont 8 scalefont setfont
 xl yb m xr xl sub 2 div -21 rm centershow}d
/ylabel
 {/Helvetica-Bold findfont 8 scalefont setfont
 llx yb m 20 yt yb sub 2 div rm 90 rotate
centershow -90 rotate}d

/idpage {/Helvetica-Bold findfont 8 scalefont
setfont
   50 500 moveto show
   3 {40 0 rmoveto show}repeat}d

/centershow
 {dup stringwidth pop 2 div neg 0 rm show}d
%%EndProlog
%%BeginScript
(5:15PM  12/30/1988)(Copyright 1988, Gerard
Kunkel)
(black plate)(FIG5-16.PS) idpage
100 100 500 460 Dimens
(Luchak Communications)Head
(Employee Breakdown by Division; Based on January
1989)Subhead
200 130 480 390 6 11 true true false true .4
Gridbox
(Divisions)ylabel
(Number of Employees Per Division)xlabel
/xpos xl d
/Helvetica findfont 8 scalefont setfont
0 50 250 {Scalenums} for
[275.33 224.83 218 117.5 97.41 54.07 34 30 22 21 ]
0 250 Bars
/Helvetica-Narrow-Bold findfont 10 scalefont
setfont
[(Distribution)(Packaging)(Manufacturing)
(Maintenance)(Sales)(Marketing)(Accounting)(Person
nel)
(Research)(Executive)] Vertlabels

showpage
%%EndScript
%%Trailer
grestore
```

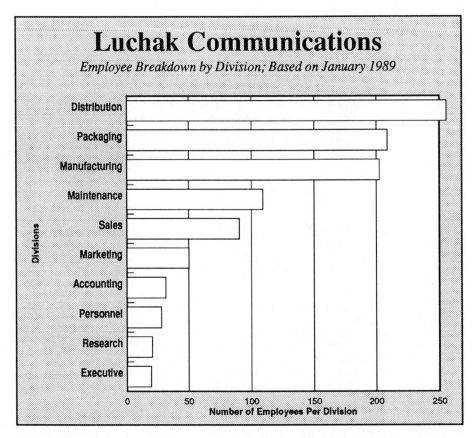

Figure 5—16

5.5.3   Adding Some Texture

The same graphic with some gray values added is much more powerful, as seen in Figure 5–17. The data becomes easier to read, and, with wisely chosen colors, emphasis can direct the viewer's eye to the data that you want show off.

Adding this gray was very simple. The only changes took place in the *Bars* routine. Instead of using 1 as the value of gray to fill these bars, I use a variable that allows this color to change. First off, the definition *sg* was created to allow this. Its starting definition was .9, or 10% light gray. Each time the routine is run, the gray is increased by 20%. This works fine when you only have five bars. However, a value of 110%, or 130% will only give you solid black. To overcome this in charts with many bars, I have added an *if* statement that checks to see if the number is less than zero. When it is less than zero, *sg* is redefined as .9.

```
/Bars
{/topscale ex d
 /botscale ex d
 /plotarray ex d
 /reverseyt 0 d
 /scalefactor topscale botscale sub d
 /scalefactor scalefactor totalheight div d
 /barwidth horizjump .7 mul d
 /barspace horizjump .15 mul d
 newpath
 xl yb m
 /y yt d
 /sg .9 d
 plotarray
    {/plot ex d
    /y y barspace sub d
    /x plot scalefactor div xl add d
    xl y m x y l
    /y y barwidth sub d
    x y l xl y l closepath
    sg 0 lt {/sg .9 d}if
    gs sg setgray fill gr 0 setgray stroke
    /sg sg .2 sub d
    /y y barspace sub d
    }forall
}def
```

5-6   The Building Blocks

Dr. George Luchak, professor emeritus at Princeton University, a good friend and relative, likes to use the expression, "Let's go back to first principles." This is a good time for *us* to go back to first principles. What Dr. Luchak is referring to is the logical base of knowledge that you start from when you embark on a problem-solving task. In this case, we have created a number of different chart and graph types that were easy to follow and had some strong relationships that could be translated into generic drawing routines.

So, what are the basic building blocks of a chart, graph, or diagram? Data and design. Taking that data and translating it into a meaningful graphic requires that you understand the data as well as the goal at hand.

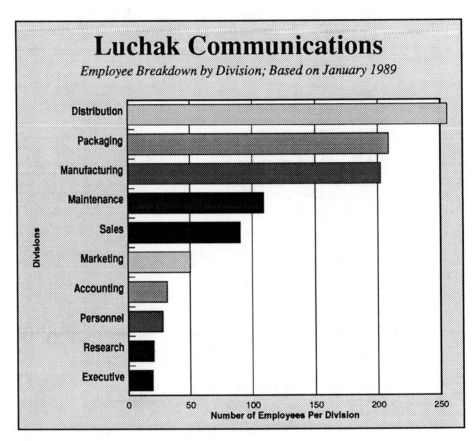

Figure 5—17

Your goal is first and foremost the most effective form of presenting the information—in the broadest sense, a means of communicating to the person who views your graphic. In seeking the best design for representing your data graphically, you will first need to define what I call the "knowns and unknowns" of the design process.

Goals are often achieved with the aid of the "knowns." In the case of magazine publishing, my area of expertise, the "knowns" are the overall design of the publication, its underlying grid, the capabilities of your production system, and the production schedule (deadlines). The "unknowns" of any design are often contained within the data. Even the best-made plans cannot account for the oddities of data presentation. At *PC Magazine*, we have developed a great deal of custom software to produce the charts and graphs. Even with the planning that goes into writing software, all of the possibilities cannot be defined in advance of having the actual data.

Before embarking on any ambitious PostScript programming exercises, you should ask yourself "What do I want to accomplish?" This may sound trite, but a well- conceived outline of the task at hand will result in a well-conceived program structure. After all, you will want to go back and debug, correct, modify, or even borrow pieces of code. If you can outline the task to be performed and write routines that perform subtasks, those routines can be transported to other programs. And if, God forbid, your first attempt at programming a graphic is not 100% correct, locating the problem will be much easier when the PostScript interpreter tells you in which routine the error occurred.

My very first "stab" at this kind of graphic PostScript program was some of the sloppiest code ever written. Who knew better? Through painstaking debugging, I realized that there was a good reason to write individual routines.

In analyzing your task, try breaking the graphic image down into its component elements. For instance, a typical bar chart is comprised of

- the overall space or box that it fits in,
- a grid for plot reference,
- the bars representing the data,
- labels,
- headline,
- and maybe a credit line for the data source.

This short list of elements is an excellent starting point for defining the routines that need to be written to create a bar chart. They may look like this:

```
BEGINNING COMMENTS
     %!PS-Adobe 2.0
     %%Title: Sample Comments
     %%Creator ...

ROUTINES
     /OutSideBox
     /Grid
     /DrawBars
     /ShowLabels
     /Headline
     /CreditLine

SCRIPT
     data ...
     showpage
```

There could and should be separate routines for each task at hand. If you separate the tasks into routines, you will be able to structure, understand, debug, and modify your code much more easily.

PostScript is an excellent language with which to construct data-dependent drawing routines. It is better, however, if all of your data is analyzed and prepared in another environment and the product of such analysis then provided to your PostScript code as absolute values. I'm referring to any calculations that are trying to define a best-fit line or a curvilinear trend line. Such mathematical procedures can be defined in PostScript with its *sine, cosine,* and *atangent* operators. But unless there is a real need to do this, there are many well-qualified spreadsheet programs that can find the plot points faster.

As you define and implement your PostScript code, try leaving room for some variables that control the overall size, proportion, color, typeface, and line weight. Building in the possibility of change from the outset will allow easy exploration of design ideas.

On a typical bar chart, you may be well-served to make all of the tint fills into variables that can be pushed onto the stack in advance of a routine's call. A color specification for the tint may be input directly into the code, defined as an algorithm, or input by an application program that you write.

In a scatter diagram, you may have precoded several bullet-types that can be called by a number or by a Boolean operator. It might look like this:

```
ROUTINES ...

    /PlotData {/btype exch def

        ...locate position...

        btype 1 eq {bullet1} if
        btype 2 eq {bullet2} if
        btype 3 eq {bullet3} if
        btype 4 eq {bullet4}
                   {bullet5} ifelse
    }def

    /bullet1 { ...routine...}def
    /bullet2 { ...routine...}def
    /bullet3 { ...routine...}def
    /bullet4 { ...routine...}def
    /bullet5 { ...routine...}def

SCRIPT ...

    [23 43 54 65 23 56
    67 87 34 56 34 91] 2 PlotData
```

```
showpage
clear
```

In this example, bullet type number 2 was chosen by pushing the integer 2 onto the stack in front of the *PlotData* routine call. The *if* operator checks to see what *btype* is equal to. If by chance *btype* is equal to a number greater than 5, the final *btype* check is an *ifelse* operator, which covers all other numeric possibilities and uses the *bullet5* routine.

If your graphic will change not only in data, but also in color, it would be best if you set up a color-specifying convention within your script. Let's say that a sample bar chart contains these elements:

- Background
- Inside grid box
- Grid lines
- Bars
- *X* and *Y* labels
- Headline

To apply a different color specification to each element, you may decide to code the *setcmykcolor*, *setrgbcolor*, or *sethsbcolor* operators (defined in Chapter 6) directly into the routines that draw them. It would also be possible to insert the color specifications just prior to the routine's call. This example demonstrates that technique:

```
0 0 .4 0 setcmykcolor
Background
.2 0 .2 0 setcmykcolor
Inside Grid Box
0 0 0 1 setcmykcolor
Grid Lines
1 0 .4 0 setcmykcolor
Bars
1 0 0 .6 setcmykcolor
X and Y Labels
0 1 1 0 setcmykcolor
Headline
```

The result here is

- light yellow background tint,
- pale green inside box,
- black grid lines,

- sea-blue bars,
- deep blue X and Y labels,
- and a bright red headline.

But what if you needed to have a black outline to the outside background box? This technique would accommodate that:

ROUTINE

```
/Background {
  llx lly moveto
  llx ury lineto
  urx ury lineto
  urx lly lineto
  closepath gsave
  setcmykcolor
  fill
  grestore
  setcmykcolor
  stroke}def
```

SCRIPT

```
0 0 0 1 0 0 .4 0 Background
```

That was fairly straightforward. Now what if you needed to specify a different color for each bar that you are plotting? The following routine fragment would accommodate this.

ROUTINE

```
/Bars {
  /Data exch def
  Data {
    /value exch def
    setcmykcolor
    ... plot data routine ...
  }forall
  }def
```

SCRIPT

```
[1  .3  0  0 1245
 1  .5  0  0 3251
 1  .7  0  0 4821
 1  1   0  0 2394
 .7 1  .3  0 2193
 .5 1  .5  0 2381] Bars
```

The same logic can be applied to all forms of PostScript programming. If you are creating graphics that use a particular font, you could put color, typeface, and other special type effects into variables, or at least into the script portion of the program. You will then be able to make all of your modifications at the bottom of the program. You will also find that placing the PostScript program into an application will be much easier when all of your variables reside in one section of the code.

5-7   Drawing a Line Graph

Putting together a line graph is a bit more complex than it might seem. With the bar graphs in the previous section it was a matter of locating a plot point and assembling a routine around that point. With a line graph, there must be a continuous connection from the first point all the way through to the last point. The connection scheme creates a polyline. You may remember this or a polygon or two from geometry. Geometry comes in very handy in designing and programming data-driven graphics.

In the case of Figure 5–18, most of the basics of the graphic are the same as the previous bar charts. There will, however, be some differences in the way items are located and drawn. As with any of my programs, there is a continuous evolution of the code. Since I always look for more efficient ways to render graphics, you will find slight (and sometimes not so slight) variations to my routines. Often, a slight change to one part of a routine will make it more efficient in the context of a new graphic. As I mentioned earlier, the number of repetitive steps within a program will determine the

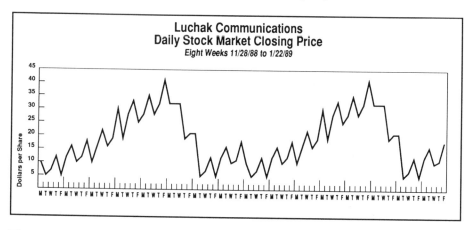

Figure 5—18

need for a routine. If a step occurs only once, a routine may not be necessary.

So, as you review these chart and graph programs, do not be alarmed when you see changes to the routines. Quite often, what was good for one program may not be good for another.

Before looking at the prologue, let's sum up the actual script that makes calls to the prologue.

```
/drawpage {                    % begin drawpage
0 0 0 1 setcmykcolor
.1 0 .2 0 50 230 548 450 1.2 box
0 0 0 1 setcmykcolor
.2 0 .4 0 80 260 532 390 80 9
true true false .4 .4 chartgridbox
0 45 dimens
0 0 0 1 setcmykcolor
(Eight Weeks 11/28/88 to 1/22/89)
(Luchak Communications)           % title
(Daily Stock Market Closing Price) label
0 0 0 1 setcmykcolor
[10 5 7 12 5 12 16 10
12 18 10 16 22 16 19
30 19 28 33 25 28 35
28 32 41 32 32 32 19
21 21 5 7 12 5 12 16
10 11 18 10 5 7 12 5
12 16 10 12 18 10 16
22 16 19 30 19 28 33
25 28 35 28 32 41 32
32 32 19 21 21 5 7 12
5 12 16 10 11 18 ]polyline    % data array
(Dollars per Share) leftscale     % y axis label
0 5 topscale {scleft} for         % y axis scale
/Helvetica-Bold findfont [4 0 0 7 0 0]makefont setfont
/ax xl def /y yb 9 sub def
[(M)(T)(W)(T)(F)]centershow                % x
axis labels
}def                           % end drawpage
```

In this example, the entire script is contained in one routine called *drawpage*. The script is structured in this manner to allow for a single-file four- color separation, one that operates very quickly and neatly. By placing all of the PostScript drawing operations in one routine, we can easily image it four times, once for each separation. In order to save the current state as we perform a *showpage* and eject the page, we trap the *showpage* operator between a *save* and *restore* operator. This keeps a record of the current VM (Virtual Memory) state and returns it when the *restore* operator is executed.

Any updates or changes to the data need take place only in this area of the code. As a result, any future uses of this code need take place only in a word processor. Later on, I will show you how to write your own application for importing data, editing data and graphics, and exporting PostScript files. This method is far more reliable than inputting data by hand.

Once this chart is contained in this manner, a separation algorithm can break it down into its component four process colors. In the first two lines of this script, you will notice the *setcmykcolor* operator. This operator is part of the new color extensions to the PostScript language. Since most output devices do not yet support these extensions, a color-separation algorithm has been included in the prologue.

The first two routines that are called from the script create the outer box and inner box with scale lines. On the line before each of these calls is the *setcmykcolor* operator and its required data.

The four integers pushed onto the stack prior to the *setcmykcolor* operator are the values of cyan, magenta, yellow, and black. In this case, solid black has been specified to outline the box. The four integers that follow the *setcmykcolor* operator are picked up by the *box* routine and specify the color value for the box fill.

```
0 0 0 1 setcmykcolor
.1 0 .2 0 50 230 548 450 1.2 box
0 0 0 1 setcmykcolor
.2 0 .4 0 80 260 532 390 80 9
true true false .4 .4 chartgridbox
```

Notice the four values that lead the set of numbers pushed onto the stack in advance of the call to the *box* routine in the second line. These integers are placed on the stack so that the *setcmykcolor* operator within the *box* routine will pick them off when executed. There is no need to exchange these numbers and define them. Whenever you know that a number is available on the stack, you can simply pull it off by using it in an operation, whether you are in a routine or not.

The next call to a routine is again preceded by a change in color. Although it is the same color as a few lines earlier, you must account for the fact that the current color was changed inside the *box* routine and reset it to black.

The *polyline* routine requires only a single array. This can be an array of any length within the PostScript-language array limits.

```
0 0 0 1 setcmykcolor
[10 5 7 12 5 12 16 10
12 18 10 16 22 16 19
30 19 28 33 25 28 35
28 32 41 32 32 32 19
21 21 5 7 12 5 12 16
```

```
10 11 18 10  5  7 12  5
12 16 10 12 18 10 16
22 16 19 30 19 28 33
25 28 35 28 32 41 32
32 32 19 21 21  5  7 12
 5 12 16 10 11 18 ]polyline     % data array
```

The major difference in the code for Figure 5–18 is the *polyline* routine. Let's skip past most of the prologue to that section.

```
% ==================================
/polyline
 {/plotarray exch def pop
```

The first operation within the *polyline* routine is the exchange of the array it requires. Since it is then entered as a definition, *plotarray*, the array itself is popped off the stack. The next two lines set the line width and start a new drawing path.

```
1.2 setlinewidth
newpath
```

The next line of code defines the starting point for the first plot. Since we are placing our plot points between tick marks, we must center the plot and its label between those marks. Mathematically, that position is exactly half the distance that we are using to plot the tick marks. Earlier in the prologue, *vertjump* was defined to handle this measure. Here we can use half of a *vertjump*, added to the left edge, to define the starting *x* coordinate. The base of the interior grid is used as the *y* coordinate. Since *xl* is our left-edge coordinate for the grid and will now be the incremental *x* coordinate for the graph line, we must have some way of returning to this number. The definition *reversexl* is set up to accomplish this. The *reversexl* definition, as well as *xl*, will be incremented to keep track of where the current *plotpoint* and origin are.

```
/xl xl vertjump 2 div add def
xl yb moveto
/reversexl 0 def
/plotcount 0 def
```

A simple way to do this would be to take a *length* reading of the *plotarray* array and then subtract that amount, times the value of *vertjump*, from the new *xl*. For the sake of demonstration, I have taken a running count of the operations of this routine with the *plotcount* definition and then used that number when it is completed. This is only to demonstrate that there are many ways to skin a cat, and some are obviously more efficient than others. In this case, the example shown is not code-efficient, but it produces the same results as an efficient method. Study this method. There may be some variations that can work within your code. Another way of handling this would be to come up with a new definition name for the location of *x* during the plotting procedure. It might look like this:

```
/plotx xl vertjump 2 div add def
```

In this manner, *xl* is never redefined but is simply used as the basis of another definition. There is also no need to keep track of how far *plotx* has traveled from *xl*. When you need to return to this point, *xl* is still available. Try modifying this code to accommodate the more practical approach I have just outlined. This is good practice for understanding a simpler construction.

A *forall* operator sets up the parameters for the plotting procedure. This PostScript operator reads the array *plotarray* and performs the procedures defined between the braces for each element of that array.

Once into the plotting procedure, the *plotcount* definition becomes critical. We have already defined *plotcount* as 0. With the first line of code, *plotcount* is redefined as one by adding 1 to it. The plot value is taken from the array *plotarray* by exchanging it. It is then defined as *plot*. The definition name *y* is used to hold the actual *y* value for the plot coordinate. Here I am using the *scalefactor* definition that I created earlier in the prologue. The value of *plot* is divided by *scalefactor* and added to *yb*, the base of the graphing area.

```
plotarray    % use array of numbers
  {/plotcount plotcount 1 add def
  /plot exch def      % read numbers one at
                      % a time
  /y plot scalefactor div yb add def
```

Questions are required within the overall *polyline* procedure to determine whether or not this is to be the first plot point. If it is, a *moveto* is performed. Otherwise, a *lineto* is performed. This is where the *plotcount* definition comes in. This use of *plotcount* is necessary but can be handled without much overhead. In this example, *plotcount* is redefined each time a new number is taken from the array. It is then checked in the two *if* statements. As the process continues, the value of *plotcount* increases. However, we need only determine if *plotcount* is one or any other value in the universe. I would recommend that a Boolean operator be used in place of this value.

```
plotcount 1 eq
  {xl y moveto advance}if
```

```
plotcount 1 gt
   {xl y lineto advance}if
}forall
```

The same procedure when using a Boolean operator would look like this:

```
/plotcount true def
plotarray   % use array of numbers
   {/plot exch def    % read numbers one at
                      % a time
  /y plot scalefactor div yb add def
  plotcount
     {xl y moveto
     /plotcount false def
     advance}if
  plotcount
     {xl y lineto
     advance}if
  }forall
  {
```

With this method, the *advance* routine can also be modified. In fact, we can combine the *advance* routine into these two operations and completely eliminate the need for it as a separate routine. Since the subject has come up, let's look at that routine.

```
% ====================================
/advance {/xl xl vertjump add def
   /reversexl reversexl vertjump add def}def

% ====================================
```

Advance performs two basic operations. The first is to redefine the value of *xl* by adding *vertjump* to it. The second is to redefine *reversexl* by adding *vertjump* to it. As I mentioned above, this routine could be eliminated in the alternate code, since neither operation would exist. Instead, the value of *vertjump* need only be added to *plotx* every time a new plot is executed in the *polyline* routine. The *polyline* routine would look like this:

```
/polyline
  {/plotarray exch def pop
   1.2 setlinewidth
   newpath
   /plotx vertjump 2 div add def
   plotx yb moveto
   /plotcount true def
     plotarray   % use array of numbers
       {/plot exch def
       /y plot scalefactor div yb add def
       plotcount
       {xl y moveto
         /plotcount false def
```

```
    /plotx plotx vertjump add def}
  {xl y lineto
    advance}ifelse
  }forall
  stroke
}def
```

Finishing up the original *polyline* routine is the *stroke* operator. After we have moved to the starting location and pathed to each plot point, we cannot forget to stroke the line. Otherwise, we will have an elaborate path with no image on the paper. In my first crack at this code, that is exactly what I forgot to take care of. I spent a good deal of time trying to figure out why there was no line on my graph. How simple, and yet how easy to overlook.

After the *stroke* operator, *xl* is redefined to back up to the original position by using the cumulative *reversexl* and the initial one-half of *vertjump* to subtract from its final value.

```
  stroke
 /xl xl reversexl sub vertjump 2 div sub def
}def
```

The complete Figure 5–18 code listing:

```
%%Title: Polyline Graph
%%Creator: Gerard Kunkel
%%CreationDate: 5:58PM  12/30/1988
%%BoundingBox: 0 0 612 792


% ===================================
%  This is a four color separation
%  routine that outputs four plates
%  from one file.
% ===================================
/seps 24 dict def
 seps begin
   /pickcolor [{pop pop pop 1 exch sub setgray}
        {pop pop exch pop 1 exch sub setgray}
        {pop 3 1 roll pop pop 1 exch sub setgray}
        {4 1 roll pop pop pop 1 exch sub setgray}]def
        /angles [105 75 90 45]def end

  /C 0 def /M 1 def /Y 2 def /K 3 def
  /colorbreaks {userdict begin
        dup seps /pickcolor get exch get
        /setcmykcolor exch def
        seps /angles get exch get
        currentscreen
        exch pop 3 -1 roll exch
        setscreen
        /setscreen {}def
```

```
        end
)bind def

%  ===================================
%  regmarks is a routine for drawing
%  a registration mark
%  ===================================
/regmarks
  {.7 setlinewidth
  /ymark exch def /xmark exch def
  /Helvetica findfont 4 scalefont setfont
  xmark 10 sub ymark 17 sub moveto 90 rotate
  (LUCHAK COMMUNICATIONS) show -90 rotate
  newpath xmark ymark 10 add moveto
    xmark ymark 10 sub lineto closepath stroke
  newpath xmark 10 sub ymark moveto
    xmark 10 add ymark lineto stroke
    xmark ymark 5 0 360 arc stroke}def

%  ===================================
%  registerpage uses the regmark
%  routine to draw four registermarks
%  ===================================
/registerpage
 {40 740 regmarks 40 50 regmarks
 580 50 regmarks 580 740 regmarks}def

%  ===================================
%  an expanded box routine with
%  variables defined by exchanging
%  coordinate numbers allows for
%  those numbers to be used in later
%  calculations
%  ===================================
/box
 {setlinewidth
  /ytbox exch def
  /xrbox exch def
  /ybbox exch def
  /xlbox exch def
  xlbox ybbox moveto
  xlbox ytbox lineto
  xrbox ytbox lineto
  xrbox ybbox lineto
  closepath gsave setcmykcolor fill grestore stroke
 }def

%  ===================================
%  this routine exchanges all the
%  parameters of the chart box and
%  grid. The grid is then further
%  broken down to horizontal ticks
%  or grid lines. The if questions
```

```
%  are looking for a Boolean true
%  or false. You may have horizontal
%  tick marks, lines, or neither if
%  both are false.
% ================================
/chartgridbox
{setlinewidth
 /insidelines exch def
 /horizlines exch def
 /horiztick exch def
 /break exch def
 /yaxiscount exch def
 /xaxiscount exch def
 /yt exch def
 /xr exch def
 /yb exch def
 /xl exch def
 newpath
 xl yt moveto
 xr yt lineto
 xr yb lineto
 xl yb lineto
 closepath gsave
 setcmykcolor fill
 grestore
 stroke
  /totalwidth xr xl sub def
  /vertjump totalwidth xaxiscount div def
  /totalheight yt yb sub def
  /horizjump totalheight yaxiscount div def
  insidelines setlinewidth
  /tick yb 6 add def
 drawvert
horizlines {/tick xr def drawhoriz}if
horiztick {/tick xl 6 add def drawhoriz}if
/ylegendline yb 20 sub def
}def

% ==================================
%  the horizontal grid line
%  or tick mark drawing routine
% ==================================
/drawhoriz
  {yaxiscount {newpath
  xl yb moveto tick yb lineto closepath stroke
  /yb yb horizjump add def}repeat
  /yb yb totalheight sub def
  }def

% ==================================
%  the vertical tick mark drawing
%  routine
% ==================================
```

```
/drawvert
  {/vertcount 1 def
  xaxiscount {newpath
  xl yb moveto xl
  vertcount 1 eq {tick 6 add}{tick} ifelse
  lineto closepath stroke
  /xl xl vertjump add def
  /vertcount vertcount 1 add def
  vertcount 6 eq {/vertcount 1 def}if
  }repeat
  /xl xl totalwidth sub def
  }def


% ==================================
%  a generic routine to centertype
% ==================================
/centertype
 {/strg exch def
  strg dup stringwidth pop
  2 div neg 0 rmoveto
  strg show pop}def


% ==================================
%  a routine to center the day-of-
%  week labels at the bottom of the
%  chart.
% ==================================
/centershow
  {/ax ax vertjump 2 div add def
  /days exch def
  {days{ax y moveto centertype
  /ax ax vertjump add def} forall
  ax xr ge {exit} if
  }loop
  }def


% ==================================
/leftscale
 {/num 6 string def
  /xlabel exch def
  /scalestep topscale botscale sub xaxiscount div def
  7 /Helvetica-Bold F
  /x xl 18 sub def
  x yb moveto 90 rotate
  xlabel show -90 rotate
  /yscale yb def 0 yb moveto
  } def


% ==================================
/scleft
  {num cvs dup stringwidth pop
  14 exch sub 0 rmoveto show
```

```
  /yscale yscale horizjump add def x yscale moveto
  } def

% ==================================
/ylabels
{/labelarray exch def pop
  /y yb 10 sub def
  labelarray
  {xl y moveto
  /label exch def
  label aload pop
  dup stringwidth pop
  2 div sub neg 0 rmoveto show pop
  /xl xl vertjump add def
  }forall
  /xl xl vertjump yaxiscount mul sub def
}def

% ==================================
/dimens
 {/topscale exch def
  /botscale exch def
  /scalefactor topscale botscale sub def
  /scalefactor scalefactor totalheight div def
  pop }def

% ==================================
/advance {/xl xl vertjump add def
  /reversexl reversexl vertjump add def}def

% ==================================
/polyline
 {/plotarray exch def pop
  1.2 setlinewidth
  newpath
  /xl xl vertjump 2 div add def
  xl yb moveto
  /reversexl 0 def
  /plotcount 0 def
   plotarray      % use array of numbers
     {/plotcount plotcount 1 add def
     /plot exch def     % read numbers one at
                        % a time
     /y plot scalefactor div yb add def
     plotcount 1 eq {xl y moveto advance}if
     plotcount 1 gt {xl y lineto advance}if
     }forall
     stroke
  /xl xl reversexl sub vertjump 2 div sub def
}def

% ==================================
/label
```

```
  {/Helvetica-Bold findfont [12 0 0 14 0 0] makefont
setfont
  xlbox ytbox moveto
  /headx xrbox xlbox sub 2 div def headx -18 rmoveto
exch
  centertype
  xlbox ytbox moveto headx -32 rmoveto centertype
  /Helvetica-Bold findfont [8 0 1 10 0 0] makefont
setfont
  xlbox ytbox moveto headx -44 rmoveto centertype
  }def

% ===================================
/F {findfont exch scalefont setfont}def

% ===================================
/names {/namearray exch def}def

% ===================================
/idpage
  {/colr exch def 1 1 1 1 setcmykcolor
  8 /Helvetica-Bold F
  60 745 moveto
  namearray {show 50 0 rmoveto}forall
  colr show .5 setlinewidth
  50 755 moveto 0 -15 rlineto 500 0 rlineto
  0 15 rlineto closepath stroke
  registerpage
}def
[(6:09PM  12/30/1988)
(FIG5-18.PS)
(Copyright 1988 Gerard Kunkel)]names

% ===================================
%%EndProlog
% ===================================


/drawpage {                  % begin drawpage
0 0 0 1 setcmykcolor
.1 0 .2 0 50 230 548 450 1.2 box
0 0 0 1 setcmykcolor
.2 0 .4 0.80 260 532 390 80 9
true true false .4 .4 chartgridbox
0 45 dimens
0 0 0 1 setcmykcolor
(Eight Weeks 11/28/88 to 1/22/89)
(Luchak Communications)              % title
(Daily Stock Market Closing Price) label  % second line
0 0 0 1 setcmykcolor
[10 5 7 12 5 12 16 10
12 18 10 16 22 16 19
30 19 28 33 25 28 35
```

```
28 32 41 32 32 32 19
21 21 5 7 12 5 12 16
10 11 18 10 5 7 12 5
12 16 10 12 18 10 16
22 16 19 30 19 28 33
25 28 35 28 32 41 32
32 32 19 21 21 5 7 12
5 12 16 10 11 18 ]polyline          % data array
(Dollars per Share) leftscale        % y axis label
0 5 topscale {scleft} for            % y axis scale
/Helvetica-Bold findfont
[4 0 0 7 0 0]makefont setfont
/ax xl def /y yb 9 sub def
[(M)(T)(W)(T)(F)]centershow          % x axis labels
}def                                 % end drawpage

K colorbreaks (black)
idpage drawpage save showpage restore
```

5.7.1   Adding a Little Life to the Graph

In Figure 5–19, I have attempted to enhance the impact of the graph
without resorting to any data distortion. By reversing the plot line out of a
dark gray background, the emphasis is put on the data line. Making
changes like this to an existing graphics file is relatively simple. The only
modifications needed have been made in the script portion of the code.

```
<insert>[(6:17PM  12/30/1988)
(FIG5-19.PS)
(Copyright 1988 Gerard Kunkel)]names
/drawpage {                % begin drawpage
0 0 0 1 setcmykcolor
.1 0 .2 .05 50 230 548 450 1.2 box
0 0 0 0 setcmykcolor
.2 0 .4 .8 80 260 532 390 80 9
true true false .4 .4 chartgridbox
0 45 dimens
0 0 0 1 setcmykcolor
(Sixteen Weeks)
(Luchak Communications)                % title
(Daily Stock Market Closing Price) label % second line
of title
0 0 0 0 setcmykcolor
2.5 setlinewidth
[10 5 7 12 5 12 16 10
```

```
12 18 10 16 22 16 19
30 19 28 33 25 28 35
28 32 41 32 32 32 19
21 21 5 7 12 5 12 16
10 11 18 10 5 7 12 5
12 16 10 12 18 10 16
22 16 19 30 19 28 33
25 28 35 28 32 41 32
32 32 19 21 21 5 7 12
5 12 16 10 11 18 ]polyline        % data array
0 0 0 1 setcmykcolor
(Dollars per Share) leftscale      % y axis label
0 5 topscale {scleft} for          % y axis scale
/Helvetica-Bold findfont
[4 0 0 7 0 0]makefont setfont
/ax xl def /y yb 9 sub def
[(M)(T)(W)(T)(F)]centershow        % x axis labels
}def                               % end drawpage

K colorbreaks (black) idpage drawpage save showpage
restore
```

In order to change the backgound of the outer box from white to a light gray tint, one integer must be changed. In the second line of the *drawpage* definition are the four color specifications for this box. There are already some color specifications for later use, but now I have added 5% black to the fill color. This value is expressed as .05, since 0 represents no color and one represents solid color.

```
/drawpage {              % begin drawpage
0 0 0 1 setcmykcolor
.1 0 .2 .05 50 230 548 450 1.2 box
```

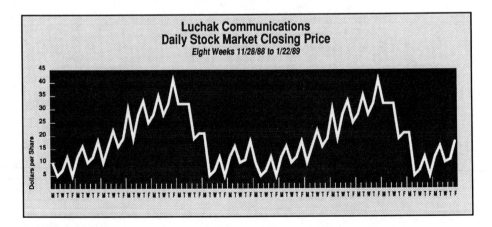

Figure 5—19

The fourth line of the *drawpage* routine contains the color specification for the interior box. The value of .8 has replaced a zero to fill the interior box with 80% black.

```
/drawpage {              % begin drawpage
0 0 0 1 setcmykcolor
.1 0 .2 .05 50 230 548 450 1.2 box
0 0 0 0 setcmykcolor
.2 0 .4 .8 80 260 532 390 80 9
true true false .4 .4 chartgridbox
```

The *polyline* array is preceded by a *setcmykcolor* operator that has a value of no color, or opaque white. In addition, the line width has been changed from the current line width to 2.5 points. This increase in width is also important to the impact of the graphic. Too fine a line would get lost in the black area, just as too fine a black line in the white background would get confused with the fine grid.

```
0 0 0 0 setcmykcolor
2.5 setlinewidth
[10 5 7 12 5 12 16 10
12 18 10 16 22 16 19
30 19 28 33 25 28 35
28 32 41 32 32 32 19
21 21 5 7 12 5 12 16
10 11 18 10 5 7 12 5
12 16 10 12 18 10 16
22 16 19 30 19 28 33
25 28 35 28 32 41 32
32 32 19 21 21 5 7 12
5 12 16 10 11 18 ]polyline        % data array
```

Immediately following the *polyline* routine call is another *setcmykcolor* that resets the color to black. This line did not appear in the original code, since the current color was already black coming out of the *polyline* routine. In this case, the labels are strongest when printed in black against the 5% black background.

```
5 12 16 10 11 18 ]polyline        % data array
0 0 0 1 setcmykcolor
(Dollars per Share) leftscale     % y axis label
0 5 topscale {scleft} for         % y axis scale
/Helvetica-Bold findfont
[4 0 0 7 0 0]makefont setfont
/ax xl def /y yb 9 sub def
[ (M)(T)(W)(T)(F)]centershow       % x axis labels
}def                              % end drawpage

K colorbreaks (black) idpage drawpage save showpage
restore
```

5.7.2 Changing the Measurement of Time

In Figure 5–20, an important change is made on the x- axis. In our original
line graph, I was incrementing days of the week, excluding weekend days.
In this case, the increment has been changed to quarterly data plots. In the
first example (Figure 5–19), a large tick mark was drawn for every fifth
entry, falling between Friday and Monday. In this new graphic, I chose to
indicate each *year* with the larger tick mark, while each quarter is a small
tick mark. The bulk of the modification takes place within the *drawvert*
routine.

```
% ==================================
/drawvert
  {/vertcount 1 def
  xaxiscount {newpath
  xl yb moveto xl
  vertcount 1 eq {tick 6 add}{tick} ifelse
  lineto closepath stroke
  /xl xl vertjump add def
  /vertcount vertcount 1 add def
  vertcount 6 eq {/vertcount 1 def}if
  }repeat
  /xl xl totalwidth sub def
  }def
```

In the first example (Figure 5–19) of the *drawvert* routine, you saw that
there was a *repeat* operator that drew a tick mark for every data point along
the x-axis. The process was repeated *xaxiscount* times. During this process,
if *vertcount* was equal to 1, then a tick mark six points larger is drawn.

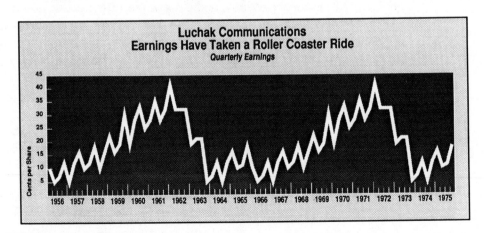

Figure 5—20

Otherwise, the normal size tick mark was drawn. As this routine was repeated, *vertcount* was incremented by one. When it reached 6 it was redefined as one, and the larger tick mark was drawn.

```
/drawvert
  {/vertcount 1 def
  xaxiscount {newpath
  xl yb moveto xl
  vertcount 1 eq {tick 6 add}{tick} ifelse
  lineto closepath stroke
  /xl xl vertjump add def
  /vertcount vertcount 1 add def
  vertcount 5 eq {/vertcount 1 def}if
  }repeat
  /xl xl totalwidth sub def
  }def
```

In Figure 5–20, the reset of *vertcount* happens at 5 as opposed to 6. This creates four units between large tick marks.

Another area of the program must be modified to accommodate the new segmenting of data points. Since this chart is measuring quarterly results over a number of years, I have chosen the year as the label for time. In Figure 5–19, I used days of the week for each increment. In that case, the distance between each label was equal to the distance between each plot point—the product of the total width of the plot area divided by the number of plots.

Here I have put the *centershow* and its script values together to show the relationship.

```
% ==================================
/centershow
  {/ax ax vertjump 4 mul 2 div add def
  /years exch def
  {years{ax y moveto centertype
  /ax ax vertjump 4 mul add def} forall
  ax xr ge {exit} if
  }loop
  }def
% ==================================
[ (1956)(1957)(1958)(1959)(1960)
(1961)(1962)(1963)(1964)(1965)
(1966)(1967)(1968)(1969)(1970)
(1971)(1972)(1973)(1974)(1975) ]centershow
```

The major difference here is the change of the *ax* definitions. Each time a label is drawn, *ax* is redefined as *ax* plus *vertjump* times 4. This moves four relative plotpoint distances to the right.

The entire code for Figure 5–20 is shown so that you can see the relationships easily.

```
gsave
%%Title: Polyline Graph
%%Creator: Gerard Kunkel
%%CreationDate: 5:58PM  12/30/1988
%%BoundingBox: 0 0 612 792

% =================================
%  This is a four color separation
%  routine that outputs four plates
%  from one file.
% =================================
/seps 24 dict def
 seps begin
  /pickcolor [{pop pop pop 1 exch sub setgray}
       {pop pop exch pop 1 exch sub setgray}
       {pop 3 1 roll pop pop 1 exch sub setgray}
       {4 1 roll pop pop pop 1 exch sub setgray}]def
       /angles [105 75 90 45]def end

  /C 0 def /M 1 def /Y 2 def /K 3 def
  /colorbreaks {userdict begin
       dup seps /pickcolor get exch get
       /setcmykcolor exch def
       seps /angles get exch get
       currentscreen
       exch pop 3 -1 roll exch
       setscreen
       /setscreen {}def
       end
}bind def

% ===================================
%  regmarks is a routine for drawing
%  a registration mark
% ===================================
/regmarks
  {.7 setlinewidth
  /ymark exch def /xmark exch def
  /Helvetica findfont 4 scalefont setfont
  xmark 10 sub ymark 17 sub moveto 90 rotate
  (LUCHAK COMMUNICATIONS) show -90 rotate
  newpath xmark ymark 10 add moveto
    xmark ymark 10 sub lineto closepath stroke
  newpath xmark 10 sub ymark moveto
    xmark 10 add ymark lineto stroke
    xmark ymark 5 0 360 arc stroke}def

% =================================
%  registerpage uses the regmark
%  routine to draw four registermarks
% =================================
/registerpage
  {40 740 regmarks 40 50 regmarks
  580 50 regmarks 580 740 regmarks}def
```

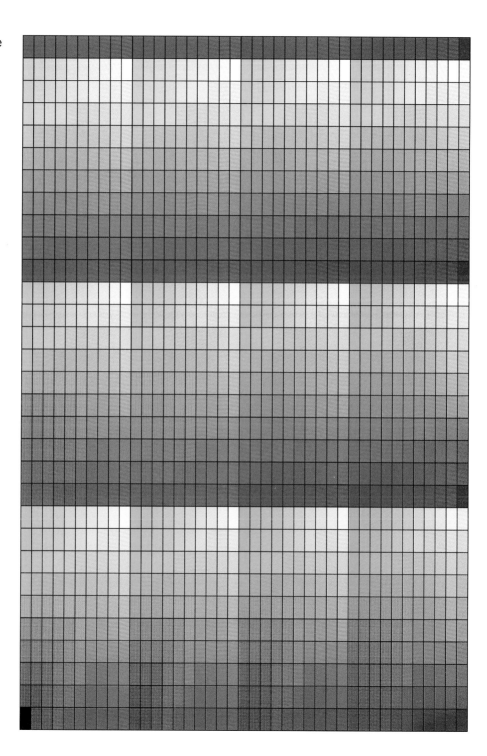

Color Plate

1

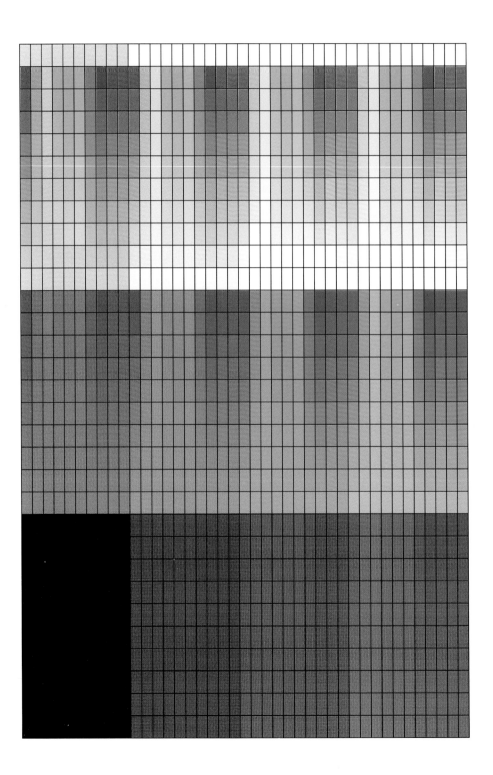

Color Plate

3

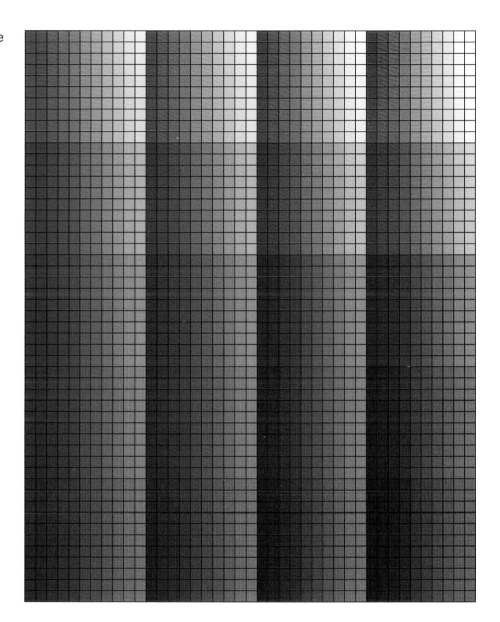

Color Plate

4

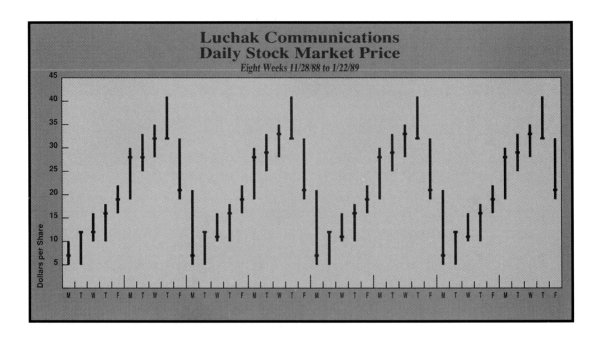

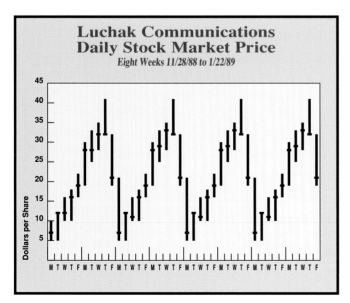

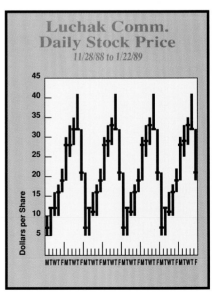

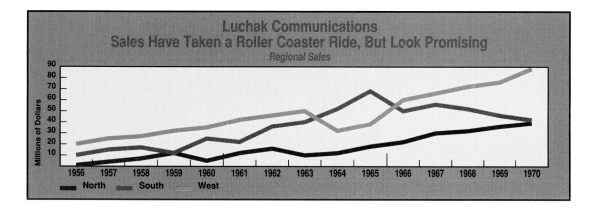

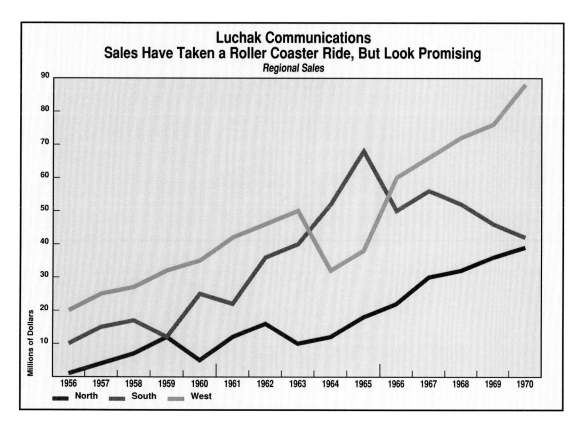

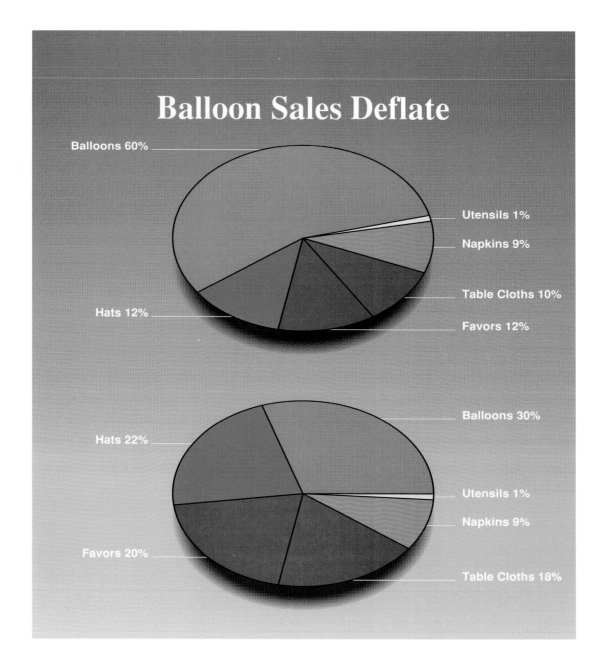

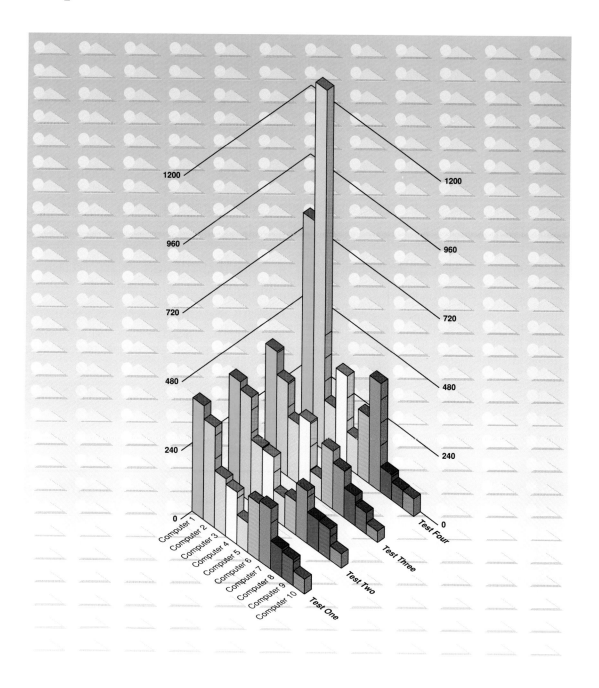

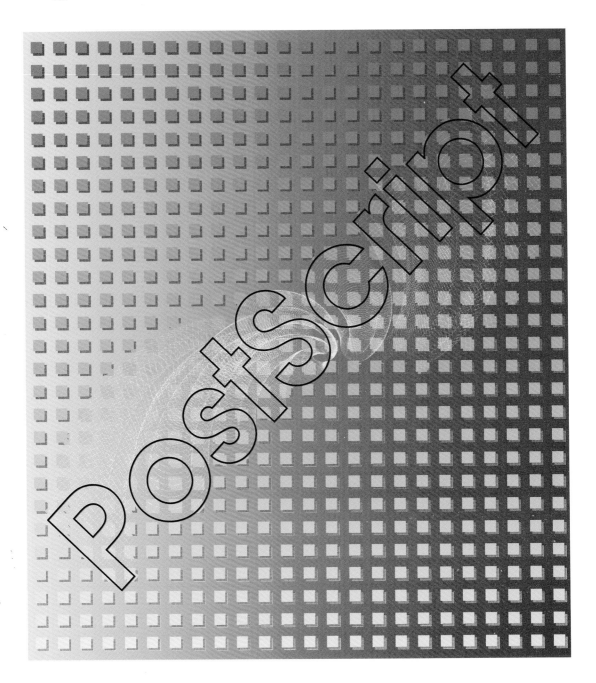

```
% ==================================
%  an expanded box routine with
%  variables defined by exchanging
%  coordinate numbers allows for
%  those numbers to be used in later
%  calculations
% ==================================
/box
 {setlinewidth
  /ytbox exch def
  /xrbox exch def
  /ybbox exch def
  /xlbox exch def
  xlbox ybbox moveto
  xlbox ytbox lineto
  xrbox ytbox lineto
  xrbox ybbox lineto
  closepath gsave setcmykcolor fill grestore stroke
}def

% ==================================
%  this routine exchanges all the
%  parameters of the chart box and
%  grid. The grid is then further
%  broken down to horizontal ticks
%  or grid lines. The if questions
%  are looking for a Boolean true
%  or false. You may have horizontal
%  tick marks, lines, or neither if
%  both are false.
% ==================================
/chartgridbox
 {setlinewidth
  /insidelines exch def
  /horizlines exch def
  /horiztick exch def
  /break exch def
  /yaxiscount exch def
  /xaxiscount exch def
  /yt exch def
  /xr exch def
  /yb exch def
  /xl exch def
  newpath
  xl yt moveto
  xr yt lineto
  xr yb lineto
  xl yb lineto
  closepath gsave
  setcmykcolor fill
  grestore
  stroke
   /totalwidth xr xl sub def
   /vertjump totalwidth xaxiscount div def
```

```
  /totalheight yt yb sub def
  /horizjump totalheight yaxiscount div def
  insidelines setlinewidth
  /tick yb 6 add def
 drawvert
horizlines {/tick xr def drawhoriz}if
horiztick {/tick xl 6 add def drawhoriz}if
/ylegendline yb 20 sub def
)def

% ===================================
%  the horizontal grid line
%  or tick mark drawing routine
% ===================================
/drawhoriz
  {yaxiscount {newpath
  xl yb moveto tick yb lineto closepath stroke
  /yb yb horizjump add def}repeat
  /yb yb totalheight sub def
  }def

% ===================================
%  the vertical tick mark drawing
%  routine
% ===================================
/drawvert
  {/vertcount 1 def
  xaxiscount {newpath
  xl yb moveto xl
  vertcount 1 eq {tick 6 add}{tick} ifelse
  lineto closepath stroke
  /xl xl vertjump add def
  /vertcount vertcount 1 add def
  vertcount 5 eq {/vertcount 1 def}if
  }repeat
  /xl xl totalwidth sub def
  }def

% ===================================
%  a generic routine to centertype
% ===================================
/centertype
 {/strg exch def
  strg dup stringwidth pop
  2 div neg 0 rmoveto
  strg show pop}def

% ===================================
%  a routine to center the day-of-
%  week labels at the bottom of the
%  chart.
% ===================================
/centershow
```

```
{/ax ax vertjump 4 mul 2 div add def
/years exch def
{years{ax y moveto centertype
/ax ax vertjump 4 mul add def} forall
ax xr ge {exit} if
}loop
}def

% ===================================
/leftscale
 {/num 6 string def
 /xlabel exch def
 /scalestep topscale botscale sub xaxiscount div def
 7 /Helvetica-Bold F
 /x xl 18 sub def
 x yb moveto 90 rotate
 xlabel show -90 rotate
 /yscale yb def 0 yb moveto
 } def

% ===================================
/scleft
  {num cvs dup stringwidth pop
  14 exch sub 0 rmoveto show
  /yscale yscale horizjump add def x yscale moveto
  } def

% ===================================
/ylabels
{/labelarray exch def
  /y yb 10 sub def
  labelarray
  {xl y moveto
  /label exch def
  label aload pop
  dup stringwidth pop
  2 div sub neg 0 rmoveto show
  /xl xl vertjump add def
  }forall
  /xl xl vertjump yaxiscount mul sub def
}def

% ===================================
/dimens
 {/topscale exch def
  /botscale exch def
  /scalefactor topscale botscale sub def
  /scalefactor scalefactor totalheight div def  % needs
totalheight
   }def

% ===================================
/advance {/xl xl vertjump add def
```

```
   /reversexl reversexl vertjump add def}def

% ====================================
/polyline
 {/plotarray exch def
  newpath
  /xl xl vertjump 2 div add def
  xl yb moveto
  /reversexl 0 def
  /plotcount 0 def
   plotarray    % use array of numbers
     {/plotcount plotcount 1 add def
      /plot exch def      % read numbers one at
                          % a time
      /y plot scalefactor div yb add def
      plotcount 1 eq {xl y moveto advance}if
      plotcount 1 gt {xl y lineto advance}if
      }forall
      stroke
  /xl xl reversexl sub vertjump 2 div sub def
}def

% ====================================
/label
 {/Helvetica-Bold findfont [12 0 0 14 0 0] makefont
setfont
  xlbox ytbox moveto
  /headx xrbox xlbox sub 2 div def headx -18 rmoveto
exch
  centertype
  xlbox ytbox moveto headx -32 rmoveto centertype
  /Helvetica-Bold findfont [8 0 1 10 0 0] makefont
setfont
  xlbox ytbox moveto headx -44 rmoveto centertype
  }def

% ====================================
/F {findfont exch scalefont setfont}def

% ====================================
/names {/namearray exch def}def

% ====================================
/idpage
 {/colr exch def 1 1 1 1 setcmykcolor
 8 /Helvetica-Bold F
 60 745 moveto
 namearray {show 50 0 rmoveto}forall
 colr show .5 setlinewidth
 50 755 moveto 0 -15 rlineto 500 0 rlineto
 0 15 rlineto closepath stroke
 registerpage
}def
```

```
% ==================================
%%EndProlog
% ==================================

[(6:17PM  12/30/1988)
(FIG5-20.PS)
(Copyright 1988 Gerard Kunkel)]names
/drawpage {              % begin drawpage
0 0 0 1 setcmykcolor .1 0 .2 .05 50 230 548 450 1.2 box
0 0 0 0 setcmykcolor .2 0 .4 .6 80 260 532 390 80 9
  true true false .4 .7 chartgridbox
0 45 dimens
0 0 0 1 setcmykcolor
(Quarterly Earnings)
(Luchak Communications)             % title
(Earnings Have Taken a Roller Coaster Ride) label  %
second line of title
0 0 0 0 setcmykcolor
3.5 setlinewidth
[10 5 7 12 5 12 16 10 12 18 10 16 22 16 19
30 19 28 33 25 28 35 28 32 41 32 32 32 19 21
21 5 7 12 5 12 16 10 11 18 10 5 7 12 5 12 16 10 12 18
10 16 22 16 19
30 19 28 33 25 28 35 28 32 41 32 32 32 19 21
21 5 7 12 5 12 16 10 11 18 ]polyline   % data array
0 0 0 1 setcmykcolor
(Cents per Share) leftscale     % y axis label
0 5 topscale {scleft} for        % y axis scale
/Helvetica-Bold findfont [7 0 0 9 0 0]makefont setfont
/ax xl def /y yb 9 sub def
[(1956)(1957)(1958)(1959)(1960)(1961)(1962)(1963)(1964)
(1965)(1966)(1967)(1968)(1969)(1970)
(1971)(1972)(1973)(1974)(1975)]centershow
% x axis labels
}def                          % end drawpage

K colorbreaks
(black) idpage
drawpage
save showpage restore
clear grestore
```

5.7.3   Multiplying the Results

In Figure 5–21 things really get exciting. More often than not, a line graph
is used when there are multiple lines of data to be plotted. In our previous
example, I plotted two-dimensional data. In this example, I will plot three
dimensions of data: time, quantity, and type. Type is expressed by the

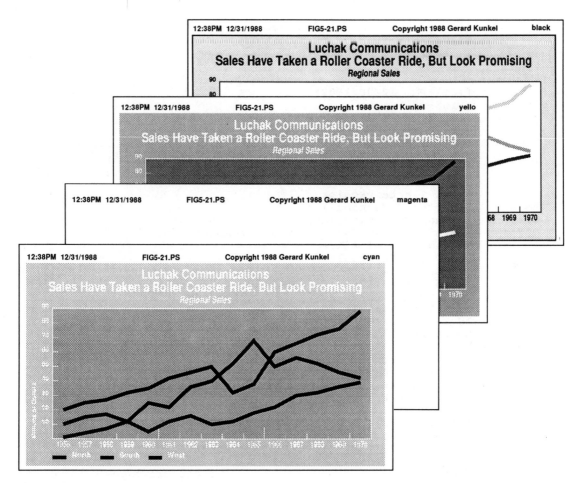

Figure 5—21

multiple lines. Evolving from a one-line graph to a two- or three-line graph is very easy. Since I have set up the data plots as a routine, we can continue to throw data at that plotting routine. In this example, any number of data lines can be added.

Let's look at the script alone. All other routines in this example are the same as in the previous examples.

```
[(12:38PM  12/31/1988)
(FIG5-21.PS)
(Copyright 1988 Gerard Kunkel)]names
/drawpage {              % begin drawpage
```

```
0 0 0 1 setcmykcolor
.1 0 .2 .05 50 230 448 450 1.2 box
0 0 0 1 setcmykcolor
.2 0 .4 0 80 260 432 400 15 9
true true false .4 .7 chartgridbox
0 90 dimens
0 0 0 1 setcmykcolor
(Regional Sales)
(Luchak Communications)            % title
(Sales Have Taken a Roller \
Coaster Ride, But Look Promising) label
3.5 setlinewidth
/Helvetica-Bold findfont 8 scalefont setfont
1 0 0 .6 setcmykcolor
[1 4 7 12 5 12 16 10
12 18 22 30 32 36 39]polyline   % data array
(North) key
1 0 .4 .3 setcmykcolor
[10 15 17 12 25 22 36
40 52 68 50 56 52 46 42]polyline   % data array
(South) key
1 0 .8 .1 setcmykcolor
[20 25 27 32 35 42 46
50 32 38 60 66 72 76 88]polyline   % data array
(West) key
0 0 0 1 setcmykcolor
(Millions of Dollars) leftscale    % y axis label
0 10 topscale {scleft} for        % y axis scale
/Helvetica-Bold findfont [7 0 0 9 0 0]makefont setfont
/ax xl def /y yb 9 sub def
[(1956)(1957)(1958)(1959)(1960)(1961)(1962)(1963)(1964)
(1965)(1966)(1967)(1968)(1969)(1970)] 1 centershow
% x axis labels
}def                              % end drawpage

K colorbreaks
(black) idpage
drawpage save showpage restore
C colorbreaks
(cyan) idpage
drawpage save showpage restore
M colorbreaks
(magenta) idpage
drawpage save showpage restore
Y colorbreaks
(yellow) idpage
drawpage save showpage restore
clear grestore
```

The only code change here is the insertion of two additional *poly-line* routines. Preceding the data for the polyline is a new color specification. Since we have overlapping lines, I chose to design this graphic in color. A color example is shown as Color Plate 5 in the center of the book.

5-8   Breaking Your Data into Slices

One of the most widely used chart types is the pie chart. When used properly, the pie chart quickly conveys cumulative and relative information as percentages of the whole. When multiple pie charts are used, changes in values across time or changes in relationships across types can be shown. In PostScript, creating a pie chart is a reasonably simple project. It does not take much code, just a lot of forethought. In fact, the most difficult aspects of this code are labeling the graphic and producing dimensional results.

In this chapter, I have started with a basic pie chart and added on features to enhance the design and increase the readability. In our first example, Figure 5–22, I have rendered a bare-bones pie chart—not very exciting to look at, but very functional. The pie is a complete circle, and the slice points are true to the data values.

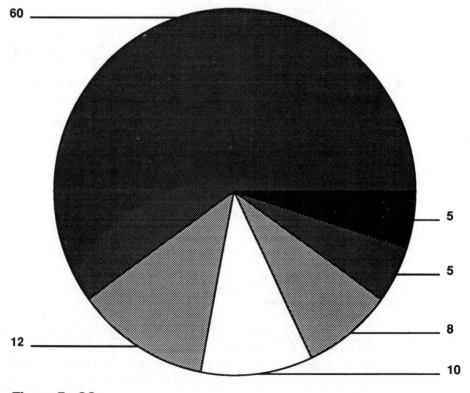

Figure 5—22

Let's take a quick look at the code for this figure.

```
%%Title: Piechart GK
%%CreationDate: 2:07PM  12/11/1988
%%Creator: Gerard Kunkel
%%BoundingBox 0 0 612 792
% PostScript routine to draw pie charts
/seps 24 dict def
 seps begin
        /pickcolor [
        {pop pop pop 1 exch sub setgray}
        {pop pop exch pop 1 exch sub setgray}
        {pop 3 1 roll pop pop 1 exch sub setgray}
        {4 1 roll pop pop pop 1 exch sub setgray}
        ]def
        /angles [105 75 90 45]def
    end

  /C 0 def
  /M 1 def
  /Y 2 def
  /K 3 def
  /colorbreaks {
        userdict begin
        dup seps /pickcolor get exch get
        /setcmykcolor exch def
        seps /angles get exch get
        currentscreen
        exch pop 3 -1 roll exch
        setscreen
        /setscreen {}def
        end
}bind def
% =======================================
/rightshow {dup stringwidth pop neg 0 rmoveto show}def
% =======================================
/pies     % array of pie slices
  {/piearray exch def
   /cumang 0 def

   piearray
   {/slicearray exch def
   slicearray aload pop
    /pieslice exch def
    /degree pieslice 100 div 360 mul def
    /c exch def
    newpath 0 0 moveto
    0 0 rad cumang cumang degree add
    arc showpercent
    /cumang cumang degree add def
    closepath gsave 0 0 0 c setcmykcolor
    fill grestore 1 1 1 1 setcmykcolor stroke
}forall
}def
% =======================================
```

```
/showpercent
  { gsave newpath 0 0 moveto
    0 0 rad cumang cumang degree 2 div add
    arcn currentpoint
    /y exch def /x exch def
    x 0 gt {newpath x y moveto rm y lineto
              stroke rm 6 add y moveto
              pieslice num cvs show}
            {newpath x y moveto lm y lineto
              stroke lm 6 sub y moveto
              pieslice num cvs rightshow}ifelse
              grestore
  }def
% ========================================
K colorbreaks
/transx 300 def /transy 400 def
/rad 150 def
/rm rad 20 add def
/lm rm neg def
/Helvetica-Bold findfont 10 scalefont setfont
/num 6 string def
1 setlinewidth
2 setmiterlimit
transx transy translate
[
[.6 60]
[.3 12]
[0 10]
[.3 8]
[.6 5]
[1 5]] pies
transx neg transy neg translate
40 700 moveto
(FIG5-22.PS   Gerard Kunkel   1:01PM  12/31/1988)show
/#copies 2 def
showpage
clear
```

As you can see, this code begins like many others. It has the standard commenting at the beginning. In this case, I have added a color separation routine, knowing that ultimately I would be producing this in full color. As I work with this file, though, I will be outputting to the Apple LaserWriter IINTX in black and white. To accommodate this printer and speed the development process, I have chosen to call upon black only when executing the *colorbreaks* routine. Look at the beginning of the script. You will see that the code line

```
K colorbreaks
```

is sent to the printer prior to any other procedure calls.

Immediately following the color separation routine is a boilerplate routine for aligning type to the right.

```
% =======================================
/rightshow {dup stringwidth pop neg 0 rmoveto show}def
% =======================================
```

The first pie-chart routine in this program is the *pies* routine. In simple terms, this routine exchanges the pie values, draws and fills the pie slice, and calls the *showpercent* subroutine to draw the label for that slice. This routine repeats itself until all of the slices are drawn.

It starts off quite simply. The array of pie-slice values is exchanged and defined as *piearray*. Then a new definition is set up, *cumang*. *Cumang* is my abbreviation of *cumulative angle*. It will be necessary in the creation of a pie chart to keep tabs on the current location, so that each subsequent pie slice properly abuts the previous slice. The *cumang* definition will be redefined for each slice of the pie that is drawn.

```
% =======================================
/pies      % array of pie slices
  {/piearray exch def
   /cumang 0 def
```

After the *cumang* definition, a *forall* loop is executed on the *piearray* array.

```
piearray
{/slicearray exch def
slicearray aload pop
 /pieslice exch def
```

Since a pie chart measures percent of whole, or parts per 100, we must convert the *pieslice* percent values into degrees. A complete circle or ellipse is a path rendered from 0 to 360 degrees. A pie slice of 100% would not be a path from 1 to 100 degrees, however, it would be a path from 0 to 360 degrees. The formula for converting percent to degrees is

```
360 divided by 100 times value
```

If the value in this example is 12, then the formula would be

```
360/100*12=43.2
```

The product, 43.2, is the width, in degrees, of that pie slice. Within the *pies* routine, the conversion takes place as

```
/degree pieslice 100 div 360 mul def
```

This may look a little backwards, but that is typical of PostScript. With postfix notation, math formulas are sent to the interpreter in reverse.

Within the *piearray* array is the gray value of the fill color. Since I am using a four-color separator for later use, I have set the values of cyan, magenta, and yellow to zero. The value of black is exchanged and defined as *c*.

```
/c exch def
```

The actual drawing begins in the next line. A new path is set up, and the coordinate 0, 0 is moved to. This is immediately followed by an *arc* operator and its values. Note that a math operator, *add*, appears within the required set of values supplied to the *arc* operator. This is done so that an addition definition need not be created. It is much simpler sometimes to introduce some simple mathematics as you are plotting a path. In this case, I am adding the definition *degree* to the current cumulative angle as the slice is drawn. This creates the first and second degrees of rotation required by the *arc* operator to draw a pie slice.

After the slice is drawn, the current *degree* value is added to *cumang* to create the updated current angle.

```
newpath 0 0 moveto
    0 0 rad cumang cumang degree add
    arc showpercent
    /cumang cumang degree add def
    closepath gsave 0 0 0 c setcmykcolor
    fill grestore 1 1 1 1 setcmykcolor stroke
}forall
}def
% =======================================
```

The next routine that is unique to the pie-chart program is the *showpercent* subroutine. This routine positions and shows the percentage of the slice being drawn. This routine is executed every time a new slice is drawn, because it is dependent upon the current location and values.

The first objective in this routine is to find the center of a slice. The same construct of operators and definitions that was used to draw the original pie slice is used here, but this time the *arc* is pathed only half the distance. Note the insertion of the division operator. Once at the halfway point, the current location is requested from the interpreter, so that I can determine whether the label should print to the left or the right of the pie chart.

The *currentpoint* operator returns the *x* and *y* coordinates and pushes them onto the stack. Now that those numbers are on the stack, we can grab them and use them as definitions, as I have done in the next line.

In the next block of code, an *ifelse* operator queries if the *x* location is greater than zero. If so, it will draw the label to the right. If not, it draws the label to the left.

```
% =========================================
/showpercent
  { gsave newpath 0 0 moveto
    0 0 rad cumang cumang degree 2 div add
    arcn currentpoint
    /y exch def /x exch def
    x 0 gt {newpath x y moveto rm y lineto
          stroke rm 6 add y moveto
          pieslice num cvs show}
         {newpath x y moveto lm y lineto
          stroke lm 6 sub y moveto
          pieslice num cvs rightshow}ifelse
          grestore
  }def
% =========================================
```

Finally, in the script, the color separator is informed that the black values are to be printed. The *x* and *y* coordinates for the location translation are provided, as well as the pie radius, the right and left margins for label alignment, and the definition of the label font.

```
% =========================================
K colorbreaks
/transx 300 def /transy 400 def
/rad 150 def
/rm rad 20 add def
/lm rm neg def
/Helvetica-Bold findfont 10 scalefont setfont
```

Further along in the script, an empty string is defined to accept the converted pie-slice values into percent labels. The line width and miter limit are defined, and the actual *x* and *y* translation is performed. These coordinates have been defined so that we may reverse the process later.

```
/num 6 string def
1 setlinewidth
2 setmiterlimit
transx transy translate
```

The array of numbers to be defined as *piearray* is marked with a bracket. Each gray fill value, combined with its percentage of the pie, is also contained in brackets. The package of all slices is then completed when the right bracket is pushed onto the stack. This array is followed by the *pies* routine call, which will pick it up and process the data.

```
[
[.6 60]
[.3 12]
[0 10]
[.3 8]
[.6 5]
[1 5]] pies
```

After the *piearray*, the location is *translate*d back to the origin so that all page identifiers, crop marks, and registration marks can be properly placed. Added to these final lines is the */#copies* definition. This is a number-of-copies "request button" that is sent to the interpreter, telling it, in this case, to print two copies of each page from now on. Note that I said, "from now on." The printer will continue to print two copies of everything until it is told otherwise, reset, or turned off.

```
transx neg transy neg translate
40 700 moveto
(FIG5-22.PS   Gerard Kunkel   1:01PM   12/31/1988)show
/#copies 2 def
showpage
clear
```

5.8.1 Which Slice Is Which?

Figure 5–22 was certainly a simple pie chart. I created it specifically to show how a mechanism for creating a pie chart would be constructed. What was lacking in that chart was a set of labels to tell you what all of those percentages were.

There are a couple of ways to go about placing text inside this graphic. You could locate each label individually, move there, and show the label. Or, as I have done in the initial drawing of the percent labels, you can let the code automatically determine where each label is to be placed.

In Figure 5–23, the pie chart has text labels added to the percent labels. Since the script is (proportionate) the "tail wagging the dog," let's look at what modifications have been done to the "tail" of this program.

```
% =======================================
K colorbreaks pop pop
/transx 300 def /transy 400 def
/rad 150 def
/rm rad 20 add def
/lm rm neg def
/Helvetica-Bold findfont 10 scalefont setfont
/num 6 string def
```

```
1 setlinewidth
2 setmiterlimit
transx transy translate
[
[(Balloons).6 60]
[(Hats).3 12]
[(Favors)0 10]
[(Table Cloths).3 8]
[(Napkins).6 5]
[(Utensils)1 5]] pies
transx neg transy neg translate
40 700 moveto
(FIG5-23.PS     Gerard Kunkel   1:06PM   12/31/1988)show
showpage
```

There have been only two modifications here. The first is obvious: the text labels have been added to the *piearray* contained in parenthesis, delimiting them as text string objects. The other modification is the change to the prologue routines *showpercent* and *pies*. Both routines have had references to the labels added to them.

In the *forall* loop within the *pies* routine, the new label is exchanged and defined as *Name*. It is placed within the loop so that each label for each plot is redefined into the *Name* label.

```
piearray
    {/slicearray exch def
     slicearray aload pop
     /pieslice exch def
     /degree pieslice 100 div 360 mul def
     /c exch def
     /Name exch def
     newpath 0 0 moveto
     0 0 rad cumang cumang degree add
     arc showpercent
     /cumang cumang degree add def
     closepath gsave 0 0 0 c setcmykcolor
     fill grestore 1 1 1 1 setcmykcolor stroke
}forall
```

The *showpercent* routine has a number of modifications made to its *ifelse* operations. The first true operation has the *Name* object followed by a space, then the converted pie-slice value, and finally a percent sign. Since the true operation of this *ifelse* question prints from left to right, no special placements are necessary. The objects can print one after the other. To adjust the awkward space left between the converted pie-slice number and the percent sign, reduce the value of *num* in its initial definition. In this program it has a value of 6, but only two spaces are necessary or desirable. Try this modification and adjust as desired.

```
% =======================================
/showpercent
  { gsave newpath 0 0 moveto
    0 0 rad cumang cumang degree 2 div add
    arcn currentpoint
    /y exch def /x exch def
    x 0 gt {newpath x y moveto rm y lineto
            stroke rm 6 add y moveto
            Name show ( )show pieslice num cvs show
            (%)show}
```

The second half of the *ifelse* operation also prints its text from left to right, but it must move to the right to fit in front of the left-hand pointer. In the original example, the width of the converted pie-slice value was calculated with a generic *mr* routine. This routine uses the *stringwidth* operator to return the width and height of the text string currently on the top of the stack. The height is thrown away with a quick *pop*. The next number on the stack, the width, is used as part of the math to move (relatively) to the left using the *rmoveto* operator.

So when the additional label information is added to the mix, each text string and number is passed through the *mr* routine to move the current point to the left by that width.

Once we are at the final point, we can then *show* the name, space, number, and percent sign.

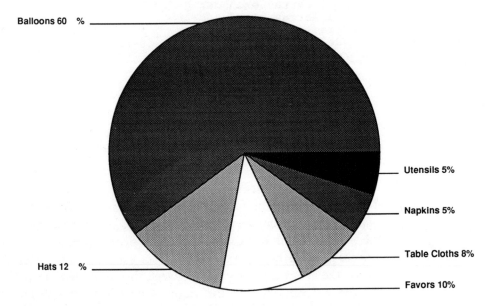

Figure 5—23

```
                    {newpath x y moveto lm y lineto
                    stroke lm 6 sub y moveto
                    pieslice num cvs
                    Name mr ( )mr num mr (%)mr
                    Name show ( )show num show (%)show}ifelse
                    grestore
            }def
%  ========================================
```

The complete listing of modified prologue and script for Figure 5–23:

```
%  ========================================
/pies      % array of pie slices
   {/piearray exch def
    /cumang 0 def

    piearray
    {/slicearray exch def
    slicearray aload pop
     /pieslice exch def
     /degree pieslice 100 div 360 mul def
     /c exch def
     /Name exch def
     newpath 0 0 moveto
     0 0 rad cumang cumang degree add
     arc showpercent
     /cumang cumang degree add def
     closepath gsave 0 0 0 c setcmykcolor
     fill grestore 1 1 1 1 setcmykcolor stroke
}forall
}def
%  ========================================
/showpercent
   { gsave newpath 0 0 moveto
     0 0 rad cumang cumang degree 2 div add
     arcn currentpoint
     /y exch def /x exch def
     x 0 gt {newpath x y moveto rm y lineto
             stroke rm 6 add y moveto
             Name show ( )show pieslice num cvs show
             (%)show}
            {newpath x y moveto lm y lineto
             stroke lm 6 sub y moveto
             pieslice num cvs
             Name mr ( )mr num mr (%)mr
             Name show ( )show num show (%)show}ifelse
             grestore
   }def
%  ========================================
K colorbreaks pop pop
/transx 300 def /transy 400 def
/rad 150 def
/rm rad 20 add def
```

```
/lm rm neg def
/Helvetica-Bold findfont 10 scalefont setfont
/num 6 string def
1 setlinewidth
2 setmiterlimit
transx transy translate
[
[(Balloons).6 60]
[(Hats).3 12]
[(Favors)0 10]
[(Table Cloths).3 8]
[(Napkins).6 5]
[(Utensils)1 5]] pies
transx neg transy neg translate
40 700 moveto
(FIG5-23.PS    Gerard Kunkel   1:06PM  12/31/1988)show
showpage
```

5.8.2   Faking Some Dimension

Figure 5–24 takes the same pie chart and scales it to become an elliptical pie chart.

```
% =======================================
K colorbreaks pop pop
1 .7 scale
/transx 300 def /transy 400 def
/rad 150 def
/rm rad 20 add def
/lm rm neg def
/Helvetica-Bold findfont 10 scalefont setfont
```

The *scale* operator allows us to take the perfect-circle pie and fake perspective. The values calculated for the original flat pie remain intact; only the appearance changes. The *x*, or width, of the *scale* operator is 1, leaving the width of the pie unchanged. The *y*, or height, is .7, rendering a compressed image.

5.8.3   Cleaning up the Labels

In Figure 5–24 the pie chart looks fairly good when scaled into an elliptical pie. The page identifier and chart labels, however, have been altered right

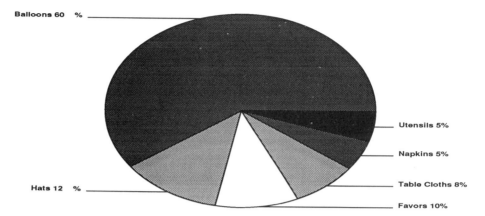

Figure 5—24

along with the pie. Since the *scale* operator can't selectively scale one object and not another, we must tell it which ones to scale.

The script for Figure 5–25, shown below, performs a *gsave* and a *grestore* around the pie-drawing operations, thereby segregating them from the rest. The *scale* operator appears within the *gsave* nest so that the pie is distorted. In this example, the page identification remains outside the *gsave* nest and prints in its normal position at its normal character height.

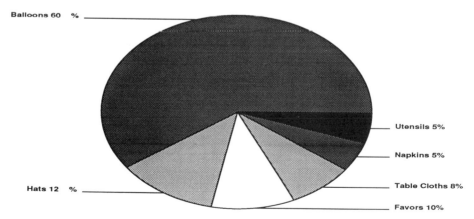

Figure 5—25

```
% =====================================
K colorbreaks pop pop
gsave
1 .7 scale
/transx 300 def /transy 400 def
/rad 150 def
/rm rad 20 add def
/lm rm neg def
/Helvetica-Bold findfont 10 scalefont setfont
/num 6 string def
1 setlinewidth
2 setmiterlimit
transx transy translate
[
[(Balloons).6 60]
[(Hats).3 12]
[(Favors)0 10]
[(Table Cloths).3 8]
[(Napkins).6 5]
[(Utensils)1 5]] pies
transx neg transy neg translate
grestore
40 700 moveto
(FIG5-25.PS    Gerard Kunkel   1:14PM  12/31/1988)show
showpage
```

Zipping right along, Figure 5–26 fixes more of the problems by adjusting the labels within the pie-drawing routines. This is accomplished by changing the font matrix with the *makefont* operator. This operator accepts a six-element array as its input. The array

```
[24 0 0 24 0 0]
```

makes a 24-point font. When you want or need to distort the typeface, the first and fourth elements can change the *x* and *y* relationships respectively. The array

```
[24 0 0 48 0 0]
```

creates a face that is 24 points wide and 48 points tall. This method of typeface modification is used in Figure 5–26 to reverse the effect of the pie scaling. What I have done here is to set up a definition for both *x* and *y* scaling so that they may be used with the *scale* operator and also used in calculating the proper font distortion. Two new routines have been introduced to handle this.

The first, *Setscale*, has been created to set up the scaling definitions.

```
% =====================================
/Setscale {/scaley exch def /scalex exch def
          scalex scaley scale}def
% =====================================
```

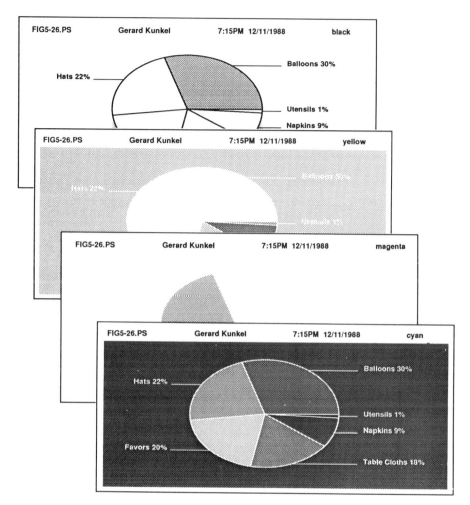

Figure 5—26

This routine exchanges the two values for *x* and *y* scaling from the script, applies object names, and then uses them with the *scale* operator to set up the distortions for the pie chart.

Gettype sets up the fonts for use in the graphic. In this routine, the *makefont* matrix is an array of absolute numbers, object variables, and math operators. The point size is determined by the amount of distortion from the desired point size. In this case, *ps*, defined as 8, is used directly inside the font matrix definition. Two other objects are defined before the font is made and set. *Percenx* and *perceny* are defined as the amount of distortion from a normal scaling. In the font matrix definition, *ps* is multiplied by *percenx* and *perceny* to place the final distorted values on the stack.

```
% =======================================
/Gettype {/ps 8 def
    /percenx 1 scalex sub 1 add def
    /perceny 1 scaley sub 1 add def
    /Helvetica-Bold findfont
    [ps percenx mul 0 0 ps perceny mul 0 0 ]
    makefont setfont}def
% =======================================
```

With these two routines set in place, any variation on the scaling factor will be automatically compensated for in the typeface calls. If you desire a much narrower pie chart, you will not need to experiment and adjust the fonts for the labels.

Two other changes have been made to Figure 5–26 that make it a much more interesting chart. A background tint and a shadow under the pie enhance the chart, again without distorting the data.

```
% =======================================
/Background {C1 M1 Y1 0 setcmykcolor
    llx lly moveto llx ury lineto
    urx ury lineto urx lly lineto
    closepath fill}def
% =======================================
/Shadow {/g .05 def /shadrad rad def
    9{newpath 0 -30 moveto
    0 -30 shadrad 0 360 arc
    closepath C1 M1 Y1 g setcmykcolor fill
    /g g .1 add def
    /shadrad shadrad 2 sub def}repeat
}def
% =======================================
```

The *Background* routine takes the color definitions set up in the script and fills a simple box for the background. Black is set to zero so that the shadow applied in the next routine can have a smooth transition from background to deep shadow. *Shadow* sets up a shadow that is equal in size to the pie chart to be layered on top of it. Nine separate fills are used, each with a darker percentage of black and two points smaller in size, to create the illusion of a soft-edge shadow. The *Background* and *Shadow* routines are executed within the scaled nest of commands. This coordinates the size and shape of the shadow to the pie.

Color is defined throughout this figure, and the color specifications are transferred from the script to the routines as each slice, the background, and shadow are drawn. The colors for the pie slices could be generated automatically, incremented from a single base or randomly. I prefer to specify my colors individually to add selective impact to important slices.

The complete listing for Figure 5–26:

```
%%Title: Piechart GK
%%CreationDate: 1:43PM  12/31/1988
%%Creator: Gerard Kunkel
%%BoundingBox 0 0 612 792
% PostScript routine to draw elliptical pie charts
/seps 24 dict def
 seps begin
        /pickcolor [
        {pop pop pop 1 exch sub setgray}
        {pop pop exch pop 1 exch sub setgray}
        {pop 3 1 roll pop pop 1 exch sub setgray}
        {4 1 roll pop pop pop 1 exch sub setgray}
        ]def
        /angles [105 75 90 45]def          % cmyk
screenangles
   end

   /C 0 def
   /M 1 def
   /Y 2 def
   /K 3 def
   /colorbreaks {
        userdict begin
        dup seps /pickcolor get exch get
        /setcmykcolor exch def
        seps /angles get exch get
        currentscreen
        exch pop 3 -1 roll exch
        setscreen
        /setscreen {}def
        end
}bind def
% =======================================
/mr {dup stringwidth pop neg 0 rmoveto}def
% =======================================
/showpercent
   { 0 0 0 1 setcmykcolor
     gsave .5 setlinewidth
     newpath 0 0 moveto
     0 0 rad cumang cumang degree 2 div add
     arcn currentpoint
     /y exch def /x exch def
     x 0 gt {newpath x y moveto rm y lineto
             stroke rm 6 add y moveto
             Name show ( )show pieslice num cvs show
             (%)show}
            {newpath x y moveto lm y lineto
             stroke lm 6 sub y moveto
             pieslice num cvs
             Name mr num mr (%)mr
             Name show ( )show num show (%)show}ifel:
             grestore
   }def
% =======================================
```

```
/pies       % array of pie slices
  {/piearray exch def
   /cumang 0 def

   piearray
   {/slicearray exch def
   slicearray aload pop
    /pieslice exch def
    /degree pieslice 100 div 360 mul def
    /K1 exch def
    /Y1 exch def
    /M1 exch def
    /C1 exch def
    /Name exch def
    newpath 0 0 moveto
    0 0 rad cumang cumang degree add
    arc showpercent
    /cumang cumang degree add def
    closepath gsave C1 M1 Y1 K1 setcmykcolor
    fill grestore 0 0 0 1 setcmykcolor stroke
}forall
}def
% =========================================
/Gettype {/ps 8 def
    /percenx 1 scalex sub 1 add def
    /perceny 1 scaley sub 1 add def
    /Helvetica-Bold findfont
    [ps percenx mul 0 0 ps perceny mul 0 0 ]
    makefont setfont}def
% =========================================
/Setscale {/scaley exch def /scalex exch def
        scalex scaley scale}def
% =========================================
/Background {C1 M1 Y1 0 setcmykcolor
    llx lly moveto llx ury lineto
    urx ury lineto urx lly lineto
    closepath fill}def
% =========================================
/Shadow {/g .05 def /shadrad rad def
    9{newpath 0 -30 moveto
    0 -30 shadrad 0 360 arc
    closepath C1 M1 Y1 g setcmykcolor fill
    /g g .1 add def
    /shadrad shadrad 2 sub def}repeat
}def
% =========================================
/names {/namearray exch def}def
% =========================================
/F {findfont exch scalefont setfont} def
% =========================================
/idpage
  {/colr exch def 1 1 1 1 setcmykcolor
  8 /Helvetica-Bold F
  90 645 moveto
  namearray {show 50 0 rmoveto}forall
  colr show .5 setlinewidth
```

```
    80 655 moveto 0 -15 rlineto 500 0 rlineto
    0 15 rlineto closepath stroke
    registerpage
    30 63 translate
    cropmarks
    -30 -63 translate
    }def
    % ==================================
    /regmarks
      {.7 setlinewidth
      /ymark exch def
      /xmark exch def
      /Helvetica findfont 5 scalefont setfont
      xmark 10 sub ymark 32 sub moveto 90 rotate
      (LUCHAK COMMUNICATIONS) show -90 rotate
      newpath
        xmark ymark 10 add moveto
        xmark ymark 10 sub lineto closepath stroke
      newpath
        xmark 10 sub ymark moveto
        xmark 10 add ymark lineto stroke
        xmark ymark 5 0 360 arc stroke
    }def
    % ==================================
    /registerpage
     {80 640 regmarks
     80 120 regmarks
     532 120 regmarks
     532 640 regmarks}def
    % ==================================
    /cropmarks {1 setlinewidth
       /width 549 def
       /height 666 def
       0 6 sub 0 m
       0 30 sub 0 l stroke
       0 0 6 sub m
       0 0 30 sub l stroke

       0 6 sub height m
       0 30 sub height l stroke
       0 height 6 add m
       0 height 30 add l stroke

       width 6 add 0 m
       width 30 add 0 l stroke
       width 0 6 sub m
       width 0 30 sub l stroke

       width 6 add height m
       width 30 add height l stroke
       width height 6 add m
       width height 30 add l stroke
    }def
    % ==================================
/drawpage {gsave
1 .7 Setscale
```

```
Gettype
/transx 300 def /transy 400 def
/rad 80 def
/rm rad 20 add def
/lm rm neg def
/num 2 string def
1 setlinewidth
2 setmiterlimit
transx transy translate
/llx -200 def /lly -200 def
/urx 200 def /ury 200 def
/C1 .6 def /M1 0 def /Y1 .1 def
Background
Shadow
[[(Balloons).5 0 0 .2 30]
[(Hats).3 .2 0 0 22]
[(Favors).1 .4 0 0 20]
[(Table Cloths).4 .4 .1 0 18]
[(Napkins).6 .2 .4 0 9]
[(Utensils).8 0 .2 0 1]] pies
transx neg transy neg translate
grestore
40 700 moveto
1 1 Setscale
Gettype
[(FIG5-26.PS)(Gerard Kunkel)(7:15PM   12/11/1988)]names
}def

K colorbreaks
(black) idpage
drawpage
save showpage restore
C colorbreaks
(cyan) idpage
drawpage
save showpage restore
M colorbreaks
(magenta) idpage
drawpage
save showpage restore
Y colorbreaks
(yellow) idpage
drawpage
save showpage restore
clear grestore
```

5.8.4   Putting Some Dimension into the Background

The Figure 5–27, there is a simple modification to the background. The *Background* routine has been replaced with a routine for a graduated color background. This routine accepts eight colors, four coordinates, and one Boolean operator as its arguments. The complete description of this routine appears in chapter 6.

```
% =====================================
/grad
  {/ud e d
   /k1 e d /y1 e d /m1 e d /c1 e d
   /k2 e d /y2 e d /m2 e d /c2 e d
   /ury e d /urx e d /lly e d /llx e d
   ud{/range ury lly s d}
     {/range urx llx s d}ifelse
   /cgrad c2 c1 s range div d
   /mgrad m2 m1 s range div d
   /ygrad y2 y1 s range div d
   /kgrad k2 k1 s range div d
   1.1 setlinewidth
   c1 m1 y1 k1 setcmykcolor
ud{range{llx lly m urx lly l
     stroke /lly lly 1 a d grada}repeat}
   {range{llx lly m llx ury l
     stroke /llx llx 1 a d grada}repeat}ifelse}d
% =====================================
/grada {c1 m1 y1 k1 setcmykcolor
  /c1 c1 cgrad a d /m1 m1 mgrad a d
  /y1 y1 ygrad a d /k1 k1 kgrad a d}d
% =====================================
```

The script portion of Figure 5–27 has been modified to accommodate the addition of the *grad* routine.

```
% =====================================
/drawpage {gsave
100 150 500 420 .5 0 .6 .3 .1 .5 .6 0 true grad
1 .7 Setscale
Gettype
...etc.
```

5-9   Creating a Scatter Diagram

Like the other chart and graph types, the scatter diagram is data-dependent. The *x* and *y* values used to plot the scatter diagram usually

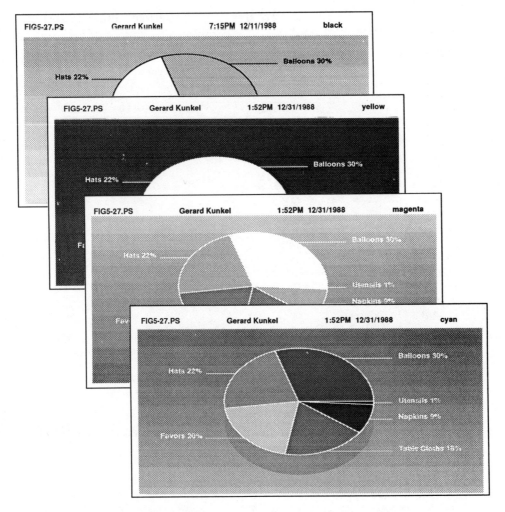

Figure 5—27

represent two qualified data sets that are logically comparable. An example of a useful scatter diagram would be the plotting of horsepower to price for a car. If horsepower were plotted from top to bottom on the grid and price were plotted from left to right, the upper-left quadrant of the diagram would show the most power for the least price. The lower right would show the least power and the greatest expense.

As you can see in Figure 5–28, the cluster of bullets within the grid is basically a confusing smattering of dots unless labels and descriptives are applied. Figure 5–28 illustrates a bare-bones scatter-plotting procedure, like the one I did at the beginning of this chapter to illustrate proper scaling techniques.

In a scatter diagram, both *x* and *y* values are needed to plot points. In previous chart and graph types, only one value was needed; the other axis was derivative of the number of points to be plotted.

Since we are changing the way that we provide data to the program, I have brought the graphic back to basics to create the groundwork for some more elaborate examples later on.

```
%!PS-Adobe 2.0
%%Title: ScatterPlot fig 5-28
%%CreationDate: 21:57PM  1/18/1989
%%Creator: Gerard Kunkel
%%BoundingBox 0 0 612 792
%%EndComments

%%BeginProlog
% =====================================
/PageSet
      {/ury exch def
       /urx exch def
       /lly exch def
       /llx exch def
       /gridwidth urx llx sub def
       /gridheight ury lly sub def
       /ylines exch def
       /xlines exch def
       /ymax exch def
       /ymin exch def
       /xmax exch def
       /xmin exch def
       /ygridnum ymax ymin sub ylines
           idiv def
       /xgridnum xmax xmin sub xlines
           idiv def
       /xfactor gridwidth
           xmax xmin sub div def
       /yfactor gridheight
           ymax ymin sub div def
       /xincrement xgridnum xfactor mul def
       /yincrement ygridnum yfactor mul def
       1 setlinewidth
       0 setgray
       3 setmiterlimit}def

%========================
/rightshow {dup stringwidth pop
      neg 0 rmoveto show}def
%========================
/centershow {dup stringwidth pop
      2 div neg 0 rmoveto show}def
%========================
/SimpleYGrid
```

```
    (/ygrid lly def
     /num 3 string def
     /scnum ymin def
     ylines 1 add {
     llx ygrid moveto
     llx gridwidth add
        ygrid lineto stroke
     llx 6 sub ygrid moveto
        scnum dup num cvs rightshow
     /ygrid ygrid yincrement add def
     /scnum scnum ygridnum add def)repeat
     }def
%==========================
/SimpleXGrid
    (/xgrid llx def
     /scnum xmin def
     xlines 1 add {
     xgrid lly moveto
     xgrid lly gridheight add lineto stroke
     xgrid lly 10 sub moveto
     scnum dup num cvs centershow
     /xgrid xgrid xincrement add def
     /scnum scnum xgridnum add def)repeat
     }def

%==========================
/ScatterData
        (/Dataarray exch def
         /datanum Dataarray length 2 idiv def
         Dataarray aload pop
         datanum {
            /y exch yfactor mul lly add def
            /x exch xfactor mul llx add def
            newpath
            x y moveto
            Drawmark
         }repeat)def

%==========================
/Drawmark
        {-2 2 rmoveto 0 -4 rlineto
        4 0 rlineto 0 4 rlineto closepath fill}def
%==========================
/idshow {
  50 440 moveto show
  50 430 moveto show
  50 420 moveto show}def


%==========================
%%EndProlog
%%BeginScript


%==========================

/Helvetica-Bold findfont 8 scalefont setfont
0 200 0 120 10 6 100 100 400 400 PageSet
```

```
SimpleYGrid
SimpleXGrid
[34 45 56 34 123 84 95 56 67 22] ScatterData
(FIG5-28.PS)
(Gerard Kunkel)
(21:12PM  1/19/1989)idshow

showpage
clear
```

Going routine by routine:

PageSet pulls a long set of numbers off the stack and uses them to determine the width and height of the graphic, as well as to calculate the scaling factors for plotting. For easier reference, I have brought the routine call up from the script portion of the program.

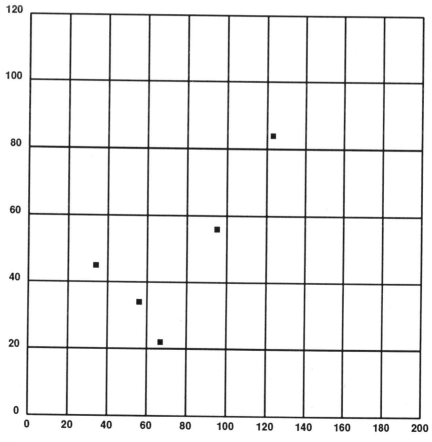

Figure 5—28

The number of gridlines is exchanged and defined as *ylines* for the left side scale, or *x*. *xlines* exchanges the number of gridlines for the bottom scale, or *y*.

Both bottom- and top-of-scale numbers are exchanged for the left and bottom scales: *ymax, ymin, xmax, xmin*. In this example, the left scale ranges from 0 to 120, and the bottom ranges from 0 to 200. These values are used in determining the scaling factors and in plotting the scale numbers on the grid.

The objects *ygridnum* and *xgridnum* calculate the value of the scale increments for each scale. For instance, the left scale ranges from 0 to 120, and we have pushed the number 6 onto the stack to define *ylines*. That means that *xgridnum* subtracts 0 from 120 and divides the result by 6. The *idiv* operator is used to divide so that the product is an integer. Since we use the value of *ylines* in a *repeat* loop, we must provide an integer, not a real number.

The scaling factors, *yfactor*, are defined as the height divided by the result of subtracting the bottom from the top value. The same applies for the *xscalegrid*, using the width, left, and right values.

Finally, *xincrement* and *yincrement* are calculated to use in drawing the gridlines. *Xgridnum* and *ygridnum* are multiplied by their respective scaling factors to produce the correct spacing between each gridline.

The remainder of the *PageSet* routine is housekeeping material.

```
% =======================================
/PageSet
    {/ury exch def
    /urx exch def
    /lly exch def
    /llx exch def
    /gridwidth urx llx sub def
    /gridheight ury lly sub def
    /ylines exch def
    /xlines exch def
    /ymax exch def
    /ymin exch def
    /xmax exch def
    /xmin exch def
    /ygridnum ymax ymin sub ylines
        idiv def
    /xgridnum xmax xmin sub xlines
        idiv def
    /xfactor gridwidth
        xmax xmin sub div def
    /yfactor gridheight
        ymax ymin sub div def
    /xincrement xgridnum xfactor mul def
    /yincrement ygridnum yfactor mul def
```

```
       1 setlinewidth
       0 setgray
       3 setmiterlimit)def
%  =======================================
0 200 0 120 10 6 100 100 400 400 PageSet
%  =======================================
```

You can take a deep breath now. I know that was quite a bit to cram into one routine, but it is all relative and is best described and put out of the way. It gets easier from here on.

After *PageSet*, two generic routines are inserted to place the left-side scale numbers and bottom scale numbers accurately. *Rightshow* and *centershow* have appeared in many other programs, and if you have gone from front to back in this book, you will have these memorized by now.

```
%==========================
/rightshow (dup stringwidth pop
      neg 0 rmoveto show)def
%==========================
/centershow (dup stringwidth pop
      2 div neg 0 rmoveto show)def
%==========================
```

The routine *SimpleYGrid* draws the grid lines that extend from left to right and positions the scale numbers to the left of those lines. Since this routine relies on increments in locations and values, two new objects have been created to accept the incremental values. The distance between each gridline is equal to *yincrement*. An object called *ygrid* is defined with the base value of the grid, *gridlly*. Each time the operation within *SimpleYGrid* is repeated, *ygrid* is increased by the value of *yincrement*.

The same holds true for the scale numbers. *Scnum* is first defined as *ymin*, the bottom value on the scale, as exchanged from the script. This value is also increased during each repetition of the operation and is converted to a string value prior to showing it on the page. Note the inclusion of the definition of *num*, an empty string three characters in length.

```
%==========================
/SimpleYGrid
    {/ygrid lly def
     /num 3 string def
     /scnum ymin def
     ylines 1 add {
     llx ygrid moveto
     llx gridwidth add
       ygrid lineto stroke
     llx 6 sub ygrid moveto
       scnum dup num cvs rightshow
```

```
/ygrid ygrid yincrement add def
/scnum scnum ygridnum add def}repeat
}def
```
%==========================

Now things are really getting simple. *SimpleXGrid* is constructed exactly the same way as *SimpleYGrid*. The only changes are that all of the x-relative objects have been replaced by y-relative objects.

```
%==========================
/SimpleXGrid
    {/xgrid llx def
    /scnum xmin def
    xlines 1 add {
    xgrid lly moveto
    xgrid lly gridheight add lineto stroke
    xgrid lly 10 sub moveto
    scnum dup num cvs centershow
    /xgrid xgrid xincrement add def
    /scnum scnum xgridnum add def}repeat
    }def

%==========================
```

ScatterData is where this program gets to be fun. The array of numbers that I set up in the script contained 10 elements, all integers. These numbers represent the *x,y* relative locations of the data. While these numbers are arbitrary, I will show later how to work with real numbers that apply to variable data types. As these numbers are shown, the first of two numbers represents the *x* value, and the second the *y* value.

This routine takes the entire array off the stack and defines it as *Dataarray*. The first operation that is performed is to measure the size of the array, divide it in two, and define the product as *datanum*. Note that the division is executed using the *idiv* operator and not just *div*. This returns an integer, which is necessary when applied to a *repeat* operator's use.

This array is *aload*ed onto the stack. The duplicate array that is also put on the stack by the *aload* operator is removed with the *pop* stack operator. Now we have all of our plotting numbers sitting on the stack waiting to be plucked off. The *repeat* operator will cycle through our process using *datanum* as the counter. This operation takes the *x* and *y* coordinates of the stack and multiplies them by our scaling factors, *xfactor* and *yfactor*. Those numbers then have the left and bottom values added to them for accurate placement.

Finally, a new path is set up, and *Drawmark* is called on to finish the plot task.

```
%==========================
/ScatterData
        {/Dataarray exch def
        /datanum Dataarray length 2 idiv def
        Dataarray aload pop
        datanum {
           /y exch yfactor mul lly add def
           /x exch xfactor mul llx add def
           newpath
           x y moveto
           Drawmark
        }repeat}def

%==========================
[34 45 56 34 123 84 95 56 67 22] ScatterData
```

The *Drawmark* routine starts from the *currentpoint* established in the *ScatterData* routine. By pulling the actual plot-point drawing routine out of the *ScatterData* routine, you can easily select and modify plot-point indicators. In this example I have chosen a simple four-point box.

```
%==========================
/Drawmark
        {-2 2 rmoveto 0 -4 rlineto
        4 0 rlineto 0 4 rlineto closepath fill}def
%==========================
```

In Figure 5–28, the boxes indicating the plot points are a bit small. Since this program is constructed in small bite-size fragments, the routine to draw a bullet can be modified to create a more attractive, easier-to-read bullet.

Figure 5–29 illustrates an alternate bullet treatment that is attained by modifying the *Drawmark* routine. The original *Drawmark* routine has been saved, and a new *Drawmark2* has taken its place. The new routine uses filled circles to come up with a dimensional appearance. Each new circle is drawn on top of the previous one in a descending order of both size and gray shade.

```
%==========================
/ScatterData
        {/Dataarray exch def
        /datanum Dataarray length 2 idiv def
        Dataarray aload pop
        datanum {
           /y exch yfactor mul lly add def
           /x exch xfactor mul llx add def
           newpath
           x y moveto
           Drawmark2
        }repeat}def
```

```
/Drawmark2
        (x y 8 0 360 arc fill
         .3 setgray
         x 1 sub y 6 0 360 arc fill
         .6 setgray
         x 2 sub y 4 0 360 arc fill
         .8 setgray
         x 3 sub y 2 0 360 arc fill
         0 setgray
}def
%=========================
```

Figure 5–30 offers up an interesting locator. *Drawmark3* is the new plot-point drawing routine. It draws a small dimensional box, instead of the more traditional bullet.

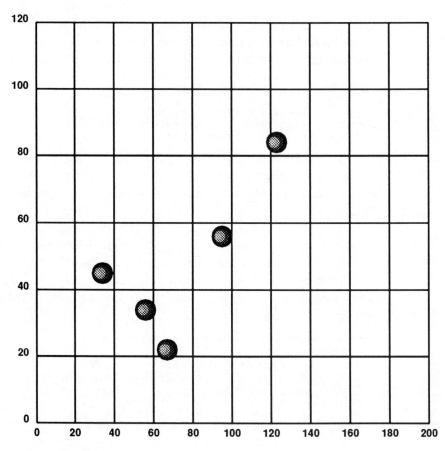

Figure 5—29

```
%===========================
/Drawmark3
        {x 7 sub y 7 sub moveto
        x 3 sub y 3 add lineto
        x 3 add y 3 add lineto
        x 7 add y 7 sub lineto
        closepath .8 setgray fill

        x 7 add y 7 add moveto
        x 3 add y 3 add lineto
        x 3 add y 3 sub lineto
        x 7 add y 7 sub lineto
        closepath 1 setgray fill
        x 7 sub y 7 sub moveto
        x 3 sub y 3 sub lineto
        x 3 add y 3 sub lineto
        x 7 add y 7 sub lineto
        closepath .7 setgray fill
        x 7 add y 7 add moveto
        x 3 add y 3 add lineto
        x 3 sub y 3 add lineto
        x 7 sub y 7 add lineto
        closepath .4 setgray fill
        x 7 sub y 7 add moveto
        x 3 sub y 3 add lineto
        x 3 sub y 3 sub lineto
        x 7 sub y 7 sub lineto
        closepath .1 setgray fill
        }def
%===========================
```

Although this is a lot of code, it is very fast and does not create any unnecessary dictionary items.

Figure 5–31 takes the same graphic and adds a few design considerations that enhance the readability of the graphic. By adjusting line weights, you can focus the reader's attention to the important areas of the diagram. For Figure 5–31, I have added a routine named *Quads*. This routine pulls no data off the stack; it merely uses the definitions already present in memory, put there by previous routines.

Quads adds a heavier outside line and heavy center lines that focus the reader on the four quadrants that are formed. When comparing *x* and *y* data, it is useful to be shown where the center is, to help compare values.

Since we have introduced various line weights, it becomes necessary to add a *setlinewidth* to the subsequent routine or, following the *Quads* routine, call in the script to set the proper line width for the *x* and *y* grid lines.

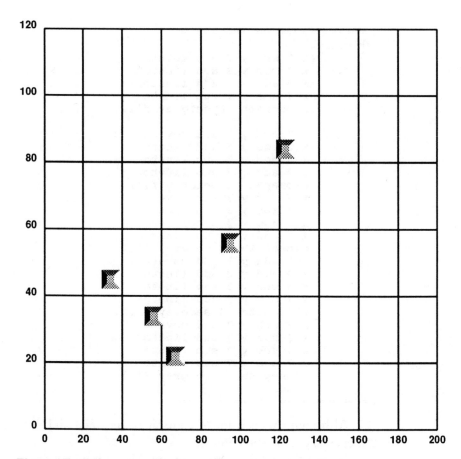

Figure 5—30

```
%============================
/Quads
     {1.6 setlinewidth
      llx lly moveto
      llx ury lineto
      urx ury lineto
      urx lly lineto
      closepath stroke
      llx gridwidth 2 div add
         lly moveto
      llx gridwidth 2 div add
        ury lineto stroke
      llx lly
        gridheight 2 div add moveto
      urx lly
        gridheight 2 div add lineto stroke
     }def
```

```
%==========================
/SimpleYGrid
     {.5 setlinewidth

...

%==========================
/Helvetica-Bold findfont 8 scalefont setfont
0 200 0 120 10 6 100 100 400 400 PageSet
Quads
SimpleYGrid
SimpleXGrid
[34 45 56 34 123 84 95 56 67 22 180 80 148 32]
ScatterData
(FIG5-31.PS)
(Gerard Kunkel)
(22:23PM  1/19/1989)idshow

showpage
```

5.9.1   Coming to Conclusions

In statistical analysis, a "best-fit" line might be calculated to represent a common relationship among data points. Linear or curvilinear lines may be calculated to best represent a result or, in business, a trend line. The formulas for plotting such a line are mathematical problems, not PostScript problems. To offer such a solution in this code would suggest my complete understanding of this area. Unfortunately, I have only enough knowledge in this area to be dangerous.

Once you have established a working scatter diagram and have determined where your origin will be, (possibly $\times = 0, y = 0$) the routine for calculating and drawing your line will be best placed before the *ScatterData* routine. I would suggest that, if you are going to plot such a line, the mathematics be performed in a spreadsheet and the data exported to your charting program.

5.9.2   What Are All Those Dots?

If you've come this far, you're almost at a complete graphic. However, this data is meaningless unless the *x*- and *y*-axes and plot points are defined. In Figure 5–32, I demonstrate how to plot and show a label for each data point. The logic here is to pass the text string along with the data, so that the two travel hand-in-hand and avoid any recalculation as a separate routine.

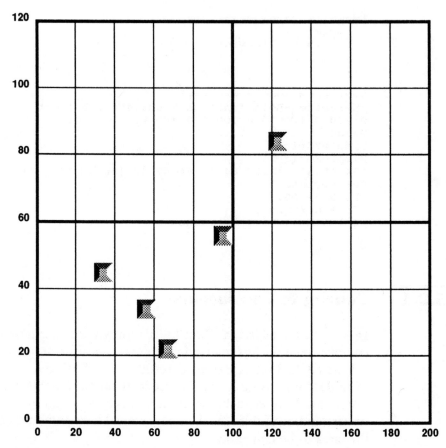

Figure 5–31

For this example, I am using generic labels to help you track the process. Since I have chosen to place each label above the data point, I can use the *x* and *y* coordinates and then add to or subtract from that location to show the label. Immediately after defining *x* and *y* in the *Dataarray* routine, the label can be shown.

The script for Figure 5–32 need only have the labels added to the *Dataarray* call.

```
%============================
/ScatterData
        {/Dataarray exch def
        /datanum Dataarray length 3 idiv def
        Dataarray aload pop
        datanum {/label exch def
          /y exch yfactor mul lly add def
          /x exch xfactor mul llx add def
          x y 10 add moveto label show
          newpath
```

```
        x y moveto
        Drawmark3
      }repeat)def
%=========================

/Helvetica-Bold findfont 8 scalefont setfont
0 200 0 120 10 6 100 100 400 400 PageSet
Quads
SimpleYGrid
SimpleXGrid
[34 45 (House A) 56 34 (House B)
123 84 (House C) 95 56 (House D)
67 22 (House E) 170 80 (House F)
148 32 (House G)] ScatterData
(FIG5-32.PS)
(Gerard Kunkel)
(21:12PM  1/19/1989)idshow

showpage
clear
```

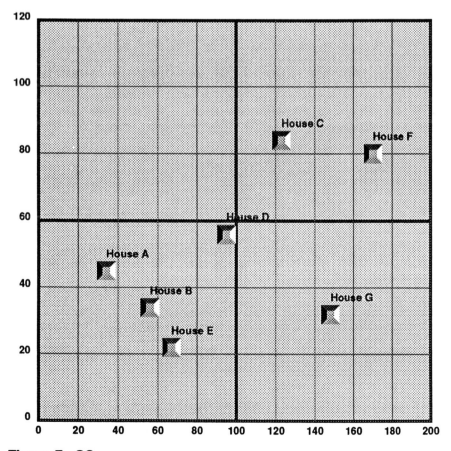

Figure 5—32

5.9.3   Completing the Picture

Figure 5–33 adds a third dimension of data. In this example, I chose to include the number of acres that the house sits on. This value is represented as the area of the circle centered on the plot point. To do this, I have modified both the *ScatterData* routine and the *Drawmark2* routine. The former now allows for a new definition, *Zemphasis*, which multiplies all of the plot circles by the same value to increase visibility. The latter draws a circle that is equal to the area (acreage) provided in the array.

```
%============================
/ScatterData
        {/Zemphasis exch def
        /Dataarray exch def
        /datanum Dataarray length 4 idiv def
        Dataarray aload pop
        datanum {/label exch def
          /y exch ygridscale mul
              botval ygridscale mul sub
              gridlly add def
          /x exch xgridscale mul
              leftval xgridscale mul sub
              gridllx add def
          /rad exch def
          x y rad add 2 add moveto label show
          newpath
          x y moveto
          Drawmark2
        }repeat}def

%==========================
/Drawmark2
        {1 setgray /z 1 def
         9 {x y rad sqrt 3.14 div Zemphasis mul
            z mul 0 360 arc fill
            1 z sub setgray /z z .05 sub def
           }repeat
         0 setgray
}def
%=========================
/Helvetica-Bold findfont 8 scalefont setfont
0 5000 100 200 10 10 100 100 400 400 PageSet
Quads
SimpleYGrid
SimpleXGrid
[2 1034 145 (House A) 1 1520 164 (House B)
10 1623 184 (House C) 4 1995 156 (House D)
5 3267 102 (House E) 14 4170 180 (House F)
2 2148 132 (House G)] 10 ScatterData
```

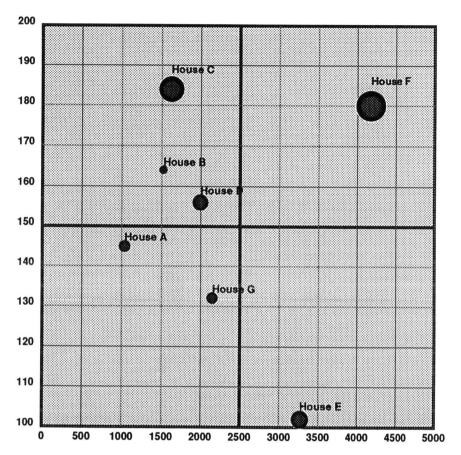

Figure 5—33

In the final version of this code, I have completed the labels for the axes. With all of the important dimensions defined up front in the *PageSet* routine, I can easily add other routines that rely on the coordinates named there.

For the *x* and *y* labels, I have used the *llx* and *lly* definitions to determine how far away the labels must be from the axes. I have also centered them on these axes, based on the width and height of the diagram. The *Xlabel* and *Ylabel* routines should be self-explanatory in their PostScript construct. The *Zlabel* routine simply locates the center of the width and adds 10 points to the height of the graphic to show the bullet size label.

For easy reference, the complete code for Figure 5–34 has been provided.

```
%!PS-Adobe 2.0
%%Title: ScatterPlot AverageLine fig 5-34
%%CreationDate: 5:22PM  1/22/1989
%%Creator: Gerard Kunkel
%%BoundingBox 0 0 612 792
%%EndComments

%%BeginProlog
% =====================================
/PageSet
     {/ury exch def
      /urx exch def
      /lly exch def
      /llx exch def
      /gridwidth urx llx sub def
      /gridheight ury lly sub def
      /ylines exch def
      /xlines exch def
      /ymax exch def
      /ymin exch def
      /xmax exch def
      /xmin exch def
      /ygridnum ymax ymin sub ylines
           idiv def
      /xgridnum xmax xmin sub xlines
           idiv def
      /xfactor gridwidth
           xmax xmin sub div def
      /yfactor gridheight
           ymax ymin sub div def
      /xincrement xgridnum xfactor mul def
      /yincrement ygridnum yfactor mul def
      .5 setlinewidth
      0 setgray
      3 setmiterlimit}def

%============================
/rightshow {dup stringwidth pop
      neg 0 rmoveto show}def
%============================
/centershow {dup stringwidth pop
      2 div neg 0 rmoveto show}def
%============================
/SimpleYGrid
     {.5 setlinewidth
      /ygrid lly def
      /num 9 string def
      /scnum ymin def
      ylines 1 add {
      .5 setgray
      llx ygrid moveto
      llx gridwidth add
        ygrid lineto stroke
```

```
            llx 6 sub ygrid moveto
            0 setgray scnum dup num cvs rightshow
            /ygrid ygrid yincrement add def
            /scnum scnum ygridnum add def)repeat
            )def
%==========================
/Ylabel {/label exch def
            llx lly moveto
            0 gridheight 2 div rmoveto
            label dup stringwidth pop
            90 rotate
            2 div neg 26 rmoveto
            show -90 rotate)def
%==========================
/SimpleXGrid
            {.5 setlinewidth
            /xgrid llx def
            /scnum xmin def
            xlines 1 add {
            .5 setgray
            xgrid lly moveto
            xgrid lly gridheight add lineto stroke
            xgrid lly 10 sub moveto
            0 setgray scnum dup num cvs centershow
            /xgrid xgrid xincrement add def
            /scnum scnum xgridnum add def)repeat
            )def
%==========================
/Xlabel {/label exch def
            llx lly moveto
            gridwidth 2 div 0 rmoveto
            label dup stringwidth pop
            2 div neg -24 rmoveto
            show )def
%==========================
/Zlabel {/label exch def
            llx ury moveto
            gridwidth 2 div 0 rmoveto
            label dup stringwidth pop
            2 div neg 10 rmoveto
            show )def
%==========================
/Quads
            {2 setlinewidth
            llx lly moveto
            llx ury lineto
            urx ury lineto
            urx lly lineto
            closepath gsave .9 setgray fill
            grestore stroke
            llx gridwidth 2 div add
              lly moveto
            llx gridwidth 2 div add
```

```
        ury lineto stroke
    llx lly
       gridheight 2 div add moveto
     urx lly
       gridheight 2 div add lineto stroke
     }def




%===========================
/ScatterData
        {/Zemphasis exch def
        /Dataarray exch def
        /datanum Dataarray length 4 idiv def

        %==================================
        % ROUTINE TO PLOT DATA
        %==================================
        Dataarray aload pop
        datanum {/label exch def
          /y exch yfactor mul ymin yfactor mul sub
              lly add def
          /x exch xfactor mul xmin xfactor mul sub
              llx add def
          /rad exch sqrt 3.14 div Zemphasis mul def
          x y rad add 2 add moveto label show
          newpath
          x y moveto
          Drawmark2
        }repeat}def

%===========================
/Drawmark2
        {1 setgray /z 1 def
         9 {x y rad z mul 0 360 arc fill
           1 z sub setgray /z z .05 sub def
          }repeat
         0 setgray
}def
%===========================
/idshow {
   50 440 moveto show
   50 430 moveto show
   50 420 moveto show}def


%===========================
%%EndProlog
%%BeginScript

%======= THE SCRIPT =========================
%======= SETUP PARAMETERS ===================
0 5000 100 200 10 10 100 100 400 400 PageSet
```

```
%======= DRAW QUADRANTS =====================
Quads

%======= DRAW Y GRID AND LABEL ==============
/Helvetica findfont 7 scalefont setfont
SimpleYGrid
/Helvetica-Bold findfont 11 scalefont setfont
(Yearly Real Estate and School Taxes)Ylabel

%======= DRAW X GRID AND LABEL ==============
/Helvetica findfont 7 scalefont setfont
SimpleXGrid
/Helvetica-Bold findfont 11 scalefont setfont
(Purchase Price in Thousands)Xlabel

%======= DRAW Z LABEL =======================
(Size of Bullet Indicates Amount of Acreage)Zlabel

%======= PLOT AND LABEL DATA ================
/Helvetica-Bold findfont 8 scalefont setfont
[7 2234 135 (House A) 8 520 164 (House B)
10 2023 124 (House C) 4 2995 186 (House D)
5 1267 102 (House E) 14 4170 110 (House F)
2 3148 155 (House G)] 10 ScatterData

%======= ID PAGE ============================
(FIG5-34.PS)
(Gerard Kunkel)
(4:27PM  1/22/1989)idshow

%======= SHOW AND CLEAR THE STACK ===========
showpage
clear
```

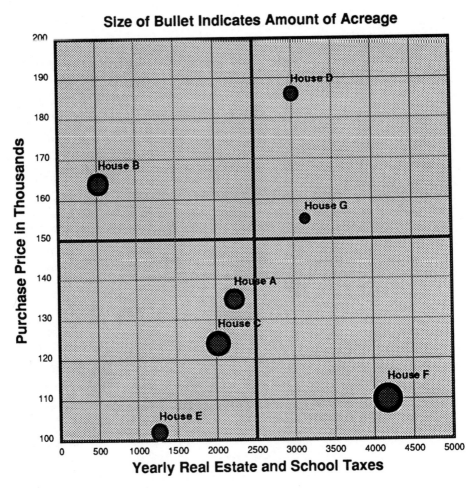

Figure 5—34

Color

6-1 Working in Color and Separating Color

This chapter of the book was the most interesting to prepare for, as well as the most challenging. To acquire enough knowledge in this area to write about it took about 12 years of working in conventional color preparation for printing, a comprehensive knowledge of the programming tools available in PostScript, constant interaction with other programmers, and about six months of trial and error. All in all, the six months of trial and error were the most fruitful.

As I have mentioned in other parts of this book, I am not what I would consider a programmer's programmer. A true programmer is someone who lives and breathes the language he or she uses. Tied to that lifestyle is a solid base of programming knowledge that crosses over into other languages. I feel that I have considerable knowledge in the PostScript language, but a limited knowledge in other languages. While all of the programs in this chapter, as well as other chapters, have been thoroughly tested and proven, they may not be judged well-structured by a seasoned programmer. In all of my programming efforts, I have been looking not for programming awards, but for practical solutions for the graphics community. I welcome any criticisms of my programming techniques or basic assumptions. After all, it is the sharing of ideas that advances the state of the art.

The programs that I present in this chapter are based on my working knowledge of color and substantial research into both color theory and PostScript control of color and screening. The knowledge of PostScript and pre-press color of several other professionals have been useful to me— namely, Michael Christie of Gerard Associates Phototypesetting, in New York; and Lloyd Shultz, Pre-press Operations Director at Ziff-Davis Publishing, also in New York. Both have been there to answer questions of detail that ultimately fit like pieces in a jigsaw puzzle, to complete the big picture.

It is important for you to understand that in all of the programming attempts for color output there was no screen display to help in the color selection process. Guesswork and color specification books were the only references available. A future project that I will undertake will be a rudimentary attempt to display the colors being selected in the PostScript output. This, however, requires the same amount of work as developing a complete software application.

The future promises a much easier working environment for Post-Script programmers. Display PostScript, the screen-display version of the page-description language, will allow you to write your text and graphics to the screen prior to printing. This should save reams of paper for you and provide a faster environment for both program and artwork development.

In this chapter I will show you how to work within PostScript's built-in color operators and also introduce you to the newer extended color operators that are present in a limited number of devices recently introduced to the market.

In the latter part of this chapter I will introduce a number of color separation techniques that have become my most treasured accomplishments.

Finally, I will discuss the use of color PostScript output devices and the Linotronic 300 as a color separation output device.

6-2   Color Models

PostScript is primarily a black-and-white programming environment. While it is true that operators exist for the red-green-blue (RGB) color model and the hue-saturation-brightness (HSB) color model, when push comes to shove PostScript talks in terms of black, white, and gray. Even in environments where color is being printed to paper from a PostScript file, it requires multiple passes of primary colors. The ink or wax being applied to the paper is merely a black-and-white image printed as color. It is the job of the interpreter in the output device to determine which pixels are to be painted on which color pass.

Let's look at the operators available in the most common PostScript-capable printing devices.

The first and most commonly used is the *setrgbcolor* operator. This operator is based on the red-green-blue color model, the same color model that is used in most computer graphics applications. This color model is prevalent due to its direct relationship to the color display that operates with subtractive color—black being zero illumination of any color and white being full illumination of all three colors. To use this operator, you must have three numbers on the stack prior to calling it. These numbers must all be between zero and one. The same applies for the HSB color operator. If you were looking for a solid red box specified with the RGB model, you would program the following.

```
1 0 0 setrgbcolor  % red
```

This line of code instructs the system to provide full intensity of red and no intensity of the other colors.

Choosing the same color in the HSB model would require the following line of code:

```
0 1 1 sethsbcolor  % red
```

Let's look at some other colors in both the RGB and the HSB models:

```
0 1 0 setrgbcolor      % green
0 0 1 setrgbcolor      % royal blue
.5 .5 .5 setrgbcolor   % medium gray
.33 0 0 sethsbcolor    % green
.66 0 0 sethsbcolor    % royal blue
0 .5 .5 sethsbcolor    % medium gray
```

6.2.1   RGB Color Array Output

The color plate, Figure C–1, shows the effect of creating a color array using *setrgbcolor* as the color operator. The following listing shows how it was created.

```
%!PS-Adobe 2.0 EPSF
%%Title: Color Tests
%%Creator: Gerard Kunkel
%%CreationDate: 3:44PM  3/1989
%%BoundingBox: 0 0 612 792

.4 setlinewidth
/box {x y moveto
x 10 add y lineto
x 10 add y 20 add lineto
x y 20 add lineto
closepath gsave fill grestore
0 0 0 setrgbcolor stroke}def

/drawscale{
  4{100 0 translate
  /b b .1 add def
  /r -0.1 def /g -0.1 def
    50 20 250 {/y exch def
     /g g .1 add def
     g 1 ge{/g 0 def}if
       100 10 200 {/x exch def
       /r r .1 add def
       r g b setrgbcolor
       r 1 gt{/r -0.1 def}if
     box}for
   }for
  }repeat
  -400 0 translate
}def
-100 0 translate
/b -0.1 def drawscale
0 200 translate
/b .3 def drawscale
0 200 translate
/b .7 def drawscale

showpage
```

6.2.2   HSB Color Array Output

The color plate, Figure C–2, shows the effect of creating a color array using *sethsbcolor* as the color operator. The following listing shows how it was created.

```
%!PS-Adobe 2.0 EPSF
%%Title: Color Tests
%%Creator: Gerard Kunkel
%%CreationDate: 3:44PM  3/1989
%%BoundingBox: 0 0 612 792
```

```
.4 setlinewidth
/box {x y moveto
x 10 add y lineto
x 10 add y 20 add lineto
x y 20 add lineto
closepath gsave fill grestore
0 0 0 sethsbcolor stroke}def

/drawscale{
  4{100 0 translate
  /b b .1 add def
  /r -0.1 def /g -0.1 def
    50 20 250 {/y exch def
     /g g .1 add def
     g 1 ge{/g 0 def}if
       100 10 200 {/x exch def
       /r r .1 add def
       r g b sethsbcolor
       r 1 gt{/r -0.1 def}if
     box}for
   }for
  }repeat
  -400 0 translate
}def
-100 0 translate
/b -0.1 def drawscale
0 200 translate
/b .3 def drawscale
0 200 translate
/b .7 def drawscale

showpage
```

6.2.3 A Printer's Color Model

Recently, Adobe introduced a specification for a third color model that directly addresses the printing and publishing trades. This model is based on the conventional color separation process, which produces four plates for printing. Each plate represents one of four printer's process colors: cyan, magenta, yellow, and black. This new operator, *setcmykcolor*, allows the programmer to specify each of the four process colors directly on the stack. The operator works like this:

```
0 1 1 0 setcmykcolor
```

This line of code sets the current CMYK color to red. In process colors, 100% magenta and 100% yellow combine to create solid red.

```
0 1 0 setrgbcolor           % green
0 0 1 setrgbcolor           % royal blue
.5 .5 .5 setrgbcolor        % medium gray
.33 0 0 sethsbcolor         % green
.66 0 0 sethsbcolor         % royal blue
0 .5 .5 sethsbcolor         % medium gray
1 0 1 0 setcmykcolor        % green
1 .6 0 0 setcmykcolor       % royal blue
0 0 0 .5 setcmykcolor       % medium gray

. . . or . . .

.5 .5 .5 0 setcmykcolor     % medium gray
```

6.2.4   CMYK Color Array Output

The color plate, Figure C–3, shows the effect of creating a color array using *setcmykcolor* as the color operator. The following listing shows how that was created.

```
%!PS-Adobe 2.0 EPSF
%%Title: Color Tests CMYK
%%Creator: Gerard Kunkel
%%CreationDate: 9:10PM  4/3/1989
%%BoundingBox: 0 0 612 792

% ----- a simple box drawing routine ---------------
.4 setlinewidth
/box {x y moveto
x 10 add y lineto
x 10 add y 10 add lineto
x y 10 add lineto
closepath gsave fill grestore
0 0 0 1 setcmykcolor stroke}def

% ----- the color palette drawing  routine ---------
/drawscale{
  4{100 0 translate           % move to starting
location
  /cyan cyan .1 add def        % increase cyan by 10%
  /mag -0.1 def
  /yel -0.1 def
  50 10 150 {/y exch def
    yel 1 lt{/yel yel .1 add def}
          {/yel 0 def}ifelse
      100 10 200 {/x exch def
      mag 1 lt{/mag mag .1 add def}
            {/mag 0 def}ifelse
```

```
        cyan mag yel k setcmykcolor
      box}for
    }for
  }repeat
  -400 0 translate
}def
/cyan 0 def
-100 0 translate
/k 0 def drawscale
0 100 translate
/k .1 def drawscale
0 100 translate
/k .2 def drawscale
0 100 translate
/k .3 def drawscale
0 100 translate
/k .4 def drawscale

showpage
```

It is important to note where you can apply the color instructions available in PostScript and where you should not use them.

6.2.5   Apple LaserWriter Family of Printers

This line of printers is used for black-and-white output only. However, they still make excellent proofing devices for color images, because the cost per print is pennies, while the cost per color print is a dollar or more. The limitation here is that these printers do not directly support the new extended color operators, *setcmykcolor* and *currentcmykcolor*. They do, however, interpret the RGB color model as levels of gray. The operators used here are *setrgbcolor* and *currentrgbcolor*. And, finally, they support the HSB color model with direct interpretation of *sethsbcolor* and *currenthsbcolor*.

If you are at all like me, you would still prefer to use the *setcmykcolor* operator. In my case, this is the color model that I grew up on. In the publishing field, color is typically defined by one or both of two models: CMYK (cyan, magenta, yellow, and black), or the Pantone Matching System (PMS).

In order to use this printer family to output black-and-white proofs of these full-color images, you must use the models directly supported by their own version of the PostScript interpreter—or write the necessary PostScript code to do the interpretation. The following code will interpret the *setcmykcolor* operator. It is important that this routine be downloaded into the printer prior to attempting to print any PostScript code that contains the *setcmykcolor* operator. Downloading can be accomplished with an off-the-shelf PostScript font downloader. This code can also be copied from the DOS command line utilizing the *copy* command. Simply copy the file to the port where the PostScript printer resides.

```
serverdict begin 0 exitserver

/cyan 0 def
/magenta 0 def
/yellow 0 def
/black 0 def

/setcmykcolor {
  /black exch def
  /yellow exch def
  /grayyellow yellow .2 mul def
  /magenta exch def
  /graymagenta magenta .4 mul def
  /cyan exch def
  /graycyan cyan .3 mul def

  /gray graycyan graymagenta add
    grayyellow add black add def

  gray 1 gt{/gray 1 def}if
  /gray gray 1 exch sub def

  gray systemdict begin setgray end

}def
```

The four values that are present on the stack before calling the *setcmykcolor* operator are taken off the stack and put in the dictionary by applying key names that represent their respective colors. Next, the three colors—cyan, magenta, and yellow—are reduced in preparation for conversion to gray. Each color has a different value based upon the relationship of its density to black's density.

```
/setcmykcolor {
/black exch def
/yellow exch def
/grayyellow yellow .2 mul def
/magenta exch def
/graymagenta magenta .4 mul def
/cyan exch def
/graycyan cyan .3 mul def
```

These new values are added together to come up with one gray value. The value of gray is checked to see if it is greater than one. If so, it is defined as one.

```
/gray graycyan graymagenta add
  grayyellow add black add def
```

```
gray 1 gt{/gray 1 def}if
```

That value is then inverted to fit within the guidelines of the *setgray* operator, and *setgray* is called.

```
/gray gray 1 exch sub def
gray systemdict begin setgray end
```

Creating a routine to accommodate *currentcmykcolor* is now very simple. Since key names have been defined for each of the four colors, we can call upon those definitions to acquire the current values.

```
/currentcmykcolor {
  cyan
  magenta
  yellow
  black
}def
```

This routine pushes the four values for cyan, magenta, yellow, and black onto the stack. These four numbers can then be used in other calculations. The complete downloadable file can be condensed and sent like this:

```
serverdict begin 0 exitserver
/cyn 0 def /mgnta 0 def /ylw 0 def /blk 0 def
/setcmykcolor {
  /blk exch def
  /ylw exch def /grayylw ylw .2 mul def
  /mgnta exch def /graymgnta mgnta .4 mul def
  /cyn exch def /graycyn cyn .3 mul def
  /gray graycyn graymgnta add grayylw add blk add def
  gray 1 gt{/gray 1 def}if
  /gray gray 1 exch sub def
  gray systemdict begin setgray end
}def
/currentcmykcolor {cyn mgnta ylw blk}def
```

6.2.6 Tektronix Phaser and QMS ColorScript Color PostScript Printing Systems

If you are using either one of these printers as the output device, you can print directly. Both of these printers interpret the extended color PostScript operators. If you are in a workgroup environment that has either of these printers and a black-and-white printer, such as the Apple LaserWriter, be sure to download the *setcmykcolor* interpreting routines into the Laser-Writer if you are specifying colors in CMYK.

6.2.7   Linotronic 100/300/500

The Linotronic laser typesetting systems can be thought of as highly sophisticated LaserWriters. They, too, do not support the newer extended color operators; so any file that is to be printed as a color separation, or color composite, will need the *setcmykcolor* operator or a color separation routine sent down prior to imaging the file. Simply sending the *setcmykcolor* interpreter will produce a black-and-white page of various gray levels. What you really need is separate pieces of paper or film output that represent what a printing shop will use for plates in the printing process.

Outputting multiple pages for multiple-color film will be covered later in this chapter. This is all possible from one PostScript file. In the meantime, let's look at the control that we have over the specification of color. Having a clear understanding of the generation of color within your PostScript code will help you understand what needs to happen on the output end when you send your file to a laser printer or typesetter.

6-3   Black Is a Color

The PostScript operator *setgray* should be very familiar by now. By implementing color into our graphics, we will actually be taking advantage of the *setgray* operator in major ways. Since *setgray* will play a role in any final color separations, I will take some time now to familiarize you with its varied uses.

We may redefine the *setgray* operator to suit our needs. For instance, we could put a limit on the range of gray values in our PostScript code. I can prevent the printer from outputting black by intercepting a black specification and redefining it as gray. This code can be downloaded into the printer so that all subsequent *setgray* calls will be redefined. This type of correction is in no way permanent or damaging. Resetting the system to its original values simply requires turning the printer off and restarting.

The following lines of PostScript code put a limit on the range of grays:

```
userdict begin
/setgray {dup dup
  0 eq{pop .1}if
  .5 ge
    {systemdict begin .7 mul setgray end}
    {systemdict begin 1.3 mul setgray end}
  ifelse
}def
end
```

This downloaded routine will allow only grays between routine .13 and .7 intensities to be printed.

We may also see the need to increase the percentage of gray from what was specified to what is actually printing. For instance, light grays, such as 10%, have no difficulty printing on an Apple LaserWriter at 300 dpi, but the Linotronic, at 1270 dpi, will actually produce a lighter gray. In some of my testing, a 2% gray was the product of a 10% specification.

To overcome this, we can use the *setgray* operator as the vehicle to adjust the gray value for our final output device, the Linotronic 300.

The following listing redefines *setgray* to allow for global gray-value adjustments. By multiplying the value by a fraction of itself, we can create a curve by which all *setgray* values are increased to compensate for printer inaccuracies. Since a value of one sent to the *setgray* operator is calling for white, that value is checked for first. If the test proves true, the computation is ignored.

```
userdict          % call user dictionary
begin             % push to top of dictionary stack
/setgray
  (dup 1 lt{      % if value is less than 1 then
    dup           % dup top value
    .1 mul        % multiply by .1
    sub           % subtract product from original value
  )if
  systemdict      % call system dictionary
  begin           % push to top of dictionary stack
  setgray         % set the gray value using new number
  end             % end use of system dictionary
  )def            % end procedure
end               % end use of user dictionary
```

6-4   Extended Color Operators

The color extensions recently added by Adobe to its PostScript language refer to the CMYK color model and match colors (which can be PMS). As if you could not tell by now, the CMYK color model is my favorite color model to work with. If you have a background in video, the RGB color model may be yours. Since we are looking at the production of images on paper or film, it makes sense to have a clear understanding of the CMYK color model. This model is the one used by printers when working in process colors.

The following is a list of color operators that you will find in full-color PostScript implementations. The most common, *setcmykcolor*, is used extensively in this book. For more information on these operators, refer to David Holzgang's book, *PostScript Programmer's Reference Guide*, published by Scott, Foresman and Company.

colorimage

width height bits/component matrix procedure [proc ncolors-1] multiproc ncolors colorimage

Like the image operator in previous releases of PostScript, the *colorimage* operator renders a sampled image. The difference here is the implementation of color. The bits/component value is the same as bits in the *image* operator. That value is applied to all colors being rendered. The procedure applied for the *colorimage* operator is actually a multiple of procedures that correspond to each of the colors being used—three for RGB, four for CMYK:

currentblackgeneration

currentblackgeneration *procedure*

reads the current state of the graphics function for black generation and returns its procedure to the operand stack. Black generation is the complement of undercolor removal, in which black is created to replace percentages of the other three printing inks. The goal is to print the same color with a smaller amount of ink. By doing so, colors can be controlled more effectively on the printing press. For instance, equal amounts of cyan, magenta, and yellow create a gray. Reproducing that same gray value out of one ink will allow much greater control:

currentcmykcolor

currentcmykcolor *cyan magenta yellow black*

reads the current state of the CMYK color specification. This operator returns four values, representing cyan, magenta, yellow, and black.

currentcolorscreen

currentcolorscreen *(cyan)frequency angle procedure*
                     (magenta)frequency angle procedure
                     (yellow)frequency angle procedure
                     (black)frequency angle procedure

This operator returns the frequency, angle, and procedure for setting the screen parameters of all four colors in CMYK order.

currentcolortransfer

currentcolortransfer *(cyan)procedure*
(magenta)procedure
(yellow)procedure
(black)procedure

The *currentcolortransfer* operator returns the current transfer functions for each of the CMYK color components.

currentundercolorremoval

currentundercolorremoval *procedure*

The *currentundercolorremoval* operator returns the procedure used to calculate the amount of color to be removed from a three-color specification when black is being created and added as a fourth color.

setblackgeneration

procedure setblackgeneration

When preceded by a valid procedure, this operator will set the current black generation.

setcmykcolor

cyan magenta yellow black setcmykcolor

The *setcmykcolor* operator is used to define the four printing-process inks as additive color. The operator must be preceded by four values ranging from zero to one. Since this is being described as additive color, a value of .2 will yield a 20% dot size.

setcolorscreen

(cyan)frequency angle procedure
(magenta)frequency angle procedure
(yellow)frequency angle procedure
(black)frequency angle procedure setcolorscreen

This operator sets the frequency, angle, and procedure parameters of all four colors in CMYK order. It is similar to the *setscreen* operator, the difference being in the amount of data that is supplied to the operator. The frequency, angle, and procedure can be different for each color, although it would logically be best if the frequency and dot shape procedure remained the same for each. Angle, naturally, would have to be set differently to accommodate the printing process. Recommended screen angle settings for four-color printing:

CYAN	15
MAGENTA	− 15
YELLOW	30
BLACK	45

The goal behind screen angling is to position the darker inks at least 30 degrees away from each other and the lighter inks at least 15 degrees away.

Frequency refers to the number of lines imaged per inch. It does not refer to resolution, which is device-specific. The ideal frequency is determined by the resolution of your output device and the requirements of your printing process. For instance, most print shops prefer screen frequencies no greater than 133 lines per inch. Depending on the equipment and speed of printing, frequencies greater than this may cause color to fill in between the dots.

setcolortransfer

(cyan)procedure
(magenta)procedure
(yellow)procedure
(black)procedure currentcolortransfer

the setcolortransfer operator sets the current transfer functions for each of the CMYK color components.

setundercolorremoval

procedure setundercolorremoval

The setundercolorremoval operator sets the procedure used to calculate the amount of color to be removed from a three color specification when black is being created and added as a fourth color.

6-5   Color Separations

I have worked with two basic approaches to separating color. One is to create one PostScript file that will output all of the necessary separations in succession. The other is to create a separate file for each color plate that is to be printed.

Another method, but one that requires too much operator intervention, is to download a color separation routine for each color required, followed by the PostScript program that represents the page.

Most often, I have worked with my own PostScript code for separated art. Recently however, I have been using a combination of off-the-shelf software, to create the PostScript files, and my own software. For instance, any program that creates a PostScript file that contains one of the color operators, and not just *setgray*, can be separated into four-color separations. Combining your code with code from PageMaker, for example, often means that different color models are being used. I prefer to work with the new *setcmykcolor* operator, while most commercially available software works with the *setrgbcolor* operator. This combination of definitions complicates the operation but does not make it impossible.

The *PC Magazine* cover for the May 30, 1989 issue was created with this technique. A combination of eight PostScript programs and PC-based PageMaker was used to create the final output file. The output file from PageMaker was written using the Micrografx PostScript Driver for Windows. This file was then passed through my separation program, which creates four separated plates, one for each process color. The entire cover was output to a Linotronic 300 at Gerard Associates in New York. From concept to film took about six design hours and three production hours. The running time on the Linotronic 300 was approximately two hours. The total output cost for this cover was under $500. Normally, a cover for the magazine can run as much as $5,000, depending on design.

The code for such a color separation is not long, nor is it terribly complex. However, there are many parameters that have been coded into it that are specific to the needs of *PC Magazine*. I will show, in the next few examples, how to separate colors and provide enough information so that you can create a color separation routine for your code.

6.5.1   Starting Small

Working with only a few page elements will help to show the effect that these color separation programs have on the page. A box, some typography, and an irregular polygon will suffice. First, I will set up the elements for the page:

```
%%BeginProlog

/box {
  /height exch def
```

```
   /width exch def
   0 height rlineto
   width 0 rlineto
   0 height neg rlineto
   closepath gsave
   1 .4 0 setrgbcolor fill
   grestore stroke}def

/typog {
   /strg exch def
   /y exch def /x exch def
   1 0 0 setrgbcolor /red 1 def
   9 {x y moveto
     strg show
     red 0 0 setrgbcolor /red red .1 sub def
     /y y 20 add def} repeat }def

/polygon {
   moveto
   /linarray exch def
   /linlen linarray length def
   linarray aload pop
   linlen 2 idiv {lineto}repeat
   closepath fill}def

%%EndProlog
/drawpage {
   .2 0 .7 setrgbcolor
   [350 400 400 300 450 300 400 100 225 100 300 425]
250 250 polygon
   0 1 0 setrgbcolor
   100 100 moveto
   100 200 box
   /Helvetica-Bold findfont 26 scalefont setfont
   120 100 (This is a color separation)typog
}def

drawpage
showpage
```

By adding a color separation routine to the file, we can output three plates—one each for red, green, and blue. Figure 6–1 shows the three separate plates printed from an Apple LaserWriter.

```
%!PS-Adobe 2.0 EPSF
%%Title: Gerard Kunkel's Color Separator
%%Creation Date: 04-04-1989
%%Creator: Gerard Kunkel
%%EndComments

% ========== FURNITURE
=================================
/R {/color 3 def
   currentscreen exch pop 15 exch setscreen }def
```

```
/G {/color 2 def
   currentscreen exch pop 45 exch setscreen }def
/B {/color 1 def
   currentscreen exch pop 0 exch setscreen }def
/setupfreq {/freq exch def currentscreen
  3 -1 roll pop freq 3 1 roll setscreen}def

90 setupfreq

% ========== REDEFINE POSTSCRIPT OPERATORS
==============
/setrgbcolor {
  color 1 eq
    {1 exch sub setgray pop pop}
    {color 2 eq
    {pop 1 exch sub setgray pop}
    {pop pop 1 exch sub setgray}ifelse
  }ifelse}def

/box {
  /height exch def
  /width exch def
  0 height rlineto
  width 0 rlineto
  0 height neg rlineto
  closepath gsave
  1 .4 0 setrgbcolor fill
  grestore stroke}def

/typog {
  /strg exch def
  /y exch def /x exch def
  1 0 0 setrgbcolor /red 1 def
  9 {x y moveto
    strg show
    red 0 0 setrgbcolor /red red .1 sub def
    /y y 20 add def} repeat }def

/polygon {
  moveto
  /linarray exch def
  /linlen linarray length def
  linarray aload pop
  linlen 2 idiv {lineto}repeat
  closepath fill}def

/showcolor {0 setgray 200 400 moveto
  /Helvetica-Bold findfont 48 scalefont setfont
  show}def

%%EndProlog
/drawpage {
  .2 0 .7 setrgbcolor
  [350 400 400 300 450 300 400 100 225 100 300 425]
250 250 polygon
```

```
     0 1 0 setrgbcolor
     100 100 moveto
     100 200 box
     /Helvetica-Bold findfont 26 scalefont setfont
     120 100 (This is a color separation)typog
}def

R (red) showcolor drawpage showpage
G (green) showcolor drawpage showpage
B (blue) showcolor drawpage showpage
```

By defining the entire script for this program as a routine, the page can be repeated within the program as many times as needed.

The three lines at the end of this program perform four tasks each. The first task is to tell the separation routine which color is to be used—"R" for example. The second task is to push the reference text string—"(red)" for example—onto the stack and print it on the page with the "showcolor" routine. The third task is to perform all of the script procedures, *drawpage*. And finally, the *showpage* operator images the page and ejects it.

The *drawpage* procedure contains all of the script procedures that we defined in our last example. Since there are a limited number of operations in this procedure, we can safely do this without pressing any system limits. It is possible, however, to put too many operations into the *drawpage* procedure and cause a *dictful* error or, depending on the type of operations, exceed other system limits.

Let's look more closely at some of the routines used to create this separation.

The first set of routines in this separation program is the color definition, with screen angles and frequency definitions added in.

```
% ========== FURNITURE
==================================
/R {/color 3 def
    currentscreen exch pop 15 exch setscreen }def
/G {/color 2 def
    currentscreen exch pop 45 exch setscreen }def
/B {/color 1 def
    currentscreen exch pop 0 exch setscreen }def
```

The three procedures for defining the different colors operate the same way. The key name definition of *color* is set to tell the separation routine which color to accept. If red is the color currently chosen, *color* will equal three. The current screen parameters are then pushed onto the stack with the *currentscreen* operator. The three objects that then sit on the stack represent screen frequency, angle, and the dot-shape procedure. We are currently

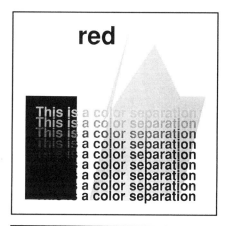

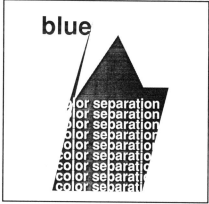

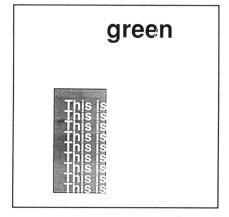

Figure 6—1

concerned with the middle value, so the top two objects are flipped with the *exch* operator. The top value, now screen angle, is popped off the stack, and the new value is pushed onto the stack. In this case, the new screen angle is 15. (You may choose another angle.)

To reset the screen values, we must once again flip the top two objects so that they are in the proper order. Once they are flipped, the *setscreen* operator is invoked, and the three objects are used to set the new screen parameters. This entire process is performed when the character "R" is pushed onto the stack. By pushing a "G" onto the stack, the green colors are set to be printed, and so on.

The number of lines per inch can and should also be set. For line art graphics, I tend to use a 90-line screen, although I can go up to a 120-line screen, depending on my printer. Since the Apple LaserWriter sets its default line screen at 60, these printouts will appear to have a higher resolution. This is not the case. The device resolution is not affected by the lines per inch. While the dots in a screen pattern appear finer, the printer is still printing them at 300 dpi.

```
/setupfreq  {/freq exch def currentscreen
  3 -1 roll pop freq 3 1 roll setscreen}def
```

```
90 setupfreq
```

The *setupfreq* procedure accesses the current screen values, just like the previous routine. In this case, however, we are concerned with the third element on the stack, the frequency. To get to that value, we need to roll the top three objects. The code *3 -1 roll* takes the third object, puts it at the top of the stack, and pushes the other two down. With the new order in place, the top object is popped off, and the new frequency value is pushed on. Now we need to put the objects back into their original order for the *setscreen* operator. This is done by using the *roll* operator again, except that this time the syntax is *3 1 roll*. This takes the top item and puts it into the third position.

The actual separation of colors does not happen in any of these routines. It actually happens in a redefinition of some of the standard color operators. In our sample program we are using *setrgbcolor* as the operator to define color; so the color separation procedure must redefine *setrgbcolor* to understand which color we want to print.

PostScript operators can be redefined to suit your needs. This form of definition resides in the current dictionary, above the system dictionary. Therefore, the PostScript interpreter will find the newest definition of the operator in the current dictionary (which it checks first) and use it, rather than the definition in the system dictionary.

```
% ========== REDEFINE POSTSCRIPT OPERATORS
==============
/setrgbcolor {
   color 1 eq                 % if color is blue
     {1 exch sub              % invert value
      setgray                 % set gray with new value
      pop pop}if              % discard other two values

   {color 2 eq                % if not blue / if color is
green
      {pop                    % discard blue value
       1 exch sub             % invert value
       setgray                % set gray with new value
       pop}                   % discard red value

                              % if not green, must be red
      {pop pop                % discard blue, green
values
       1 exch sub             % invert value
       setgray}ifelse         % set gray with new value
   }ifelse}def
```

6.5.2   Insert Separate Downloadable Separator

Downloading a separate color-separation program before sending your file to the printer can reduce the amount of data sent to your printer throughout the day. By downloading the separation routine as a file and then following it with the single character to delineate the color, you can send your PostScript files down without actually attaching the separation routine. The separation routine will remain in the printer until it is powered down or redefined.

This is particularly handy since you can then send an "R", "G", or "B" to reset the color to be printed. Remember, this code does not give you color output, just a black printout that represents the amount of that color for each specification.

The following code shows a simple color separator to create four plates—one each for cyan, yellow, magenta, and black.

```
%!PS-Adobe 2.0 EPSF
%%Title: Gerard Kunkel's Color Separator
%%Creation Date: 04-04-1989
%%Creator: Gerard Kunkel
%%EndComments

%   condense some commonly used operators
/ld {load def}def /color 0 def /ex /exch ld
```

```
%  define a commonly used operation
/3pop {pop pop pop}def

%  parameters for undercolor removal
/magentaUCR .3 def
/yellowUCR .07 def
/blackUCR .4 def

%  define screen angles for each of the
%  four process colors
/C {/color 3 def
  currentscreen ex pop
  15 ex setscreen }def
/M {/color 2 def
  currentscreen ex pop
  45 ex setscreen }def
/Y {/color 1 def
  currentscreen ex pop
  0 ex setscreen }def
/K {/color 0 def
  currentscreen ex pop
  -15 ex setscreen }def

%  define the screen frequency in lines per inch
/setupfreq  {/freq exch def currentscreen
  3 -1 roll pop freq 3 1 roll setscreen}def
90 setupfreq

%  begin redefining standard PostScript operators
userdict begin

/setgray {color 0 eq{systemdict begin setgray end}
    {pop systemdict begin 1 setgray end}ifelse}def

/setrgbcolor {color 0 eq
    {createK systemdict begin setgray end 3pop}
    {createK pop correctMY color 1 sub
      index systemdict begin setgray end
3pop}ifelse}def

/correctMY {rgb2cym
  1 index yellowUCR mul sub 3 1 roll
  1 index magentaUCR mul sub 3 1 roll
  3 1 roll rgb2cym}def

/createK{rgb2cym
  smallest 3 index smallest /least ex def pop pop
  /percent_UCR least blackUCR sub
  dup 0 lt {pop 0}if def
  3{ percent_UCR sub 3 1 roll }repeat rgb2cym
  percent_UCR 1.25 mul 1 ex sub}def

%  invert RGB to CMY colors
/rgb2cym {3{1 ex sub 3 1 roll}repeat}def
```

```
/smallest {2 copy lt {1}{0}ifelse index}def
end
C
%   download PostScript print file
M
%   download the same PostScript print file
Y
%   download the same PostScript print file
K
%   download the same PostScript print file
```

When creating a downloadable header, or color separator, there is one major difference in the way you structure your code. To secure consistent control over the *setgray* operation, you must use the user dictionary (*userdict*) and the system dictionary (*systemdict*). The following code fragment from our last listing shows how *setgray* and *setrgbcolor* have been redefined, this time using *systemdict* to perform the final gray-value setting. Note that *setgray* itself is redefined to set the gray value only when black has been chosen. In both cases, the final *setgray* operation goes down to the system dictionary.

Both of these definitions have been placed in the user dictionary. This will ensure that subsequent programs will find this operator first and not find the one residing in the system dictionary.

```
userdict begin
/setgray {color 0 eq{systemdict begin setgray end}
    {pop systemdict begin 1 setgray end}ifelse}def
/setrgbcolor {color 0 eq
    {createK systemdict begin setgray end 3pop}
    {createK pop correctMY color 1 sub
      index systemdict begin setgray end
3pop}ifelse}def
...
end
```

6.5.3   Modifying Existing Colors

Since the PostScript language is constructed with colors specified as combinations of primary colors within a color model, you can control and edit those colors as a group or individually. For instance, the color specification *0 0 0 setrgbcolor* sets the current color to white. If you needed to globally respecify white as another color, you could do so by adding the following code to the beginning of the program.

```
/setrgbcolor
  {exch                % exchange top two elements
   .4 add              % add .4 to GREEN value
   dup 1 gt {pop 1}if  % make sure it is not more
than 1
   exch                % exchange top two elements
   setrgbcolor         % set color
  }def
```

This is certainly not a practical application of this capability, but it is important to understand that existing PostScript operators may be redefined temporarily to suit the needs of your program. The result of this code produces a green tint to all of the original colors. This technique can be thought of as a rudimentary color correction.

Such color corrections are important in the real world. In the publishing field, we often require adjustments to color separations to accommodate press gain at the time of printing. *Press gain* is an industry term used to describe the color density that is gained when a publication is printed on the printing press.

In our earlier example, we separated some basic shapes and text. If you needed to adjust those colors to accommodate your printing process, you could do one of two things. First, rewrite the color specification in the PostScript program; second, make a global adjustment to the separation program so that all colors are changed across the board.

If you have many color specifications in a single output file or have many programs that require this kind of adjustment, the second method of adjustment is the most practical. For instance, my output from the Linotronic 300 has been giving me about a 3% dot where 10% has been specified. To get the 10% that I really want, I could go in and adjust all of the color specifications to rectify this shortcoming. However, it would be better if I could do this for all files going through the system and continue to specify colors exactly as I want them.

The following technique allows the user to specify how much to increase dot size to compensate for the inaccuracy of the Linotronic typesetter.

```
userdict
/setgray {dup 1 exch sub .1 mul add
  systemdict begin setgray end
  }def
end
```

Since all color separations eventually come down to setting a dot size via the *setgray* operator, this will apply to all colors when separating. If, for some reason, you did not want the same adjustments for all colors, then you could make this adjustment conditional. In all of my examples of PostScript color separation, you will notice that the code keeps track of which color it is working on by use of a key name definition for each plate of separation. The latter example shows color defined by the key name *color*. To write a conditional dot-size adjustment within this routine, you would check to see if the key name *color* and the color value matched. If so, the adjustment takes place. The following code makes a different adjustment for cyan, magenta, and yellow than it does for black.

```
userdict
/setgray {
  color 0 eq
  {dup 1 exch sub .05 mul add}
  {dup 1 exch sub .1 mul add}ifelse
  systemdict begin setgray end
  }def
end
```

The *ifelse* operator checks to see if the color is black, *color* equals zero. If cyan were the color that needed special attention, then we can check to see if *color* equals 3. In this example, the increase in dot size is only half as much for black as it is for the other colors. This is accomplished by simply changing the value for multiplication. There may be situations where you would need to specify a different adjustment for each color. The following code checks for each color and then provides a separate multiplication factor for each.

```
userdict
/setgray {
  color 0 eq
  {dup 1 exch sub .05 mul add}
  {color 1 eq
    {dup 1 exch sub .2 mul add}
    {color 2 eq
      {dup 1 exch sub .07 mul add}
      {dup 1 exch sub .1 mul add}ifelse
    }ifelse
  }ifelse
  systemdict begin setgray end
  }def
end
```

This latest version sets up three nested *ifelse* statements to check all four colors. If the result of the query is true, the procedure is executed. If not, the program proceeds on to the next *ifelse*. The last *ifelse* will execute the first procedure, if true, or execute the second procedure, if false.

6.5.4   RGB Conversion

In order to create four separated plates for your printer, you will need to convert any reference to the RGB color model to CMYK. Since most off-the-shelf applications create RGB type files in PostScript, you will have to include this conversion to play it safe.

The following PostScript color separation routine accepts *setrgbcolor* and *sethsbcolor* operators for color definition and converts their color values to the CMYK color model. This routine does not use the *setcmykcolor* operator. Rather, it uses the *setgray* operator to image four black-and-white representations of each color plate.

```
% ========== FURNITURE
====================================
/ld {load def}def /color 0 def /ex /exch ld
/3pop {pop pop pop}def /sdict /systemdict ld

% ========== PERCENT OF UNDERCOLOR
REMOVAL===============
/magentaUCR .3 def
/yellowUCR .07 def
/blackUCR .4 def

% ========== COLOR AND SCREEN SETUPS
====================
/C {/color 3 def currentscreen ex pop 15 ex
setscreen }def
/M {/color 2 def currentscreen ex pop 45 ex
setscreen }def
/Y {/color 1 def currentscreen ex pop 0 ex setscreen
}def
/K {/color 0 def currentscreen ex pop -15 ex
setscreen }def

/currentblack 1 def

/setupfreq  {/freq exch def currentscreen
  3 -1 roll pop freq 3 1 roll setscreen}def
90 setupfreq

% ========== PUT DEFINITIONS INTO USER DICT
=============
userdict begin

% ========== REDEFINE POSTSCRIPT OPERATORS
=============
/sethsbcolor {sdict begin
  sethsbcolor currentrgbcolor end
  userdict begin setrgbcolor end}def

/setrgbcolor
  {color 0 eq
```

```
      {createK sdict begin setgray end 3pop}
      {createK pop correctMY color 1 sub
          index sdict begin setgray end 3pop}
    ifelse}def

% ========== CORRECT YELLOW AND MAGENTA
=================
/correctMY {rgb2cym
   1 index yellowUCR mul sub 3 1 roll
   1 index magentaUCR mul sub 3 1 roll
   3 1 roll rgb2cym}def

% ========== CALCULATE PERCENT OF BLACK REPLACEMENT
=====
/createK{rgb2cym
   smallest 3 index smallest /least ex def pop pop
   /percent_UCR least blackUCR sub
   dup 0 lt {pop 0}if def
   3{ percent_UCR sub 3 1 roll }repeat rgb2cym
   percent_UCR 1.25 mul 1 ex sub}def

% ========== CONVERT RGB TO CMY
==========================
/rgb2cym {3{1 ex sub 3 1 roll}repeat}def

% ========== LOOK FOR SMALLEST VALUE
====================
/smallest {2 copy lt {1}{0}ifelse index}def

end

Y     % set current separation to yellow

% insert standard PostScript program file here
% can contain RGB, HSB, or gray color models
```

6.5.5 Color Trapping

Color trapping is a difficult process, even in conventional terms. In traditional mechanical preparation of preseparated color art, an amberlith or rubylith overlay was produced to mask out areas that would print as a separate color. These masks were adhered to an acetate film and were carefully scored so that a thin membrane of translucent film could be removed. The remaining masked area represented the color areas. If you were creating screen tints of this color, a conventional photoscreening process would have to take place later.

Trapping during the cutting of overlays was usually done along a black line. The tint area would surprint slightly into the black line. Color ink surprinting a black line will usually not show in the final printed piece.

Creating a trap in a computer system requires some serious planning. Ideally, you will know from the outset whether or not your colors will trap to a black line. This is usually a question of design. If you are trapping to a black line, you can consider a technique I developed for one of my color separators that simply prints lines at the specified width for black and then prints a line of zero thickness when printing the other color plates.

This technique has worked very successfully. The tradeoff (there are always tradeoffs) is that the use of any color lines in your artwork is affected by the code.

Another approach is another offspring of the traditional techniques. Spreading the yellow plate or selectively spreading a color will fill in any gaps that may occur when printing goes off register. Again, every technique has its tradeoffs. This one will work fine if you can define the elements that are to be spread, and the color. Spreading the width of a line is rather simple. Downloading the following code into the *userdict* prior to printing will increase the line width for black to create a color overlap.

```
/setlinewidth {
color 0 eq
{systemdict begin .2 add setlinewidth end}
{systemdict begin setlinewidth end}
ifelse
}def
```

This technique becomes particularly difficult when you need to trap type to the background color. You cannot increase the current point size and expect similar results. This would not only produce large characters, but strings of characters would extend longer because of the increased size. The only way to do it this way would be to get the character outline via the *charpath* operator, increase the line-weight for that typeface, and then fill the characters. This will greatly slow the system and is not advised. Such global character path operations can prove disastrous.

Another way to handle trapping to text is to surprint the characters across the background. PostScript does not have any built-in operators for creating a surprint, however, there are some tricks that you can use to create this effect.

6.5.6 Text Surprints

I have developed one sure-fire way to create text surprints (text that prints over a background color), but, as in all of these solutions, there are tradeoffs. This technique requires that all text be printed in either black or white. Any type specified in color will not work.

This technique relies upon the color separation routine outlined previously. By turning the *show* operator on and off, depending upon which color you are printing, you can create the surprint effect. The following *userdict* code will carry out the necessary selections.

```
/show {color 0 eq
{sdict begin show end}
{sdict begin pop end}
ifelse}def
```

The complete color separator takes into account that you may have knockout white type with your black type. The code below, the final separation routine, assumes that you have black or white type only and that all rules are black. This will create all the necessary four-color separations for the RGB, HSB, gray, and CMYK color models. This color separator was also used to create the color separations in the color plate section of this book. This and other routines are available on disk to save the time it would take to keystroke them. See the order form in the back of this book.

```
%!PS-Adobe 2.0 EPSF
%%Title: Gerard Kunkel's Color Separator
%%Creation Date: 04-04-1989
%%Creator: Gerard Kunkel
%%EndComments

% This particular color separation program increases the
% current line width when the setlinewidth operator
% is called in subsequent programs.
% All black lines surprinted. All color lines deleted
% All type is assumed black or white in this version
% All black type will surprint color

% ========== FURNITURE
===================================

/ld {load def}def /color 0 def /ex /exch ld
/3pop {pop pop pop}def /sdict /systemdict ld

% ========== PERCENT OF UNDERCOLOR
REMOVAL================
/magentaUCR .3 def
/yellowUCR .07 def
/blackUCR .4 def

% ========== COLOR AND SCREEN SETUPS
=====================
```

```
/C {/color 3 def currentscreen ex pop 15 ex
setscreen }def
/M {/color 2 def currentscreen ex pop 45 ex
setscreen }def
/Y {/color 1 def currentscreen ex pop 0 ex setscreen
}def
/K {/color 0 def currentscreen ex pop -15 ex
setscreen }def

/currentblack 1 def

/setupfreq  {/freq exch def currentscreen
  3 -1 roll pop freq 3 1 roll setscreen}def
90 setupfreq

% insert a call to "checkscreen" after someone
else's
% header file. For instance, a header to a
MicroGrafx
% output file may include some setscreen calls. This
% routine will reset the screens to your settings.

/checkscreen
  {color 0 eq
   {currentscreen ex pop -15 ex setscreen 90
setupfreq}
   {color 1 eq
    {currentscreen ex pop 0 ex setscreen 90
setupfreq}
    {color 2 eq
     {currentscreen ex pop 45 ex setscreen 90
setupfreq}
     {currentscreen ex pop 15 ex setscreen 90
setupfreq
    }ifelse
   }ifelse
  }ifelse
}def

% ========== PUT DEFINITIONS INTO USER DICT
==============
userdict begin

% ========== REDEFINE POSTSCRIPT OPERATORS
==============
/setgray {
    color 0 eq
    {sdict begin adjustdot setgray end}
    {pop sdict begin 1 setgray end}
    ifelse}def

/setlinewidth {
    color 0 eq
    {sdict begin .2 add setlinewidth end}
```

```
        {currentblack 1 eq
          {sdict begin setlinewidth end}
          {sdict begin 0 setlinewidth pop end}ifelse}
        ifelse}def

    /show {color 0 eq
        {sdict begin show end}
        {currentblack 1 eq
          {sdict begin show end}
          {sdict begin pop end}ifelse}
        ifelse}def

    /ashow {color 0 eq
        {sdict begin ashow end}
        {currentblack 1 eq
          {sdict begin ashow end}
          {sdict begin 3pop end}ifelse}
        ifelse}def

    /awidthshow {color 0 eq
        {sdict begin awidthshow end}
        {currentblack 1 eq
          {sdict begin awidthshow end}
          {sdict begin 3pop 3pop end}ifelse}
        ifelse}def

    /adjustdot {dup 0 eq
      {}{dup 1 exch sub .1 mul add}ifelse}def

    /check4white {4 copy add add add 0 eq
      {/currentblack 1 def}{/currentblack 0
    def}ifelse}def

    /check4whitergb {3 copy add add 3 eq
      {/currentblack 1 def}{/currentblack 0
    def}ifelse}def

    /sctcmykcolor {color 0 eq
      {check4white 1 ex sub
       sdict begin adjustdot setgray end 3pop}
      {color 1 eq
        {check4white pop 1 ex sub
         sdict begin adjustdot setgray end pop pop}
        {color 2 eq
          {check4white pop pop ex pop 1 ex sub
           sdict begin setgray end}
          {check4white 3pop 1 ex sub
           sdict begin adjustdot setgray end}ifelse
          }ifelse
        }ifelse
    }def

    /sethsbcolor {sdict begin
      sethsbcolor currentrgbcolor end
```

```
userdict begin setrgbcolor end}def

/setrgbcolor
  {color 0 eq
    {check4whitergb 3 copy add add 0 eq % was 3
      {sdict begin 0 setgray end 3pop}
      {createK sdict begin adjustdot setgray end
3pop}
    ifelse}
    {check4whitergb 3 copy add add 0 eq
      {sdict begin 1 setgray end 3pop}
      {createK pop correctMY color 1 sub
        index sdict begin adjustdot setgray end 3pop}
    ifelse}
  ifelse}def

% ========== CORRECT YELLOW AND MAGENTA
=================
/correctMY {rgb2cym
  1 index yellowUCR mul sub 3 1 roll
  1 index magentaUCR mul sub 3 1 roll
  3 1 roll rgb2cym}def

% ========== CALCULATE PERCENT OF BLACK REPLACEMENT
=====
/createK{rgb2cym
  smallest 3 index smallest /least ex def pop pop
  /percent_UCR least blackUCR sub
  dup 0 lt {pop 0}if def
  3{ percent_UCR sub 3 1 roll }repeat rgb2cym
  percent_UCR 1.25 mul 1 ex sub}def

% ========== CONVERT RGB TO CMY
========================
/rgb2cym {3{1 ex sub 3 1 roll}repeat}def

% ========== LOOK FOR SMALLEST VALUE
====================
/smallest {2 copy lt {1}{0}ifelse index}def

% ========== END USER DICT DEFINITIONS
=================
% ========== REGISTRATION ROUTINE FOR SEPARATIONS
=======
/names {/namearray exch def}def /F {findfont exch
scalefont setfont}def
/sepsid {/colr exch def 1 1 1 1 setcmykcolor
  cropmarks registerpage
  sdict begin 1 setlinewidth end
  llx 20 add ury 25 add moveto 0 -15 rlineto 570 0
rlineto
  0 15 rlineto closepath stroke
  /Helvetica-Bold findfont 8 scalefont setfont llx
30 add ury 15 add moveto
```

```
    namearray {sdict begin show end 30 0
rmoveto}forall
    colr sdict begin show end }def
/centshow {dup stringwidth pop 2 div neg 0 rmoveto
show}def
/regmarks { /ym exch def /xm exch def
    /Helvetica findfont 5 scalefont setfont 1 1 1 1
setcmykcolor
    xm 15 sub ym 24 sub moveto xm 8 sub ym 24 sub
lineto
    xm 8 sub ym 24 add lineto xm 15 sub ym 24 add
lineto
    closepath fill 0 0 0 0 setcmykcolor
    xm 10 sub ym moveto 90 rotate (GERARD KUNKEL)
centshow -90 rotate
    1 1 1 1 setcmykcolor newpath xm ym 10 add moveto
    xm ym 10 sub lineto closepath stroke
    newpath xm 10 sub ym moveto xm 10 add ym lineto
stroke
    xm ym 5 0 360 arc stroke}def
/registerpage {llx 10 sub ury 15 add regmarks
    llx 10 sub lly 15 sub regmarks
    urx 20 add lly 15 sub regmarks
    urx 20 add ury 15 add regmarks}def
/cropmarks {
    /llx 40 def /lly 40 def % lower left corner
    /urx 572 def /ury 752 def % upper right corner
    llx 6 sub lly moveto llx 30 sub lly lineto stroke
    llx lly 6 sub moveto llx lly 30 sub lineto stroke
    llx 6 sub ury moveto llx 30 sub ury lineto stroke
    llx ury 6 add moveto llx ury 30 add lineto stroke
    urx 6 add lly moveto urx 30 add lly lineto stroke
    urx lly 6 sub moveto urx lly 30 sub lineto stroke
    urx 6 add ury moveto urx 30 add ury lineto stroke
    urx ury 6 add moveto urx ury 30 add lineto
stroke}def

end            % end userdict entries

Y              % call for yellow separations

% ===== REDEFINE SHOWPAGE OPERATOR
====================
/showpage {
initgraphics
[(Gerard Kunkel)(separation of an existing file)
(ISSUE#10)(04-04-1989)]names
(YELLOW )sepsid
systemdict begin showpage end}def
```

Figure 6–2 shows four black-and-white pages representing what separated positive plates would look like when printed.

Figure 6—2

6.5.7 Adjusting for the Limitations of a Linotronic Output Device

When you specify 10% of some color or black, you expect to get 10%. The truth is that, on a paper laser printer, you will get a little more than 10%, and on the Linotronic laser typesetter you will get less than 10%. In fact, in my initial tests with the Linotronic, the output gave a reading of 2% on a densitometer. When this film went to printers plates, the 2% dot completely disappeared.

On the other end of the gray scale, the darker grays were imaging fairly well. Since the lighter shades of gray are disappearing, it would be desirable to specify a slightly darker value to compensate. Ideally, you would then get the gray you originally desired.

The inaccuracy of dot size can not be blamed entirely on the device. The quality of paper or film and developing plays a big role. However, if you find that there is a consistent problem with dot size, you can create a PostScript curve to adjust the dot size. A curve approach to increasing the dot size would affect the light grays greatly but would not affect the darker grays very much.

The following line of code creates a mathematical curve based on the gray value being sent to the PostScript interpreter.

```
/adjustdot {dup 0 eq
  {}{dup 1 exch sub .1 mul add}ifelse}def
```

The *adjustdot* routine simply duplicates the top value on the stack—the *setgray* value that is to be imaged—and subtracts that value from 1. The remainder is then multiplied by .1. That product is added to the original value on the top of the stack. Below are three examples of the effect of the adjust-dot routine.

Original Dot Size	Dot After *adjustdot*	Amount of increase
.1	.19	90%
.5	.55	10%
.9	.91	1%
0	0	0%

Figure 6–3 illustrates the effect of an adjustment to the *setgray* operator. The mathematics here is simple: 10% of the inverse gray value is added to the actual gray value. The resulting value is used to set the gray value. The following code listing is used to generate Figure 6–3.

```
%!PS-Adobe 2.0
%%Title:Graduated Screen Test
%%CreationDate: 21:50PM  2/1/1989
%%Creator: Gerard Kunkel
%%BoundingBox: 0 0 612 792
%%EndComments
```

```
/ld {load def} def /d /def ld
/l /lineto ld /m /moveto ld /e /exch ld
/a /add ld /s /sub ld /np /newpath ld
/rm /rmoveto ld /rl /rlineto ld

/setupfreq
  {/freq exch def
  currentscreen
  3 -1 roll pop
  freq 3 1 roll
  setscreen}def

/grad
  {/ud e d
   /k1 e d /k2 e d
   /ury e d /urx e d /lly e d /llx e d
   ud{/range ury lly s d}
     {/range urx llx s d}ifelse
   /kgrad k2 k1 s range div d
   1.1 setlinewidth
   k1 abs setgray
   ud{range{llx lly m urx lly l
       stroke /lly lly 1 a d grada}repeat}
     {range{llx lly m llx ury l
       stroke /llx llx 1 a d grada}repeat}ifelse
}d
/grada {k1 abs setgray
  /k1 k1 kgrad a d
}d

/F {findfont e scalefont setfont}d

/namearray {/names exch def}def

/idpage
 {/colr e d
 8 /Helvetica-Bold F
 90 545 m
 1 1 1 1 setcmykcolor
 names{show 30 0 rm}forall
 colr show
 .5 setlinewidth
 80 555 m 0 -15 rl 500 0 rl
 0 15 rl closepath stroke
 }d

/regmarks
   {.7 setlinewidth
   /ym e d  /xm e d
   5 /Helvetica F
   xm 12 s ym 17 s m 90 rotate
   (PC MAGAZINE) show -90 rotate
   np xm ym 10 a m
     xm ym 10 s l closepath stroke
```

```
    np xm 10 s ym m
      xm 10 a ym l stroke
      xm ym 5 0 360 arc stroke}d

/registerpage
 {80 520 regmarks
 80 80 regmarks
 545 80 regmarks
 545 520 regmarks}d

[ (21:50PM  4/30/1989)
(graduated gray test)
(Copyright 1988 Gerard Kunkel) ]namearray

registerpage
12 /Helvetica-Bold F

40 setupfreq
0 setgray
100 100 180 500 0 1 true grad
100 80 moveto (no adjustment) show

/setgray {dup 1 exch sub .1 mul sub
  systemdict begin setgray end}def
200 100 280 500 0 1 true grad
200 80 moveto (.1 adjustment) show

/setgray {dup 1 exch sub .3 mul sub
  systemdict begin setgray end}def
300 100 380 500 0 1 true grad
300 80 moveto (.3 adjustment) show

/setgray {dup 1 exch sub .5 mul sub
  systemdict begin setgray end}def
400 100 480 500 0 1 true grad
400 80 moveto (.5 adjustment) show

showpage
```

6.5.8   Taking Care of the Showpage Operator

The downloaded color separator reviewed in this chapter puts a page identifier on the top of the page. Since this information needs to be imaged on the page that comes to the printer later, we need to print this after the page has been imaged. The cleanest way to insert the page identifier on not only one page, but multiple pages, is to redefine the *showpage* operator in the user dictionary. In the code extracted from the separator, you can see the identifier information as well as an *initgraphics* call. This call resets all

no adjustment   .1 adjustment   .3 adjustment   .5 adjustment

Figure 6—3

of the graphic parameters of the system: line weight, scale, gray value, and so on. The final line pushes the *systemdict* to the top of the dictionary stack, so that the real *showpage* can then be executed.

```
/showpage {
initgraphics        % initialize graphics state
[(Gerard Kunkel)    % begin array of names
(separation of an existing file)
```

```
(ISSUE#10)
(04-04-1989)]names  % end array of names
(YELLOW )sepsid     % identify separation plate
systemdict          % call system dictionary
begin               % push to top of dictionary stack
showpage            % call original "showpage"
end}def             % restore dictionary stack
```

6-6   Halftone Screen Control

Graduated tint backgrounds or "fills" have become a popular graphic device recently and will probably stay with us through the nineties. Creating an even flow of color or gray in PostScript requires a good understanding of the halftoning machinery. In Figure 6–4, I have output a PostScript program that resets the halftoning lines per inch in a repetitive graduated tint. The tinting instructions are the same in each; only the lines per inch have changed.

The code for this output is shown below to allow you to experiment with line screens and choose your own best fit.

```
%!PS-Adobe 2.0
%%Title:Graduated Screen Test
%%CreationDate: 21:50PM  2/1/1989
%%Creator: Gerard Kunkel
%%BoundingBox: 0 0 612 792
%%EndComments

% ===== CONDENSE SOME OPERATORS =======
/ld {load def} def /d /def ld
/l /lineto ld /m /moveto ld /e /exch ld
/a /add ld /s /sub ld /np /newpath ld
/rm /rmoveto ld /rl /rlineto ld

% ===== SET LINES-PER-INCH ============
/setupfreq
  {/freq exch def
  currentscreen
  3 -1 roll pop
  freq 3 1 roll
  setscreen}def

% ===== GRADUATED TINT ROUTINE ========
/grad
  {/ud e d
  /k1 e d /k2 e d
  /ury e d /urx e d /lly e d /llx e d
  ud{/range ury lly s d}
```

```
   {/range urx llx s d}ifelse
 /kgrad k2 k1 s range div d
   1.1 setlinewidth
   k1 abs setgray
   ud{range{llx lly m urx lly l
      stroke /lly lly l a d grada}repeat}
    {range{llx lly m llx ury l
      stroke /llx llx l a d grada}repeat}ifelse
}d
/grada {k1 abs setgray
  /k1 k1 kgrad a d
}d

% ===== GENERIC FONT SETTING ROUTINE ==
/F {findfont e scalefont setfont}d

% ===== PAGE IDENTIFICATION ROUTINE ===
/idpage
 {/colr e d
 8 /Helvetica-Bold F
 90 545 m
 1 1 1 1 setcmykcolor
 names{show 30 0 rm}forall
 colr show
 .5 setlinewidth
 80 555 m 0 -15 rl 500 0 rl
 0 15 rl closepath stroke
}d

% ===== REGISTRATION MARKS ============
/regmarks
  {.7 setlinewidth
  /ym e d  /xm e d
  5 /Helvetica F
  xm 12 s ym 17 s m 90 rotate
  (PC MAGAZINE) show -90 rotate
  np xm ym 10 a m
    xm ym 10 s l closepath stroke
  np xm 10 s ym m
    xm 10 a ym l stroke
    xm ym 5 0 360 arc stroke}d

/registerpage
 {80 520 regmarks
 80 80 regmarks
 545 80 regmarks
 545 520 regmarks}d

% ===== ARRAY OF ID INFO =============
/namearray {/names exch def}def
[(21:50PM  1/30/1989)
(graduated color test)
(Copyright 1988 Gerard Kunkel)]namearray
```

```
% ===== END OF PROLOG / BEGIN SCRIPT ==
%%EndProlog
registerpage
10 /Helvetica-Bold F
15 setupfreq
100 100 150 500 0 1 true grad
0 setgray
100 80 moveto (15 linescreen) show
40 setupfreq
175 100 225 500 0 1 true grad
0 setgray
175 80 moveto (40 linescreen) show
60 setupfreq
250 100 300 500 0 1 true grad
0 setgray
250 80 moveto (60 linescreen) show
80 setupfreq
325 100 375 500 0 1 true grad
0 setgray
325 80 moveto (80 linescreen) show
110 setupfreq
400 100 450 500 0 1 true grad
0 setgray
400 80 moveto (110 linescreen) show
133 setupfreq
475 100 525 500 0 1 true grad
0 setgray
475 80 moveto (133 linescreen) show
showpage
```

As you can see by the output, the fewer lines per inch, the greater the smoothness of the tint background. If the lines per inch are too many, relative to the output resolution, the halftoning machinery attempts to place a dot that is too close in size to the previous line of dots. When the change in dot size finally occurs, the change is extremely noticeable, and the tint appears to have bands in it. The banding effect is a result of selecting a lines-per-inch value too great for the output resolution.

The Apple LaserWriter uses a default lines-per-inch value of 60. Resetting this value to 45 produces a smoother graduation of color. However, if the same code is to be output to a Linotronic device at 1270 resolution, 90 lines per inch will create a very smooth graduated tint. Figure 6–5 demonstrates the effect that the same code has on the Linotronic system at 1270 dpi.

As you can see, the greater the resolution, the more available pixels there are to form a single dot. This allows a greater degree of accuracy in dot size and more smoothness in the creation of graduated tints.

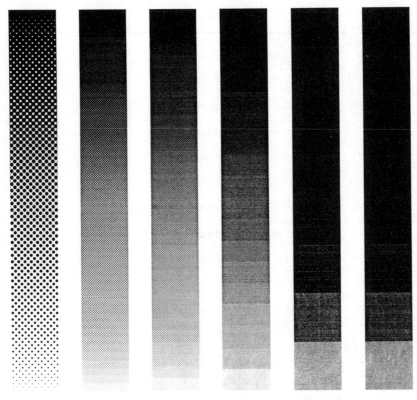

15 linescreen   40 linescreen   60 linescreen   80 linescreen   110 linescreen 133 lines

Figure 6—4
Apple LaserWriter output

6.6.1   Changing Screen Frequency

The routine that sets the frequency is a simple one.

```
/setupfreq
  {/freq exch def
  currentscreen
  3 -1 roll pop
  freq 3 1 roll
  setscreen}def
```

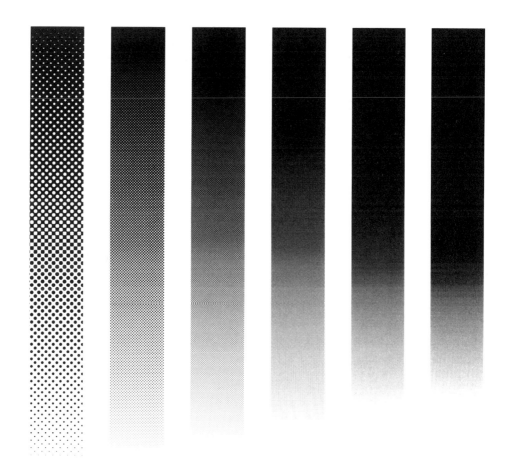

15 linescreen   40 linescreen   60 linescreen   80 linescreen   110 linescreen   133 lines

Figure 6—5
Linotronic output of the same code

The *setupfreq* routine first exchanges a value from the stack. That number is stored in a the key name value *freq*. The current screen values—frequency, angle, and spot function—are pushed onto the stack by using the *currentscreen* operator. The numbers now on the stack are rolled to put the screen frequency number at the top. That number is *pop*ped. Then *freq* is placed on the stack in place of the number.

The *freq* value is then rolled back down to its original position so that the *setscreen* operator can take its three values and reset the linescreen.

6.6.2 Graduated Tints

Now that we can see the value of understanding the screen function in PostScript, let's look closely at the complete graduated tint program.

This graduated tint program does not take full advantage of the PostScript language, since it does not use the *image* operator. I found it considerably easier to create a full-color graduated tint by painting a series of single-point lines that change color in each succession.

The *image* operator will paint only one pass of gray or color, while this method paints it once for all colors by using the available color operators. This is a well-tested technique that has been proven in regular application at the magazine. At both low- and high-resolution outputs, the tints were smooth from end to end. Of course, the proper linescreen has to be used for the appropriate resolution. Refer to Figure 6–6 for guidance to this code. The graduated tints in the color plate section of this book have used this PostScript set of routines. See Figures C–6, C–7, and C–8 for color reference.

Figure 6–6 shows the complete code for a full-color graduated tint.

```
%!PS-Adobe 2.0
%%Title:Graduated Screen Test
%%CreationDate: 21:50PM  2/27/1989
%%Creator: Gerard Kunkel
%%BoundingBox: 0 0 612 792
%%EndComments

/seps 24 dict def
  seps begin
        /colorselect [
        {pop pop pop
           1 exch sub setgray}
        {pop pop exch pop
           1 exch sub setgray}
        {pop 3 1 roll pop pop
           1 exch sub setgray}
        {4 1 roll pop pop pop
           1 exch sub setgray}
        ]def
        /angles [15 60 30 0]def          %
setcmykcolor screenangles
  end

  /C 0 def /M 1 def /Y 2 def /K 3 def
  /colorbreaks {
        userdict begin
        dup seps
        /colorselect get exch get
        /setcmykcolor exch def
```

```
        seps
        /angles get exch get
        currentscreen
        exch pop 3 -1 roll exch
        setscreen
        end
}bind def

% ===== GRADUATED TINT ROUTINE =======
/grad
  % start with information exchanges
  {/ud exch def      % up/down?

   /k1 exch def       % start black at
   /y1 exch def       % start yellow at
   /m1 exch def       % start magenta at
   /c1 exch def       % start cyan at

   /k2 exch def       % finish black at
   /y2 exch def       % finish yellow at
   /m2 exch def       % finish magenta at
   /c2 exch def       % finish cyan at

   /ury exch def       % upper-right y
   /urx exch def       % upper-right x
   /lly exch def       % lower-left y
   /llx exch def       % lower-left x

   % if ud is true then range will equal
   % upper-right y minus lower-left y
   % else range will equal
   % upper-right x minus lower-left x
   ud{/range ury lly sub def}
     {/range urx llx sub def}ifelse

   % incremental color changes are
   % calculated by finish color less
   % the starting color divided
   % by range.
   /cgrad c2 c1 sub range idiv def
   /mgrad m2 m1 sub range idiv def
   /ygrad y2 y1 sub range idiv def
   /kgrad k2 k1 sub range idiv def

   1.1 setlinewidth

   % set four color
   c1
   m1
   y1
   k1 setcmykcolor

   % if ud is true then perform the
   % first procedure, else perform
   % the second.
```

```
        ud{range
            {llx lly moveto
             urx lly lineto
             stroke
             /lly lly 1 add def grada}repeat}
           {range
             {llx lly moveto
              llx ury lineto
              stroke
              /llx llx 1 add def grada}repeat}
        ifelse}d

% grada sets the new color
% for the next line
/grada {
  cl ml yl kl setcmykcolor

  /cl cl cgrad add def
  /ml ml mgrad add def
  /yl yl ygrad add def
  /kl kl kgrad add def
}def

/F {findfont exch scalefont setfont} def

/idpage
  {10 /Helvetica-Bold F
  .5 setlinewidth
  /namearray exch def
  60 544 moveto
  1 1 1 1 setcmykcolor
  namearray
    {show 30 0 rmoveto} forall
  50 555 moveto
  0 -15 rlineto
  500 0 rlineto
  0 15 rlineto
  closepath stroke
}def

/regmarks
  {.7 setlinewidth
  /ymark exch def
  /xmark exch def
  /Helvetica findfont 5 scalefont setfont
  xmark 20 sub ymark 17 sub moveto
  90 rotate
  (COMPANY NAME) show
  -90 rotate
  newpath
    xmark ymark 10 add moveto
    xmark ymark 10 sub lineto
    closepath stroke
  newpath
    xmark 10 sub ymark moveto
```

```
    xmark 10 add ymark lineto
    stroke
    xmark ymark 5 0 360 arc stroke
}def

/registerpage {
  40 40 regmarks
  40 540 regmarks
  540 540 regmarks
  540 40 regmarks}def

/drawpage {
1 1 1 1 setcmykcolor registerpage
100 100 150 500 1 0 0 0 0 1 0 0 true grad
175 100 225 500 0 1 0 0 0 0 1 0 true grad
250 100 300 500 0 0 1 0 1 0 0 0 true grad
325 100 375 500 0 0 0 1 0 0 0 0 false grad
400 100 450 500 0 1 0 0 1 0 0 1 false grad
475 100 525 500 1 0 0 0 1 0 0 1 false grad}def

%%EndProlog
C colorbreaks drawpage
[(CYAN)(1:30PM  5/13/1989)(PostScript Book)] idpage
showpage
M colorbreaks drawpage
[(MAGENTA)(1:30PM  5/13/1989)(PostScript Book)]
idpage showpage
Y colorbreaks drawpage
[(YELLOW)(1:30PM  5/13/1989)(PostScript Book)]
idpage showpage
K colorbreaks drawpage
[(BLACK)(1:30PM  5/13/1989)(PostScript Book)] idpage
showpage
showpage
```

The *grad* routine performs most of the work in this process. The beginning is quite simple to understand. This series of exchanges and key name definitions is pulling values off the stack to provide information to the subroutines within.

The first exchanged item is a Boolean operator that will determine if the tint is to run up and down, or, left and right. The next eight exchanges define the starting and ending colors in CMYK colors.

The four corners of the tinted area are determined by the next four values taken from the stack and defined as the familiar llx, lly, urx and ury. taken from the stack and defined as the familiar *llx*, *lly*, *urx*, and *ury*.

```
/grad
{/ud exch def
 /k1 exch def
 /y1 exch def
 /m1 exch def
 /c1 exch def
```

```
/k2 exch def
/y2 exch def
/m2 exch def
/c2 exch def
/ury exch def
/urx exch def
/lly exch def
/llx exch def
```

The first subroutine uses the *ud* key name definition in determining the Boolean question for up/down or left/right tint sweeps. If *ud* is true, then the range of color sweep will be calculated according to the overall height. If *false*, then the range is calculated according to the overall width. The key name *range* is used to store the result of this calculation.

```
ud{/range ury lly sub def}
  {/range urx llx sub def}ifelse
```

The *range* definition is used in the next four lines of code to help calculate the exact value of tint change for each line painted in the graduated tint. To get this number, the first starting color value is subtracted from the ending color value. That result is then divided by *range*. This final number is stored as *cgrad* in the first line. This value will typically be less than .01. This will not be a problem for the half-toning machinery.

```
/cgrad c2 c1 sub range div def
/mgrad m2 m1 sub range div def
/ygrad y2 y1 sub range div def
/kgrad k2 k1 sub range div def
```

After the color increment has been determined and stored, the line width and the CMYK color are set. The four values pushed onto the stack are key name definitions representing the four starting values for cyan, magenta, yellow, and black.

```
1.1 setlinewidth

c1
m1
y1
k1 setcmykcolor
```

The next subroutine relies on the *ud* definition for direction. If *ud* is true, then the first bracketed procedure is executed; if not, then the second. The first routine strokes a horizontal line and then increases the *y* value to get set for the next stroking. This process is repeated for the value of *range*. If *range* equals 100, then 100 lines are stroked. The last operation within either of these procedures is a call to *grada*, our next routine.

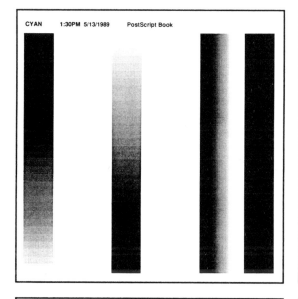

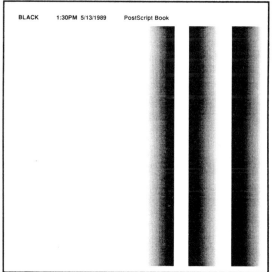

Figure 6—6

```
ud{range
    {llx lly moveto
     urx lly lineto
     stroke
     /lly lly 1 add def grada}repeat}
  {range
    {llx lly moveto
     llx ury lineto
     stroke
     /llx llx 1 add def grada}repeat}
ifelse}d
```

The *grada* routine is the place where the color is reset for the next line and the CMYK color values are recalculated. The second half of the *grada* routine adds the incremental value to the starting value and accumulates through the *repeat* operation in the *grad* procedure. After all of the repeats, equal to *range*, the starting color value will equal the ending color value.

```
/grada {
  c1 m1 y1 k1 setcmykcolor
  /c1 c1 cgrad add def
  /m1 m1 mgrad add def
  /y1 y1 ygrad add def
  /k1 k1 kgrad add def
}d
```

Finally, in the script portion of the code, 12 values and one Boolean are pushed onto the stack in advance of calling the *grad* procedure. Dissecting the string of values, we can see that the first four represent the lower-left corner *x* and *y;* the second four represent the starting CMYK color values; and the third four values represent the ending CMYK color values. This particular string will produce a graduated tint that is 50 points wide and 400 points tall. It starts at the top with 100% cyan and sweeps down to 100% magenta.

```
100 100 150 500 1 0 0 0 0 1 0 0 true grad
```

6-7   Output Devices

6.7.1   Apple LaserWriter Family

The most widely used family of PostScript printers is the Apple line of LaserWriters. While these printers are extremely reliable, they do not have the latest CMYK color operators. It is possible, however, to make them CMYK-compatible by downloading a simple set of PostScript routines.

The following PostScript code can be downloaded to the Apple LaserWriter to enable CMYK information to be converted into shades of gray.

```
%!PS-Adobe 2.0 EPSF
%%Title: setcmykcolor for LaserWriter
%%Creator: Gerard Kunkel
%%CreationDate: 5-13-89

serverdict begin 0 exitserver  % download and save
in memory

/setcmykcolor {
  /black exch def
  /yellow exch .1 mul def    % 10 percent gray value
  /magenta exch .3 mul def   % 30 percent gray value
  /cyan exch .2 mul def      % 20 percent gray value
  /grayval black yellow add magenta add cyan add def
  grayval 1 gt{pop 1}if
  1 grayval sub setgray
  }def
```

The first active line of this code allows for this code to be permanently downloaded (until the next power-down). The value zero is the password, standard from the factory. If you or your network manager has changed that password, be sure to change this code to match.

6.7.2   Tektronix Phaser CP and QMS ColorScript

These two wax transfer print engines are PostScript-compatible with the latest color operators, thereby simplifying the codework necessary to print color PostScript files. Both printers are ideal color proofers, although color correctness is far from ideal. The match from typical RGB to color print is quite good, but the relationship to final printed material is not. Care should be taken when proofing with a color device as a prelude to four-color printing.

6.7.3   Linotronic 100/300/500

Output from the Linotronic device will yield substantially greater resolutions and therefore cleaner, sharper typography and graphics. The most common resolution used is 1270 dpi. These devices are capable of outputting at resolutions up to 2540 dpi. If you are looking for fast output at a medium quality, 635 dpi can be specified when requesting Lino output.

Since the Linotronic devices offer film as an output medium, the output can be used as the final film ready for press plates. The quality of output can vary wildly on this output, depending greatly upon the chemical process of developing the final film. I would recommend that you use a qualified Linotronic output service that has had a track record in film output. Usually, a typesetting company will be your best choice, since they have experience in producing quality type and usually have worked with negative film.

When creating PostScript output code, a single page may be produced several different ways. Some of the output possibilities are:

1. Black-and-white paper output, ready for mechanicals.

2. Black-and-white film output, ready for stripping or plate making (positive or negative, right or wrong reading).

3. Two-color film, one piece of film for each color. This film can be screened for each color value or output as solid areas for conventional screening. Film is recommended for any color work, because paper output is not as accurate when trying to align your color plates during the stripping and printing process.

4. Three-color film. The same mathematics will apply as for the two-color, simply adding one more variable.

5. Four-color film for process color printing. This would be the most common color application. One piece of film per color is output, with the proper screen angles to avoid moire patterns of the screened dots.

6. Four-color with a fifth match color. This is a technique often used when a PMS (Pantone Matching System) color is to be used. Often, that color will be gold or silver, colors difficult to simulate in any other color-mixing process.

There are Linotronic-specific PostScript operations that are beyond the scope of this book. However, all of the code mentioned in this book will output to a Linotronic series printer. (*setcmykcolor* requires a separate downloaded header; see Section 5 of this chapter). Your Linotronic service bureau will have all of the necessary skills to rotate your image or invert the image to a negative.

6-8 Controlling Your Color Files

As you begin to work with preseparated color PostScript files, you will notice a plethora of paper mounting in the output tray. Revision after revision, we have all become paper pushers, printing our files to check the work. Assuming you are using a black-and-white laser printer or a Linotronic 300, there will be no way to tell which page is which color—or, in the case of multiple versions, which version is which—without having a page identification scheme. The best solution to printing color-separated files is to print them in color. The best solution to printing them with a black-and-white printer is to properly identify each page with color notation and version information.

Ideally, you would be printing out to a color PostScript printer such as the QMS ColorScript or the Tektronix Phaser color PostScript printer. Granted, these printers start at $12,000 and rise sharply from there, but it is not unlikely that these printers will wind up in your operation if you require a reasonable volume of color proofs.

At *PC Magazine,* we found that the typical preseparated color PostScript output file required four or five black-and-white passes before the file was ready to send to our Linotronic 300 supplier. Once output to film, we needed to check color. This was done with a 3M Color Key proofing device. At a Color Key cost of about $40.00 per job, this became a very expensive part of the production cycle. While it is true that this cost was always there—whether we produced computer-generated art or conventional mechanicals—we have constantly looked for money-saving alternatives that incorporate computers.

The question raised is a simple one. How many color keys will it take to justify the $12,000 needed to buy a Tektronix Phaser color PostScript printer?

Answer: 12000 cost / 40 per color key = 300 pieces of art.

Add to that number the ink and paper costs and some routine maintenance, and you have about 320 pieces of art needed to justify the purchase. At *PC Magazine* we average 35 pieces of art each issue. In addition, we produce about 10 full- color pages on computer, with the anticipation of producing all pages on computer in the first few months of 1990. That means that within 10 magazine issues, or roughly six months, we will begin to see a cost savings.

If you have a production volume close to this one, similar cost savings can be reached within this time frame. But the real reason you want to have a color printer in-house is the immediacy of seeing your work in color. Rather than waiting 24 to 48 hours to proof color, you need wait only minutes. Necessary corrections can begin immediately and not jeopardize any production deadlines.

While you wait to get a color printer in hand, and even when you have one, you will need to keep track of each page of output. Making this process as automatic as possible will help ensure a consistent presentation, accurate labeling, and, ultimately, correct film stripping and printing.

6.8.1   Page Identification

The most important part of creating four-color separations is the registration and identification of the four individual color plates. In this chapter, we will show a variety of routines that can be customized to fit your needs.

It is important to keep track of the version of your code, as well as the file name and (when producing four-color) which color plate is printing. To do this properly, an automatic date-and-time stamp and file name transfer are required. Without them, manual input of such information is recommended. Such identifications reduce the confusion of multiple versions floating around a workgroup. And if files are to be shared by various people, output pages will also need to be identified by the user's name.

If you are writing your code from your own application, use the computer's clock for the correct time. By adding in a single line of code to write a PostScript line, you can have each output file automatically time-stamped. You may also pick up the DOS file name currently in use or request one at print time.

In BASIC, this routine would look like this:

```
print "/date("date$") def"
print "/time("time$") def"
print "/filenam("file$") def"
print "filenam show date show time show"
```

Depending on how your output port was opened, this PostScript code could print directly to your PostScript printer or to a file on disk for later printing. (See the section on BASIC to learn how to write PostScript files from BASIC programs).

If your total PostScript code is short, printing directly to the printer will usually be successful. Larger PostScript programs may encounter printer timeout errors, waiting for the PostScript code to be interpreted. In such cases, it is best to write the file to disk and use a PostScript downloader to control the communication flow. There are numerous PostScript down-

job name	time: 9:00am	date: 4-1-1989	version 1

Figure 6–7

loaders on the market. One is available from Adobe and is packaged with their downloadable fonts. Another possibility is to write your own communications link to the printer and receive error information.

In the example above, BASIC will print to a file a combination of characters from BASIC string variables and PostScript operators. When the file is completely written, it will look like straight PostScript. This file is nothing but ASCII characters and can be opened in any word processor for further review or modification. The example above will print something like this when the variables are defined.

```
/date(6-18-89) def
/time(10:00:00am) def
/filenam(testfile.eps) def
    filenam show date show time show
```

Below is a complete PostScript program that will print a set of page identifiers, shown in Figure 6–7. This is a black-and-white solution to page identification and is useful for tracking file name, version, date, time, and artist's name.

```
% routine to draw an identification on page
% the array of labels can be passed from an
application
% date, time, filename, should always be included
% a sequential update of version is recommended

% this routine requires the F font routine
% it also assumes you are outputing an 8.5x11 inch
page

%!PS-Adobe 2.0
%%Title:IDPAGE
%%Creator: Gerard Kunkel
%%CreationDate: 9:00am 6-18-89
%%EndComments
%%BeginProlog

/F {findfont exch scalefont setfont}def

/idpage
 {10 /Helvetica-Bold F
 .5 setlinewidth
 /namearray exch def
 60 744 moveto
 namearray
   {show 50 0 rmoveto}forall
```

```
50 755 moveto
0 -15 rlineto
500 0 rlineto
0 15 rlineto
closepath stroke
}def

%%EndProlog

[(job name)(time: 9:00am)
(date: 4-1-1989)(version 1)] idpage

showpage
```

If you are writing the variables in BASIC:

```
print
"[("file$")("time$")("date$")("vers$")] idpage"
```

There are two constant variable names, *time$* and *date$*, that are used in this code to return the current system-level date and time.

Try adding more identification names to the *idpage* function call. Since *idpage* reads an array off the stack and then executes a *forall* procedure, any number of items may be added to the array. The width of the identifier is a limiting factor at about 430 points (roughly 6 inches). Try changing either the type point size or the space between each item to reduce the overall width. The space between items is determined by the *50 zero rmoveto* statement inside the *forall* loop.

The same page identification can be used when producing a four-color separation. With four pages, the goal is to have the same identification appear on each output page. The only item that changes is the reference to the color. For instance, you would want each page to have the date, time, version, file name, and so on, but the individual color plates should be uniquely identified as cyan, magenta, yellow, or black. This is accomplished by having a unique color identifier passed to the *idpage* function for each page that is printed, as shown in Figure 6–8.

```
%!PS-Adobe 2.0
%%Title:IDPAGE
%%Creator: Gerard Kunkel
%%CreationDate: 9:00am 6-18-89
%%EndComments
%%BeginProlog
%FIGURE 6-8.PS

/seps 24 dict def
  seps begin
        /pickcolor [
        {pop pop pop
            1 exch sub setgray}
        {pop pop exch pop
```

```
            1 exch sub setgray}
        {pop 3 1 roll pop pop
            1 exch sub setgray}
        {4 1 roll pop pop pop
            1 exch sub setgray}
        ]def
        /angles [105 75 90 45]def          %
setcmykcolor screenangles
  end

  /C 0 def /M 1 def /Y 2 def /K 3 def
  /colorbreaks {
        userdict begin
        dup seps
        /pickcolor get exch get
        /setcmykcolor exch def
        seps
        /angles get exch get
        currentscreen
        exch pop 3 -1 roll exch
        setscreen
        /setscreen {}def
        end
}bind def

/F {findfont exch scalefont setfont}def

/names {/namearray exch def}def

/idpage
 {/colr exch def
 .5 setlinewidth
 10 /Helvetica-Bold F
 60 744 moveto 1 1 1 1 setcmykcolor
 namearray
    {show 50 0 rmoveto}forall
 colr show
 50 755 moveto
 0 -15 rlineto
 500 0 rlineto
 0 15 rlineto
 closepath stroke
}def

/drawpage { % series of color drawing routines
  }def

%%EndProlog
[(date)(time)(filename)(version #)]names
C colorbreaks (CYAN) idpage
drawpage gsave showpage grestore
M colorbreaks (MAGENTA) idpage
drawpage gsave showpage grestore
Y colorbreaks (YELLOW) idpage
drawpage gsave showpage grestore
K colorbreaks (BLACK) idpage
drawpage gsave showpage grestore
```

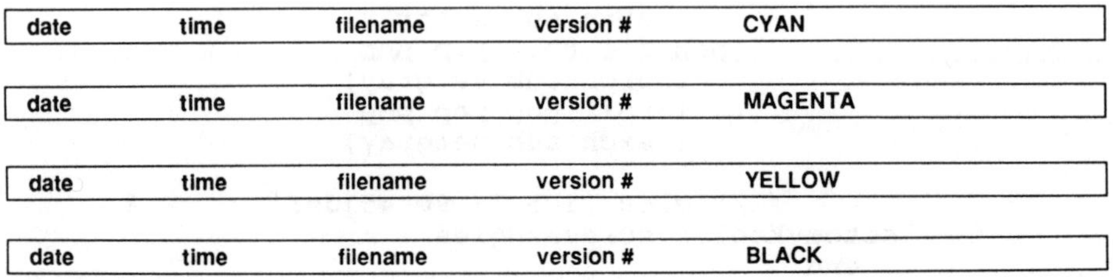

date	time	filename	version #	CYAN

date	time	filename	version #	MAGENTA

date	time	filename	version #	YELLOW

date	time	filename	version #	BLACK

Figure 6—8

Note that in this code, the only function that is actually drawing to the page is the *idpage* routine. When using this color-separation routine, the reference to *setcmykcolor* must appear after the *colorbreaks* routine is called. Otherwise, an error will occur due to the fact that the *setcmykcolor* extended operator is defined in the *colorbreaks* routine. If you are using a device that supports the extended PostScript color operators, such as the Tektronix Phaser Card and CP, you will not need the color-separation routine. But be aware that this works only when the interpreter can understand *setcmykcolor*.

As *idpage* is executed, it picks the string naming the color off the stack and defines it as *colr*. For each pass of color, the appropriate string is inserted preceding the *idpage* routine call.

```
/idpage
{/colr exch def
```

then defines the type style and point size using the *F* function.

```
8 /Helvetica-Bold F
```

Locating a starting point, the current color is defined as solid cyan, magenta, yellow, and black.

```
60 740 moveto 1 1 1 1 setcmykcolor
```

The *forall* procedure prints each identification in the array called *namearray*, moving 50 points to the right after each string. Since the color has been set to solid for all four colors, the names will then print on their appropriate separations. The name of the color is changed each time because *colr* is redefined with each pass.

```
namearray
{show 50 0 rmoveto}forall
```

After the last string in *namearray*, the *colr* variable is printed.

```
colr show
```

And, finally, a box is drawn to trap all the identifications

```
50 755 moveto
0 -15 rlineto
500 0 rlineto
0 15 rlineto
closepath stroke
}def
```

6.8.2   Register Page Routines

In traditional mechanical art preparation, registration marks are added to the edges of the art to be scanned along with the artwork. This allows the film preparation house and the printer to register the separated reproductions properly by aligning the registration marks. These marks are typically composed of circles with crosshairs through the center. They look much like the sight on a gun. They may be any shape or even character, as long as they are outside the artwork area and are fine enough in line weight to allow for precise alignment when lining up the film negatives or when actually printing. We have seen cases where the registration marks are actually type, or a company logo. (In this case the company was a professional film stripper servicing the publishing industry.)

A set of four registration marks is typical, one for each corner. Two may be acceptable if placed on opposite sides, but four or more are desirable.

The following set of routines creates a four-color registration with four marks, one in each corner.

The first routine, *regmarks*, defines a single mark. In this case a company name has been added to the mark as an additional identifier of the artwork's creator.

```
/regmarks
  {.7 setlinewidth
  /ymark exch def  /xmark exch def
  /Helvetica findfont 5 scalefont setfont
  xmark 20 sub ymark 17 sub moveto
  90 rotate
  (COMPANY NAME) show
  -90 rotate
  newpath
    xmark ymark 10 add moveto
    xmark ymark 10 sub lineto
    closepath stroke
  newpath
    xmark 10 sub ymark moveto
    xmark 10 add ymark lineto
    stroke
    xmark ymark 5 0 360 arc stroke
}def
```

The second routine locates and draws the four registration marks. Note that the location of the *regmarks* is entered onto the stack preceding the object's name. The procedure defined as *registerpage* reads and defines the *y* location first, then the *x*. Then it uses them as *x* and *y* on the stack before the *moveto* and *lineto* operator calls.

```
/registerpage
  {40 740 regmarks
  40 50 regmarks
  580 50 regmarks
  580 740 regmarks}def
```

Since there is a repetition of locations and operator calls, a more compressed form of this code may be written. For this example, the long version is more descriptive. You may also want to address these numbers as indents from the edge of your imaging page. If you are defining the page size with your application, it may be more useful to define the *regmarks* location as

```
leftedge 10 add bottomedge 10 add regmarks
```

thereby eliminating the need to individually define the location of *registermarks* if you change the size of your paper. This code fragment assumes that you are defining your page dimensions as *leftedge, rightedge, topedge,* and *bottomedge*.

By adding *1 1 1 1 setcmykcolor* and *registerpage* to your page-drawing routine, the four marks will be added to each of the four color plates, as shown in Figure 6–9.

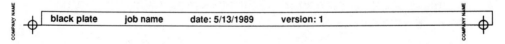

Figure 6—9

```
% Page registration routine
% FIGURE 6-9

/seps 24 dict def
  seps begin
        /pickcolor [
        {pop pop pop
           1 exch sub setgray}
        {pop pop exch pop
           1 exch sub setgray}
        {pop 3 1 roll pop pop
           1 exch sub setgray}
        {4 1 roll pop pop pop
```

```
            1 exch sub setgray}
        ]def
        /angles [105 75 90 45]def           %
setcmykcolor screenangles
  end

  /C 0 def /M 1 def /Y 2 def /K 3 def
  /colorbreaks {
        userdict begin
        dup seps
        /pickcolor get exch get
        /setcmykcolor exch def
        seps
        /angles get exch get
        currentscreen
        exch pop 3 -1 roll exch
        setscreen
        /setscreen {}def
        end
}bind def

/F {findfont exch scalefont setfont} def

/idpage
  {10 /Helvetica-Bold F
  .5 setlinewidth
  /namearray exch def
  60 744 moveto
  1 1 1 1 setcmykcolor
  namearray
    {show 30 0 rmoveto} forall
  50 755 moveto
  0 -15 rlineto
  500 0 rlineto
  0 15 rlineto
  closepath stroke
}def

/regmarks
  {.7 setlinewidth
  /ymark exch def
  /xmark exch def
  /Helvetica findfont 5 scalefont setfont
  xmark 20 sub ymark 17 sub moveto
  90 rotate
  (COMPANY NAME) show
  -90 rotate
  newpath
    xmark ymark 10 add moveto
    xmark ymark 10 sub lineto
    closepath stroke
  newpath
    xmark 10 sub ymark moveto
    xmark 10 add ymark lineto
```

```
    stroke
    xmark ymark 5 0 360 arc stroke
}def

/registerpage {
  40 40 regmarks
  40 740 regmarks
  540 740 regmarks
  540 40 regmarks}def

%%EndProlog
K colorbreaks

1 1 1 1 setcmykcolor registerpage
[(black plate)(job name)
(date: 5/13/1989)(version: 1)] idpage
showpage
```

6.8.3   Color Bars

When you are controlling the output identification, it is also important to add some other useful color-control guides. We have already printed the color name on the output page, but that is a name that must be searched for when working with the final film. There are some other methods for identifying the color that are much more visual and therefore allow faster identification.

The following code segment will print a set of color bars on each of the four output pages, which, when combined, form a set of color controls that will aid in the printing process. This code is shown as four black printouts in Figure 6–10.

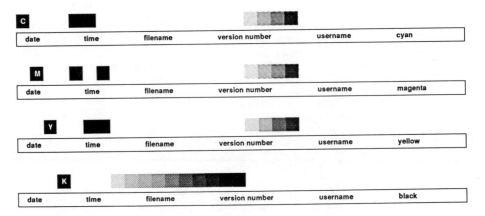

Figure 6—10

First, each color is identified in a separate solid-color box—for example, a solid cyan box identified with a white "C" printed in the center. This form of identification helps assure that the proper output page is used with the appropriate ink when printing.

The same method may be used in spot color artwork.

```
% COLOR BAR SAMPLE
% FIGURE 6-9
%!PS-Adobe 2.0
%%Title:IDPAGE
%%Creator: Gerard Kunkel
%%CreationDate: 9:00am 6-18-89
%%EndComments
%%BeginProlog

/seps 24 dict def
 seps begin
        /pickcolor [
        {pop pop pop
           1 exch sub setgray}
        {pop pop exch pop
           1 exch sub setgray}
        {pop 3 1 roll pop pop
           1 exch sub setgray}
        {4 1 roll pop pop pop
           1 exch sub setgray}
        ]def
        /angles [105 75 90 45]def
        % setcmykcolor screenangles
   end

  /C 0 def /M 1 def /Y 2 def /K 3 def
  /colorbreaks {
        userdict begin
        dup seps /pickcolor get exch get
        /setcmykcolor exch def
        seps /angles get exch get
        currentscreen
        exch pop 3 -1 roll exch
        setscreen
        /setscreen {}def
        end
}bind def

/F {findfont exch scalefont setfont}bind def

/names {/namearray exch def}def

/idpage
 {/colr exch def .5 setlinewidth
 8 /Helvetica-Bold F 1 1 1 1 setcmykcolor
 60 745 moveto
 namearray {show 50 0 rmoveto}forall
 colr show
```

```
50 755 moveto
0 -15 rlineto
500 0 rlineto
0 15 rlineto
closepath stroke
}def

/box
  {setcmykcolor moveto lineto lineto lineto
   closepath fill} bind def

%%EndProlog

/drawpage
{50 760 50 775 65 775 65 760 1 0 0 0 box
0 0 0 0 setcmykcolor 55 765 moveto (C) show
65 760 65 775 80 775 80 760 0 1 0 0 box
0 0 0 0 setcmykcolor 70 765 moveto (M) show
80 760 80 775 95 775 95 760 0 0 1 0 box
0 0 0 0 setcmykcolor 85 765 moveto (Y) show
95 760 95 775 110 775 110 760 0 0 0 1 box
0 0 0 0 setcmykcolor 100 765 moveto (K) show
110 760 110 775 125 775 125 760 1 1 0 0 box
125 760 125 775 140 775 140 760 1 0 1 0 box
140 760 140 775 155 775 155 760 0 1 1 0 box
155 760 155 775 170 775 170 760 0 0 0 .1 box
170 760 170 775 185 775 185 760 0 0 0 .2 box
185 760 185 775 200 775 200 760 0 0 0 .3 box
200 760 200 775 215 775 215 760 0 0 0 .4 box
215 760 215 775 230 775 230 760 0 0 0 .5 box
230 760 230 775 245 775 245 760 0 0 0 .6 box
245 760 245 775 260 775 260 760 0 0 0 .7 box
260 760 260 775 275 775 275 760 0 0 0 .8 box
275 760 275 775 290 775 290 760 0 0 0 .9 box
290 760 290 775 305 775 305 760 0 0 0 1 box
305 760 305 775 320 775 320 760 .1 .1 .1 0 box
320 760 320 775 335 775 335 760 .3 .3 .3 0 box
335 760 335 775 350 775 350 760 .5 .5 .5 0 box
350 760 350 775 365 775 365 760 .7 .7 .7 0 box
}def                    % end drawpage
[ (date)(time)(filename)
(version number)(username)]names

C colorbreaks (cyan) idpage
drawpage save showpage restore
M colorbreaks (magenta) idpage
drawpage save showpage restore
Y colorbreaks (yellow) idpage
drawpage save showpage restore
K colorbreaks (black) idpage
drawpage save showpage restore
```

7

Basic Interaction

7-1 Using BASIC to Create Your PostScript Files

Now that you have some programs in PostScript, you may want to change them periodically to create new art. You can certainly open up the PostScript text file and selectively edit the code, but this has a few problems associated with it.

The greatest problem is the introduction of error. Any time a file is opened, you open the door for a bad keystroke or, even worse, a deletion that is unrecoverable. This is a fine method for program development, but any volume production should take place in a more protected environment. Consider the following PostScript code:

```
100 100 translate
/Times-Roman findfont 8 scalefont setfont
0 0 moveto
(Job Number: 80245 -- Operator: John Doe)show
0 -20 rmoveto
(4-18-89 -- 10:10am)show
showpage
```

If this were to repeat for each new use of this code, you would not want to manually keystroke each change directly in the code. The best alternative is to create an application program that writes the PostScript file for you, based on input at the application level. We have chosen BASIC as our programming environment to guarantee the greatest level of reader comprehension. The same code above as a short BASIC program would be:

```
cls
line input "Enter a filename: ";filename$
line input "Enter your page identification:
";pageid$
print "Hit any key to create file, hit ESC to exit."
aloop:
a$=inkey$
if a$=asc$(27) then goto ender else goto printit
goto aloop
printit:
open filename$ for output as #1
print #1 "100 100 translate"
print #1 "/Times-Roman findfont 8 scalefont setfont"
print #1 "0 0 moveto"
print #1 "("pageid$")show"
print #1 "0 -20 rmoveto"
print #1 "("date$" and "time$")show"
print #1 "showpage"
write
close #1

ender:
cls
stop
```

This works fine for updating textual information in your PostScript files, but the following method is much more useful when manipulating graphics. Consider this code:

```
cls
line input "Enter a filename: ";filename$
line input "Enter your page identification:
";pageid$
line input "Enter your data array: ";darray$
line input "Enter the lower left x coordinate:
";llx$
line input "Enter the lower left y coordinate:
";lly$
line input "Enter the upper right x coordinate:
";urx$
line input "Enter the upper right y coordinate:
";ury$
print "Hit any key to create file, hit ESC to exit."
aloop:
a$=inkey$
if a$=asc$(27) then goto ender else goto printit
goto aloop
printit:
open filename$ for output as #1
print #1, "%!PS-Adobe 2.0"
```

```
print #1, "%%Title: SimplePlot"
print #1, "%%CreationDate: 12-12-88"
print #1, "%%Creator: Gerard Kunkel"
print #1, "%%BoundingBox 0 0 612 792"
print #1, "%%EndComments"
print #1, ""
print #1, "%%BeginProlog"
print #1, "%========================="
print #1, "/PageSet"
print #1, " {/ury exch def /urx exch def "
print #1, "      /lly exch def /llx exch def"
print #1, "      /width urx llx sub def "
print #1, "      /scalejump exch def"
print #1, "      /gridlines exch def"
print #1, "      /topval exch def"
print #1, "      /botval exch def"
print #1, "      1 setlinewidth "
print #1, "      0 setgray "
print #1, "      3 setmiterlimit}def"
print #1, ""
print #1, "%========================="
print #1, "/SimpleGrid"
print #1, " {/ygrid lly def "
print #1, "      gridlines {"
print #1, "      llx ygrid moveto llx width add
ygrid lineto"
print #1, "      /ygrid ygrid scalejump add def
}repeat"
print #1, "  }def"
print #1, ""
print #1, "%========================="
print #1, "/PlotData "
print #1, " {/Dataarray exch def"
print #1, " /widthjump width Dataarray length div
def"
print #1, "    /x llx def"
print #1, " Dataarray"
print #1, " {/Plot exch def"
print #1, "      /Plot Plot gridscale mul def"
print #1, "      x Plot moveto Drawmark "
print #1, "      /x x widthjump add def "
print #1, "      }forall"
print #1, ""
print #1, "%========================="
print #1, "/Drawmark"
print #1, " {-2 2 rmoveto 0 -4 rlineto"
print #1, "      4 0 rlineto 0 4 rlineto closepath
fill}def"
print #1, ""
print #1, "%========================="
print #1, "%%EndProlog"
print #1, "%%BeginScript"
print #1, ""
print #1, "0 125 5 25 "llx$;lly$;urx$;ury$ "
```

```
PageSet"
print #1, "SimpleGrid"
print #1, darray$" PlotData"
print #1, "/Times-Roman findfont 8 scalefont
setfont"
print #1, "50 740 moveto"
print #1, "("pageid$")show"
print #1, "0 -20 rmoveto"
print #1, "("date$" and "time$")show"
print #1, "showpage"
write
close #1
ender:
cls
stop
```

In the beginning of this code is a set of line inputs that collect some of the important variables for the PostScript script.

```
line input "Enter a filename: ";filename$
line input "Enter your page identification:
";pageid$
line input "Enter your data array: ";darray$
line input "Enter the lower left x coordinate:
";llx$
line input "Enter the lower left y coordinate:
";lly$
line input "Enter the upper right x coordinate:
";urx$
line input "Enter the upper right y coordinate:
";ury$
```

These BASIC variables are then applied later when an output file is opened and the PostScript code is written to disk. Upon inspection, you will see that the variables have now been wed into the PostScript procedural calls. Other variables can be input as well.

This method of data insertion gets us very close to an application program that allows for fast and easy update of data-driven graphics.

7-2 Application #1: A PostScript PROLOG Writer

Avid PostScript programmers often duplicate their efforts by rewriting the same information over and over again. Typically this will be the header information and some well-tested and oft-used routines. Having come to this conclusion from personal experience, I programmed a PROLOG writer. It is nothing more than a simple BASIC program that writes a PostScript header and all of the requested routines from my "greatest hits" collection.

The concept is simple. The program is a simple keyboard-interactive program that allows you to check off the routines that you will be using in your PostScript program. By saving a file, you are writing the PostScript prologue. You will then need to go in and write the particular procedure calls to the routines. It is easy to modify this BASIC code to add in your favorite routines. Follow these steps to add in the hypothetical "EXAMPLE" routine:

1. Open the .BAS file into Microsoft's QuickBASIC editor.

2. Scroll to locate the main screen. (The code looks just like the compiled screen image pictured in Figure 7–1.)

3. Change a screen cell to read "EXAMPLE". Use cell number 7 for this example. (The cells run sequentially from top to bottom and left to right.)

1989 G Kunkel	POSTSCRIPT PROLOG CODE WRITER			filename.ext
SPECIAL	GEOMETRY	CHARTS	TYPE	
SAVE	POLYGON	LINECHRT	FL RIGHT	.....
CMYK	FPOLYGON	VBARCHRT	FL CENTR	.....
REGISTER	BOX	HBARCHRT	JUSTIFY	.....
PAGE IDs	FillBOX	PIECHART	TY UP	.....
FOUNTAIN	CIRCLE	SCATTER	TY DOWN	.....
CLIPPING	FCIRCLE	HIGH-LOW	SHADOW	.....
.....	POLYLINE	BUBBLE	SPACED	.....
.....	ARC	3D BARS	.....	.....
.....	.....	.....	.....	.....

Figure 7–1
PROLOG.BAS
Main screen of the PostScript prologue writer showing the compiled program before making entries.

4. Find the pointer reference lower down in the code by searching for "ptr7". This BASIC routine is where you will insert your "EXAMPLE" code.

In Figure 7–1, the main screen of the PROLOG writer shows the routines available for file creation. By scrolling to the available selections and pressing the space bar, the user can toggle between "yes" and "no" choices. When completed, the "SAVE" box in the upper-left corner can be selected to write the file.

Figure 7–2, shows a typical screen display after the selection of routines has been made (marked by "x"s). Figure 7–3 shows the output code from this selection.

The following code is the complete BASIC listing of PROLOG.BAS. When compiled in Microsoft's QuickBASIC IV, the resulting EXE file will allow you to create your own prologues. By changing the PostScript code

```
ENTER YOUR POSTSCRIPT FILENAME: fig7-3

        SPECIAL         GEOMETRY        CHARTS          TYPE

   [ ]  SAVE            POLYGON         LINECHRT    X   FL RIGHT        .....
   X    CMYK            FPOLYGON        VBARCHRT    X   FL CENTR        .....
   X    REGISTER    X   BOX             HBARCHRT    X   JUSTIFY         .....
   X    PAGE IDs    X   FillBOX         PIECHART        TY UP           .....
        FOUNTAIN    X   CIRCLE          SCATTER         TY DOWN         .....
        CLIPPING    X   FCIRCLE         HIGH-LOW        SHADOW          .....
        .....           POLYLINE        BUBBLE          SPACED          .....
        .....           ARC             3D BARS         .....           .....
        .....           .....           .....           .....           .....
```

Figure 7–2
PROLOG.BAS
Main screen of the PostScript prologue writer showing the compiled program AFTER making entries. The save selection has been made and the program is waiting for a filename.

```
%!PS-Adobe 2.0 EPSF
%%Title: test.ps
%%Creator: Gerard Kunkel's Prolog Writer
%%CreationDate: 20:07:48 05-16-1989
%%BoundingBox: 0 0 612 796

%            BEGIN PROLOG

% ===================================
% ===== furniture
% ===================================
1 setlinewidth 0 setgray 1 setlinejoin

% ===================================
% ===== cmyk color separations for lineart
% ===================================
/seps 24 dict def seps begin
  /pickcolor [{pop pop pop 1 exch sub setgray}
  {pop pop exch pop 1 exch sub setgray}
  {pop 3 1 roll pop pop 1 exch sub setgray}
  {4 1 roll pop pop pop 1 exch sub setgray}]def
  /angles [105 75 90 45]def    % cmyk screenangles
end

/C 0 def /M 1 def /Y 2 def /K 3 def
/colorbreaks {userdict begin
  dup seps /pickcolor get exch get
  /setcmykcolor exch def seps /angles get exch get
  currentscreen exch pop 3 -1 roll exch
  setscreen /setscreen {}def end
}bind def

% /drawpage{    % BEGIN POSTSCRIPT ROUTINES

% ===================================
% ===== place register marks on page
% ===================================
/regmarks
{.5 setlinewidth
/ymark exch def
/xmark exch def
newpath xmark ymark moveto
 xmark ymark 20 sub lineto closepath stroke
newpath xmark 10 sub ymark 10 sub moveto
 xmark 10 add ymark lineto
closepath stroke xmark ymark 5 0 360 arc stroke
}bind def

/registerpage
 {40 740 regmarks
 40 50 regmarks
 580 50 regmarks
 580 740 regmarks}bind def
```

Figure 7–3

```
% =====================================
% ===== print page identifications
% =====================================
/F {findfont exch scalefont setfont}def
/names {/namearray exch def}def
/idpage{/colr exch def 8 /Helvetica-Bold F
 60 745 moveto
 1 1 1 1 setcmykcolor
 namearray {show 50 0 rmoveto}forall
 colr show .5 setlinewidth
 .5 setlinewidth  50 755 moveto 0 -15 rlineto 500 0 rlineto
 0 15 rlineto closepath stroke}def
[(date)(time)(filename)]names

% =====================================
% ===== box
% =====================================
/cbox
{setlinewidth setcmykcolor moveto lineto lineto lineto
 closepath gsave setcmykcolor fill grestore stroke}bind def
% .3 .5 .7 1 100 300 100 100 200 100 200 300 0 1 .7 .5 .3 cbox


% =====================================
% ===== filled color box
% =====================================
/fbox
{setlinewidth setcmykcolor moveto lineto lineto lineto
 closepath gsave setcmykcolor fill grestore stroke}def
% .5 .5 .5 .5 100 300 100 100 200 100 200 300 .1 .1 .1 .1 1 fbox

% =====================================
% ===== color circle
% =====================================
/ccircle
{setlinewidth setcmykcolor 0 360 arc stroke}def
% 100 100 12 .1 .1 .1 .1 1 ccircle

% =====================================
% ===== filled color circle
% =====================================
/fccircle
{setlinewidth setcmykcolor 0 360 arc fill}def
% 100 100 12 .1 .1 .1 .1 1 fccircle

% =====================================
% ===== color polyline
% =====================================
/polyline {
setlinewidth setcmykcolor /plarray exch def plarray aload pop
/plots exch count def /plotcount 1 def plots {plotcount 1 eq
```

Figure 7—3
(continued)

```
{moveto}{lineto}ifelse /plotcount 0 def}repeat closepath stroke}def
% [123 145 167 188 199 204] .5 .5 .5 .5 3 polyline

% ===================================
% ===== flush right
% ===================================
/FRshow {dup stringwidth pop neg 0 rmoveto show}def
% (Flush Right String)FRshow


% ===================================
% ===== flush center
% ===================================
/FCshow {dup stringwidth pop 2 div neg 0 rmoveto show}def
% (Flush Center String)FCshow


% ===================================
% ===== color shadow type
% ===================================
/shadow { % 4-color version
 /type exch def 3 -3 rmoveto setcmykcolor type show
 0 0 moveto setcmykcolor type show}def
% 1 0 1 0 1 1 0 .5 (test words) shadow
% ===================================
registerpage
% ===================================
[(black plate)(name)(date)(version #1)] names
% ===================================
}def          % END PROLOG

C colorbreaks     % CYAN PAGE
(cyan) idpage drawpage showpage

M colorbreaks
(magenta) idpage drawpage showpage

Y colorbreaks
(yellow) idpage drawpage showpage

K colorbreaks
(black) idpage drawpage showpage
```

Figure 7–3
(*concluded*)

insertions and their screen references, you will be able to customize this program to fit your needs.

There is a complete version of PROLOG.BAS source code available by mail. There is an ordering coupon in the back of this book.

```
cls
color1=1

header:
locate 1,1
```

```
print ``_____``
print ``_   1989 G Kunkel    POSTSCRIPT PROLOG CODE WRITER        filename.ext _``
print ``_____``
if writefile=1 then goto afterbody
body:
print ``      SPECIAL        GEOMETRY        CHARTS          TYPE              ``
print ``  _____``
print `` |  | SAVE     |   | POLYGON  |   | LINECHRT |   | FL RIGHT |   | ..... |``
print `` |  _____     _____       _____       _____               ``
print `` |  | CMYK     |   | FPOLYGON |   | VBARCHRT |   | FL CENTR |   | ..... |``
print `` |  _____     _____       _____       _____               ``
print `` |  | REGISTER |   | BOX      |   | HBARCHRT |   | JUSTIFY  |   | ..... |``
print `` |  _____     _____       _____       _____               ``
print `` |  | PAGE IDs |   | FillBOX  |   | PIECHART |   | TY UP    |   | ..... |``
print `` |  _____     _____       _____       _____               ``
print `` |  | FOUNTAIN |   | CIRCLE   |   | SCATTER  |   | TY DOWN  |   | ..... |``
print `` |  _____     _____       _____       _____               ``
print `` |  | CLIPPING |   | FCIRCLE  |   | HIGH-LOW |   | SHADOW   |   | ..... |``
print `` |  _____     _____       _____       _____               ``
print `` |  | ..... |     | POLYLINE |   | BUBBLE   |   | SPACED   |   | ..... |``
print `` |  _____     _____       _____       _____               ``
print `` |  | ..... |     | ARC      |   | 3D BARS  |   | ..... |     | ..... |``
print `` |  _____     _____       _____       _____               ``
print `` |  | ..... |     | ..... |     | ..... |     | ..... |     | ..... |``
print ``  _____``;
locate 25,2:print ``      Spacebar to Mark Selection    Enter to Select
Press ESC to Exit``;
ptr=1:wiper=6:wipec=3:r=6:c=3:dim x$(45):wipeptr=1
blank$=``
``
for n=1 to 45:x$(n)=``    ``:next

afterbody:
mainloop:
a$=inkey$
if a$=``''`` then goto mainloop
if asc(a$)=32 and ptr=2 then gosub changecolor:goto mainloop
if asc(a$)=32 then gosub changex:goto mainloop
if asc(a$)=13 and ptr=1 then gosub writefile :goto mainloop
if asc(a$)=15 then gosub ender:goto mainloop
if a$=chr$(27) then gosub ender:goto mainloop
if len(a$)=2 goto funkey:goto mainloop
gosub clik:goto mainloop
funkey:
b$=right$(a$,1)
if b$=chr$(75) then gosub leftkey        `left cursor
if b$=chr$(77) then gosub rightkey       `right cursor
if b$=chr$(80) then gosub downkey        `down cursor
if b$=chr$(72) then gosub upkey          `up cursor
goto mainloop

clik:sound(200),1:sound(100),1:return

changecolor:
color 7,0
```

```
x$(ptr)='' X ''
color1=color1+1
if color1>3 then color1=1
select case color1
  case 1:color1$='' CMYK ''
  case 2:color1$='' B&W ''
  case 3:color1$='' RGB ''
  case else
end select
locate 8,7:print color1$
return

changex:
color 0,7
if x$(ptr)='' X '' then x$(ptr)=''    '' else x$(ptr)='' X ''
if ptr=1 then gosub writefile
if ptr=2 then gosub changecolor
locate r,c:print x$(ptr)
return mainloop

upkey:ptr=ptr-1:r=r-2:
if ptr<1 then ptr=45:r=22:c=48
if ptr=9 then c=3:r=22
if ptr=18 then c=18:r=22
if ptr=27 then c=33:r=22
if ptr=38 then c=48:r=22
gosub testptr
return
downkey:ptr=ptr+1:r=r+2
if ptr=10 then c=18:r=6
if ptr=19 then c=33:r=6
if ptr=28 then c=48:r=6
if ptr=37 then c=63:r=6
gosub testptr
return

leftkey:ptr=ptr-9:c=c-15
gosub testptr
return
rightkey:ptr=ptr+9:c=c+15
gosub testptr
return

testptr:
if ptr<1 then ptr=45:c=63:r=22
if ptr>45 then ptr=1:c=3:r=6
locate r,c
color 0,7:print x$(ptr)
locate wiper,wipec
color 7,0:print x$(wipeptr)
wipeptr=ptr:wiper=r:wipec=c
return

cm:
print #1,''''
```

```
print #1,''% ================================''
print #1,''% ===== ''name$
print #1,''% ================================''
return

meter:locate 2,x:print ''_'':x=x+1:return

writefile:
x=12
locate 2,2:print blank$;
locate 2,3:print ''ENTER YOUR POSTSCRIPT FILENAME: '';
locate 2,35:line input file$

locate 2,2:print blank$;
if file$='''' then beep:return
locate 2,61:print ''FILE:''file$
locate 2,3:print ''PROGRESS:''
locate 2,60:print '':''
open file$ for output as #1

print #1,''%!PS-Adobe 2.0 EPSF
print #1,''%%Title: ''file$
print #1,''%%Creator: Gerard Kunkel's Prolog Writer''
print #1,''%%CreationDate: ''time$'' ''date$
print #1,''%%BoundingBox: 0 0 612 796"
print #1,''
print #1,''%              BEGIN PROLOG''

beginroutines:

name$=''furniture'':gosub cm:gosub meter
print #1,''1 setlinewidth 0 setgray 1 setlinejoin''

ptr2:if x$(2)=''   '' then goto ptr3
if color1=2 then goto ptr3
name$=''cmyk color separations for lineart'':gosub cm
print #1,''/seps 24 dict def seps begin''
print #1,''  /pickcolor [{pop pop pop 1 exch sub setgray}''
print #1,''  {pop pop exch pop 1 exch sub setgray}''
print #1,''  {pop 3 1 roll pop pop 1 exch sub setgray}''
print #1,''  {4 1 roll pop pop pop 1 exch sub setgray}]def''
print #1,''  /angles [105 75 90 45]def    % cmyk screenangles''
print #1,''end ''
print #1,''''
print #1,''/C 0 def /M 1 def /Y 2 def /K 3 def''
print #1,''/colorbreaks {userdict begin''
print #1,''  dup seps /pickcolor get exch get''
print #1,''  /setcmykcolor exch def seps /angles get exch get''
print #1,''  currentscreen exch pop 3 -1 roll exch''
print #1,''  setscreen /setscreen {}def end''
print #1,''}bind def''
print #1,''''
print #1,''% /drawpage{    % BEGIN POSTSCRIPT ROUTINES''
```

```
ptr3:gosub meter
if x$(3)=''    '' then goto ptr4
if color1=2 then goto ptr4
name$=''place register marks on page'':gosub cm
print #1,''/regmarks''
print #1,''{.5 setlinewidth''
print #1,''/ymark exch def''
print #1,''/xmark exch def''
print #1,''newpath xmark ymark moveto''
print #1,'' xmark ymark 20 sub lineto closepath stroke''
print #1,''newpath xmark 10 sub ymark 10 sub moveto''
print #1,'' xmark 10 add ymark lineto''
print #1,''closepath stroke xmark ymark 5 0 360 arc stroke''
print #1,''}bind def''
print #1,''''
print #1,''/registerpage''
print #1,'' {40 740 regmarks''
print #1,'' 40 50 regmarks''
print #1,'' 580 50 regmarks''
print #1,'' 580 740 regmarks}bind def''
print #1,''''

ptr4:gosub meter
if x$(4)=''    '' then goto ptr5
name$=''print page identifications'':gosub cm
print #1,''/F {findfont exch scalefont setfont}def''
print #1,''/names {/namearray exch def}def''
print #1,''/idpage{/colr exch def 8 /Helvetica-Bold F''
print #1,'' 60 745 moveto ''
if color1=1 then print #1,'' 1 1 1 1 setcmykcolor '' else print #1,'' 0
setgray ''
print #1,'' namearray {show 50 0 rmoveto}forall  ''
print #1,'' colr show .5 setlinewidth
print #1,'' .5 setlinewidth  50 755 moveto 0 -15 rlineto 500 0 rlineto ''
print #1,'' 0 15 rlineto closepath stroke}def''
print #1,''[(date)(time)(filename)]names''

ptr5:gosub meter
if x$(5)=''    '' then goto ptr6

ptr6:gosub meter
if x$(6)=''    '' then goto ptr7

ptr7:gosub meter
if x$(7)=''    '' then goto ptr8

ptr8:gosub meter
if x$(8)=''    '' then goto ptr9

ptr9:gosub meter
if x$(9)=''    '' then goto ptr10

ptr10:gosub meter: rem polygon
if x$(10)=''    '' then goto ptr11
```

```
ptr11:gosub meter: rem filled polygon
if x$(11)=''    '' then goto ptr12

ptr12:gosub meter
if x$(12)=''    '' then goto ptr13
name$=''box'':gosub cm
if x$(12)='' X '' and color1=1 then goto ptr12C
print #1,''/box''
print #1,''{setlinewidth setgray moveto lineto lineto lineto stroke}bind def''
print #1,''% 100 300 100 100 200 100 200 300 0 1 box''
print #1,''''
goto ptr13

ptr12C:
print #1,''/cbox''
print #1,''{setlinewidth setcmykcolor moveto lineto lineto lineto''
print #1,'' closepath gsave setcmykcolor fill grestore stroke}bind def''
print #1,''% .3 .5 .7 1 100 300 100 100 200 100 200 300 0 1 .7 .5 .3 cbox''
print #1,''''

ptr13:gosub meter
if x$(13)=''    '' then goto ptr14
if color1=1 then goto ptr13c
name$=''filled box'':gosub cm
print #1,''/fbox''
print #1,''{setlinewidth setgray moveto lineto lineto lineto''
print #1,'' closepath gsave setgray fill grestore stroke}def''
print #1,''% .5 100 300 100 100 200 100 200 300 0 1 fbox''
goto ptr14

ptr13c:
name$=''filled color box'':gosub cm
print #1,''/fbox''
print #1,''{setlinewidth setcmykcolor moveto lineto lineto lineto''
print #1,'' closepath gsave setcmykcolor fill grestore stroke}def''
print #1,''% .5 .5 .5 .5 100 300 100 100 200 100 200 300 .1 .1 .1 .1 1 fbox''

ptr14:gosub meter
if x$(14)=''    '' then goto ptr15
if color1=1 then goto ptr14c
name$=''circle'':gosub cm
print #1,''/circle''
print #1,''{setlinewidth setgray 0 360 arc stroke}def''
print #1,''% 100 100 12 0 1 circle''
goto ptr15

ptr14c:
name$=''color circle'':gosub cm
print #1,''/ccircle''
print #1,''{setlinewidth setcmykcolor 0 360 arc stroke}def''
print #1,''% 100 100 12 .1 .1 .1 .1 1 ccircle''
```

```
ptr15:gosub meter
if x$(15)=''    '' then goto ptr16
if color1=1 then goto ptr15c
name$=''filled circle'':gosub cm
print #1,''/fcircle''
print #1,''{setlinewidth setgray 0 360 arc fill}def''
print #1,''% 100 100 12 0 1 fcircle''
goto ptr16

ptr15c:
name$=''filled color circle'':gosub cm
print #1,''/fccircle''
print #1,''{setlinewidth setcmykcolor 0 360 arc fill}def''
print #1,''% 100 100 12 .1 .1 .1 .1 1 fccircle''

ptr16:gosub meter
if x$(16)=''    '' then goto ptr17
if color1=1 then goto ptr16c
name$=''polyline'':gosub cm
print #1,''/polyline {''
print #1,''setlinewidth setgray /plarray exch def plarray aload pop ''
print #1,''/plots exch count def /plotcount 1 def plots {plotcount 1 eq''
print #1,''{moveto}{lineto}ifelse /plotcount 0 def}repeat closepath
stroke}def''
print #1,''% [123 145 167 188 199 204] .5 3 polyline''
goto ptr17

ptr16c:
name$=''color polyline'':gosub cm
print #1,''/polyline {''
print #1,''setlinewidth setcmykcolor /plarray exch def plarray aload pop ''
print #1,''/plots exch count def /plotcount 1 def plots {plotcount 1 eq''
print #1,''{moveto}{lineto}ifelse /plotcount 0 def}repeat closepath
stroke}def''
print #1,''% [123 145 167 188 199 204] .5 .5 .5 .5 3 polyline''

ptr17:gosub meter
if x$(17)=''    '' then goto ptr18
name$=''arc'':gosub cm

ptr18:gosub meter
if x$(18)=''    '' then goto ptr19
name$=''line chart'':gosub cm

ptr19:gosub meter
if x$(19)=''    '' then goto ptr20
name$=''vertical bar chart'':gosub cm

ptr20:gosub meter
if x$(20)=''    '' then goto ptr21
name$=''horizontal bar chart'':gosub cm
```

```
ptr21:gosub meter
if nf(21)=''    '' then goto ptr22
name$=''pie chart'':gosub cm

ptr22:gosub meter
if x$(22)=''    '' then goto ptr23
name$=''scatter chart'':gosub cm

ptr23:gosub meter
if x$(23)=''    '' then goto ptr24
name$=''high low chart'':gosub cm

ptr24:gosub meter
if x$(24)=''    '' then goto ptr25
name$=''bubble chart'':gosub cm

ptr25:gosub meter
if x$(25)=''    '' then goto ptr26
name$=''3d charts'':gosub cm
ptr26:gosub meter
if x$(26)=''    '' then goto ptr27

ptr27:gosub meter
if x$(27)=''    '' then goto ptr28

ptr28:gosub meter
if x$(28)=''    '' then goto ptr29
name$=''flush right'':gosub cm
print #1,''/FRshow {dup stringwidth pop neg 0 rmoveto show}def''
print #1,''% (Flush Right String)FRshow''

ptr29:gosub meter
if x$(29)=''    '' then goto ptr30
name$=''flush center'':gosub cm
print #1,''/FCshow {dup stringwidth pop 2 div neg 0 rmoveto show}def''
print #1,''% (Flush Center String)FCshow''

ptr30:gosub meter
if x$(30)=''    '' then goto ptr31
name$=''justified type'':gosub cm

ptr31:gosub meter
if x$(31)=''    '' then goto ptr32
name$=''vertical type (up)'':gosub cm

ptr32:gosub meter
if x$(32)=''    '' then goto ptr33
name$=''vertical type (down)'':gosub cm

ptr33:gosub meter
if x$(33)=''    '' then goto ptr34
if color1=1 then goto ptr33c
name$=''shadow type'':gosub cm
print #1,''/shadow {      % black and white version''
```

```
print #1,'' /type exch def 3 -3 rmoveto 0 setgray type show''
print #1,'' 0 0 moveto 1 setgray type show}def''
print #1,''% (test words) shadow''
goto ptr34

ptr33c:
name$=''color shadow type'':gosub cm
print #1,''/shadow {  % 4-color version''
print #1,'' /type exch def 3 -3 rmoveto setcmykcolor type show''
print #1,'' 0 0 moveto setcmykcolor type show}def''
print #1,''% 1 0 1 0 1 1 0 .5 (test words) shadow''

ptr34:gosub meter
if x$(34)=''   '' then goto ptr35

ptr35:gosub meter
if x$(35)=''   '' then goto ptr36

ptr36:gosub meter
if x$(36)=''   '' then goto ptr37

ptr37:gosub meter
if x$(37)=''   '' then goto ptr38

ptr38:gosub meter
if x$(38)=''   '' then goto ptr39

ptr39:gosub meter
if x$(39)=''   '' then goto ptr40

ptr40:gosub meter

ptr1end:gosub meter
if x$(3)=''   '' then goto ptr2end
print #1,''% ===================================''
print #1,''registerpage''

ptr2end:gosub meter
if x$(4)=''   '' then goto ptr3end
print #1,''% ===================================''
print #1,''[(black plate)(name)(date)(version #1)] names''

ptr3end:gosub meter
if x$(1)=''   '' then goto ptr4end

ptr4end:gosub meter
if color1=2 then goto ptr5end
if x$(2)=''   '' then goto ptr5end
print #1,''% ===================================''
print #1,''}def          % END PROLOG''
print #1,''''
print #1,''C colorbreaks      % CYAN PAGE''
print #1,''(cyan) idpage drawpage showpage ''
print #1,''''
```

```
print #1,''M colorbreaks''
print #1,'' (magenta) idpage drawpage showpage''
print #1,''''
print #1,''Y colorbreaks''
print #1,'' (yellow) idpage drawpage showpage''
print #1,''''
print #1,''K colorbreaks''
print #1,'' (black) idpage drawpage showpage
print #1,''''

ptr5end:gosub meter
ptrend:gosub meter

print #1,''''
close #1
ender:
locate 2,2:print blank$;
locate 2,2:print '' EXIT PROGRAM (Y/N)''
exitloop:a$=inkey$:if a$='''' then goto exitloop
if a$=''Y'' then goto endit
if a$=''y'' then goto endit
writefile=1
return header

endit:
cls
end
```

7-3   Application #2: A Headline Writer

The following code written for Microsoft's QuickBASIC 4.0 (IBM-compatible) will generate an application that creates encapsulated Post-Script files. This particular program enables headline condensing, expanding, obliquing, and bolding. See Figure 7–4 for an example of the screen image when this code is compiled. The highlighted selection, "TYPE-FACE", shows that Helvetica bold oblique has been chosen. Hitting the space bar at this point will cycle the selection through various PostScript typefaces. By editing the BASIC source code, you can add other PostScript typefaces that are available on your printer.

Figure 7–5 shows the same program with the edit window displayed. This window is accessed via the F5 key. Complete text editing is available in this window, including the ability to add kerning marks. Positive and

```
┌─────────────────────────────────────────────────────────────────┐
│ /Helvetica-BoldOblique  POSTSCRIPT HEADLINE CODE WRITER  default.EPS │
├─────────────────────────────────────────────────────────────────┤
│   FILENAME: default              POINT SIZE: 36                   │
│   TYPEFACE: /Helvetica-BoldOblique    LEADING: 46                 │
│   BOLDNESS: 1                 SKEW IN DEGREES: 0                  │
│   PRINTER: Color               CONDENSING %: 10                  │
│  GLOBAL KRN: 8                ALIGNMENT: Flush Left              │
│      LLX: 0                         C: 100                       │
│      LLY: -321                      M: 20                        │
│      URX: 524.6                     Y: 40                        │
│      URY: 28.80                     K: 10                        │
│  F1-WRITE EPS   F2-SAVE   F3-OPEN   F4-WRITE GRID   F5-ENTER TEXT │
│  xxxxxxxx                                                         │
└─────────────────────────────────────────────────────────────────┘
```

Figure 7—4
KERN.BAS
Main screen of the PostScript custom headline writer showing the compiled program AFTER making entries. The cursor is sitting on the type selection and the program is waiting for a typeface selection to be made.

negative kern values can be inserted between characters and words. Positive kerning is represented by a "less-than" symbol and negative kerning by a "greater-than" symbol.

Figure 7–6 shows a PageMaker screen display with an encapsulated PostScript file representing a headline created with KERN.EXE, the compiled version of KERN.BAS

Figure 7–7 shows the typography that was created with this program.

The following program listing is the complete KERN.BAS program. Since this book focuses on PostScript and not BASIC, I will not go into the details of the BASIC programming. However, I will take the opportunity to show you how to create logical gates that determine the composition of the PostScript code.

```
' POSTSCRIPT HEADLINE WRITER
' COPYRIGHT 1988 GERARD KUNKEL
'

top: cls
dim d$(10,2):dim t$(7):kfact=1
blank2$=''
''
blank$=''                          ''
blank3$=''
r=5:c=15:wiper=5:wipec=15
d$(1,1)=''default'':exten$=''.EPS''
face=1:dr=1:dc=1:align=1:printer=1
dim kern1(7)
dim kern2(7)
dim linestring$(7)
gosub repaintscreen
gosub openit
gosub getkey
goto top

repaintscreen:
color 7,0
locate 1,1
print ''_____''
print ''_ 1988 G Kunkel      POSTSCRIPT HEADLINE CODE WRITER       filename.ext _''
print ''_____''
body:
print ''_____'';
print ''¦   FILENAME:                    POINT SIZE:                  ¦'';
print ''_____'';
print ''¦   TYPEFACE:                    LEADING:                     ¦'';
print ''_____'';
print ''¦  BOLDNESS:                 SKEW IN DEGREES:                 ¦'';
print ''_____'';
print ''¦   PRINTER:                 CONDENSING %:                    ¦'';
print ''_____'';
print ''¦ GLOBAL KRN:                    ALIGNMENT:                   ¦'';
print ''_____'';
print ''¦      LLX:                      C:                           ¦'';
print ''¦                                                             ¦'';
print ''¦      LLY:                      M:                           ¦'';
print ''¦                                                             ¦'';
print ''¦      URX:                      Y:                           ¦'';
print ''¦                                                             ¦'';
print ''¦      URY:                      K:                           ¦'';
print ''_____'';
print ''¦  F1-WRITE EPS    F2-SAVE    F3-OPEN    F4-WRITE GRID   F5-ENTER TEXT ¦'';
print ''_____'';
return

update:
color 7,0
locate 25,3:print blank2$;
```

```
locate 2,65:print ''                ''
locate 2,65:print d$(1,1)''.EPS'';
locate 25,3:print ''xxxxxxxx'';
return

crcheck:
if dr=2 and dc=2 then gosub qbox:gosub repaintscreen:gosub refresh
if dr=4 and dc=2 then gosub qbox:gosub repaintscreen:gosub refresh
if dr=2 and dc=1 then gosub newface
if dr=4 and dc=1 then gosub newprinter
if dr=5 and dc=2 then gosub alignment
return

newface:
face=face+1
if face>8 then face=1
select case face
  case 1:d$(2,1)=''/Helvetica''
  case 2:d$(2,1)=''/Helvetica-Bold''
  case 3:d$(2,1)=''/Helvetica-Oblique''
  case 4:d$(2,1)=''/Helvetica-BoldOblique''
  case 5:d$(2,1)=''/Times-Roman''
  case 6:d$(2,1)=''/Times-Bold''
  case 7:d$(2,1)=''/Times-Italic''
  case 8:d$(2,1)=''/Times-BoldItalic''
end select
locate 7,15:print blank$
locate 7,15:print d$(2,1)
return newkey


newprinter:
printer=printer+1
if printer>2 then printer=1
select case printer
  case 1:d$(4,1)=''Black and White''
  case 2:d$(4,1)=''Color''
end select
locate 11,15:print blank$
locate 11,15:print d$(4,1)
return newkey

alignment:
align=align+1
if align>4 then align=1
select case align
  case 1:d$(5,2)=''Flush Left''
  case 2:d$(5,2)=''Flush Right''
  case 3:d$(5,2)=''Centered''
  case 4:d$(5,2)=''Letter Spaced''
  end select
locate 13,57:print blank$
locate 13,57:print d$(5,2)
return newkey
```

```
getkey:
outon$='' .EPS'' :color 0,7
locate r,c:print blank$
color 7,0
v$=d$(dr,dc)
if d$(1,2)<>'''' and d$(2,2)='''' then d$(2,2)=d$(1,2)
gosub testx
sound (170),.1
newkey:
a$=inkey$
if a$='''' then goto newkey

if asc(a$)=13 then d$(dr,dc)=v$:gosub crcheck:gosub update:goto getkey
if asc(a$)=8 then num=len(v$)-1:gosub backspace:sound (400),.3:goto newkey
if asc(a$)=27 then gosub ender:goto getkey
if len(a$)=2 goto funkey:goto getkey
v$=v$+a$
locate 2,3:print v$
goto newkey

backspace:
if num<0 then num=0
v$=left$(v$,num):
locate 2,3:print blank$:
locate 2,3:print v$:
return

'=============================== extended characters ==================
funkey:
sound (600),.1
b$=right$(a$,1)
k=asc(b$)
select case k
  case 59
    gosub writefile
  case 60
    gosub saveit
  case 61
    gosub openit
  case 62
    gosub writegrid
  case 63
      gosub entertext
      gosub repaintscreen
      gosub refresh
  case 75
    gosub leftkey       'left cursor
  case 77
    gosub rightkey      'right cursor
  case 80
    gosub downkey       'down cursor
  case 72
    gosub upkey         'up cursor
```

```
    case 71
      gosub homekey
    case 73
      gosub pgup
    case 81
      gosub pgdn
    case 79
      gosub endkey
    case else
  end select
  goto getkey

  '============================= cursor keys ===================
  leftkey:
  wipedr=dr:wipedc=dc
  wiper=r:wipec=c:dc=dc-1
  if dc<1 then dc=2
  gosub testx
  return

  upkey:
  wipedr=dr:wipedc=dc
  wiper=r:wipec=c:dr=dr-1
  if dr<1 and dc=1 then dr=9:dc=2
  if dr<1 and dc=2 then dr=9:dc=1
  gosub testx
  return

  rightkey:
  wipedr=dr:wipedc=dc
  wiper=r:wipec=c:dc=dc+1
  if dc>2 then dc=1
  gosub testx
  return

  downkey:
  wipedr=dr:wipedc=dc
  wiper=r:wipec=c:dr=dr+1
  if dr>9 and dc=2 then dr=1:dc=1
  if dr>9 and dc=1 then dr=1:dc=2
  gosub testx
  return

  homekey:
  pgup:
  wipedr=dr:wipedc=dc
  wiper=r:wipec=c:dr=1:dc=1
  gosub testx
  return

  endkey:
  pgdn:
  wipedr=dr:wipedc=dc
```

```
wiper=r:wipec=c:dr=9:dc=2
gosub testx
return


ender:
locate 2,3:print blank$;
locate 2,3:print ''EXIT PROGRAM (Y/N)''
for z= 1 to 2
sound (600),1
sound (180),1
sound (100),2
next
exitloop:a$=inkey$:if a$='''' then goto exitloop
if a$=''Y'' then goto endit
if a$=''y'' then goto endit
writefile=1
locate 2,3:print blank$
return

openit:
filename$=d$(1,1)+''.KRN''
locate 2,3:print ''OPENING FILE      ''
open filename$ for input as #1
for x=1 to 9
for y=1 to 2
input #1, d$(x,y)
next
next
for t=1 to 7
input #1, t$(t)
next
for t=1 to 7
lent=len(t$(t))
for z=1 to lent
if mid$(t$(t),z,1)=''\'' then mid$(t$(t),z,1)='',''
next
next
close #1
locate 2,3:print ''COMPLETED      ''
gosub defd10
gosub refresh
gosub update
return

saveit:
filename$=d$(1,1)+''.KRN''
locate 2,3:print ''SAVING FILE      ''
open filename$ for output as #1
for x=1 to 9
for y=1 to 2
print #1, d$(x,y)'','';
next
next
```

```
for t=1 to 7
lent=len(t$(t))
for z=1 to lent
if mid$(t$(t),z,1)='','' then mid$(t$(t),z,1)=''\''
next
x$=t$(t)
if right$(t$(t),1)=chr$(13) then x$=left$(t$(t),lent-1)
print #1, x$'','';
next
write
close #1
locate 2,3:print ''COMPLETED          ''
return

endit:
cls
end

'    add in shell to print file from DOS

writegrid:
gridtest=1

writefile:
exten$=''.EPS''
filename$=d$(1,1)+exten$
open filename$ for output as #1
locate 2,3: print blank$:locate 2,3:print ''WRITING FILE''
print #1, ''%!PS-Adobe 2.0''
print #1, ''%%Title: ''d$(1,1)
print #1, ''%%CreationDate:''date$;'' Time: ''time$
print #1, ''%%Creator: Gerard Kunkel 1988''
if gridtest=1 then print #1, ''%%BoundingBox: 0 0 612 792'' :goto afterbbox
print #1, ''%%BoundingBox: ''d$(6,1)'' ''d$(7,1)'' ''d$(8,1)'' ''d$(9,1)
locate 2,3: print blank$:locate 2,3:print ''WRITING BBOX''
afterbbox:
print #1, ''gsave''
if gridtest=0 then goto aftergrid
locate 2,3: print blank$:locate 2,3:print ''WRITING GRID''
lly=val(d$(7,1))
llx=val(d$(6,1))
ury=val(d$(9,1))
urx=val(d$(8,1))

print #1, ''25 300 translate''
print #1, ''1.5 setlinewidth 0 setgray''
print #1, ''/llx ''llx'' def /lly ''lly'' def /urx ''urx'' def /ury ''ury''
def''
print #1, ''''
print #1, ''llx lly moveto llx ury lineto''
print #1, ''urx ury lineto urx lly lineto''
print #1, ''closepath stroke''
print #1, ''/drawgrid {/lly ''val(d$(7,1))''  def''
print #1, ''   llx increment urx {''
```

```
print #1, ``    llx lly moveto llx ury lineto stroke''
print #1, ``    /llx llx increment add def}for''
print #1, ``    /llx ``val(d$(6,1))'' def''
print #1, ``  lly increment ury {``
print #1, ``    llx lly moveto urx lly lineto stroke''
print #1, ``    /lly lly increment add def}for}def''
print #1, ``.3 setlinewidth''
print #1, ``/increment 12 def drawgrid''
print #1, ``/increment 72 def drawgrid''
aftergrid:
if printer=1 then goto BWprint
if printer=2 then goto colorprint
beep:close #1:return

BWprint:
locate 2,3: print blank$:locate 2,3:print ``WRITING B&W''
print #1, using ``#.##'';1-(val(d$(9,2))*.01)
print #1, `` setgray''
goto aftercolor

colorprint:
locate 2,3: print blank$:locate 2,3:print ``WRITING COLOR''
print #1, using ``#.##''; (val(d$(6,2))*.01)
print #1, using ``#.##''; (val(d$(7,2))*.01)
print #1, using ``#.##''; (val(d$(8,2))*.01)
print #1, using ``#.##''; (val(d$(9,2))*.01)
print #1, `` setcmykcolor''

aftercolor:

print #1, bold `` setlinewidth''
print #1, ``3 setmiterlimit /y 0 def''
print #1, ``/T {dup stringwidth pop /tw exch def''
print #1, ``    false charpath gsave fill grestore stroke''
print #1, ``    /kfactor exch def''
print #1, ``    /twf tw kfactor mul def /track track twf add def''
print #1, ``    track y moveto }def''
print #1, ``/newline {/y y ``d$(2,2)'' sub def /track 0 def track y
moveto}def''
print #1, ````
charwidth=val(d$(1,2))-(val(d$(1,2))*(val(d$(4,2))*.01))
skew=cos(charwidth)*val(d$(3,2))
skew=abs(skew)
print #1, d$(2,1) `` findfont [``charwidth'' 0 ``skew
print #1, using ``###.##'';val(d$(1,2))
print #1, `` 0 0]''
print #1, ``makefont setfont''
print #1, ````
print #1, ``/track 0 def''
print #1, ``0 y moveto''

lin=1:lincount=1
linestring$(lin)=''''
kern1(lin)=0
```

```
kern2(lin)=0
kfact=1-(global*.01)
textlen=len(d$(10,1))

getlineinfo:
for x=1 to textlen
  t$=mid$(d$(10,1),x,1)
  if t$=chr$(13) then lin=lin+1:goto nextgli
  if t$=chr$(60) then kern1(lin)=kern1(lin)+1:goto nextgli
  if t$=chr$(62) then kern2(lin)=kern2(lin)+1:goto nextgli
  linestring$(lin)=linestring$(lin)+t$
locate 2,3:print ``Line: ``lin``> ``linestring$(lin)
nextgli:
next

if align=2 then gosub FlushRight:gosub ReadFR
if align=3 then gosub FlushCenter
if align=4 then gosub LetterSpace

for x=1 to textlen
gosub FlushLeft
next
goto endfile

FlushLeft:
ReadStrings:
  t$=mid$(d$(10,1),x,1)
  if t$=chr$(13) then goto leading
  checkkern:
    t2$=mid$(d$(10,1),x+1,1)
    if t2$=chr$(60) then x=x+1:kfact=kfact-.05:goto checkkern
    if t2$=chr$(62) then x=x+1:kfact=kfact+.05:goto checkkern
    print #1, kfact``(``t$``)T ``;
    kfact=1-val(d$(5,1))*.01
nextReadStrings:
return

FlushRight:
lin=1
print #1, ``/locateFR {stringwidth pop /strwidth exch def``
print #1, `` /track strwidth ``kern1(lin)`` ``charwidth`` .05 mul mul sub
def``
print #1, `` /track track ``kern2(lin)`` ``charwidth`` .05 mul mul add def``
print #1, `` /track urx track sub def}def``
return

ReadFR:
print #1, ``(``linestring$(lin)``) locateFR``
print #1, ``track y moveto``
goto ReadStrings
return

FlushCenter:
return
```

```
LetterSpace:
return

endfile:
print #1, ``grestore''
write
close #1
locate 2,3:print blank$:locate 2,3:print ``COMPLETED''
gosub repaintscreen
gosub refresh
return

leading:
lin=lin+1
if lin=7 then return
print #1, ``newline''
select case align
  case 1
  goto nextReadStrings
  case 2
  goto ReadFR
end select
return


testx:
if dc=1 then c=15 else c=57
r=dr*2+3
v$=d$(dr,dc)
color 7,0
locate wiper,wipec
print blank$
locate wiper,wipec
print using ``\                   \'';d$(wipedr,wipedc)
color 0,7
locate r,c:print blank$
locate r,c:print using ``\                 \'';d$(dr,dc)
locate 2,3:print blank$
locate 2,3:print d$(dr,dc)
return

refresh:
for z=1 to 18
sound (170),.3
gosub downkey
next
return

qbox:
locate 12,4:print ``_____'';
for l=10 to 4 step -1
locate l,4:print ``_____'';
locate l+1,4:print ``|                                       |'';
next
```

```
locate 6,6:print ''Do You Want the System ''
locate 7,6:print ''Calculate an Estimated ''
locate 8,6:print ''Bounding Box? ''
qboxloop:c$=inkey$:if c$='''' then goto qboxloop
if c$=''y'' or c$=''Y'' then gosub calc else return

calc:
' ============= lly =============

lt=0
lins=0
for t=1 to 7
if t$(t)='''' then goto skiplins
lins=lins+1

skiplins:
next
d=val(d$(2,2))
d=0-(d*lins-1)
d$(7,1)=str$(d)
if lins=1 then d=d*.4:d$(7,1)=str$(d)
'============== urx =============
t$=d$(10,1)
lt=0:x=0:chklen=len(t$)

for t=1 to 7
tlen=0
tloop:x=x+1
if x>chklen then goto endoftloop
if mid$(t$,x,1)=chr$(13) then goto nextline
if mid$(t$,x,1)=chr$(60) then tlen=tlen-1.1
if mid$(t$,x,1)=chr$(62) then tlen=tlen-.9
tlen=tlen+1
if tlen>lt then lt =tlen
goto tloop
nextline:
next
endoftloop:
cw=val(d$(1,2))-(val(d$(1,2))*(val(d$(4,2))*.01))
cw=cw*.8
globalkern=(1-(val(d$(5,1))*.01))
d$(8,1)=str$((cw * lt)*globalkern)
d$(9,1)=str$(val(d$(1,2))*.8)
d$(8,1)= left$(d$(8,1),6)
d$(9,1)= left$(d$(9,1),6)
return

entertext:
ptr=1
lin=7
color 7,0
locate 16,4:print
''_____'';
for l=14 to 5 step -1
```

```
locate 1,4:print ''__ TEXT EDITING WINDOW
                                          '';
locate l+1,4:print ''|
|'';
next
for t=1 to 7
locate lin+(t-1),7:print t$(t)
next
t=1

newkey2:
begin$=t$(t):e$=''''
ptr=len(t$(t))+1

newkey2b:
col=ptr+6
locate lin,7:print blank3$
locate lin,7:print t$(t)

newkey3:
color 7,0
a$=inkey$
locate lin,col:print mid$(t$(t),ptr,1)
if a$='''' then goto newkey3
color 0,7
if asc(a$)=13 then gosub newline:goto newkey2
if asc(a$)=8 then gosub backspace2:sound (400),.3:goto newkey2b
if asc(a$)=27 then gosub defd10:return
if len(a$)=2 then gosub funkey2:a$='''':else ptr=ptr+1
t$(t)=begin$+a$+e$
num=len(t$(t))
begin$=left$(t$(t),ptr-1)
if num>0 then e$=mid$(t$(t),ptr,num-(ptr-1))
goto newkey2b

defd10:
d$(10,1)=''''
for t=1 to 7
if t$(t)='''' then goto skip13
if right$(t$(t),1)<>chr$(13) then t$(t)=t$(t)+chr$(13)
skip13:
d$(10,1)=d$(10,1)+t$(t)
next
return


clearline:
locate lin,7:print blank3$
locate lin,7:print t$(t)
return

del:
num=len(t$(t))
begin$=left$(t$(t),ptr-1)
```

```
e$=mid$(t$(t),ptr+1,num-(ptr-2))
t$(t)=begin$+e$
return

backspace2:
num=len(t$(t))
if num<1 then num=1
ptr=ptr-1:if ptr<1 then ptr=1:return
begin$=left$(t$(t),ptr-1)
e$=mid$(t$(t),ptr+1,num-(ptr-1))
t$(t)=begin$+e$
return

newline:
gosub clearline
t$(t)=t$(t)+chr$(13)
lin=lin+1
t=t+1:ptr=1
if lin>11 then:beep:lin=lin-1:t=t-1
return


funkey2:
sound (600),.1
b$=right$(a$,1)
k=asc(b$)
select case k
  case 59
        gosub writefile
  case 60
        gosub saveit
  case 61
        gosub openit
  case 62
        gosub writegrid
  case 75
        gosub leftkey2        'left cursor
  case 77
        gosub rightkey2       'right cursor
  case 80
        gosub downkey2        'down cursor
  case 72
        gosub upkey2          'up cursor
  case 71
        gosub homekey2
  case 73
        gosub pgup2
  case 81
        gosub pgdn2
  case 83
        gosub del
  case 79
        gosub endkey2
  case else
```

```
end select
return

'============================ cursor keys ====================
leftkey2:
ptr=ptr-1:if ptr<1 then ptr=1
return

upkey2:
gosub clearline
lin=lin-1
t=t-1
if t<1 then t=1:lin=lin+1
begin$=t$(t):e$=''''
if ptr>len(t$(t)) then ptr=len(t$(t))+1
return

rightkey2:
ptr=ptr+1:if ptr>num then ptr=num+1
return

downkey2:
gosub clearline
lin=lin+1
t=t+1
if t>7 then t=7:lin=lin-1
begin$=t$(t):e$=''''
if ptr>len(t$(t)) then ptr=len(t$(t))+1
return

homekey2:
pgup2:
gosub clearline
lin=5:t=1:ptr=1
begin$=t$(t):e$=''''
return

endkey2:
pgdn2:
gosub clearline
lin=11:t=7:ptr=1
begin$=t$(t):e$=''''
return
```

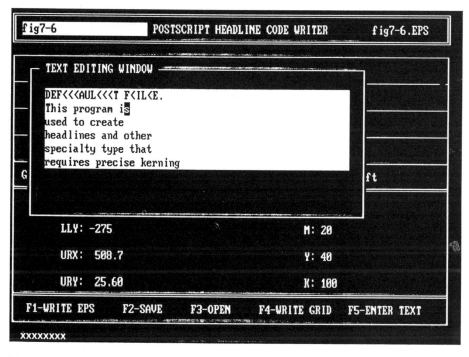

Figure 7–5
KERN.BAS
Main screen of the PostScript custom headline writer showing the compiled
program AFTER making entries. The EDIT WINDOW has been called and type
changes are being made. The less-than symbols indicate kerning units.

7.3.1 The KERN program default File

The following code is the comma-delimited default file, DEFAULT-
.KRN. To operate KERN.EXE, you will need to have this file available in
the same directory. This file should be input in a regular word processor
and saved as an ASCII file without any style formatting.

```
default,36,/Times-BoldItalic,46,1,0,Color,10,8,Flush Left,0,100,-
321,20,524.6,40,28.80,10,Default file for them,for you and i,and this is the
second,line and now the third,line of type\ and,it goes,on\ and on\ and on.,
```

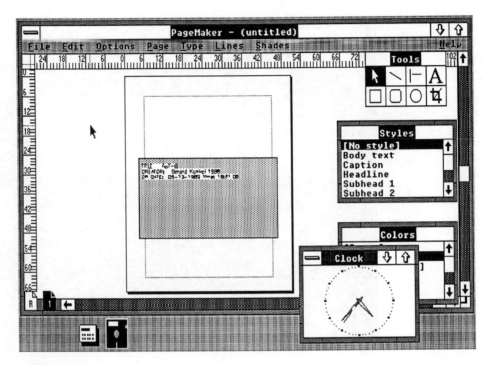

Figure 7—6
KERN.BAS
A PageMaker page with the encapsulated file from KERN.EXE. The bounding box is an estimated size calculated by KERN. The typography will appear when printed to a PostScript printer.

DEFAULT FILE.

This program is used to create headlines and other specialty type that requires precise kerning

Figure 7–7

CHAPTER 8

Encapsulated PostScript

8-1   Encapsulating PostScript

Jim Von Ehr of Altsys in Plano, TX, extended the overall power and flexibility of PostScript when he wrote the specifications for encapsulated PostScript. This subset of the standard PostScript Document Structuring Conventions is exactly what it sounds like, a segment of PostScript code that is encapsulated into an existing PostScript file.

The usefulness of this file type may not be immediately obvious, but if you are a desktop-publishing user, you will greatly appreciate the expanded possibilities presented to you. Capabilities that are not readily available to you in DTP may be possible in EPS (encapsulated PostScript).

Think of this capability in these terms: Anything that you see created in this book, as well as any creations that you design, can be encapsulated and imported into a DTP package and combined with text, graphics, or other imported files.

This screen image (Figure 8–1) shows the combination of a number of encapsulated files with PageMaker text, a halftone, and some PageMaker primitive graphics.

This LaserWriter output (Figure 8–2) shows the complete image. As you can see, those mysterious encapsulated PostScript gray boxes in PageMaker contained the code necessary to generate the detailed logos. This is by far the most practical way to create this type of page—or any page that contains repetitive graphic forms or graphics that are otherwise not available in PageMaker.

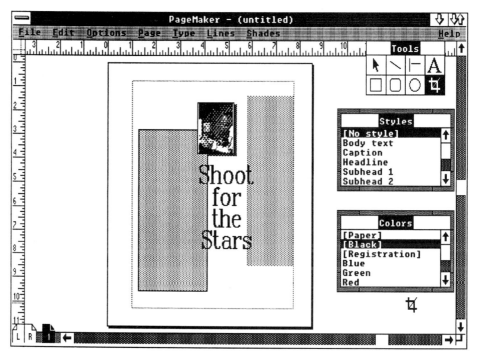

Figure 8—1

PageMaker, as well as many other PC-based and Macintosh-based publishing packages, allows for conforming encapsulated PostScript files to be imported. Nonconforming images will not be read in most cases. In some cases, a nonconforming file will be readable at the time of import, but not writable when printing. Any errors in the EPS file that occur at the interpretation stage of printing will cause the output system to halt.

First, let's look at those PostScript operator commands that should *not* be used within an encapsulated file.

banddevice	*initclip*	*note*	*setdevice*
copypage	*initgraphics*	*nulldevice*	*setccbatch*
erasepage	*initmatrix*	*quit*	*setmatrix*
exitserver	*legal*	*renderbands*	*showpage*
framedevice	*letter*	*setpageparms*	*stop*
grestoreall			

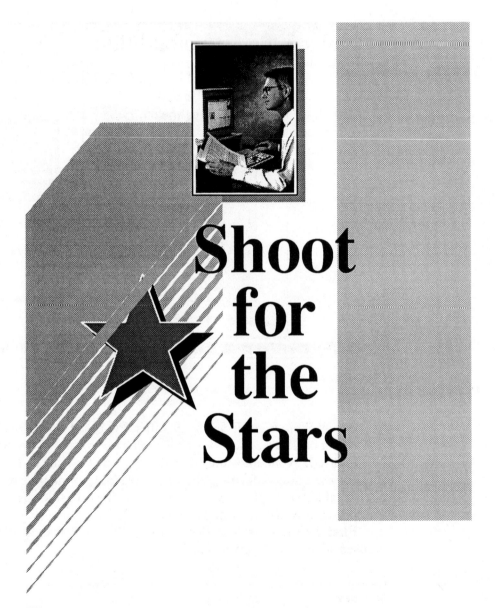

Figure 8—2

NOTE: Some applications disable the *showpage* operator. It is recommended, however, that this operator not be used when creating files for encapsulation.

8-2   Writing a Conforming File

Now that we know what NOT to include in an encapsulated file, let's look at what we must and should include.

Below is a brief look at the conforming construct and commenting required (and some desired) to create an encapsulated PostScript file that can be imported and printed.

At the very beginning of any PostScript file, there should be some identifying information—basic information such as the version of PostScript that you are conforming to, the date, the time, the creating applications name, any copyright information, and so forth. These indentifiers must be there in an EPS file. This is the information that the importing application will read to determine file type, size, and labeling information.

```
%!PS-Adobe-2.0 EPSF 1.2
%%Title: Encapsulated File
%%Creator: My Application
%%CreationDate: 10:00:00 12-06-88
%%BoundingBox: 0 0 612 792
%%EndComments
```

The header comments listed above can exist in any PostScript file. It is good practice to include this information in all of your files regardless of any intent to encapsulate and import. This is a structuring convention that will aid in keeping track of your PostScript file versions and names.

Let's look at these line by line.

```
%!PS-Adobe-2.0 EPSF 1.2
```

This is the identifying line that properly informs the importing software application as to which version of Adobe's PostScript you are conforming to.

```
%%Title: Encapsulated File
```

The Title is your title name. This comment, as well as all other comments, should be no longer than 256 characters.

```
%%Creator: My Application
```

The Creator comment line is where you indicate your name or the name of your application that is generating this file.

```
%%CreationDate: 10:00:00 12-06-88
%%BoundingBox: 0 0 612 792
```

The creation date is surely obvious. *BoundingBox* is by far the most critical of the comment fields imported. This array of four numbers informs the importing software as to the dimensions of the image area. As in other PostScript conventions, the four numbers are *llx, lly, urx,* and *ury,* defining two points of a box—the lower left and upper right corners. Anything outside these dimensions will not print.

```
%%EndComments
```

The *EndComments* field lets the system know that you have now completed the header comments.

At this point you can begin your procedure set. Remember to NOT include a *showpage* in your EPS file. While conforming import applications are required to disable the *showpage* operator, some do not do so. Omitting it will avoid any problems.

8.2.1   Clean Stacks

Since EPS files are normal PostScript files that have been encapsulated with the intent to add them to other PostScript code, care must be taken to avoid reaching the stack limits of PostScript.

When programming, assume that the importing program has already consumed some portion of the maximum memory available. Specifically, watch out for too many nested layers of *save/restore* and *gsave/grestore*. With a limit of eight layers, you can run out rather quickly, especially if you intend to add additional layers of encapsulation. After all, some application programs allow for both import and export of encapsulated files.

Another simple rule to follow is to regularly clean your stack. Keep an equivalent number of *pops* within your routines to empty out any unused data. I am probably one of the greatest offenders of this rule. In short programs I have the bad habit of writing the file so that it will image on the page, but never checking the stack to see what garbage I have left in my path.

In order to check your work, enter an interactive state with the PostScript interpreter and dump your PostScript code down. Then issue the command *pstack*. This will display the current stack contents. Assuming your page has been showpaged, the stack should be empty.

8-3 Attached Images

Most applications that read EPS files represent them on the screen as a gray box. This gray box is equal in size to the *BoundingBox* information that you have provided. In addition, some of the header comments are read by the application and added to the box as text comments. Usually, the file's title, creator, and creation date are printed inside the gray bounding box.

It is possible on both the Macintosh and PC platforms to attach a picture of your PostScript file so that the application can display an image rather than the gray box. (This is, of course, providing that the importing application is set up to do so, and most are.) The image attached to the EPS file is created by the application that generated the EPS file. For instance, on the Macintosh platform, if you were to create a simple box filled with a gray shade as an EPS file, you could also create the same image using the QuickDraw library routines. This image drawn on the screen can than be saved as a PICT file in the resource fork of the EPSF (encapsulated PostScript file) file. When this EPSF file is read by the importing application, it will read the PICT information and display that within the EPSF's bounding box.

A similar approach is possible on a PC platform, but it is decidedly more difficult. Two file formats are available, TIFF and Windows Metafile (WMF). Since there is no resource fork available in a PC-based file, a file header must be written that the importing application can read. This file header format looks like this:

```
HEADER

Byte
Number   Description
--------------------------------------------------
-------------
0-3 Must be hex C5D0D3C6 ("EPSF") byte0 =C5
4-7 Byte position in file for start of PostScript
code
8-11 Byte length of PostScript code
12-15 Byte position in file for start of MetaFile
16-19 Byte length of MetaFile code
20-23 Byte position in file for start of TIFF file
24-27 Byte length of TIFF code
28-29 Checksum of header (XOR of bytes 0-27)(ignored
if FFFF)

NOTE: Since you would never have both MetaFile and
TIFF code both representing your screen display, it
```

```
is assumed that either the MetaFile or the TIFF
position and length fields are zero; the non-zero
section is the one which should be used by the
importing application.

BODY
PostScript section
Metafile or TIFF section
```

For more information concerning encapsulated PostScript, write to

Altsys Corporation
Attn: Jim Von Ehr
720 Avenue F, Suite 108, Dept EPS
Plano, Texas 75074

Complete structuring conventions are available.

8-4 Interacting With PageMaker Using Encapsulated PostScript

All of the tips and techniques illustrated in this book can be applied to the world of desktop publishing. The encapsulated PostScript file format is your "hook" into these packages. Almost every DTP package supports the .EPS file format (file type EPSF on the Macintosh).

Since an encapsulated PostScript file can be created with any ASCII word processor, such as Windows Notepad, you can immediately hook into PageMaker or Ventura with an encapsulated version of your company logo or other extensively used piece of art.

I did just that for *PC Magazine*. In fact, the very first file that I encapsulated was a box. Start small and grow. The objective with that file was to make sure that I fully understood the proper code format for encapsulation. Once the simple box was imported, it was easy to see the possibilities. You may consider starting with something as simple as a box. I was lucky because our logo was framed in a box. Since PostScript defines encapsulated files as painted pixels within a bounding box, this is also the most logical place for anyone to start. After all, you will eventually have to contain your art within a box, visible or not.

From my original box came the *PC Magazine* logo. Working interactively, I was able to perfect the look of the PostScript-generated logo. When

I was ready, I created my EPS comment lines and specified the *Bounding-Box* dimensions. Figure 8–3 shows a PageMaker screen of what I saw when I imported the *PC Magazine* logo and added some other smaller logos.

Figure 8–4 shows the output from PageMaker to an Apple Laser-Writer IINT.

The code below shows exactly what was necessary to create a successful EPS file. This code will work fine on a Macintosh. The only requirement is that the file type be written as EPSF so that the importing application understands that it is an encapsulated PostScript file.

```
%%Title:   LOGOUSA4
%%Creator:  Gerard   Kunkel
%%CreationDate:    09-12-1989    19:29:25
%%BoundingBox:  100  100  260   306
%%EndComments

%%BeginProlog
/sc  1  def  /logolines  2  sc  mul  def
/x   100  def  /y  100  def  /4pop{4{pop}repeat}def
/m  {moveto}def  /l  {lineto}  def
/cgfgs  {closepath  gsave  fill  grestore  stroke}def
/cf  {closepath  fill}def
/box  {newpath  100  25  m  100  306  l
      260  306  l  260  25  l  cgfgs}def
/ecbox{newpath  104  29  m  104  98  l
      256  98  l  256  29  l  cgfgs}def
/inbox  {newpath  104  104  m  104  302  l
      256  302  l  256  104  l  closepath  stroke}def
/lns  {newpath  x  y  m  /y1  48  def  /x1  156  def
      {y1  200  le{4  y1  m  x1  y1  l  /y1  y1
       17.2  add  def}{exit}  ifelse}loop
       closepath  stroke}def
/PC{newpath  10  55  m  10  196  l  39  196  l
       39  55  l  cgfgs  newpath  39  196  m  76  196  76
       174  28  arcto  4pop  76  108  50  108  28  arcto
       4pop  39  108  l  39  126  l  49  126  49  140
       8  arcto  4pop  49  178  39  178  8  arcto
       4pop  38  178  l  cgfgs  newpath  122  139  m
       150  139  l  150  196  122  196  28  arcto
       4pop  108  196  l  82  196  82  172  28  arcto
       4pop  82  55  108  55  28  arcto  4pop
       150  55  150  112  28  arcto  4pop
       150  112  l  122  112  l  122  73  117  73  4  arcto
       4pop  112  73  112  81  4  arcto  4pop
       112  178  114  178  4  arcto  4pop
       122  178  122  172  4  arcto  4pop
       cgfgs  7.5  10  m}def
/Mag  {/zz  sc  3  div  def
       /Helvetica-Bold  findfont
       [27  0  0  45  0  0]  makefont
       setfont  (MA)show
       currentpoint  exch  1  sub  exch  m
```

```
      (GAZINE) show
      7.5 77 add 10 m (MA)show
      currentpoint exch 1 sub exch m
      (GAZINE) show }def
%%EndProlog

systemdict  begin  .2  setlinewidth  end
0  setgray  box
systemdict  begin  logolines  setlinewidth  end
1  setgray  ecbox  inbox
x  y  translate  lns  PC  Mag

showpage
```

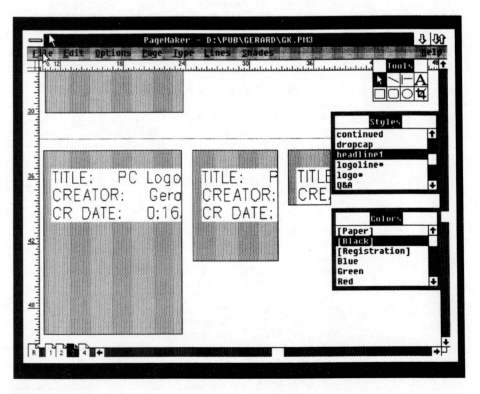

Figure 8—3

Figure 8—4

In this example, I have not shown the EPS file integrated with other more standard PageMaker elements. Figure 8–5 illustrates this integration nicely. The JETSET newsletter page has a number of imported elements and an EPS file, as well as PageMaker-generated text and graphics.

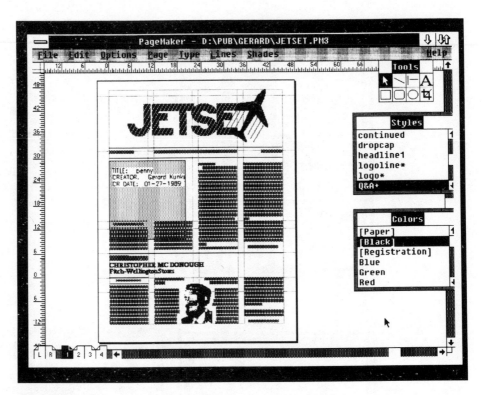

Figure 8–5
Encapsulated PostScript Working With PageMaker

The JETSET logo was created in Micrografx Designer, and the photo was scanned with a Microtek 300C halftone scanner and stored as a TIFF file. The encapsulated PostScript file was used to create a modified headline typeface that is not available in PageMaker. This EPS file was generated by my KERN.BAS program, which is outlined and listed in chapter 7, section 3. This is a good example of why you would want to program in PostScript and why you might then want to encapsulate it.

Note that the EPS bounding box in Figure 8–5 is overlapping the upper part of the text in the first and second columns. This is acceptable because the box is larger than the actual image area for the display type. In fact, if you are working quickly and want to save some time, you can specify a bounding box that is equal to the size of the paper you will be printing on.

We often do this at the magazine to save time. When you know exactly where to position the art within the page, you can explicitly start the image there or translate the image to that point. Either way, you will be successful.

The final output (Figure 8–6) shows the type in place and all of the text still printing where it should.

As you can see, using the encapsulated PostScript specification can enhance your desktop publishing documents. Logos, special graphic and typographic effects, and often-used graphic items can be streamlined and controlled in EPS format. In chapter 9 I will show the full breadth of interaction with desktop publishing using self-created PostScript code. The examples there are practical extensions of desktop publishing. In essence, this technique expands the drawing and formatting capabilities of the desktop publishing package.

8-5 Sending Color Information Through

What we have discussed so far is encapsulated PostScript that prints black-and-white images. This is essential when you are dealing with older hardware and software. With the advent of PageMaker 3.0, Ventura Professional Extension, Micrografx Designer 2.0, and Aldus Freehand, encapsulated PostScript with color specifications has become a reality and in many cases a necessity. For a thorough explanation of color specification and separation, see chapter 6. In this chapter, we will discuss the proper method of passing color information through to your application.

As was discussed earlier in this chapter, the document structuring of a file helps the importing application to work with your EPS file. In the case of color files, there is no standard for initial commenting of encapsulated files. The Altsys Corporation has offered a specification. At the time this book was prepared, however, no confirmation had been given by Adobe Systems, the company that produces the PostScript interpreters and licenses their use.

Without having the final specification in hand, I will at least try to give you enough information to let you start using color in your EPS files.

December 1988   Your monthly guide to the best the world has to offer   Vol. 1 No. 12

Penny-Pinching LANs

BY TIMOTHY SMITH

This month, JET SET focuses on shopping in Asia. Our lead story: shopping strategies for Southeast Asia's busiest city, Hong Kong. Though any time is a good time to stroll the endless malls and arcades of Central and Kowloon, the moderate temperatures of autumn and winter make outdoor walking far more pleasant than it is during the sultry summer months. Remember, Hong Kong is at the same latitude as the Bahamas.

Smart shoppers start off at one of the vast, air-conditioned shopping centers to get a feel for prices before plunging into the more obscure areas to hunt bargains. Among the best choices is the Landmark on Hong Kong Island. Packed with hundreds of upscale boutiques, this is where you'll find a full selection of European designer clothing, handcrafted luggage, and leather goods. The complex is connected by walkway to several hotels in the area.

If you ride the old street tram to the East you'll run into Casueway Bay, where you'll find some interesting Chinese and Japanese department stores. Shoes may be the best bargains there.

Across the harbor near the Star Ferry Pier in Kowloon you'll find the largest shopping center in all of Asia. Actually, the complex consists of three huge malls: Harbour City, Ocean Centre, and Ocean Terminal. These centers cater to arriving cruise ship passengers as well as to Kowloon tourists, so you're sure to find an international parade of shoppers crowding the endless corridors. Shopping fanatics may choose to stay at the Hong Kong Hotel, which sits atop the complex.

After a thorough exploration of Nathan Road (and a rest in the famous Peninsula Hotel lobby), you may want to head over to Tsimshatsui East, the newest shopping district in

(Continued on page 3)

CHRISTOPHER MC DONOUGH
Fitch-Wellington Stores

BY J.N. CANARD

London-born Christopher McDonough has been General Manager, Asian Operations of the Finch-Wellington chain of department stores for sixteen years. Finch-Wellington has had branches in Tokyo, Singapore, and Hong Kong since 1964. Recently, he shared his some of his unique views on Hong Kong shopping in an interview at his Kowloon headquarters.

Q. Hong Kong is a Chinese city, but with an amazingly international collection of shops and shoppers. Finch-Wellington is a British store. Do you find that Britons who've traveled so far will shop at a store that reminds them of home?

A. Only when they find rather a good bargain. Our crowds are mostly American. You see, I find that most Americans long to acquire a certain British style whereas the Brit-ish strive for an American look. While Londoners are at the Ralph Lauren outlets, Americans are in my store buying cashmere sweaters, Burberry trenchcoats, and Liberty of London neckties. Quite remarkable, actually.

Q. So Americans come to Hong Kong to indulge in a little

(Continued on page 2)

Figure 8—6

Fortunately, this process is extremely simple. Unfortunately, most of the application packages available today do not support the new color extensions. Some products, however, are being launched with the new specification. For instance, the Tektronix Phaser Color print system, a family of products that are PostScript-compatible, fully supports color PostScript specifications. HSB, RGB, and CMYK color models are interpreted, as well as the original *setgray* operator. For these examples of color encapsulated PostScript, I will use the Tektronix Phaser system as the output device. Taking these files and using them on a black-and-white printer is much more difficult and is covered in the chapters on BASIC programming and enhancing desktop publishing packages.

If you have read the chapter on color separation (Chapter 6), you will be much better prepared to understand this chapter.

The following encapsulated PostScript file can easily be converted to be drawn in color.

```
%!PS-Adobe 2.0
%%Creator: Gerard Kunkel
%%Title: PC Survey Logo
%%CreationDate: 0:16AM  2-3-1988
%%BoundingBox: 0 0 66.5 30
%%EndComments

/box {newpath
  0 0 moveto 0 30 lineto
  66 30 lineto 66 0 lineto
  closepath fill
}def

/inbox {newpath
  1 1 moveto 1 29 lineto
  65 29 lineto 65 1 lineto
  closepath stroke
}def

.7 setlinewidth
0 setgray box
1 setgray inbox
8.5 9.5 translate 0 0 moveto
/Times-Bold findfont [12 0 0 16 0 0] makefont
setfont
(SURVEY) show
```

In this example, a black box is drawn, a white line is inserted inside the box, and, finally, the word SURVEY is placed in white. The original intent for this little logo was to have white characters and inside line in a royal blue box. Let's fix this file so that it "thinks color." To change this encapsulated PostScript file means changing the reference to *setgray* to color:

```
.7 setlinewidth
1 .4 0 .1 setcmykcolor box
0 0 0 0 setcmykcolor inbox
8.5 9.5 translate 0 0 moveto
/Times-Bold findfont [12 0 0 16 0 0] makefont
setfont
(SURVEY) show
```

In this example I have chosen my favorite color model, CMYK. The same can be done with the other color models. Here is the same example with RGB.

```
.7 setlinewidth
0 .6 1 setrgbcolor box
1 1 1 setrgbcolor inbox
8.5 9.5 translate 0 0 moveto
/Times-Bold findfont [12 0 0 16 0 0] makefont
setfont
(SURVEY) show
```

When the accepting application receives this information, it simply performs a *gsave* and *grestore* on either side of it. This is to save the current state while performing the instructions in your code.

Using the *setrgbcolor* operator will guarantee no errors, since the earlier versions of the PostScript interpreter will understand that instruction. The newer *setcmykcolor* will cause an error, since the older interpreters did not include any reference to this operator. Some newer PostScript clones, however, such as the Tektronix Phaser System, will directly accept the *setcmykcolor* operator.

If you understand and can specify in RGB color, then do so. Coming from a publishing background, I think in terms of CMYK, the printer's process ink colors. The mixing of these inks is as natural to me as picking Crayola crayons. For anyone with a video discipline, the RGB color model will probably be more acceptable. In addition, the translation of color specification in RGB format in PostScript code and a computer or video display is a one-to-one relationship that does not require any translation.

The following code is an example of a detailed graphic that contains color definitions. This file was passed through PageMaker to generate the image shown in Figure C–5 in the color page inserts.

```
gsave
%%Title: Stock Market High-low graph
%%Creator: Gerard Kunkel
%%CreationDate: 3:44PM  12/30/1988
%%BoundingBox: 50 130 348 550
```

```
/box
 {setlinewidth
  /ytbox exch def
  /xrbox exch def
  /ybbox exch def
  /xlbox exch def
  xlbox ybbox moveto
  xlbox ytbox lineto
  xrbox ytbox lineto
  xrbox ybbox lineto
  closepath gsave setcmykcolor fill grestore stroke
}def


% ===================================
/chartgridbox
{setlinewidth
 /insidelines exch def
 /horizlines exch def
 /horiztick exch def
 /break exch def
 /yaxiscount exch def
 /xaxiscount exch def
 /yt exch def
 /xr exch def
 /yb exch def
 /xl exch def
 newpath
 xl yt moveto
 xr yt lineto
 xr yb lineto
 xl yb lineto
 closepath gsave
 setcmykcolor fill
 grestore
 stroke
  /totalwidth xr xl sub def
  /vertjump totalwidth xaxiscount div def
  /totalheight yt yb sub def
  /horizjump totalheight yaxiscount div def
  insidelines setlinewidth
  /tick yb 6 add def
 drawvert
horizlines {/tick xr def drawhoriz}if
horiztick {/tick xl 6 add def drawhoriz}if
/ylegendline yb 20 sub def
}def

% ===================================
/drawhoriz
  {yaxiscount {newpath
  xl yb moveto tick yb lineto closepath stroke
  /yb yb horizjump add def}repeat
  /yb yb totalheight sub def
  }def
```

```
% ===================================
/drawvert
   {/vertcount 1 def
   xaxiscount {newpath
   xl yb moveto xl
   vertcount 1 eq {tick 6 add}{tick} ifelse
   lineto closepath stroke
   /xl xl vertjump add def
   /vertcount vertcount 1 add def
   vertcount 6 eq {/vertcount 1 def}if
   }repeat
   /xl xl totalwidth sub def
   }def

% ===================================
/centertype
  {/strg exch def
   strg dup stringwidth pop
   2 div neg 0 rmoveto
   strg show}def

% ===================================
/centershow
   {/ax ax vertjump 2 div add def
   {ax y moveto centertype
   /ax ax vertjump add def} forall
   }def

% ===================================
/leftscale
  {/num 6 string def
   /xlabel exch def
   /scalestep topscale botscale sub xaxiscount div
def
   7 /Helvetica-Bold F
   /x xl 18 sub def
   x yb moveto 90 rotate
   xlabel show -90 rotate
   /yscale yb def 0 yb moveto
   } def

% ===================================
/scleft
   {num cvs dup stringwidth pop
   14 exch sub 0 rmoveto show
   /yscale yscale horizjump add def x yscale moveto
   } def

% ===================================
/ylabels
{/labelarray exch def
   /y yb 10 sub def
   labelarray
```

```
    {xl y moveto
    /label exch def
    label aload pop
    dup stringwidth pop
    2 div sub neg 0 rmoveto show
    /xl xl vertjump add def
    }forall
    /xl xl vertjump yaxiscount mul sub def
}def

% ==================================
/dimens
 {/topscale exch def
  /botscale exch def
  /scalefactor topscale botscale sub def
  /scalefactor scalefactor totalheight div def
  }def

% ==================================
/drawclose
 {-3 -1 rmoveto 0 2 rlineto 6 0 rlineto
  0 -2 rlineto closepath fill /plotcount 0 def
  /xl xl vertjump add def
  /reversexl reversexl vertjump add def
}def

% ==================================
/highlowplot
 {/plotarray exch def
  2 setlinewidth
  newpath
  /xl xl vertjump 2 div add def
  xl yb moveto
  /reversexl 0 def
  /plotcount 0 def

    plotarray    % use array of numbers

     {/plotcount plotcount 1 add def
     /plot exch def      % read numbers one at
                         % a time
     /y plot scalefactor div yb add def % needs yb
     plotcount 1 eq
       {xl y moveto}if
     plotcount 2 eq
       {xl y lineto}if
     plotcount 3 eq
       {xl y moveto drawclose}if
     }forall

  /xl xl reversexl sub vertjump 2 div sub def
}def
```

```
% ==================================
/label
 {/Helvetica-Bold findfont [12 0 0 14 0 0] makefont
setfont
  xlbox ytbox moveto
  /headx xrbox xlbox sub 2 div def headx -18 rmoveto
exch
  centertype pop
  xlbox ytbox moveto headx -32 rmoveto centertype
pop
  /Helvetica-Bold findfont [8 0 1 10 0 0] makefont
setfont
  xlbox ytbox moveto headx -44 rmoveto centertype
  }def

% ==================================

%%EndProlog
% ==================================


/drawpage {                  % begin drawpage
0 0 0 1 setcmykcolor .1 0 .2 0 50 130 348 550 .5 box
0 0 0 1 setcmykcolor .2 0 .4 0 80 160 332 490 20 9
true true false .4 .7 chartgridbox
0 45 dimens
0 1 1 0 setcmykcolor
(Four Weeks of Trading)
(XYZ Trading Corporation)        % title
(Daily Stock Market Price) label  % second line of
title
1 .6 0 0 setcmykcolor
[10 5 7 12 10 12 16 10 12 18 14 16 22 18 19
30 21 28 33 28 28 35 28 32 41 32 32 32 19 21
21 15 17 17 15 15 16 10 11 18 11 16 22 16 21
29 19 28 31 25 29 35 28 34 41 32 40 45 39 41
]highlowplot   % data array
(Dollars per Share) leftscale    % y axis label
0 5 topscale {scleft} for        % y axis scale
/Helvetica-Bold findfont [4 0 0 7 0 0]makefont
setfont
/ax xl def /y yb 9 sub def
[ (M)(T)(W)(T)(F)
(M)(T)(W)(T)(F)
(M)(T)(W)(T)(F)
(M)(T)(W)(T)(F)
]centershow                      % x axis labels
}def                             % end drawpage

drawpage
```

The bounding box information at the top of the file is the same dimensions as the outer box of the graph. This makes the placement of PageMaker-generated graphics very easy. Irregularly shaped objects within rectangular bounding boxes but without attached graphics for reference make the addition of other graphics much more difficult.

You will notice in Figure 8–7 that there are text blocks surprinting the bounding box drawn by PageMaker. This does not damage the file or confuse the system. PageMaker thinks of it as any other object in the publication. It can be moved, scaled, or distorted, just like any other image. It can also be sent to the front or the back. The one thing that this file cannot do is knockout other elements when specifying second color knockouts.

Should you desire, the encapsulated PostScript file could be the top most layer and overprint some lower-layer elements, such as tint areas or other graphics. Figure 8–8 shows this technique in action.

This is actually the default import for graphics. If you are a PageMaker user now, you will be familiar with that fact. What that means is that the

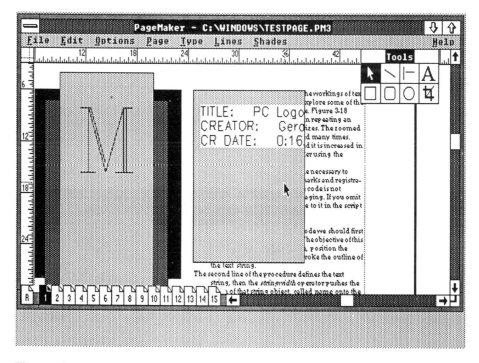

Figure 8—7

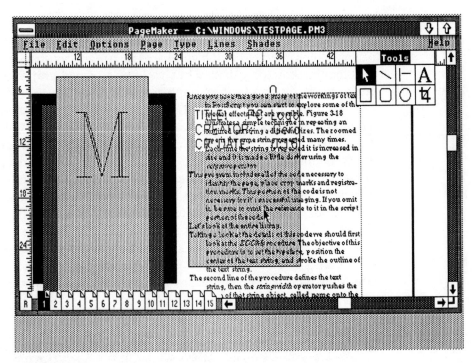

Figure 8—8

imported graphic is always on top of what is already on the page. You will have to send the graphic to the back implicitly if you want your text to surprint it.

8-6   Hardware Possibilities

In previous chapters I have referred to some hardware and software products that can assist in producing graphics and desktop publishing documents. Most notable is the Tektronix Phaser System. This system is available for the Macintosh- and IBM-compatible computing platforms. The system configurations differ slightly for each platform, but the concepts are basically the same.

The Tektronix system uses its own PostScript interpreter clone. On the IBM platform, the controller resides on an add-in board in your AT or

386 machine, and the color laser engine (laser printer) is attached to a communications port on it. An additional parallel printer port is available for plugging in an A- or B-sized black-and-white laser engine.

This system is unique (as of this writing) in that it interprets the newer color extensions to PostScript, including the *setcmykcolor* operator.

The Phaser plug-in adapter card is an eight-bit board that will work in a standard AT-type bus. The board boasts eight megabytes of RAM for the Postscript interpreter, one port for the Phaser CP, and another for an optional black-and-white laser printer. Since all of the PostScript interpretation takes place on the Phaser card in the host computer, most non-PostScript-compatible laser printers will work. At $6,995, this interpreter board is still a bargain when you consider its power.

The Phaser CP is the color thermal wax transfer engine in the family. The CP sells for $6,000 and is offered, at no discount, with the interpreter card for $12,995. By the way, if you already have a Tek 4693D or DX, the Phaser Card will give you PostScript compatibility without having to purchase the Phaser CP print engine.

Setup for the Phaser system is simple. The plug-in board has a complete set of documentation to help change jumpers if you encounter some interrupt conflicts with mice, network cards, or other adapters. Follow a simple set of menus to install the software and utilities and update your AUTOEXEC.BAT file; hook up the provided cable; and color prints can start to flow.

This is a big machine. You may consider giving it a table all its own! And don't begin to imagine it's portable. Two people will be needed when moving becomes necessary.

The Phaser card interprets all of the standard PostScript operators. In addition, it interprets the extended color PostScript operators, including *setcmykcolor*. When printing to the optional black-and-white printer, the Phaser card translates the color values into the appropriate gray values.

The Phaser CP offers a four-pass (cyan, magenta, yellow, and black) ribbon or a three-pass (magenta, yellow, and cyan) ribbon. Fortunately, the CP contains the electronics to understand which ribbon has been installed, and no user intervention or software setup is necessary.

Tektronix recommends using the latest verison of the Micrografx PostScript driver for Windows. The driver is bundled with the installation software.

Like most other PostScript printer clones, the Phaser offers the standard 35 resident fonts. Resetting the font matrix directly in PostScript code showed the system to be fast and reliable.

Every new system has some room for improvement. In the case of the Phaser, downloadable fonts is that area. Currently, the system provides support for BitStream type 3 downloadables without hints (intelligent scaling information). Ideally, the Adobe downloadable outline fonts with hints would be fully supported.

Another caveat, with a planned resolve, is networking support. Right now, the Phaser system supports only 3Com networks. This system is best utilized in a network environment. At $13,000, and about $1.00 per output page, (quality paper is expensive, and so are the ribbons), it would be a waste to put this device in the hands of one person. Novell users—all of them, I'm sure—would welcome direct support for their systems.

There are already a significant number of popular software packages that will support the Phaser, such as PageMaker 3.0. Through the HPGL interface, other programs such as AutoCad can be directly supported. Using Harvard Business Graphics or Micrografx Windows Graph, the CP can produce high-quality acetate transparencies for overhead projections.

Originally, the Phaser family of PostScript/HPGL output solutions was to include the Phaser LP, a 300 dpi B-sized black-and-white printer. Contrary to some press statements, Tektronix will not be offering this printer but will be supporting other popular A- and B-sized black-and-white laser printers through the Phaser card's parallel port.

Tektronix is also offering a Macintosh version of the Phaser system called the Phaser Color PrintStation for $15,995. In addition to everything available on the PC-based product, the PrintStation has a 40MB hard disk and hooks directly into AppleTalk as a print server.

In summation, the Phaser family of products marks an important price-performance breakthrough in the PostScript color printer arena. Since the system lives in both IBM- and Apple-compatible environments, this system becomes a "natural" for workgroup systems that use 3Com as the bilingual interpreter.

For more information, contact:

Phaser System
Tektronix, Inc.
PO Box 1000
Wilsonville, Oregon 97070
(503) 685-3585

CHAPTER 9

Enhancing DTP

9-1   Enhancing Desktop Publishing Packages

Off-the-shelf desktop publishing packages have continually increased in power and flexibility, and will continue to do so. As users' capabilities increase, the demands on software vendors to create new features become great. These new features become the tools to compete in a saturated market. But when do these manufacturers stop and say that the functionality of their product has reached its peak? After all, too many features can make a product too difficult to use.

As a reaction to this growth problem, some developers have launched— or plan to launch—professional versions of their product which embody the new and more powerful features. This allows the company to market the original product at a lower price and entice users to come on board for an upward ride into more advanced packages.

Even as desktop publishing increases in power and functionality, certain tasks will still be more efficient outside the DTP environment. There are currently numerous packages that create file formats readable by desktop publishing software. They are there to execute specific tasks. One, for instance—Micrografx' Windows Graph (IBM PC)—is a data-driven graphics package that will accept data from Lotus spreadsheets, let you draw a chart or graph, and then send it over to PageMaker (IBM PC). PageMaker accepts a wide variety of import file formats, such as .PIC, .WMF, and, of course, .EPS.

With task-specific software currently available, you may be surprised to hear me suggest that some tasks are still more efficient when written directly in encapsulated PostScript. In this chapter I will show you some specific examples and then show how to work with them within the PageMaker environment.

In previous chapters we looked at conforming encapsulated PostScript files. PageMaker, Ventura, and numerous other DTP programs read encapsulated files. For the programming-savvy out there, the .TIFF format can be attached to an EPS file for inclusion in PageMaker. This allows PageMaker to display the graphic image as generated by your application. For further details on creating this type of file, contact:

Altsys Corporation
720 Avenue F, Suite 109
Plano, TX 75074

9-2   A Universally Accepted Logo

A good reason for creating an encapsulated PostScript file for the desktop publishing environment is to create a library of consistent images. A company logo is an excellent candidate for encapsulation. Typically, logos have certain limitations imposed on them so that the company image is constantly reinforced with the public. Take IBM, for example. Blue has been its corporate color since the beginning of time. The logo form itself is an ever-consistent shape. Variations exist only from color to black-and-white and proportional changes in logo size. With these limitations, IBM would fare well in "hard coding" the logo form and color combinations into PostScript.

Apple Computer is another fine example of a company with an ironclad logo. Once again, color and black-and-white versions exist, and the logo can change size proportionally.

In our example, we will take the logotype for *PC Magazine* and go through the various steps of creating and testing the code, encapsulating the code, and altering the colors to fit the corporate design objectives.

Since this logo is already designed, we will look at the best, most efficient way of translating the image into PostScript.

This logo is ideal for encapsulated PostScript. It is extremely geometric in design and contains an altered Helvetica for its typeface. The corporate considerations are simple. The bullet list below outlines the graphical limitations on use.

- The color of the logo shall be 100% magenta, 100% yellow, printed on a white background when process color is available for reproduction.

- The color of the logo shall be 100% PMS 185 printed on a white background when only match colors are available for reproduction.

- The color of the logo shall be 100% black printed on a white background when no color is available for reproduction.

- Four predetermined sizes are provided for each variation of the logo. These sizes must be adhered to and can be varied only with permission from the Design Director.

With this information and the logo design in hand, we can proceed with the coding necessary to create the various logos. In each case we will rely on as many of the similarities in constructing these logos as possible. These similarities will naturally become our drawing routines. Figure 9–1 shows a PageMaker screen with the encapsulated logos on a page. Figure 9–2 shows the laser printer output from that page.

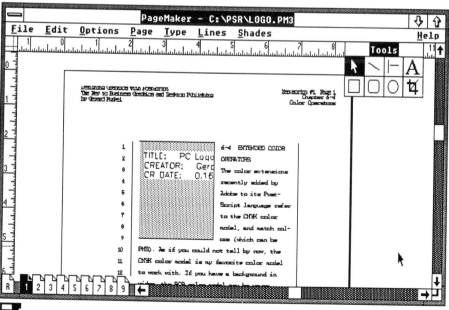

Figure 9–1

6-4 EXTENDED COLOR
OPERATORS
The color extensions
recently added by
Adobe to its Post-
Script language refer
to the CMYK color
model, and match col-
ors (which can be
PMS). As if you could not tell by now, the
CMYK color model is my favorite color model
to work with. If you have a background in
video, the RGB color model may be yours.
Since we are looking at the production of
images through to paper or film, it makes
sense to have a clear understanding of the
CMYK color model. This model is the one used
by printers when working in process colors.

The following list of color operators that
you will find in full-color PostScript implementations. The most common, *setcmykcolor*, is
used extensively in this book. For more information on these operators refer to David

Figure 9—2

9-3   A Typographic Trick

Aside from logotypes, PostScript's unique typographic controls allow for some very interesting techniques that can enhance your desktop publishing package. In Figure 9–3, I have created a shadow technique that will allow a tiny PostScript routine to be encapsulated and placed in PageMaker.

To create the same effect in PageMaker or any desktop publishing package is difficult, and it is nearly impossible to recreate consistently. Once again, the level of precision and control is at its highest when a logo can be designed and implemented mathematically. In this case, the distance from the type to its shadow is locked into our PostScript routine so that any reuse of this code with new type will yield exactly the same spacing.

```
%%Title:ShadowType
%%Creator: Gerard Kunkel Copyright 1988
%%CreationDate: December 1988
%%BoundingBox: 0 0 612 792
%%EndComments
%%BeginProlog
/ShadowType
 {/stg exch def /ps exch def
  /Helvetica-Bold findfont [ps 0 4 ps 0 0] makefont
setfont
  100 100 moveto .9 setgray stg show
  /Helvetica-Bold findfont [ps 0 0 ps 0 0] makefont
setfont
  100 100 moveto 0 setgray stg show
}def

30 (Economic Watch) ShadowType
```

Figure 9–4 shows another typographic trick, zooming type. The routine *ZOOMType* was used in conjunction with other routines to create Figure C–8. This kind of repetitive imaging is child's play for PostScript. You can see that very little in the way of code is required for this effect. Note that all of these encapsulated PostScript files have a *BoundingBox* of 8 1/2 x 11 inches.

Zooming type would be next-to-impossible in a desktop publishing package. And as Figure C–8 shows, if you combine that effect with outline type and rotation, you have probably pushed past the limits of any publishing system.

any books on the subject of the PostScript language should begin, let me aknowledge, and indeed praise, John Warnok for the development of such a versatile and flexible page description language. John created the PostScript language when they recognized a need for standards. PostScript is quickly becoming the standard for describing a page to be printed. The initial successful implementation of PostScript was embodied in the Apple LaserWriter. Within its circuitry lies the licensed PostScript interpreter, the heart of any PostScript imaging system. This interpreter is a chip. The chip contains the software necessary to r

PostS can not be inde interpreted by have a softw hardware for p acutely obvio

more descript

I have in other ende book publishe

The c handling large and producin have lead to i solutions. Wo ics is extreme fun. For the business. Pos savings in typ control over complex arra into graphics, drawings now far superior to any hand drawn work.

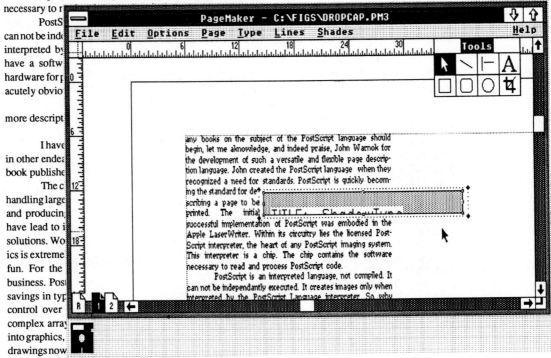

Some of you have probably been using PostScript for some time without realizing it. The introduction of PageMaker for the Macintosh, combined with the Apple LaserWriter, put application level PostScript control in the hands of tens of thousands. And in turn, desktop publishing was born.

This book is written exclusively for you, the desktop publisher. AND, Linotronic output houses, graphic designers, graphic artists, publication designers, cartographers, statisti-

Figure 9—3

```
%%Title:ZOOMType
%%Creator: Gerard Kunkel Copyright 1988
%%CreationDate: December 1988
%%BoundingBox: 0 0 612 792
%%EndComments
%%BeginProlog
/ZOOMType
 {/stg exch def
  /ps exch def
  /z .9 def
  9{300 300 moveto
    /Helvetica-Bold findfont [ps 0 0 ps 0 0]
makefont setfont
    z setgray
    stg centershow
    /z z .1 sub def /ps ps 2 add def}repeat
 }def

/centershow
 {dup stringwidth pop 2 div neg 0 rmoveto show}def

30 (Economic Watch) ZOOMType
```

The other issue to consider when working with desktop publishing software is the size of your output files. Since DTP packages handle PostScript as a generic set of tools to construct a page with, this and other graphics can use a lot of memory when translated into code. By encapsulating your routine, you will save massive amounts of memory and increase throughput.

A good example of this is the *PC Magazine* benchmark charts. The in-house software that I have written for these charts encapsulates Post-Script routines to draw the images. The original computer renderings in off-the-shelf software created output files in excess of one megabyte, or one million bytes of information. The current files average about 30K, or 30,000 bytes of information. Since we transmit our files to a remote Linotronic output, service size means dollars. A reduction of 97% in files size means considerable savings on connect time.

Figure 9–5 shows another application where PostScript can lend a helping hand in DTP. Distorting type for a special effect is usually not possible in a DTP package. The routine *SquatType* takes each character that is passed to it and applies the point size width, *ps*, and height, *psy*. In this particular example, the width of each character remains the same throughout, while the height continually decreases as the line progresses.

any books on the subject of the PostScript

language should begin, let me aknowledge, and indeed praise, John Warnok for the development of such a versatile and flex-ible page description language. John created the PostScript lan-guage when they recognized a need for standards. PostScript is quickly becoming the standard for describing a page to be printed. The initial successful implementation of PostScript was embodied in the Apple LaserWriter. Within its circuitry lies the licensed PostScript interpreter, the heart of any Post-Script imaging system. This interpreter is a chip. The chip contains the s̶

code.

Post̶ can not be inc̶ interpreted b̶ have a softw̶ hardware for̶ acutely obvi̶

more descrip̶

I hav̶ in other ende̶ book publish̶

The ̶ handling larg̶ and producir̶ have lead to̶ solutions. W̶ ics is extrem̶ fun. For the̶ business. Po̶ savings in ty̶ control over̶ complex arr̶ into graphics̶

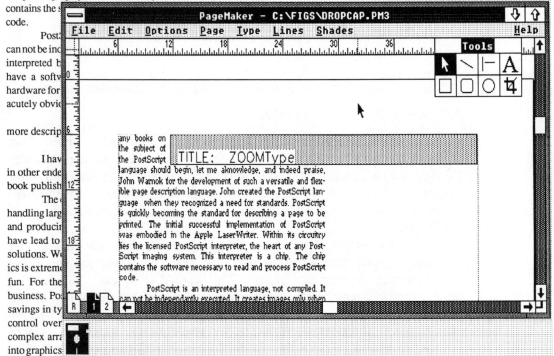

drawings now take minutes. And the quality of plot and line are far superior to any hand drawn work.

Some of you have probably been using PostScript for some time without realizing it. The introduction of PageMaker for the Macintosh, combined with the Apple LaserWriter, put application level PostScript control in the hands of tens of thousands. And in turn, desktop publishing was born.

This book is written exclusively for you, the desktop publisher. AND, Linotronic output houses, graphic designers,

Figure 9—4

```
%%Title:SquatType
%%Creator: Gerard Kunkel Copyright 1988
%%CreationDate: December 1988
%%BoundingBox: 0 0 612 792
%%EndComments
%%BeginProlog

/SquatType
 {/stg exch def
  /ps exch def
  /psy ps def
  /z .9 def
  /Helvetica-Bold findfont [ps 0 0 psy 0 0] makefont
setfont
   stg true charpath gsave .9 setgray fill grestore
stroke
  currentpoint moveto
 }def

0 setgray
200 300 moveto
30 30 (E)SquatType
29 30 (c)SquatType
28 30 (o)SquatType
27 30 (n)SquatType
26 30 (o)SquatType
25 30 (m)SquatType
24 30 (i)SquatType
23 30 (c)SquatType
22 30 ( )SquatType
21 30 (W)SquatType
20 30 (a)SquatType
19 30 (t)SquatType
18 30 (c)SquatType
17 30 (h)SquatType
```

9-4   Drop Caps

Of particular annoyance in many DTP packages is the inability to create embedded drop caps automatically. In those packages that can create a text wrap, the drop cap option may still not exist. The screen display on most systems also complicates the process by not providing an accurate representation of what will actually print. One method that I have developed to overcome this is to create a library of encapsulated initial caps in different typefaces that have a *BoundingBox* equal to the size of the character.

any books on the subject of the PostScript language should begin, let me aknowledge, and indeed praise, John Warnok for the development of such a versatile and flexible page description language. John created the PostScript language when they

ECONOMIC WATCH

recognized a need for standards. PostScript is quickly becoming the standard for describing a page to be printed. The initial successful implementation of PostScript was embodied in the Apple LaserWriter. Within its circuitry lies the licensed PostScript interpreter, the heart of any PostScript imaging system. This interpreter is a chip. The chip contains the software necessary to read and process PostScript code.

PostScript is an interpreted language, not compiled. It can not be inc...
interpreted b...
have a softw...
hardware for...
acutely obvic...

more descrip...

I hav...
in other ende...
book publish...

The...
handling larg...
and producir...
have lead to...
solutions. W...
ics is extreme...
fun. For the...
business. Po...
savings in ty...
control over...
complex arr...
into graphics...
drawings nov...
far superior t...

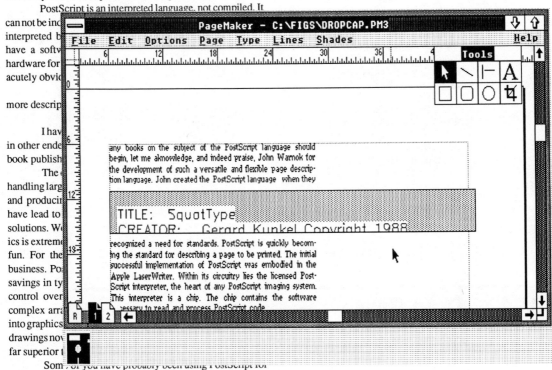

Som... of you have probably been using PostScript for some time without realizing it. The introduction of PageMaker for the Macintosh, combined with the Apple LaserWriter, put application level PostScript control in the hands of tens of thousands. And in turn, desktop publishing was born.

Figure 9—5

PageMaker is well suited to importing this EPS drop cap because of its text wrap option. This small EPS file with a predefined text wrap can be imported quickly and placed accurately.

Determining the size of the *BoundingBox* was easy. I simply used the *FontBBox* program from chapter 3 to acquire the complete list of character sizes for the font that I was using. The height and width information was used to create the dimensions of the *BoundingBox*.

An added bonus to this method of importing drop caps is that the initial cap can be further scaled, once imported. Even though the image is scaled, the character, its *BoundingBox,* and the text wrap relationships all remain intact.

Figure 9–6 shows a PageMaker screen with an encapsulated drop cap in place within some text.

Figure 9–7 shows that page as printed.

Below is Figure 9–8, a simple drop cap encapsulated program used in Figure 9–6 and 9–7.

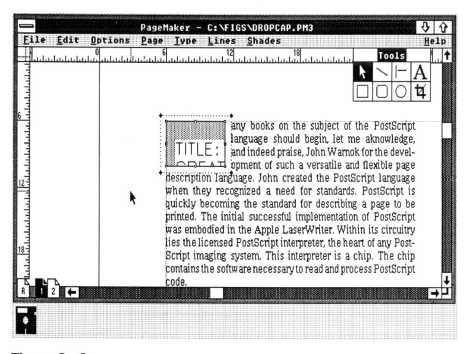

Figure 9–6

Many books on the subject of the PostScript language should begin, let me aknowledge, and indeed praise, John Warnok for the development of such a versatile and flexible page description language. John created the PostScript language when they recognized a need for standards. PostScript is quickly becoming the standard for describing a page to be printed. The initial successful implementation of PostScript was embodied in the Apple LaserWriter. Within its circuitry lies the licensed PostScript interpreter, the heart of any PostScript imaging system. This interpreter is a chip. The chip contains the software necessary to read and process PostScript code.

PostScript is an interpreted language, not compiled. It can not be independantly executed. It creates images only when interpreted by the PostScript Language interpreter. So why have a software language that is dependant on a piece of hardware for printing? The answer to this question will become acutely obvious as you read this book.

more descriptives on PS

I have tapped into my experience at PC Magazine, and in other endeavors, to create what I beleive is the most useful book published about creating graphics with PostScript.

The challenges that I have faced at PC Magazine are of handling large volumes and meeting tight deadlines. Designing and producing approximately 5000 editorial pages per year have lead to interesting, and in all cases, extremely efficient solutions. Working with computers to design and create graphics is extremely rewarding. For computer jocks like me, this is fun. For the publication I work for, this is business, big business. PostScript implementations often mean substantial savings in typesetting, and art creation. It also means greater control over quality. Our three-dimensional bar charts are complex arrays of information. When numbers are translated into graphics, conventional drawings may take days. Computer drawings now take minutes. And the quality of plot and line are far superior to any hand drawn work.

Some of you have probably been using PostScript for some time without realizing it. The introduction of PageMaker for the Macintosh, combined with the Apple LaserWriter, put application level PostScript control in the hands of tens of thousands. And in turn, desktop publishing was born.

This book is written exclusively for you, the desktop publisher. AND, Linotronic output houses, graphic designers, graphic artists, publication designers, cartographers, statisti-

Figure 9—7

```
%%Title:B Drop Cap
%%Creator: Gerard Kunkel Copyright 1988
%%CreationDate: May 1989
%%BoundingBox: 0 0 612 792
%%EndComments
%%BeginProlog

0 setgray
1 setlinewidth
/Times-Bold findfont 36 scalefont setfont
0 0 moveto
(B) true charpath
gsave
.9 setgray
fill
grestore
stroke
```

Figure 9–8

9-5   Chart Graphics

The data-driven chart graphics in chapter 5 can be encapsulated and placed in a PageMaker file. In fact, this makes a good deal of sense. These graphics might typically fall within another document or report. Since the encapsulated PostScript file can be imported and then moved and scaled, the composition of a page is exceptionally flexible and time-saving.

Figure 9–9 shows a page with a graphic inserted within the text area on the PageMaker screen.

Figure 9–10 shows the same page when output to a PostScript laser printer.

9-6   Printing and Editing the DTP's PostScript File

I have found that changes to a finished page never stop coming in. Every opportunity given to a copy-editing department will yield further corrections. In a production environment where pages must be sent to the printer and the reader on time—or else—you develop tricks that make meeting the deadlines possible.

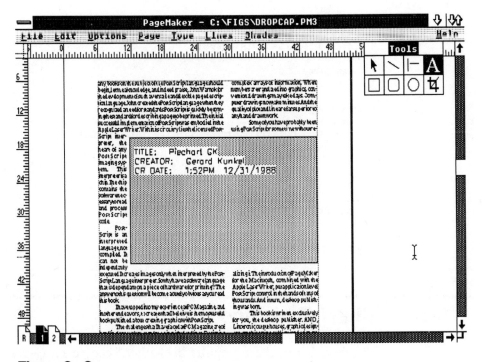

Figure 9—9

Since *PC Magazine* pages are printed to PostScript files for final transmission to the remote Linotronic, we have the opportunity to view or even edit the code. This is indeed a very dangerous proposition if you are not well-versed in PostScript. If you are up for the challenge or simply want to see how others have programmed in PostScript, open that PostScript file in a word processor and take a look.

9.6.1   Search and Replace in the Code

Once the file is open, a search-and-replace is possible. This technique is often used for last-minute corrections at the magazine. The typical application is the changing of a spelling throughout a story or graphic. Also used, but not frequently, is the changing of a color or line weight.

any books on the subject of the PostScript language should begin, let me aknowledge, and indeed praise, John Warnok for the development of such a versatile and flexible page description language. John created the PostScript language when they recognized a need for standards. PostScript is quickly becoming the standard for describing a page to be printed. The initial successful implementation of PostScript was embodied in the Apple LaserWriter. Within its circuitry lies the licensed PostScript interpreter, the heart of any PostScript imaging system. This interpreter is a chip. The chip contains the software necessary to read and process PostScript code.

PostScript is an interpreted language, not compiled. It can not be independantly executed. It creates images only when interpreted by the PostScript Language interpreter. So why have a software language that is dependant on a piece of hardware for printing? The answer to this question will become acutely obvious as you read this book.

I have tapped into my experience at PC Magazine, and in other endeavors, to create what I beleive is the most useful book published about creating graphics with PostScript.

The challenges that I have faced at PC Magazine are of handling large volumes and meeting tight deadlines. Designing and producing approximately 5000 editorial pages per year have lead to interesting, and in all cases, extremely efficient solutions. Working with computers to design and create graphics is extremely rewarding. For computer jocks like me, this is fun. For the publication I work for, this is business, big business. PostScript implementations often mean substantial savings in typesetting, and art creation. It also means greater control over quality. Our three-dimensional bar charts are

complex arrays of information. When numbers are translated into graphics, conventional drawings may take days. Computer drawings now take minutes. And the quality of plot and line are far superior to any hand drawn work.

Some of you have probably been using PostScript for some time without re-

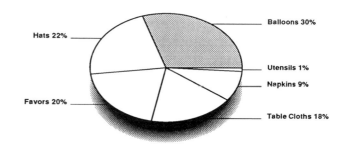

alizing it. The introduction of PageMaker for the Macintosh, combined with the Apple LaserWriter, put application level PostScript control in the hands of tens of thousands. And in turn, desktop publishing was born.

This book is written exclusively for you, the desktop publisher. AND, Linotronic output houses, graphic designers, graphic artists, publication designers, cartographers, statisticians, stock analysts, and programmers. I have intentionally put programmers last because this is a programming language that allows all creative individuals to become electronic publishing ''power users'', as we fondly call them at PC Magazine. The reason this language is so accessible to so many people

Figure 9—10

PostScript Operators Arranged by Operator Type

Array Operators

Stack Requirements	Operator	Stack Remainder	Definition
—	[	mark	pushes a mark object onto the stack.
mark any_o . . . any_n	]	array	creates a new array of $n + 1$ objects out of the objects any_o to any_n stored above the topmost *mark* on the stack.
array	**aload**	a_o . . a_n array	successively pushes all $n + 1$ elements of *array* or *packedarray* onto the operand stack, where $n + 1$ is the number of elements in *array* or *packedarray*, and finally pushes the array itself.
packedarray	**aload**	a_o . . a_n packed- array	
int	**array**	array	creates *array* that initially contains *int* null objects as entries.
any_o . . any_n array	**aload**	array	fills *array* with any_o through any_n, where *array* has a length of $n + 1$.
array1 array2	**copy**	subarray2	copies all elements of *array1* or *packed-array* into *array2*.
packedarray array2	**copy**	subarray2	

Array Operators (continued)

Stack Requirements	Operator	Stack Remainder	Definition
—	**currentpacking**	bool	returns a boolean value that indicates whether array packing is currently in effect or not.
array proc packedarray proc	**forall** **forall**	— —	enumerates every element of the first operand and executes *proc* for each of those elements.
array index packedarray index	**get** **get**	any any	looks up the *index* in *array* or *packedarray* and returns the element identified by *index* (counting from zero).
array index count packedarray index count	**getinterval** **getinterval**	subarray subarray	duplicates a section of the operand *array* or *packedarray* beginning at the element identified by *index* (counting from zero) and extending for *count* elements.
array packedarray	**length** **length**	int int	returns *int* as the number of elements that make up *array* or *packedarray*.
—	**mark**	mark	pushes a mark object onto the stack.
any_1 . . . any_n n	**packedarray**	packedarray	creates *packedarray* out of the elements any_1 through any_n.
array index value	**put**	—	stores *value* into *array* at the position identified by *index* (counting from zero).
array1 index array2	**putinterval**	—	replaces a section of the operand *array1* beginning at the element identified by *index* (counting from zero) with the contents of *array2*.
bool	**setpacking**	—	sets the array packing mode to *bool*.

Control Operators

Stack Requirements	Operator	Stack Remainder	Definition
—	**count-execstack**	int	counts the number of objects on the execution stack and returns that integer, *int*, to the top of the operand stack.

Control Operators (continued)

Stack Requirements	Operator	Stack Remainder	Definition
any	**exec**	—	immediately executes the object on the top of the operand stack.
array	**execstack**	subarray	places all the elements of the current execution stack into *array*, overwriting the initial elements.
—	**exit**	—	terminates execution of the currently active instance of a looping context.
init incr limit proc	**for**	—	executes *proc* repeatedly and, at each execution, provides a variable number on the operand stack.
packedarray proc string proc	**forall** **forall**	— —	enumerates every element of the first operand and executes *proc* for each of those elements.
bool proc	**if**	—	executes *proc* if *bool* is *true;* otherwise pops both operands and does nothing.
bool proc1 proc2	**ifelse**	—	executes *proc1* if *bool* is *true* and executes *proc2* if *bool* is *false.*
proc	**loop**	—	executes *proc* continuously until *proc* terminates execution internally.
—	**quit**	—	terminates operation of the interpreter or of the current PostScript program.
int proc	**repeat**	—	executes *proc int* times. The *int* operand must be a non-negative integer and may be 0, in which case repeat does not execute *proc* at all.
—	**start**	—	is the procedure executed by the PostScript interpreter when it first starts execution.
—	**stop**	—	terminates execution of the currently active instance of a stopped context, which is a procedure or other executable object invoked by a **stopped** operator.
any	**stopped**	bool	executes *any*, which is usually a procedure or an executable file but may be any executable object.

Conversion Operators

Stack Requirements	Operator	Stack Remainder	Definition
num string	**cvi** **cvi**	int int	converts a number, *num,* or a string that is equivalent to a number, *string,* into the integer value, *int.*
any	**cvlit**	any	converts the object *any* on the top of the operand stack to have the literal attribute.
string	**cvn**	name	converts the *string* operand to a PostScript *name* that is lexically identical to *string.*
num string	**cvr** **cvr**	real real	converts a number, *num,* or a string that is equivalent to a number, *string,* into the real number, *real.*
num base string	**cvrs**	substring	converts *num* into a string equivalent according to the number system whose base number or radix is given by *base.*
any string	**cvs**	substring	converts *any* arbitrary object into a string representation and stores the result in *string,* overwriting the initial portion in *string.*
any	**cvx**	any	converts the object *any* on the top of the operand stack to have the executable attribute.
array packedarray file string	**executeonly** **executeonly** **executeonly** **executeonly**	array packedarray file string	reduces the access attribute of the operand to execute-only.
composite object file	**noaccess** **noaccess**	composite object file	changes the access attribute of *composite object* or *file* to allow no access of any kind.
composite object file	**rcheck** **rcheck**	bool bool	tests the access attribute of the operand to see whether the access attribute of the operand is either read-only or unlimited.
composite object file	**readonly** **readonly**	composite object file	changes the access attribute of *composite object* or *file* to allow only read access.

Conversion Operators (continued)

Stack Requirements	Operator	Stack Remainder	Definition
any	**type**	typename	returns *typename*, which is a PostScript name object that specifies the type of *any*.
composite object file	**wcheck** **wcheck**	bool bool	tests the access attribute of the operand to see whether the access attribute of the operand is unlimited.
any	**xcheck**	bool	tests whether *any* has the executable or literal attribute.

Coordinates

Stack Requirements	Operator	Stack Remainder	Definition
matrix	**concat**	—	concatenates *matrix* with the CTM.
matrix1 matrix2 matrix3	**concatmatrix**	matrix3	returns the result of multiplying *matrix1* by *matrix2* as *matrix3*.
matrix	**currentmatrix**	matrix	replaces the value of *matrix* with the current transformation matrix (CTM) from the current graphics state.
matrix	**defaultmatrix**	matrix	replaces the value of *matrix* with the default coordinate transformation matrix for the output device.
dx dy	**dtransform**	dx' dy'	transforms the distance vector, (*dx*, *dy*), into device space using the current transformation matrix (CTM), and returns the equivalent distance vector for the device onto the operand stack as (*dx'*,dy').
dx dy matrix	**dtransform**	dx' dy'	transforms the distance vector, (*dx*, *dy*), using *matrix* as a transformation matrix, and returns the equivalent distance vector after the transformation onto the operand stack.

Coordinates (continued)

Stack Requirements	Operator	Stack Remainder	Definition
matrix	**identmatrix**	matrix	replaces the contents of *matrix* with the identity matrix [1.0 0.0 0.0 1.0 0.0 0.0].
dx dy	**idtransform**	ux uy	transforms the distance vector, (*dx, dy*), in device coordinates into user coordinates, using the inverse of the current transformation matrix (CTM), and returns the new distance vector for the user coordinates to the operand stack as (*ux, uy*).
dx′ dy′ matrix	**idtransform**	dx dy	transforms the distance matrix, (*dx′, dy′*) into user space using the inverse of *matrix* as a transformation matrix, and returns the equivalent distance vector after the transformation as (*dx, dy*).
—	**initmatrix**	—	restores the current transformation matrix (CTM) to the default matrix for the current output device.
matrix1 matrix2	**invertmatrix**	matrix2	replaces *matrix2* with the inverse of *matrix1*.
dx dy	**itransform**	ux uy	transforms the device coordinates, (dx, dy), into user coordinates using the inverse of the current transformation matrix (CTM), and returns the new coordinates to the operand stack as (ux, uy).
—	**matrix**	matrix	generates an identity transformation matrix, *matrix*, and places it on the operand stack.
angle	**rotate**	—	rotates the user coordinates around their origin by *angle*.
angle matrix	**rotate**	matrix	adjusts the values in *matrix* by the rotation transformation matrix and returns the modified matrix back to the operand stack. No change is made to the CTM.
sx sy	**scale**	—	scales the user coordinates around their origin by *sx* along the x axis and *sy* along the y axis.

Coordinates (continued)

Stack Requirements	Operator	Stack Remainder	Definition
sx sy matrix	**scale**	matrix	adjusts the values in *matrix* by the scaled transformation matrix and returns the modified matrix back to the operand stack. No change is made to the CTM.
matrix	**setmatrix**	—	replaces the current transformation matrix (CTM) in the current graphics state with the value of *matrix*.
x y	**transform**	x′ y′	transforms the distance vector, (x, y), into device space, using the current transformation matrix (CTM), and returns the equivalent distance vector for the device onto the operand stack as (x′, y′).
x **y** matrix	**transform**	x′ y′	transforms the position (x, y), using *matrix* as a transformation matrix, and returns the equivalent position after the transformation onto the operand stack as (x′, y′).
tx ty	**translate**	—	translates the current origin of the user coordinates to the point (tx, ty), which becomes the new origin.
tx ty matrix	**translate**	matrix	adjusts the values in *matrix* by the appropriate transformation matrix and returns the modified matrix back to the operand stack. No change is made to the CTM.

Device Operators

Stack Requirements	Operator	Stack Remainder	Definition
—	**#copies**	int	defines the number of copies of a page of output that are produced when a **showpage** operator is executed.
matrix width height proc	**banddevice**	—	installs a band buffer as the raster memory for an output device and sets certain parameters for that device.

Device Operators (continued)

Stack Requirements	Operator	Stack Remainder	Definition
—	**copypage**	—	outputs one copy of the current page onto the current output device without erasing the current page or changing the graphics state.
matrix width height proc	**framedevice**	—	installs a frame buffer as the raster memory for an output device and sets certain parameters for that device.
—	**nulldevice**	—	installs the 'null device' as the default output device.
proc	**renderbands**	—	renders bands of raster data from raster memory to the current output device.
—	**showpage**	—	produces the current page on the current output device.

Dictionary Operators

Stack Requirements	Operator	Stack Remainder	Definition
dict	**begin**	—	pushes *dict* onto the dictionary stack and makes it the current dictionary.
dict1 dict2	**copy**	dict2	copies all elements of *dict1* into *dict2*.
—	**countdictstack**	int	counts the number of dictionaries on the dictionary stack and returns that integer, *int*.
—	**currentdict**	dictionary	returns a duplicate of the current dictionary to the operand stack.
key value	**def**	—	associates *key* with *value* in the current dictionary.
int	**dict**	dict	creates an empty dictionary with a maximum capacity of *int* entries and places the created dictionary onto the operand stack.

Dictionary Operators (continued)

Stack Requirements	Operator	Stack Remainder	Definition
array	**dictstack**	subarray	places all elements of the dictionary stack into *array*, overwriting the inital elements.
—	**end**	—	pops the current dictionary off the dictionary stack and makes the dictionary that was immediately below the current dictionary.
—	**errordict**	dict	returns the dictionary *dict*, which is the *errordict* dictionary.
dict proc	**forall**	—	enumerates every (key, value) pair in *dict*, pushing both elements onto the operand stack, and then executes *proc*.
dict key	**get**	any	looks up the *key* in *dict* and returns the associated value.
dict key	**known**	bool	searches the PostScript dictionary, *dict*, for an occurrence of *key* and returns the boolean value *true* if it is found and *false* otherwise.
dict	**length**	int	returns *int* as the current number of key-value pairs in *dict*.
key	**load**	value	searches for *key* in every dictionary on the dictionary stack and returns *value* that is associated with the first occurrence of *key*.
dict	**maxlength**	int	returns *int* as the maximum number of key-value pairs that *dict* can hold, as defined by the dict operator that created *dict*.
dict key value	**put**	—	uses *key* and *value* and stores them as a key-value pair into *dict*.
—	**statusdict**	dict	returns the dictionary *dict*, which is the *statusdict* dictionary.
key value	**store**	—	searches the dictionary stack in the ordinary way, looking for a match to *key*.

Dictionary Operators (continued)

Stack Requirements	Operator	Stack Remainder	Definition
—	**systemdict**	dict	returns the dictionary *dict*, which is the *systemdict* dictionary.
—	**userdict**	dict	returns the dictionary *dict*, which is the *userdict* dictionary.
key	**where**	*if found:* dict true *if not found:* false	searches the dictionary stack and returns the dictionary that contains an entry that is associated with *key*, if that dictionary exists on the dictionary stack.

Error Messages

Stack Requirements	Operator	Stack Remainder	Definition
	dictfull	(error process)	occurs when the referenced dictionary is already full and a PostScript operation attempts to store another object into it.
	dictstack-overflow	(error process)	occurs when the dictionary stack already contains the maximum number of active dictionary entries and a **begin** operation attempts to store another dictionary on it.
	dictstack-underflow	(error process)	occurs when the dictionary stack contains the minimum number of active dictionary entries, *userdict* and *systemdict*, and an **end** operation attempts to remove a dictionary from it.
	exec-stackoverflow	(error process)	occurs when the execution stack has grown too large; procedure invocation is nested deeper than the interpreter allows.
	handleerror	(error processor)	is a procedure defined in *errordict* that is executed to report error messages and error information in a standard way.

Error Messages (continued)

Stack Requirements	Operator	Stack Remainder	Definition
	interrupt	(error process)	processes an external interrupt to halt execution of a PostScript program.
	invalidaccess	(error process)	occurs when an attempt has been made to access a composite object or a file object in a way that violates the access attribute for that object.
	invalidexit	(error process)	occurs when an attempt has been made to execute an **exit** for which there is no dynamically enclosing looping context.
	invalidfile-access	(error process)	occurs when the access string supplied to the **file** operator is unacceptable.
	invalidfont	(error process)	occurs when a PostScript font operator determines that a font dictionary is malformed in some way.
	invalidrestore	(error process)	occurs when an attempt has been made to **restore** a saved state under invalid conditions.
	ioerror	(error process)	occurs when a processing error has occurred during execution of one of the file operators.
	limitcheck	(error process)	occurs when an implementation limit has been exceeded.
	nocurrentpoint	(error process)	occurs when an operator requires a current point but the current path is empty and therefore the current point is undefined.
	rangecheck	(error process)	occurs when a numeric operand is outside the range expected by the operator.
	stackoverflow	(error process)	occurs when the number of operands on the operand stack exceeds the implementation-defined maximum number.
	stack-underflow	(error process)	occurs when the interpreter attempts to remove an operand on the operand stack and the operand stack is already empty.

Error Messages (continued)

Stack Requirements	Operator	Stack Remainder	Definition
	syntaxerror	(error process)	occurs when the PostScript input scanner (or *tokenizer*) encounters program text that does not follow the syntax rules for PostScript.
	timeout	(error process)	occurs when the PostScript interpreter exceeds some implementation-defined time value.
	typecheck	(error process)	occurs when the type of some operand is not the type expected by the operator in question.
	undefined	(error process)	occurs when a name used in a dictionary key cannot be found in the current dictionary context.
	undefined-filename	(error process)	occurs when a string used as a name for a **file** or a **run** operator cannot be found or cannot be opened.
	undefined-result	(error process)	occurs when a numeric computation would produce an undefined result (such as division by zero) or one that cannot be represented as a PostScript number (such as the inverse transformation of a non-invertible matrix).
	unmatched-mark	(error process)	occurs when an operator expects a mark object on the operand stack, but none is present.
	unregistered	(error process)	occurs when an operator object has been executed for which the interpreter has no built-in process or procedure.
	VMerror	(error process)	occurs when an error has occurred in handling or accessing the virtual memory (VM) of the output device.

File Operators

Stack Requirements	Operator	Stack Remainder	Definition
any	=	—	produces a string representation of *any* on the standard output file.
any	= =	—	produces an edited string representation of *any* on the standard output file.
file	**bytesavailable**	int	returns the number of bytes immediately available from *file*.
file	**closefile**	—	closes *file*; that is, breaks the association between the file object and the underlying file itself.
—	**currentfile**	file	returns the current file object.
bool	**echo**	—	specifies whether the characters that are received from the standard input file are written to the standard output file during interactive mode operation.
—	**executive**	—	places the PostScript interpreter into the interactive access mode, if the interpreter provides that mode of access.
filestring accessstring	**file**	file	returns the file object *file* that is identified by the file name *filestring* with access rights defined by *accessstring*.
—	**flush**	—	forces any characters stored in a buffer for the standard output file to be output immediately.
file	**flushfile**	—	If *file* is an output file, flushfile causes any buffered characters to be sent immediately. If *file* is an input file, flushfile reads the file and discards all input until it reaches end-of-file.
string	**print**	—	writes *string* onto the standard output file.
—	**prompt**	—	produces the prompt that is displayed to the user during the interactive mode.

File Operators (continued)

Stack Requirements	Operator	Stack Remainder	Definition
|- any_1 . . . any_n	**pstack**	|- any_1 . . . any_n	produces an edited string representation of all objects on the operand stack, any_n through any_1, onto the standard output file.
file	**read**	*if not end-of-file:* byte true *if end-of-file:* false	reads a single character from the designated *file* and returns it to the operand stack as an integer value.
file string	**readhexstring**	substring bool	reads characters from the designated *file* into *string* until all space in *string* is filled or until end-of-file.
file string	**readline**	substring bool	reads characters from the designated *file* into *string* until either a *newline* character (which indicates the end of a line) or until end-of-file is reached.
file string	**readstring**	substring bool	reads characters from the designated *file* into *string* until all space in *string* is filled or until end-of-file.
file	**resetfile**	—	resets the file by discarding all buffered characters that are associated with *file*.
filestring	**run**	—	executes the contents of the file identified by *filestring*.
|- any_1 . . . any_n	**stack**	|- any_1 . . . any_n	produces a string representation of all objects on the operand stack, any_n through any_1, onto the standard output file.
file	**status**	bool	returns the boolean value *true* if *file* is still associated with an open file and returns *false* otherwise.
file	**token**	*if found:* any true *if not found:* false	reads characters from *file*, interpreting them according to the PostScript syntax rules, until it has constructed a complete PostScript object, which is returned to the operand stack as result *any*.

File Operators (continued)

Stack Requirements	Operator	Stack Remainder	Definition
file byte	**write**	—	writes a single character, *byte*, to the designated *file*.
file string	**writehexstring**	—	writes characters from the designated *string* into *file* until all the characters in *string* are transmitted.
file string	**writestring**	—	writes characters from the designated *string* into *file*.

Font Operators

Stack Requirements	Operator	Stack Remainder	Definition
wx wy string	**ashow**	—	prints *string* in a similar way to the **show** operator, except that, during the printing process, **ashow** adds *wx* to the *x* width of each character and *wy* to the *y* width.
cx cy char wx wy string	**awidthshow**	—	prints the characters in *string* in a manner similar to **show** but combines the effects of **ashow** and **widthshow.**
—	**currentfont**	font	returns the current font dictionary from the current graphics state.
proc string	**cshow**	—	invokes *proc* once for each operation of the font mapping algorithm on each character in *string*.
key font	**definefont**	font	registers *font* as a font dictionary associated with *key*, which is usually a name literal.
key	**findencoding**	array	obtains the encoding array from the font identified by *key* and returns it to the operand stack.
key	**findfont**	font	obtains a font dictionary, *font*, that is associated with the *key* in the **FontDirectory** and places it on the operand stack.

Font Operators (continued)

Stack Requirements	Operator	Stack Remainder	Definition
—	**FontDirectory**	dict	returns the global directory of fonts as *dict*.
proc string	**kshow**	—	prints *string* in a similar way to the **show** operator, except that for every character in *string*, **kshow** invokes *proc*.
font matrix	**makefont**	newfont	applies *matrix* to *font* and produces *newfont*, whose characters are transformed by the values in *matrix* when they are printed.
—	**rootfont**	font	returns the root composite font that has been selected by the most recent **setfont**.
font1 scale	**scalefont**	font2	scales *font1* by the scale factor *scale* to generate a new font, *font2*, whose characters are magnified equally along both axes when they are imaged.
font	**setfont**	—	sets *font* as the current font dictionary in the current graphics state.
string	**show**	—	paints the characters that are elements of *string* on the current page at the current point using the current font.
—	**Standard-Encoding**	array	returns the standard PostScript encoding vector as *array*.
string	**stringwidth**	wx wy	calculates the cumulative change in the current point that would occur if **string** was printed in the current font by using show.
cx cy char string	**widthshow**	—	prints the characters in *string* in a manner similar to **show,** but in addition, if the integer value of the character currently being imaged matches the integer value *char*, the values *cx* and *cy* are added to the current point after imaging the character and before imaging the next character.

Font Cache Operators

Stack Requirements	Operator	Stack Remainder	Definition
—	**cachestatus**	bsize bmax msize mmax csize cmax blimit	reports the measurements for current consumption and maximum limit of several types of font cache resources.
—	**current-cacheparms**	mark lower upper	returns the current cache parameters, *lower* and *upper,* on the operand stack, preceded by a *mark.*
wx wy llx lly urx ury	**setcachedevice**	—	passes width and bounding box information for a character to the PostScript font machinery.
w0x w0y llx lly urx ury w1x w1y vx vy	**setcachedevice** **setcache-device2**	— —	passes character metric information for an individual character to the PostScript font machinery.
num	**setcachelimit**	—	sets *num* as the maximum number of bytes that may be taken up by the bitmap of a single cached character.
mark lower upper	**setcache-params**	—	sets the current cache parameters to the integer values on the operand stack that are above a *mark.*
wx wy	**setcharwidth**	—	performs a function similar to **setcachedevice** but provides only character width information to the PostScript font machinery.

Graphics Operators

Stack Requirements	Operator	Stack Remainder	Definition
—	**currentblack-generation**	proc	returns the current black generation procedure, *proc,* from the current graphics state.

Graphics Operators (continued)

Stack Requirements	Operator	Stack Remainder	Definition
—	currentcmykcolor	cyan magenta yellow black	returns the four components of the current color parameter from the current graphics state according to the cyan-magenta-yellow-black model.
—	currentcolorscreen	rfreq rangle rproc gfreq gangle gproc bfreq bangle bproc grayfreq grayangle grayproc	returns the twelve color halftone screen components from the current graphics state.
—	currentcolortransfer	rproc gproc bproc grayproc	returns the four color transfer functions that define the current color in the current graphics state.
—	currentdash	array offset	returns the current dash setting from the current graphics state.
—	currentflat	num	returns the current flatness parameter from the current graphics state.
—	currentfont	font	returns the current font dictionary from the current graphics state.
—	currentgray	num	returns the gray value of the current color parameter from the current graphics state.
—	currenthsbcolor	hue sat bright	returns the three components of the current color parameter from the current graphics state according to the hue-saturation-brightness model.
—	currentlinecap	int	returns the current line cap parameter in the current graphics state.
—	currentlinejoin	int	returns the current line join parameter in the current graphics state.
—	currentlinewidth	num	returns the current line width parameter in the current graphics state.

Graphics Operators (continued)

Stack Requirements	Operator	Stack Remainder	Definition
—	**current-miterlimit**	num	returns the current miter limit parameter in the current graphics state.
—	**currentpoint**	x y	returns the coordinates of the current point in the current graphics state as *x* and *y*.
—	**current-rgbcolor**	red green blue	returns the three components of the current color parameter from the current graphics state according to the red-green-blue model.
—	**currentscreen**	freq angle proc	returns the three components of the current halftone screen from the current graphics state.
—	**currenttransfer**	proc	returns the transfer procedure, *proc*, being used by the current graphics state.
—	**currentunder-colorremoval**	proc	returns the current undercolor removal function from the current graphics state.
—	**grestore**	—	restores the graphics state to the state that is on the top of the graphics state stack and pops the graphics state stack.
—	**grestoreall**	—	restores the graphics state to the one created by the last unmatched **save,** popping all states on the stack that were produced by any **gsave** operations made after the **save.**
—	**gsave**	—	saves a copy of the current graphics state and all its associated values on the top of the graphics state stack.
—	**initgraphics**	—	resets the most common variables in the graphics state to their initial, default values for the current output device.
proc	**setblack-generation**	—	sets the current black generation function in the current graphics state to *proc*.

Graphics Operators (continued)

Stack Requirements	Operator	Stack Remainder	Definition
cyan magenta yellow black	**setcmykcolor**	—	sets the values *cyan, magenta, yellow,* and *black* as the four components that define the current color parameter in the current graphics state according to the cyan-magenta-yellow-black (CMYK) model.
rfreq rangle rproc gfreq gangle gproc bfreq bangle bproc grayfreq grayangle grayproc	**setcolorscreen**	—	sets the twelve color halftone screen components in the current graphics state.
rproc gproc bproc grayproc	**setcolortransfer**	—	sets the four color transfer functions that define the current color in the current graphics state.
array offset	**setdash**	—	sets the current dash setting in the current graphics state according to the *array* and *offset* operands.
num	**setflat**	—	sets *num* as the current flatness parameter in the current graphics state.
font	**setfont**	—	sets *font* as the current font dictionary in the current graphics state.
num	**setgray**	—	sets *num* as the gray value of the current color in the current graphics state.
hue sat bright	**sethsbcolor**	—	sets the values *hue, sat,* and *bright* as the three components that define the current color parameter in the current graphics state according to the hue-saturation-brightness model.
int	**setlinecap**	—	sets the current line cap parameter in the current graphics state.
int	**setlinejoin**	—	sets *int* as the current line join parameter in the current graphics state.
num	**setlinewidth**	—	sets *num* as the current line width parameter in the current graphics state.
num	**setmiterlimit**	—	sets *num* as the current miter limit parameter in the current graphics state.

Graphics Operators (continued)

Stack Requirements	Operator	Stack Remainder	Definition
red green blue	**setrgbcolor**	—	sets the values *red*, *green*, and *blue* as the three components of the current color parameter from the current graphics state according to the red-green-blue model.
freq angle proc	**setscreen**	—	sets the values *freq*, *angle*, and *proc* as the three components of the current halftone screen from the current graphics state.
proc	**settransfer**	—	sets *proc* as the transfer procedure to be used by the current graphics state.
proc	**setundercolor-removal**	—	sets the current undercolor removal procedure in the current graphics state to *proc*.
bool1 bool2	**and**	result	performs a logical and of *bool1* and *bool2* and returns the boolean value *result*.
int shift	**bitshift**	result	shifts the binary representation of *int* to the left for *shift* bits and returns *result*, which is an integer.
any1 any2	**eq**	bool	compares the top two objects on the operand stack, *any1* and *any2*, and returns the value *bool*, which is *true* if the objects are equal and returns *false* otherwise.
—	**false**	false	returns the boolean object *false*.
num1 num2 string1 string	**ge** **ge**	bool bool	compares the first operand to the second operand and returns the boolean value *true* if the first is greater than or equal to the second and returns *false* otherwise.
num1 num2 string1 string2	**gt** **gt**	bool bool	compares the first operand to the second operand and returns the boolean value *true* if the first is greater than the second and returns *false* otherwise.

Graphics Operators (continued)

Stack Requirements	Operator	Stack Remainder	Definition
num1 num2 string1 string2	le le	bool bool	compares the first operand to the second operand and returns the boolean value *true* if the first is less than or equal to the second and returns *false* otherwise.
num1 num2 string1 string2	lt lt	bool bool	compares the first operand to the second operand and returns the boolean value *true* if the first is strictly less than the second and returns *false* otherwise.
any1 any2	ne	bool	compares the top two objects on the operand stack and returns the boolean value *true* if the objects are not equal and returns *false* otherwise.
bool1	not	bool2	performs the logical negation of *bool1* and returns the boolean value *bool2*.
bool1 bool2	or	result	performs a logical 'inclusive or' of *bool1* and *bool2* and returns the boolean value *result*.
—	true	true	returns the boolean object *true*.
bool1 bool2	xor	result	performs a logical 'exclusive or' of *bool1* and *bool2* and returns the boolean value *result*.

Mathematical Operators

Stack Requirements	Operator	Stack Remainder	Definition
num1	abs	num2	returns the absolute value of *num1*.
num1 num2	add	sum	adds two numbers, *num1* and *num2*, together to give result *sum*.
num denom	atan	angle	returns the angle whose tangent is *num* divided by *denom*.

Mathematical Operators (continued)

Stack Requirements	Operator	Stack Remainder	Definition
num1	**ceiling**	num2	returns the least integer value that is greater than or equal to *num1*. The type of *num2* is the same as the type of *num1*.
angle	**cos**	real	returns the cosine of *angle*, which is taken as an angle in degrees.
num1 num2	**div**	quotient	divides *num1* by *num2*, giving result *quotient*.
base exponent	**exp**	real	raises *base* to the *exponent* power and returns the result *real*.
num1	**floor**	num2	returns as *num2* the greatest integer value less than or equal to *num1*.
int1 int2	**idiv**	result	divides *num1* by *num2* and returns the integer portion of the quotient as *result*; any remainder is discarded.
num	**ln**	real	returns the natural logarithm of *num*.
num	**log**	real	returns the common logarithm of *num*.
int1 int2	**mod**	remainder	returns the remainder of the division of *int1* by *int2*.
num1 num2	**mul**	product	multiplies *num1* by *num2*, giving result *product*.
num	**neg**	−num	reverses the sign of *num*.
—	**rand**	int	generates a random integer within an implementation-defined range.
num1	**round**	num2	rounds *num1* to the nearest integer value, *num2*.
—	**rrand**	int	returns an integer value, *int*, that represents the current state of the pseudo-random number generator used by the interpreter.
angle	**sin**	real	returns the sine of *angle*, which is taken to be an angle in degrees.

Mathematical Operators (continued)

Stack Requirements	Operator	Stack Remainder	Definition
num	**sqrt**	real	returns the square root of *num*, which must be a non-negative number.
int	**srand**	—	takes the integer value, *int*, and initializes the current state of the pseudo-random number generator used by the interpreter to that number.
num1 num2	**sub**	diff	subtracts *num2* from *num1*, giving result *diff*.
num1	**truncate**	num2	truncates the value of *num1* toward zero by removing the fractional part.

Memory Operators

Stack Requirements	Operator	Stack Remainder	Definition
saveobj	**restore**	—	resets virtual memory (VM) to the state it was in when the *saveobj* was created by the save operator.
—	**save**	saveobj	creates a *saveobj* that preserves and represents the current state of virtual memory (VM).
—	**vmstatus**	level used maximum	returns the current status of virtual memory resources (VM) in the current output device.

Miscellaneous Operators

Stack Requirements	Operator	Stack Remainder	Definition
proc	**bind**	proc	replaces executable operator names in *proc* with the actual operators themselves.
—	**null**	null	pushes a *null* object onto the stack.
—	**usertime**	int	returns the value of a clock that increments one unit for every millisecond of execution time.
—	**version**	string	returns a string that identifies the version of the PostScript interpreter that is running in the current output device.
x y rad ang1 ang2	**arc**	—	appends a counterclockwise circular arc to the current path.
x y rad ang1 ang2	**arcn**	—	appends a clockwise circular arc to the current path.
p1x p1y p2x p2y rad	**arcto**	t1x t1y t2x t2y	appends an arc of a circle to the current path, generally preceded by a straight line segment.
string bool	**charpath**	—	makes character path outlines for the characters in *string* as if it were shown at the current point using show.
—	**clip**	—	intersects the inside of the current path with the inside of the current clipping path to produce a new, smaller current clipping path.
—	**clippath**	—	sets the current path to be identical to the current clipping path.
—	**closepath**	—	closes the current subpath by appending a straight line segment from the current point to the starting point of the subpath.
d1x d1y d2x d2y a2x a2y	**curveto**	—	adds a curved line segment, described by a pair of Bezier cubic equations, to the current path.
—	**currentpoint**	x y	returns the coordinates of the current point in the current graphics state.

Miscellaneous Operators (continued)

Stack Requirements	Operator	Stack Remainder	Definition
—	**eoclip**	—	intersects the inside of the current path with the inside of the current clipping path to produce a new, smaller current clipping path.
—	**flattenpath**	—	replaces the current path with a new path where all the curved line segments are approximated by straight lines.
—	**initclip**	—	replaces the clipping path in the current graphics state with the default clipping path for the current output device.
x y	**lineto**	—	appends a straight line segment to the current path, extending from the current point to the point defined by (x, y).
x y	**moveto**	—	moves the current point to (x, y) and starts a new subpath of the current path in the current graphic state.
—	**newpath**	—	initializes the current path, making it empty and making the current point undefined.
—	**pathbbox**	llx lly urx ury	returns the bounding box of the current path in user coordinates.
mvproc lnproc cvproc csproc	**pathforall**	—	enumerates all the elements of the current path, using the procedure operands, *mvproc*, *lnproc*, *cvproc*, and *csproc*.
rd1x rd1y rd2x rd2y ra2x ra2y	**rcurveto**	—	adds a curved line segment, described by a pair of Bezier cubic equations, to the current path in the same manner as the **curveto** operator, except that the operands are relative to the current point rather than absolute coordinates.
—	**reversepath**	—	replaces the current path with a new version of the path that has all the segments of each subpath enumerated in reverse order.

Miscellaneous Operators (continued)

Stack Requirements	Operator	Stack Remainder	Definition
rx ry	**rlineto**	—	adds a straight line segment to the current path in the same manner as the **lineto** operator, except that the operands are relative to the current point rather than absolute coordinates.
rx ry	**rmoveto**	—	starts a new subpath of the current path by moving to a new current point defined by the operands (rx, ry) which are relative to the current point.
—	**strokepath**	—	replaces the current path with a new path that outlines the area that would be painted by applying **stroke** to the current path.

Painting Operators

Stack Requirements	Operator	Stack Remainder	Definition
width height samp matrix proc$_1$ [. . . proc$_{ncolors}$] multiproc ncolors	**colorimage**	—	renders a sampled image with one, three, or four color components onto the current page.
—	**eofill**	—	paints the inside of the current path with the current color.
—	**erasepage**	—	erases the entire contents of the current page.
—	**fill**	—	paints the inside of the current path with the current color.
width height samp matrix proc	**image**	—	renders a sampled image onto the current page.
width height invert matrix proc	**imagemask**	—	renders an image onto the page, using the source data as a mask of one-bit samples that governs where to apply paint (in the current color) to the page.

Painting Operators (continued)

Stack Requirements	Operator	Stack Remainder	Definition
—	**stroke**	—	paints a line defined by the current path, of a thickness given by the current linewidth as set by **setlinewidth,** using the current color.

String Operators

Stack Requirements	Operator	Stack Remainder	Definition
string target	**anchorsearch**	*if found:* post match true *if not found:* string false	determines if the initial part of *string* matches the string *target*.
string1 string2	**copy**	substring2	copies all elements of *string1* into *string2*.
string proc	**forall**	—	enumerates every element of the first operand and executes *proc* for each of those elements.
string index	**get**	any	looks up the *index* in *array*, *packedarray*, or *string* and returns the element identified by *index* (counting from zero).
string index count	**getinterval**	substring	duplicates a section of the operand *string*, beginning at the element identified by *index* (counting from zero) and extending for *count* elements.
string	**length**	int	returns *int* as the number of elements that make up the value of *string*.
string index value	**put**	—	stores *value* into *string* at the position identified by *index* (counting from zero).

String Operators (continued)

Stack Requirements	Operator	Stack Remainder	Definition
string1 index string2	**putinterval**	—	replaces a section of the operand *string1* beginning at the element identified by *index* (counting from zero) with the contents of *string2*.
string target	**search**	*if found:* post match pre true *if not found:* string false	determines if any part of *string* matches the string *target*.
int	**string**	string	creates a string with length *int* and initializes each element of the string with the binary value 0.
string	**token**	*if found* post any true *if not found:* false	reads characters from *string*, interpreting them according to the PostScript syntax rules, until it has constructed a complete PostScript object, which is returned to the operand stack as result *any*.

Stack Operators

Stack Requirements	Operator	Stack Remainder	Definition
$\vdash$ any$_1$ . . . any$_n$	**clear**	$\vdash$	pops all objects from the operand stack.
mark obj$_1$ . . . obj$_n$	**cleartomark**	—	pops all objects from the operand stack above the first *mark* object on the stack.
any$_1$ . . . any$_n$ int	**copy**	any$_1$ . . . any$_n$ any$_1$ . . . any$_{int}$	when the top element on the operand stack is a non-negative integer *int*, **copy** pops *int* and then duplicates the top *int* elements of the operand stack.
$\vdash$ any$_1$ . . . any$_n$	**count**	$\vdash$ any$_1$ . . . any$_n$ n	counts the number of objects on the operand stack and returns that integer, *n*, to the top of the stack.

Stack Operators (continued)

Stack Requirements	Operator	Stack Remainder	Definition
mark obj_1 . . . obj_n	**counttomark**	mark obj_1 . . . obj_n n	counts the number of objects on the operand stack above the first *mark* and returns that integer, n to the top of the stack.
any	**dup**	any any	duplicates the topmost object on the operand stack.
any1 any2	**exch**	any2 any1	exchanges the two top objects on the operand stack to reverse their order.
any_n . . . any_0 n	**index**	any_n . . . any_0 any_n	uses the non-negative integer n as a pointer into the operand stack and duplicates the nth object on the stack, counting from the top element as 0.
any	**pop**	—	removes the top element from the operand stack.
any_{n-1} . . . any_0 n int	**roll**	$any_{(int-1)}$ . . . any_0 any_{n-1} . . . any_{int}	performs a circular shift of the contents of the operand stack.

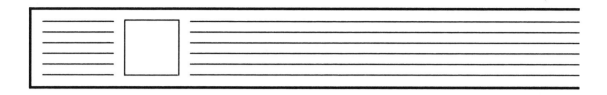

Index

NOTES

NOTES

NOTES